SHAPING RIGHT

In fundamental rights adjudication, a court first has to determine whether the interest at stake falls within the scope of the fundamental right invoked. Whether or not an individual interest falls within the scope or ambit of one of the fundamental rights protected by the European Convention on Human Rights determines whether or not the European Court of Human Rights (ECtHR) can decide on the merits of a case.

This volume brings a variety of legal scholars together to examine the scope of fundamental rights. Topics range from the nature of human rights and the real or imagined risk of rights inflation to theories of positive obligations and social and economic rights. It contains contributions of a theoretical nature as well as analytical overviews of the ECtHR's approach. In addition, comparisons are made with domestic, EU and international law.

EVA BREMS is Professor of Human Rights Law at Ghent University, Belgium. Her research interests include many areas of human rights law, at the international, European and domestic levels.

JANNEKE GERARDS is Research Professor of Fundamental Rights Law at the Law Faculty of Radboud University, Nijmegen, the Netherlands. Her research focuses on fundamental rights, judicial argumentation, judicial review and constitutional law.

SHAPING RIGHTS IN THE ECHR

The Role of the European Court of Human Rights in Determining the Scope of Human Rights

Edited by

EVA BREMS

and

JANNEKE GERARDS

CAMBRIDGE
UNIVERSITY PRESS

CAMBRIDGE
UNIVERSITY PRESS

University Printing House, Cambridge CB2 8BS, United Kingdom

Cambridge University Press is part of the University of Cambridge.

It furthers the University's mission by disseminating knowledge in the pursuit of education, learning and research at the highest international levels of excellence.

www.cambridge.org
Information on this title: www.cambridge.org/9781107618374

First published 2013
First paperback edition 2015

A catalogue record for this publication is available from the British Library

Library of Congress Cataloguing in Publication data
Shaping rights in the ECHR : the role of the European Court of Human Rights in determining the scope of human rights / edited by Eva Brems, Janneke Gerards.
p. cm.
Includes index.
ISBN 978-1-107-04322-0 (hardback)
1. European Court of Human Rights. 2. Human rights – Europe. 3. Civil rights – Europe. 4. Human rights. I. Brems, Eva, editor of compilation. II. Gerards, J. H. (Janneke H.), editor of compilation. III. Title: Shaping rights in the ECHR.
KJC5138.S53 2014
341.4′8094 – dc23 2013039530

ISBN 978-1-107-04322-0 Hardback
ISBN 978-1-107-61837-4 Paperback

CONTENTS

CONTRIBUTORS

ODDNÝ MJÖLL ARNARDÓTTIR is Professor of Human Rights Law at the University of Iceland, Reykjavik, Iceland. Her chapter was written as part of her research project on the margin of appreciation, which was funded by the Icelandic Research Fund.

EIRIK BJORGE is Shaw Foundation Junior Research Fellow, Jesus College, University of Oxford, United Kingdom.

EVA BREMS is Professor of Human Rights Law at Ghent University, Belgium.

MARIS BURBERGS is a PhD researcher at the Human Rights Centre of Ghent University, Belgium.

ANTOINE BUYSE is an associate professor and senior researcher at the Netherlands Institute of Human Rights (SIM), Utrecht University, the Netherlands. His chapter was written as part of his VENI research project on conflict dynamics and free speech, funded by the Netherlands Organisation for Scientific Research (NWO).

JANNEKE GERARDS is Professor of Fundamental Rights Law at the Radboud University of Nijmegen, the Netherlands.

EDUARDO GILL-PEDRO is a doctoral candidate at Lund University's Faculty of Law, Sweden. Prior to commencing his doctoral studies, he worked as a legal advisor in a civil liberties organisation in the United Kingdom.

XAVIER GROUSSOT is Professor of EU Law at the Faculty of Law of Lund University, Sweden and guest professor at the University Panthéon-Assas (Paris II), France.

LAURENS LAVRYSEN is a PhD student at the Human Rights Centre of Ghent University, Belgium. His research is funded by the Research Foundation Flanders (FWO) and takes place within the framework of the European Research Council-funded project 'Strengthening the European Court of Human Rights: More Accountability through Better Legal Reasoning'.

INGRID LEIJTEN is a PhD researcher and junior lecturer at the Department of Constitutional and Administrative Law of the Leiden University School of Law, the Netherlands.

PAUL LEMMENS is a judge at the European Court of Human Rights and a professor at the University of Leuven, Belgium.

GEORGE LETSAS is a Reader in Philosophy of Law and Human Rights, University College London, United Kingdom.

ALASTAIR MOWBRAY is Professor of Public Law, School of Law, University of Nottingham, United Kingdom.

MARTIN SCHEININ is Professor of International Law and Human Rights at the European University Institute, Florence, Italy.

GERHARD VAN DER SCHYFF is a senior lecturer in the Department of Public Law, Jurisprudence and Legal History of the Law School at Tilburg University in the Netherlands.

STIJN SMET is a PhD candidate at the Human Rights Centre of Ghent University, Faculty of Law, Belgium.

ACKNOWLEDGEMENTS

The current volume contains a great and rich range of ideas regarding the way in which fundamental rights are given shape by the European Court of Human Rights. We are very grateful to all contributors for having written such thought-provoking chapters and for their active participation in the expert meeting on the scope of rights that we organised in March 2012. This workshop could not have taken place without the organisational support of many people, in particular Martine Dewulf, Maris Burbergs and Ingrid Leijten. For the production of the final book, we are much indebted to Finola O'Sullivan and Elizabeth Spicer. They have made the various chapters into a beautiful book, which we very much hope that you will enjoy reading and which will form the basis for further debate on this important topic.

1

Introduction

JANNEKE GERARDS AND EVA BREMS

1. The importance of 'shaping rights' – and the difficulties related to it

In fundamental rights adjudication, a court usually determines first whether the interest at stake is protected by a fundamental rights provision – i.e. whether it falls within the scope of the fundamental right that is invoked – before considering whether the right has been restricted and, if so, whether this restriction was justified. Sometimes this is easy and straightforward. For example, if the complaint concerns prohibited publication of a book in which state secrets are disclosed, it is relatively obvious that this prohibition affects the freedom of expression. In other cases, determining the applicability of fundamental rights provisions is much more difficult and controversial. It may be asked, for example, whether pure hate speech or fighting words are protected by the freedom of expression; or whether refusing to provide a detainee with dental care amounts to 'inhuman and degrading treatment'.

Answering such questions requires interpretation: the court will have to determine what the fundamental rights provision that is invoked really means, and what it is intended to protect. This interpretative task is a particularly difficult one, as fundamental rights provisions are notoriously formulated in a very general and abstract fashion. Thus the text of fundamental rights provisions offers little guidance to a court that has to determine whether a set of facts comes within the scope of their protection.

The courts' task is made even more difficult by the very nature of fundamental rights. It is well accepted that most fundamental rights are not absolutes, but can be limited if such limitations are sufficiently justified by objective and weighty reasons, such as the protection of other

Note to the reader: all judgments and decisions of the European Court of Human Rights to which reference is made in this work are easily accessible through the HUDOC database on the Court's website: www.echr.coe.int.

fundamental rights or of important general interests. One major question is whether the assessment of the reasonableness of an interference with a fundamental right could and should form part of the definition of that right, or whether definition and justification should be strictly separated. On one hand, it is clear that the actual meaning of a fundamental right in a particular case can only be determined by looking at the case as a whole, including the justification. When considering the prohibition of a book disclosing state secrets, in the end the actual scope of the freedom of expression is determined both by the definition of that freedom and the balance that is struck between that freedom and the state's interests in keeping state secrets. After all, authors only know the extent to which they can really exercise freedom of expression if the limits to the exercise of that right are delineated. If the definition of a fundamental right does not contain any express limitation clause, this is even more important. In determining the scope of the prohibition of inhuman and degrading treatment, it is seemingly inescapable that elements of justification will be included in the courts' interpretation. For example, to determine whether the use of violence to suppress a prison riot amounted to inhuman and degrading treatment, courts must determine whether the violence used was unavoidable and not excessive. Almost unavoidably, then, elements of reasonableness and justification enter the determination of scope. Simultaneously, it can be argued that definition of scope and assessment of reasonableness require very different methods of interpretation. Whilst it could be argued that the definition of fundamental rights must be determined using classic interpretation methods (textual interpretation, teleological interpretation), the test of reasonableness involves an assessment of the aim pursued, the necessity for interference to achieve the aim, and a test of balancing or reasonableness. Moreover, it has been contended that the burden of proof for the stage of definition should be different from that for the assessment of justification: where it is up to the applicant to demonstrate that a given act or omission really interferes with his or her fundamental rights, it is the government's task to provide an objective justification for this as soon as it is clear that such a right is indeed at stake.

Hence, the process of 'shaping rights' raises many important questions, both of a conceptual and theoretical nature and of a more practical, case-law character. From a conceptual perspective, for example, it obviously must be asked to what extent 'pure' definition of the scope of fundamental rights really can and should be distinguished from the assessment of justification. Indeed, the question as to the most appropriate approach particularly arises in relation to 'absolute' rights (such as the prohibition of inhuman treatment) and in relation to notions such as that of positive obligations. Moreover, it can be queried whether it makes a difference if the case relates to 'classic' fundamental rights, such as the right to privacy or fair trial, or to fundamental rights of a social and economic character.

These questions are relevant for all fundamental rights provisions, regardless of whether they are laid down in national constitutions or in international treaties. For the European Convention on Human Rights (ECHR or Convention), however, they have particular importance. Whether or not an individual interest is brought within the scope or ambit of one of the fundamental rights protected by the Convention determines whether the European Court of Human Rights (ECtHR or Court) is competent to decide the merits of a case. Moreover, the questions raised have special relevance because the Convention contains both 'absolute' fundamental rights and fundamental rights with limitation clauses; the notion of positive obligations has been particularly strongly developed; and social and economic fundamental rights increasingly form part of the Convention rights. Especially in those situations, the conceptual questions how these rights should be 'shaped', and how the Court should proceed in these cases, are of great importance. And finally, discussions concerning the scope of the Convention are highly relevant to the Court's role and position as a supranational court. Some scholars and politicians have criticised the Court for widening the scope of the Convention to such an extent that even non-fundamental rights have now been included, and it has been questioned how legitimately a European human rights court may decide such cases.

Interestingly, however, legal doctrine has shown relatively little interest in the conceptual and practical issues related to the structure of fundamental rights and the process of 'shaping rights'. Thus far, academic literature has tended to focus either on the interpretative principles used by the ECtHR, or on the test of justification (including the test of proportionality and the margin of appreciation doctrine). Given the importance of the determination of scope to the Court's adjudication in fundamental rights cases, there is great value in bringing together the state of the art in legal scholarship on the fundamental questions surrounding the scope of fundamental rights.

2. Shaping rights: four central themes

The general theme of how to determine the scope of fundamental rights raises a wide variety of important scholarly questions having a very different nature, which should all be addressed in order to provide both in-depth and sufficiently broad insight into the theme as a whole. To address the topic of shaping rights by the ECtHR in a comprehensive, yet accessible, manner this volume centres around four central themes that merit in-depth exploration. Read in their entirety, the contributions relating to the four themes provide a broad and deep insight into how the scope of fundamental rights is determined.

2.1 Conceptual, structural and constitutional issues

The first issues to be addressed in a volume on the scope of rights are, of course, conceptual, structural and constitutional ones. As mentioned briefly above, there is much debate possible on whether elements of 'balancing' fundamental rights against other interests should play a role in determining the scope of rights; whether a 'bifurcated' approach is preferable; and how and to what extent the structure of fundamental rights provisions should affect the Court's assessment of individual applications. It is important to bring these various possible debates to the fore, as this will both give insight into, and enable sound criticism of, the way the Court defines and gives shape to the Convention.

Furthermore, opinions strongly diverge on how fundamental rights should be defined. Different views are possible as to the perspective that should be taken by the ECtHR in defining fundamental rights provisions. If the aim is to effectively protect individual rights, the scope of fundamental rights should be defined as widely as possible and the Court should declare almost all complaints with a fundamental rights aspect admissible as falling within the scope of the Convention. From a constitutional or institutional perspective, however, such a wide definition may bring about problems of division of competences between the ECtHR and national authorities.

For this reason, the scope of Convention rights should be studied from a normative, legal theoretical and constitutional perspective, as well as from a descriptive and historical perspective. It is only possible to value the determination of fundamental rights by the Court if we see clearly how the ECtHR perceives its own role in this regard, how its case law has developed over the decades and how its approaches can theoretically, conceptually and constitutionally be valued. This volume therefore starts with a number of contributions that specifically focus on these issues.

2.2 Developments in the case law of the European Court of Human Rights

Second, it is important to recognise that the European Court of Human Rights has created a large body of case law related to determining the scope of rights. It has developed economic and social guarantees as part of the classic rights protected by the Convention, it has broadened their scope by introducing procedural obligations into, for example, the right to life and the right to respect for one's private life, and it has defined substantive positive obligations in addition to the inherently negative obligations that were originally read into the Convention. The result of these developments is a significant expansion of the scope of the Convention, as well as an important change in the character of the obligations it places on states. When exploring how the Court gives shape to Convention rights, obviously it is of great interest to analyse such developments critically and evaluate their consequences for the protection of fundamental rights in Europe.

expansion of scope of the ECHR

2.3 Similar issues in different systems – a 360° comparison

In European debates on fundamental rights, it is sometimes suggested that only the European Convention on Human Rights is strongly expanding and that only the European Court of Human Rights has to answer difficult questions relating to the definition and scope of human rights. Of course, this is far from true – similar issues arise at the national (constitutional) level, at the international level of human rights protection and at the level of the European Union. Moreover, international, national and EU laws on (the scope of) fundamental rights strongly influence the case law of the Court.

To obtain a complete picture of the way in which European fundamental rights are being shaped, to allow for relevant comparisons with the ECtHR's approach, and to estimate the importance of the Court's approach for the definition of fundamental rights by national and international courts, it is important to study the determination of the scope of fundamental rights on these levels, therefore, and to look at the influence thereof on the case law of the Court. A '360° comparison' can enrich the debate on the shaping of rights by the Court, as well as provide a sound basis for further research into the definition of the scope of rights on the international, EU and national levels.

2.4 A closer look at specific Convention rights

Finally, it is interesting to see to what extent and in what manner the theoretical, national and international debates, as well as the impact of the general developments in the Court's case law, impact on that case law. This is true in particular since the impact appears to differ for the various Convention rights. For 'absolute' provisions, such as the prohibition of torture, defining the scope of a right is more important than for 'relative' provisions, such as the right to respect for one's private life. Moreover, even where the questions that have come up in relation to, for example, the Court's definition of private and family life overlap with questions that have arisen in relation to the prohibition of non-discrimination or the right to a fair trial, the case law on each of these provisions shows some very particular aspects. To obtain more insight into the explanations for differences in the Court's approach, several provisions of the Convention on which the case law discloses a strong extension of scope have been selected as case studies of a sort. For all of these, an analysis is made of the relevant case law to see whether explanations can be found for the expansion of scope as well as to provide a basis for conclusions to be drawn on the consequences and evaluation of such expansion. In all of these analyses, parallels are drawn between the case law of the Court and the conceptual, constitutional and theoretical issues discussed previously.

3. Findings: a compilation

This volume presents the insights and analyses of sixteen scholars on the four central themes discussed above. To do justice to the depth and richness of their writings, it is of course necessary to read their contributions in full. Nevertheless, a short compilation of the most important findings of all these chapters may provide a broader insight into the questions raised and (tentative) answers proposed relating to the shaping of fundamental rights by the European Court of Human Rights.

3.1 Conceptual, structural and constitutional issues relating to the scope of rights

In his chapter, Alastair Mowbray sets the stage for the various conceptual, constitutional and analytical contributions by presenting a historical analysis of the development of the scope of the Convention by the ECtHR. Examining the process by which the Convention was drafted, Mowbray finds that, amongst the numerous stakeholders, there were both competing attitudes towards the ambit of the rights and freedoms guaranteed and divergent views of the ultimate objective(s) of the ECHR. He then identifies some of the major forces underpinning the Court's interpretation and application of the Convention to make it apt for modern European societies: technological progress, changing social relationships and the evolution of human rights standards. Mowbray argues that the Court has to steer a challenging path between judicial activism and judicial restraint, in which it generally interprets and applies the Convention in accordance with contemporary needs. However, where states have signalled their intention to revise the breadth of a Convention right through the process of negotiating and ratifying additional Protocols (for example regarding the death penalty), or where a particular Convention right was drafted with a clearly limited ambit and no subsequent enhancement of that right has conclusively emerged in the relevant practice of the Member States (e.g. sanctioning marriages between same-sex couples), the Court has been cautious not to interpret the Convention contrary to the will of the states.

George Letsas continues with a legal-theoretical and conceptual analysis of the structure of, and fundamental rights provisions under, the Convention. Starting from a number of hypothetical cases, he sets out to check the European Court's mode of judicial reasoning against an ideal model. He builds this model on the basis of theoretical insights concerning the nature of rights in general. In particular, he distinguishes between *prima facie* rights and *pro tanto* rights. He says that the former appear to be rights, i.e. to constitute reasons not to interfere with the right-holder's liberty, but that in the circumstances they are not rights. Once the circumstances surrounding the situation of the alleged right-holder are known, it transpires that there was actually no right and hence no reason *not* to have interfered with someone's liberty. *Pro tanto* rights on the other hand are weighty reasons for others not to interfere with the right-holder in certain ways. But the weight need not be absolute. *Pro tanto* rights can be balanced against other *pro tanto* considerations. Letsas criticises the Court for failing to make this distinction, and on occasion upholding pseudo-rights. In addition, Letsas argues that the Court would risk making a second mistake, that of failing to take seriously some *pro tanto* rights, if it were to focus more on 'scope' analysis.

Gerhard van der Schyff also provides a legal-theoretical and conceptual analysis, but he focuses on the structure of Convention rights and the 'bifurcated' approach that distinguishes between *defining* fundamental rights (i.e. determining their scope) and *assessing the reasonableness* of interferences with such rights. In particular, van der Schyff is interested in answering the question whether, from a legal-theoretical perspective, Convention rights should be defined extensively or rather more narrowly. He starts out by distinguishing between one-stage, illimitable rights and two-stage, limitable rights, noting that in the ECHR the latter by far outnumber the former. He then argues that a narrow interpretation of scope may be appropriate for one-stage rights, yet is not desirable for two-stage rights. Following Alexy, van der Schyff submits that everything that exhibits at least one characteristic connected to the values of a right must be taken to form part of its protected conduct and interests. Formal interpretations must be followed by leaving aside value judgements as to the intended purpose, nature and quality of elements contending for protection. Engaging with opponents of his thesis, in particular Gerards, van der Schyff contends that as a rule narrow scopes come about through 'hidden' balancing, rendering legal reasoning non-transparent. He adds that the same phenomenon also implies that narrow scopes do not reduce the Court's case load.

Gerards enters into a debate with van der Schyff by arguing that legal-theoretical arguments should not be the only arguments to be taken into account by the ECtHR when defining Convention rights. In her view, the Court should also take account of constitutional, legal-political and subsidiarity considerations. Her chapter examines the argument according to which the problems caused by the Court's case load could in part be addressed by a more rigorous (narrow) interpretation of the scope of Convention rights. Gerards argues that there is not so much a direct, as an indirect relationship between the growing scope of the Convention and institutional concerns regarding the Court. Such concerns are mainly caused by the fact that, as a result of the widening of the

Convention's scope, the Court often admits individual complaints that require a complex assessment of national policies and an evaluation of intricate legal issues. Moreover, the number of individual applications may have increased as a result of relative lack of clarity offered by the Court on the precise scope of application of certain Convention rights. Therefore, Gerards proposes that the Court should limit its supervisory role to cases that concern core fundamental rights, that it should delineate new rights and obligations precisely and that it should formulate detailed and substantive standards for the applicability of specific Convention rights. In doing these things, the Court should employ a bifurcated approach, distinguishing the stage of definition clearly from the stage of justification. At this point, Gerards and van der Schyff appear to agree.

3.2 Scope and more – developments in the case law of the ECtHR

Over the years, the Court has come to deal with a great many cases on 'social' issues such as social welfare, health care, and the environment. A closer look, however, shows that often it does not define exactly what the Convention requires in these fields. In this light, Ingrid Leijten's chapter criticises the current approach taken by the ECtHR. She agrees with various other authors that usually the Court should start from a bifurcated approach, but she then goes on to argue that using such an approach is neither always desirable, nor always possible where requirements of a more economic and social kind are involved. For that reason, she searches for a different possible approach to be taken by the ECtHR in future cases on social and economic (aspects of) rights. Leijten finds inspiration for developing this different perspective in the context of the International Covenant on Social, Economic and Cultural Rights. In her view, the concept of 'minimum core obligations' developed by the Committee on Social, Economic and Cultural Rights can generate more workable definitions of rights. Adopting a similar approach might help the ECtHR to provide more clarity as to the meaning of fundamental rights, while not overstepping the boundaries of its difficult task.

The chapter written by Eva Brems throws light on the often-overlooked phenomenon of hidden procedural safeguards embedded in the substantive Convention rights. In numerous fields of its case law, the Court has in fact added a procedural layer to the scope of substantive Convention rights, by deriving state obligations of a procedural nature from substantive ECHR provisions. The main driver for this development appears to be the wish to make human rights guarantees more effective. The chapter first clarifies the reach of procedural obligations under substantive Convention rights, distinguishing between the requirement that a procedure be available and the more specific procedural guarantees that the Court requires. It goes on to analyse the impact of the 'proceduralisation' of substantive rights and the role this plays within the Court's case law.

Since the breakthrough *Marckx* judgment, the Court has found positive obligations under almost every Convention right. Despite the widespread application of the positive obligations doctrine, the Court has stated that it does not have to develop a general theory of the positive obligations which may flow from the Convention. In his chapter on the way in which it 'shapes' positive obligations, Laurens Lavrysen submits that the Court's lack of a sound and general theory has resulted in a case-to-case-approach that goes too far in this direction and gives little guidance to national courts and practitioners. He argues that the Court should take a more structured approach. Taking into account the bifurcated nature of human rights, Lavrysen proposes to apply a symmetrical approach to positive and negative obligations. In this regard, he stresses that the scope of Convention rights should be kept 'clean', meaning that elements from the second stage of the analysis, in particular proportionality and legality, should not be introduced in the first stage.

Finally, Antoine Buyse focuses on the one particular Convention provision that is specifically intended to remove certain activities from its scope. This is the 'abuse clause' – Article 17 – which forecloses human rights protection when these rights are being used to deny (other people's) human rights. Although this provision would seem to offer the Court an opportunity to define clear borders for application of the Convention, Buyse shows that there are many practical and theoretical difficulties related to the case law on this article. In particular, he analyses the Court's application of Article 17 in the light of its case law on Article 10 ECHR, which protects the freedom of expression. He shows that, in applying the abuse of rights philosophy in its material assessment under Article 10, in fact the Court blurs categorical and balancing aspects of judicial decision-making. In his view, a different approach would be desirable, in which the Court would not apply Article 17 directly to place certain types of speech outside the scope of Convention protection, but rather use the abuse of rights element as a weighty argument in assessing the justification for limiting certain types of speech. If it would do this, and if the justification test would involve 'structured balancing of interests', Buyse holds, the disadvantages of the current uses of Article 17 would be offset.

3.3 360° comparison

The ECtHR employs forty-seven judges, most of whom have previously held a judicial or academic position at the national level. That is to say, their legal reasoning has been shaped to a greater or lesser extent by their domestic legal culture. Hence it is to be expected that the legal reasoning of the Court would borrow explicitly or implicitly from some of the highest jurisdictions at the national level, and that this would be displayed in its reasoning with respect to the scope of rights, amongst other areas. The chapter of Eirik Bjorge examines the matter from the viewpoint of the United Kingdom. Relying upon the dialogue between the UK Supreme Court and Strasbourg, he argues that the ECtHR is inclined to accept the national courts' approach to the definition of ECHR rights when it is clear from their judgments that they have attempted in good faith to uphold Convention rights or to strike a fair balance between what is necessary in a democratic society and the right of the individual in issue. Thus, national courts' approaches can have important impact on the determination of the scope of rights by the ECtHR.

With the entry into force of the Lisbon Treaty on 1 December 2009, the EU Charter of Fundamental Rights has become a legally binding, core element of the Union's legal order. How will these 'new' rights impact on the 'old' human rights in Europe? And more importantly, what impact will this have on the scope of protection for the fundamental rights of EU citizens, who now have two legally binding instruments both claiming to protect them, and two supranational courts to turn to? Xavier Groussot and Eduardo Gill-Pedro examine these questions by first comparing the material and personal scope of the Charter with the Convention. Next, they look in detail at Article 52(3) of the Charter, which can be described as 'the homogeneity clause', tasked with ensuring that the coming into force of the Charter does not undermine the protection provided by the ECHR and that the two legal orders can co-exist harmoniously. Groussot and Gill-Pedro state that coherence between these two fundamentally different legal orders is not achievable, and that, in the end, it will prove impossible to fully harmonise the scope of protection of the two European fundamental rights instruments, since they operate from fundamentally different normative frameworks. Nonetheless, they argue that it is of crucial importance that a *modus vivendi* is found between the two courts to ensure harmony.

The ECHR is but one of many human rights treaties binding upon European states. In particular, at the level of the United Nations numerous – general and specific – human rights treaties have been adopted, to which most Council of Europe Member States adhere. In his contribution to this volume, Martin Scheinin examines how coherent is the scope of various human rights as defined at the UN and Council of Europe levels. Scheinin promotes an 'interdependence approach' based on the idea of universal and indivisible human rights. This does not mean that the scope of every human rights provision should be interpreted in the widest possible way but rather that every human rights provision should be interpreted as being compatible with all other human rights. In addition, Scheinin proposes an integrated view of human rights obligations. The scope of human rights is not determined only by admissibility decisions, but also by deciding on the merits of the case, which would allow for feedback loops from the ECtHR's earlier case law. In his view, to do justice to this holistic view would require a World Court of Human Rights, since such a court would be in the best position to secure a harmonised interpretation of human rights.

3.4 A closer look at specific rights

The ECtHR has repeatedly stated that the rights found in Article 3 of the Convention are 'absolute' and 'subject to no exceptions whatever', a mantra that has also been endorsed in the academic literature. In his chapter, however, Stijn Smet argues that there are compelling reasons for questioning these assumptions and for exploring the implications. To that end, he first paints a picture of what a truly absolute prohibition of torture and inhuman or degrading treatment would entail. He then provides an analysis of the Court's case law to demonstrate that currently it does not live up to the promise of such an absolute right. Given the problems of this internally inconsistent approach, Smet then goes on to analyse how the Court could amend its reasoning in order to bring it in line with its own principled stance on the 'absolute nature of the right under Article 3'. In his view, the Court might generally achieve a reconciliation between the absolute prohibition and its application by paying increased attention to the object and purpose of Article 3 and by relying exclusively on the elements that it has principally identified as being relevant to the Article's threshold question. In other cases, staying faithful to the principled, absolute nature of Article 3 would require the Court to make a clear normative choice. In Smet's view, only then would application of Article 3 truly be a question of scope only, as it is supposed by the Court to be.

The chapter written by Paul Lemmens contains an analysis of the extensive case law of the Court under Article 6 – by far the Convention's most frequently invoked provision. The issue of the scope of Article 6 involves several specific questions. First, there is the matter of the limitation of its applicability to certain procedures of a 'civil' nature, and others of a 'criminal' nature, notions that have been given autonomous meaning, yet that even today leave a number of procedures outside the reach of Article 6. Then there are the sub-rights of the right to a fair trial, quite a few of which are enumerated in the text of the provision. Yet nevertheless the Court has created or discovered additional sub-rights – in particular the right of access to court, thus broadening or at least detailing the scope of Article 6. Finally, delimiting the scope of the enumerated sub-rights also gave rise to interesting case law. For all of these topics, Lemmens analyses the case law of the Court to see which factors and elements have determined the scope of Article 6. He concludes his chapter with several thoughts on the relationship between the general right to a fair trial and its many sub-rights.

Article 8 ECHR nominally protects private life, family life, the home and correspondence, yet over time it has come to protect numerous specific interests, such as gender identity, name, reputation and self-determination. The aim of the analysis carried out by Maris Burbergs is to provide a better understanding of how Article 8 became the nursery in which new rights are born. In his chapter, he first shows how the scope of Article 8 continues to develop – for example, in 2010 and 2011 the Court recognised several 'new' interests as being covered by the Article, including the right to choose the circumstances of becoming a parent (right to give birth at home), the right to assisted suicide, the right to abortion and the right of access to IVF facilities. Burbergs concentrates on the factors that play a role in widening the scope of the Article. He concludes that the Court's approach is less a highly principled one than one that strongly relies on previous case law. The developments can take a tree-like form where a branch provides a base for another branch or branches to grow on, but the reasoning can also become 'cloudy' where a cluster of rights from previous cases is presented and then the new right is introduced. By using these metaphors, Burbergs claims, it is easier to understand the transformation processes of Article 8 of the Convention.

According to long-standing case law of the Court, the protective scope of Article 14 (non-discrimination) only reaches those areas that come within the 'ambit' of other Convention rights. Over time, as a result of the Court's case law, the 'ambit' of the Convention has been greatly extended by the Court to include a multitude of fundamental rights issues. However, up to now the ambit doctrine and its impact have been somewhat neglected in the literature on the Convention. In her chapter, Oddný Mjöll Arnardóttir endeavours to fill this gap by analysing the Court's case law on the 'ambit' of the Convention. In particular, she finds that Article 14 may 'magnify' other Convention rights: it may help to detect additional violations or aggravating elements within the minimum entitlements provided by the scope of Convention rights; it may help to discover legitimate interests that are closely linked to Convention rights even though they fall outside the more precisely defined scope of such rights and have not been recognised in domestic developments; and it may support domestic developments above the minimum standards provided by the Convention rights. Against this background, Arnardóttir also addresses the difference in material scope between Article 14 and Protocol 12, which contains a self-standing, independent prohibition of discrimination. In her view, the Court's case law shows that the difference between these articles is slowly diminishing in many important fields of protection, most notably in relation to social security benefits. While these developments at the definitional level of analysis may seem to open 'floodgates' for wide-reaching non-discrimination claims in the socio-economic sphere, Arnardóttir concludes that the margin of appreciation doctrine at the justificatory level of analysis functions as a gatekeeper and maintains an appropriate balance in the case law.

PART 1

Conceptual, structural and constitutional issues relating to the scope of rights

2

Between the will of the Contracting Parties and the needs of today

Extending the scope of Convention rights and freedoms beyond what could have been foreseen by the drafters of the ECHR

ALASTAIR MOWBRAY

This chapter will ascertain the intentions of the drafters of the European Convention on Human Rights (hereafter the ECHR or Convention)[1] and then examine a number of factors that have resulted in the judicial expansion of the rights and freedoms enshrined in its text. The genesis of the Convention predates the creation of the inter-state organisation the Council of Europe.[2] In 1948 a collection of non-governmental groups, favouring unity in western Europe, held the 'Congress of Europe'.[3] The Congress ended with a five-point declaration that included: '. . . (2)[w]e desire a Charter of Human Rights guaranteeing liberty of thought, assembly and expression as well as the right to form a political opposition; (3) [w]e desire a Court of Justice with adequate sanctions for the implementation of the Charter . . . '.[4] During the next year a triumvirate of rapporteurs drafted a European Convention on Human Rights and a Statute of the European Court of Human Rights (hereafter the Court) for the 'European Movement'.[5] Following the establishment of the Council of Europe these two drafts were submitted to the highest political body of the Council, the Committee of Ministers. In turn the Committee of

1 Convention for the Protection of Human Rights and Fundamental Freedoms, CETS No. 005, Rome 4 November 1950.

2 Statute of the Council of Europe, CETS No. 001, London 5 May 1949.

3 In The Hague from 7–10 May 1948.

4 See A. Mowbray, *Cases, Materials & Commentary on the ECHR*, 3rd edn (Oxford University Press, 2012), Ch. 1.

5 M. Pierre-Henri Teitgen (French), Sir David Maxwell-Fyfe (British) and Professor Fernand Dehousse (Belgian).

Ministers authorised the discussion of the development of such a Convention by the Council's Consultative Assembly.[6] The ensuing debates revealed the rapporteurs, taking account of the political need to secure state agreement to the substance of the Convention, adopting circumscribed views towards the scope of the Convention's guarantees. For example, Teitgen considered that the Convention should embody a 'collective guarantee' of a limited set of rights: 'security of person; freedom from arbitrary arrest; freedom from slavery and servitude; freedom of speech and expression; freedom of religious belief, practice and teaching; freedom of association and assembly; the natural rights derived from marriage and paternity and those pertaining to the family, the sanctity of the home, equality before law, protection from discrimination on account of religion, race, national origin, political or philosophical opinion; freedom from arbitrary deprivation of property'.[7] To ensure swift ratification by the states he advocated leaving these rights undefined in the Convention. Maxwell-Fyfe emphasised that they were 'negative rights or freedoms'. Furthermore, he stressed that '[o]ur list, it is true, contains none of the so-called economic or social rights which appear in the UNO Declaration.[8] Such rights would, in my view, be too controversial and difficult of enforcement even in the changing state of social and international development in Europe, and their inclusion would jeopardise the acceptance of the Convention.'[9]

Despite the cautious approach of these leading members of the Consultative Assembly, the Committee of Ministers established its own group of legal experts to produce a draft Convention. The experts worked from the proposals of the Assembly but, reflecting the disagreement amongst the states, alternative drafts were produced embodying general or defined rights and alternative approaches to the creation and role of the Court. A conference of senior officials, representing their own state's interests, was convened in June 1950 to seek to resolve these differences.

6 Now renamed the Parliamentary Assembly.

7 First Session of the Consultative Assembly – 10 August to 8 September 1949: *Collected Edition of the Travaux Preparatoires*, Vol. 1, ed. A.H. Robertson, (The Hague: Martinus Nijhoff, 1975).

8 The Universal Declaration of Human Rights, UNGA Res 217 A(III), 10 December 1948. For an analysis of the links between the ECHR and the UDHR see A. Mowbray, 'The European Convention on Human Rights' in *International Human Rights: Six Decades After the UDHR and Beyond*, M.A. Baderin and M. Ssenyonjo (eds), (Aldershot: Ashgate, 2010).

9 See note 7.

According to Bates two schools of thought on the Convention emerged at the conference.[10] Belgium, France, Ireland and Italy supported a Convention containing unelaborated rights and an international judicial supervisory system, whilst Greece, Norway, the Netherlands and the UK (with some support from Denmark and Sweden) wanted defined rights and were sceptical about European judicial supervision. The UK was insistent that the rights in the Convention had to be precisely defined.[11] Unable to reach unanimous agreement the officials produced a draft reflecting (various) majority views that elaborate the rights, especially the limitation clauses enabling states to interfere with the exercise of guaranteed rights. The guarantee of political liberties was deleted. The independent supervisory system was diluted to enable the Committee of Ministers to decide complaints.

The Committee of Ministers accepted the compromises agreed by their senior officials together with provision for an optional right of petition by aggrieved individuals to the proposed Commission. The Consultative Assembly was unhappy that the draft Convention had removed the guarantee of political liberties and that no rights to property or education had been included. A preamble, drafted by a British delegate, was also supported by the Assembly. In response the Committee of Ministers decided to include the preamble and consider adding the further rights at a later date.[12]

We can discern, from this overview of the complex drafting history of the Convention,[13] that amongst the numerous stakeholders, to use contemporary language, there were both competing attitudes towards the ambit of the rights and freedoms guaranteed and divergent views of the ultimate objective(s) of the ECHR. Regarding the Convention's substantive guarantees Greer has observed that, '[a]lthough the discussions were inevitably influenced by the intellectual and political debates about rights which had been in progress since the early modern period, they were overwhelmingly driven by the urgent need to find workable institutions and procedures which all parties could accept, rather than by grand theories about the relationship between the individual, the state, and civil

[10] E. Bates, *The Evolution of the ECHR* (Oxford University Press, 2010), pp. 89–90.

[11] E. Wicks, 'The UK Government's Perceptions of the ECHR at the Time of Entry', [2000] *Public Law* 438.

[12] In what became Protocol No. 1, (Paris, 20 March 1952).

[13] See also A.W.B. Simpson, *Human Rights and the End of Empire* (Oxford University Press, 2001).

society'.[14] He believed the creators had four objectives for the Convention. First, it was a 'symbolic statement of the identity signatory states had of themselves',[15] which contrasted with Nazism and the communist totalitarianism of the Soviet empire. Second, the ability of Member States to bring complaints against other parties was designed to be an 'early warning device' where weak democracies were beginning to decline into authoritarianism. Third, the Convention was designed to help maintain peace amongst the Member States by deterring the development of belligerent dictatorial regimes. Fourth, it was intended to promote unity amongst the Member States by enhancing their shared values. Bates has also discerned ambiguity in the ECHR, as some proponents envisaged the Convention as a 'collective pact against totalitarianism' whilst others conceived it as a European Bill of Rights. But, '[f]rom the perspective of 1950 one would guess that most saw the Convention as more of an inter-State pact against totalitarianism than anything else, with the international system of control unlikely to be invoked other than in extreme cases.'[16]

Given this absence of unanimity amongst the drafters regarding the scope of the rights guaranteed, or indeed the precise purpose of the Convention, it would be futile to argue that the ECHR should today be primarily interpreted in accordance with the original intent of its creators.[17] Therefore, we shall now focus on some of the major forces underpinning the Court's interpretation and application of the Convention to modern European societies. These include rising human rights standards, to which Member States may have directly contributed – for example the Council of Europe's present-day opposition to the death penalty – and the evolution of different forms of personal relationship (e.g. single-parent families) which are primarily the result of changes in civil society.

1. Technological progress

Obviously, public authorities, just like private persons, continually make use of new technologies and some of these have the potential to seriously threaten the balance between legitimate governmental interests

[14] S. Greer, *The ECHR: Achievements, Problems and Prospects* (Cambridge University Press, 2006), p. 17.

[15] *Ibid.*, at p. 56. [16] See note 10 at p. 104.

[17] For a detailed examination of criticism of the Court for failing to afford sufficient weight to the drafters' intentions see D. Nicol, 'Original Intent and the ECHR', [2005] *Public Law* 152.

and personal liberties.[18] Therefore, it was inevitable that the Court has been confronted with the challenging role of determining whether particular utilisations of technology by state agents have infringed the Convention rights of individuals. One area of technological evolution that has generated a stream of litigation before the Court is the secret surveillance of persons by state officials. In regard to the interception of private communications the original Court extended the scope of Article 8 to cover telephone calls in *Klass and others* v. *Germany*.[19] The plenary Court held that '[a]lthough telephone conversations are not expressly mentioned in paragraph 1 of Article 8, the Court considers, as did the Commission, that such conversations are covered by the notions of "private life" and "correspondence" referred to by this provision'.[20] It believed that state interception constitutes a 'menace' to the freedom of communication between users of telecommunications systems. 'Powers of secret surveillance of citizens, characterising as they do the police state, are tolerable under the Convention only in so far as strictly necessary for safeguarding the democratic institutions.'[21] Consequently, the Court rigorously examined whether there was a clear legal basis underpinning the West German system of interception and if there were adequate institutional safeguards against the abuse of secret surveillance. The judges were unanimous in finding that the German system met these two requirements, and that consequently no breach of Article 8 had occurred.

The judgment in *Klass* is significant for disclosing the Court's willingness to update the application of the Convention to embrace newer forms of communications and the symbiotic evolution of the technology of secret surveillance. The jurisprudential methodology it deployed when analysing whether the German interception system complied with Article 8 was applied in a number of subsequent cases in which other states were found to have violated that provision in intercepting telephone calls.[22] In the recent complaint by *Iordachi and others* v. *Moldova*,[23] the unanimous Chamber found, *inter alia*, a failure by domestic courts to properly scrutinise governmental requests for interception warrants (99.2 per cent of the requests in 2007 had been granted) and that Moldovan law

[18] See T. Murphy (ed.), *New Technologies and Human Rights* (Oxford University Press, 2009) for a number of views on different aspects of the broader issue.

[19] ECtHR 6 September 1978. [20] *Ibid.*, at para. 41. [21] *Ibid.*, at para. 42.

[22] For example, in *Malone* v. *United Kingdom*, ECtHR 2 August 1984 and *Kruslin* v. *France*, ECtHR 24 April 1990.

[23] ECtHR 11 February 2009.

governing the interception of communications lacked clarity regarding the types of offence in respect of which it could be authorised.

The full-time Court has also followed its predecessor in extending Article 8 to modern communication technologies and their interception by public officials. For example, in *Kennedy* v. *UK*,[24] the united Chamber noted that '[i]t is not disputed that mail, telephone and email communications, including those made in the context of business dealings, are covered by the notions of "private life" and "correspondence" in Article 8(1)'.[25] However, the Court rejected the applicant's complaints that his communication in all three of these forms had been intercepted by the police and/or the domestic security service in breach of Article 8. The Chamber did not find that Kennedy had established a reasonable likelihood that his communications had been intercepted by state agencies. Additionally, in *Kennedy* neither the conduct of public officials nor the surveillance regime violated Article 8. Nevertheless, the Court continues to subject new forms of communications surveillance to a close scrutiny following the requirements outlined in *Klass*.

Generally, the full-time Court has also applied a similar set of principles to the constantly evolving technology of surveillance devices used by state officials. In *Khan* v. *UK*,[26] the police had hidden a listening device on the premises of a suspected heroin dealer. The device recorded the complainant discussing his involvement in the illegal importing of heroin. Subsequently, he was convicted, on the basis of that recording, and sentenced to three years' imprisonment. The Chamber was unanimous in finding a breach of Article 8 as no domestic law had regulated the use of such devices by the police at the time the recording was made.[27] Hence, the interference with the complainant's private life had not been 'in accordance with the law' as required by Article 8(2). Consequently, state agents cannot use covert surveillance technology that has merely been authorised under administrative arrangements.

Later, in *Bykov* v. *Russia*,[28] a Grand Chamber was united in finding a violation of Article 8 in respect of the use of a concealed radio-transmitting device. A person went to the Federal Security Service (FSB) alleging that

[24] ECtHR 18 May 2010. [25] *Ibid.*, at para. 118. [26] ECtHR 12 May 2000.

[27] Between the House of Lords rejecting the complainant's appeal and the Court determining his complaint the British Parliament had enacted legislation governing police utilisation of such devices and established an independent complaints system for aggrieved individuals who believed they had been subject to covert surveillance.

[28] ECtHR (GC) 21 January 2009.

the applicant, a prominent businessman and politician, had ordered him to kill a former business associate of the applicant. The FSB and the police pretended to murder the associate and then sent the informant to the applicant's estate with a hidden radio-transmitter on his person. The police recorded the informant's conversation with the applicant. The recording was played at the applicant's trial, but his conviction for 'incitement to commit a crime involving a murder' was based upon other evidence. After reciting the well established jurisprudence requiring secret surveillance operations to be regulated by clear domestic legal rules that curtail arbitrary interferences with personal privacy, the Grand Chamber held that:

> [i]n the Court's opinion, these principles apply equally to the use of a radio-transmitting device, which, in terms of the nature and degree of the intrusion involved, is virtually identical to telephone tapping.[29]

The Grand Chamber went on to conclude that Russian law had failed to provide adequate safeguards for the use of these devices in covert operations.

The use of a concealed Global Positioning System (GPS) tracking device by the police was examined by a Chamber in *Uzun* v. *Germany*.[30] The authorities suspected the applicant was a member of a left-wing terrorist cell and he was consequently placed under covert visual, video and telephone surveillance. In addition the Federal Prosecutor General ordered that a hidden GPS tracking device should be built into the car of a fellow suspect. The GPS device enabled the authorities to recover data once every minute disclosing the location of the car and its speed. The GPS device was operational for three months until the applicant (and the owner of the car) were arrested. During the applicant's trial data from the GPS device was used, together with video and personal surveillance evidence, to establish that he had placed bombs near the homes of members of Parliament and at other locations. He was convicted of attempted murder and causing explosions, and given a sentence of thirteen years' imprisonment. Before the Chamber the government contended that the use of the GPS device had not interfered with the applicant's private life as it had merely recorded the location of the car. However, the Chamber rejected that narrow perspective of the protection accorded to a person's private life under the Convention:

[29] *Ibid.*, at para. 79. [30] ECtHR 2 September 2010.

> The Court further notes that by the surveillance of the applicant via GPS, the investigation authorities, for some three months, systematically collected and stored data determining, in the circumstances, the applicant's whereabouts and movements in the public sphere. They further recorded the personal data and used it in order to draw up a pattern of the applicant's movements, to make further investigations and to collect additional evidence at the places the applicant had travelled to, which was later used at the criminal trial against the applicant...
>
> In the Court's view, GPS surveillance is by its very nature to be distinguished from other methods of visual or acoustical surveillance which are, as a rule, more susceptible of interfering with a person's right to respect for private life, because they disclose more information on a person's conduct, opinions or feelings. Having regard to the principles established in its case-law, it nevertheless finds the above-mentioned factors sufficient to conclude that the applicant's observation via GPS, in the circumstances, and the processing and use of the data obtained thereby in the manner described above amounted to an interference with his private life as protected by Article 8(1).[31]

Therefore, when applying Article 8(2) to the authorities' actions, the Chamber adopted a more lenient approach:

> it finds that these rather strict standards, set up and applied in the specific context of surveillance of telecommunications... *Iordachi and Others*... are not applicable as such to cases such as the present one, concerning surveillance via GPS of movements in public places and thus a measure which must be considered to interfere less with the private life of the person concerned than the interception of his or her telephone conversations... It will therefore apply the more general principles on adequate protection against arbitrary interference with Article 8 rights...[32]

Given that the German Code of Criminal Procedure empowered the use of 'other special technical means' of surveillance in investigations of grave crimes,[33] and that the applicant had been able to challenge the legality of the use of the GPS evidence during his trial and subsequent appeals, the Chamber was unanimous in finding that the interference with the applicant's private life had been 'in accordance with the law' and a proportionate measure for the legitimate aims of, *inter alia*, preventing crime and protecting public safety. Hence no violation of Article 8 had occurred – so the type of information recorded by a covert surveillance

[31] *Ibid.*, at paras 51–2. [32] *Ibid.*, at para. 66.

[33] Note that in 2000 the Code had been amended to require judicial authorisation of surveillance measures operating for more than one month.

device will affect the intensity of the Court's review. This is a significant refinement in the case law.

Another technological revolution that could hardly have been imagined a generation ago, let alone at the time the Convention was drafted, is the creation and use of DNA profiles of individuals in the criminal justice system.[34] A Grand Chamber applied Article 8 to the English utilisation of DNA records in *S and Marper* v. *UK*.[35] In England the police were empowered to take DNA cell samples (usually obtained via a mouth swab) from any person arrested for a 'recordable offence' and a digital profile of those samples was stored on the national DNA database (for use in future criminal investigations). A cell sample had been taken from S at the age of eleven, when he was arrested for an alleged attempted robbery. Subsequently he was acquitted of the charge, but his sample and DNA profile were retained by the authorities. Marper had been arrested for allegedly harassing his partner and undergone similar DNA processing. He was not charged, but his DNA data was retained. Before the Grand Chamber the UK government contended that the retention of DNA samples and profiles for the criminal justice purposes laid down in domestic law did not come within the scope of private life under Article 8. However, the united Grand Chamber determined that DNA cell samples contain 'sensitive' information, including health issues. Consequently, '[g]iven the nature and the amount of personal information contained in cellular samples, their retention *per se* must be regarded as interfering with the right to respect for the private lives of the individuals concerned.'[36] Although DNA profiles contained less information than cell samples, the Grand Chamber ruled that the profiles disclosed genetic relationships between individuals that was sufficient for their retention by the authorities to fall within the right to private life of those persons. The government's claim that the applicants' samples and profiles had been retained for the legitimate aim of preventing crime was accepted by the Grand Chamber. But the Grand Chamber stated that:

> the protection afforded by Article 8 of the Convention would be unacceptably weakened if the use of modern scientific techniques in the criminal-justice system were allowed at any cost and without carefully balancing the potential benefits of the extensive use of such techniques against important private-life interests.[37]

[34] Deoxyribonucleic acid. [35] ECtHR (GC) 4 December 2008.
[36] *Ibid.*, at para. 73. [37] *Ibid.*, at para. 112.

The Grand Chamber went on to conclude that the extensive powers of retention granted to the authorities in England did not strike a 'fair balance' between the private life interests of the applicants and the wider public interest,[38] and so Article 8 had been breached. Hence this is another area of governmental utilisation of technology in which the Court has required adequate safeguards to be observed by public authorities if Convention rights are not to be infringed.

2. Changing social relationships

Just as we have seen in the above section how constantly developing technology has required the Court to refine its application of Convention rights, so the six decades since the drafting of the ECHR have witnessed unforeseeable evolutions in the social relationships between persons living in the Member States (and in other states)[39] that also necessitated reforms in the jurisprudence. A vivid illustration of this process is the Court's expanding notion of the relationships that constitute 'family life' for the purposes of Article 8. In the early case of *Marckx* v. *Belgium*,[40] the original Court took a progressive view, holding that an unmarried mother and her daughter (a single-parent family in modern parlance) were a family and could invoke the protection of Article 8 (and Article 14) to successfully challenge domestic legal discrimination against illegitimate children.

> The Court concurs entirely with the Commission's established case-law on a crucial point, namely that Article 8 makes no distinction between the 'legitimate' and the 'illegitimate' family. Such a distinction would not be consonant with the word 'everyone', and this is confirmed by Article 14 with its prohibition, in the enjoyment of the rights and freedoms enshrined in the Convention, of discrimination grounded on 'birth'. In addition, the Court notes that the Committee of Ministers of the Council of Europe regards the single woman and her child as one form of family no less than others (Resolution(70)15 of 15 May 1970) . . .[41]

[38] More generally, see A. Mowbray, 'A Study of the Principle of Fair Balance in the Jurisprudence of the European Court of Human Rights', (2010) 10(2) *Human Rights Law Review* 289.

[39] See for example *Abdulaziz, Cabales and Balkandali* v. *United Kingdom*, ECtHR 28 May 1985.

[40] ECtHR 13 June 1979 and for Ms Marckx's personal account of her complaint see M.A. Goldhaber, *A People's History of the European Court of Human Rights* (New Brunswick, NJ: Rutgers University Press, 2007), Ch. 1.

[41] *Ibid.*, at para. 31.

Subsequently, the Court has maintained a robust approach to the protection of such children.[42]

In *X, Y and Z* v. *UK*,[43] the applicants were a postoperative transsexual and his long-term female partner together with the latter's daughter, who had been born through the use of Artificial Insemination by Donor (AID). The respondent government argued that they were not a 'family', relying on Commission jurisprudence that same-sex couples did not fall within that concept. However, building upon its judgment in *Marckx*, the Court declared that:

> the notion of 'family life' in Article 8 is not confined solely to families based on marriage and may encompass other *de facto* relationships (see the *Marckx* v. *Belgium* judgment . . .). When deciding whether a relationship can be said to amount to 'family life', a number of factors may be relevant, including whether the couple live together, the length of their relationship and whether they have demonstrated their commitment to each other by having children together or by any other means . . . [44]

Having regard to the facts that X and Y had lived together for over fifteen years, had jointly applied to the National Health Service for Y to undergo AID treatment and that X had acted as Z's 'father' since her birth the Court was unanimous in concluding that they constituted a family for the purposes of Article 8. The family relationships in this case were a product of both social changes and medical/technological progress.[45]

In the more recent case of *Schalk and Kopf* v. *Austria*,[46] the Court reversed its (and the former Commission's) previous stance towards whether same-sex couples are able to claim that their relationships amount to 'family life'.[47] Taking account of the 'rapid evolution of social attitudes towards same-sex couples' that had occurred in numerous Member States over the previous decade and recent European Union legal developments:[48]

42 For a contemporary example see *Genovese* v. *Malta*, ECtHR 11 October 2011.

43 ECtHR (GC) 22 April 1997. 44 *Ibid*., at para. 36.

45 Note, the Grand Chamber was deeply divided over the assessment of restrictions on medically assisted procreation in the recent case of *SH and others* v. *Austria*, ECtHR (GC) 3 November 2011.

46 ECtHR 24 June 2010.

47 On this topic see A. Mowbray, 'An Examination of the European Court of Human Rights' Approach to Overruling its Previous Case Law', (2009) 9(2) *Human Rights Law Review* 179.

48 See note 46 at para. 93.

> the Court considers it artificial to maintain the view that, in contrast to a different-sex couple, a same-sex couple cannot enjoy 'family life' for the purposes of Article 8. Consequently the relationship of the applicants, a cohabiting same-sex couple living in a stable *de facto* partnership, falls within the notion of 'family life', just as the relationship of a different-sex couple in the same situation would.[49]

It is noticeable that the Court was applying broadly similar criteria to those articulated in *X, Y and Z* when assessing whether the applicants' relationship amounted to 'family life'. But when the Chamber came to examine the substance of the applicants' complaints, that they were not able to marry or have their partnership recognised by Austrian law, the Court found itself constrained by the language and historical origins of the Convention. In respect of the right to marry, enshrined in Article 12 of the ECHR, the Chamber observed that the text uses the terms 'men and women':

> However, in contrast, all other substantive Articles of the Convention grant rights and freedoms to 'everyone' or state that 'no one' is to be subjected to certain types of prohibited treatment. The choice of wording in Article 12 must thus be regarded as deliberate. Moreover, regard must be had to the historical context in which the Convention was adopted. In the 1950s marriage was clearly understood in the traditional sense of being a union between partners of different sex.[50]

As the Chamber found no present-day consensus amongst the Member States on the right of same-sex couples to marry – only six states permitting such marriages – the Court was unanimous in concluding that the applicants had not suffered a violation of Article 12. A bare majority of the Chamber, four judges to three, also found no breach of Article 8 in conjunction with Article 14, given the Chamber's judgment concerning the scope of Article 12. Significantly, the Grand Chamber refused the applicants' request for the case to be reconsidered under Article 43.[51]

Schalk and Kopf thus discloses the willingness of the Court to expand the coverage of 'family life' to embrace single-sex partnerships in accordance with contemporary social mores. However, it also provides a dramatic example of the reluctance of the Court to depart from the specific language of the Convention, adopted with a clear intent by the drafters, where

[49] *Ibid.*, at para. 94. [50] *Ibid.*, at para. 55.
[51] On this process see A. Mowbray, 'An Examination of the Work of the Grand Chamber of the European Court of Human Rights', [2007] *Public Law* 507.

there has been no subsequent evolution in the relevant domestic laws of most of the Member States.[52] Therefore, the judgment may be viewed as an illustration of the Court respecting the will of the states rather than the applicants' contention (supported by non-governmental organisation (NGO) third parties) that the needs of today require states to permit civil marriage for same-sex couples.

3. Evolution in human rights standards

The Court has been confronted with many situations where complainants have argued that since the drafting of the Convention relevant human rights standards have become enhanced and therefore ECHR rights and freedoms should be interpreted in the light of contemporary practice. We shall, briefly, examine three examples of how the Court has dealt with such claims.

The death penalty was a regularly used judicial punishment when the Convention was drafted. Consequently, the right to life guaranteed by Article 2 of the ECHR expressly permitted this form of punishment: '[n]o one shall be deprived of his life intentionally save in the execution of a sentence of a court following his conviction of a crime for which this penalty is provided by law'.[53] Yet over the ensuing decades increasing numbers of Member States abandoned the use of the death penalty. As a result, from the late 1980s the Court was faced with a series of high-profile cases in which the applicants (and third-party NGOs)[54] submitted that the Court should interpret Article 2 in the context of modern disapproval of the death penalty. In *Soering* v. *UK*,[55] the German applicant challenged the legality of his extradition to the USA to face capital murder charges. The Court acknowledged that:

> *[d]e facto* the death penalty no longer exists in time of peace in the Contracting States. In the few Contracting States which retain the death penalty in law for some peacetime offences, death sentences, if ever imposed, are

[52] On the topic of the European consensus, see K. Dzehtsiarou, 'Does Consensus Matter? Legitimacy of European Consensus in the Case Law of the European Court of Human Rights', [2011] *Public Law* 534.

[53] Art. 2(1).

[54] On the important contributions of NGOs to the development of the Court's jurisprudence, see R.A. Cichowski, 'Civil Society and the European Court of Human Rights' in J. Christoffersen and M.R. Madsen (eds), *The European Court of Human Rights between Law and Politics* (Oxford University Press, 2011).

[55] ECtHR 7 September 1989.

> nowadays not carried out. This 'virtual consensus in Western European legal systems that the death penalty is, under current circumstances, no longer consistent with regional standards of justice', to use the words of Amnesty International,[56] is reflected in Protocol No. 6 to the Convention,[57] which provides for the abolition of the death penalty in time of peace . . .
>
> Subsequent practice in national penal policy, in the form of a generalised abolition of capital punishment, could be taken as establishing the agreement of the Contracting States to abrogate the exception provided for under Article 2(1) . . . However, Protocol No. 6, as a subsequent written agreement, shows that the intention of the Contracting Parties as recently as 1983 was to adopt the normal method of amendment of the text in order to introduce a new obligation to abolish capital punishment in time of peace . . . [58]

Therefore, the Court considered that it was unable to rule that the death penalty in peacetime violates Article 2 (or *per se* breaches Article 3) even when the current penal practice of the Member States was taken into consideration.

A decade and a half later in *Öcalan* v. *Turkey*,[59] concerning the former leader of the PKK (Workers' Party of Kurdistan) who had been sentenced to death (subsequently commuted to a sentence of life imprisonment), Öcalan's lawyer argued that by then the practice of Member States was even more overwhelming in abandoning the death penalty. The Grand Chamber endorsed the Chamber's view that:

> [s]uch a marked development could now be taken as signalling the agreement of the Contracting States to abrogate, or at the very least to modify, the second sentence of Article 2(1), particularly when regard is had to the fact that all Contracting States have now signed Protocol No. 6 and that it has been ratified by forty-one States. It may be questioned whether it is necessary to await ratification of Protocol No. 6 by the three remaining States before concluding that the death penalty exception in Article 2 has been significantly modified. Against such a consistent background, it can be said that capital punishment in peacetime has come to be regarded as an unacceptable . . . form of punishment which is no longer permissible under Article 2.[60]

[56] A third-party intervener.
[57] Protocol No. 6 to the Convention for the Protection of Human Rights and Fundamental Freedoms concerning the Abolition of the Death Penalty, Strasbourg, 28 April 1983.
[58] See note 55 at paras 102 and 103.
[59] ECtHR (GC) 12 May 2005.
[60] *Ibid.*, at para. 163.

But, echoing the approach in *Soering*, the Grand Chamber noted that the Member States had continued their process of abolishing the death penalty via protocols through the subsequent agreement of Protocol No. 13,[61] which provides for the complete ending of the death penalty. Therefore, the Grand Chamber refrained from formally ruling on whether Article 2(1) no longer permits the death penalty. So, again, we saw the Court adopting a cautious attitude towards the continuing legality of the death penalty under Article 2, whilst recognising the increasingly strong practice of Member States to abandon the punishment.

A united Chamber further strengthened the Court's condemnation of the death penalty in *Al-Saadoon and Mufdhi* v. *UK*.[62] The applicants were Iraqi nationals suspected of having killed two British servicemen a few weeks after the Multi-National Force occupied Iraq in 2003. The applicants were detained by the British forces in Iraq and eventually handed over to the Iraqi government to face trial on war crimes charges, for which the death penalty was a punishment available to the Iraqi courts (the British government had made representations to the Iraqi government expressing opposition to the restoration/use of the death penalty in Iraq). The Chamber acknowledged further evolution in the Member States' rejection of the death penalty since *Öcalan*:

> All but two of the Member States have now signed Protocol No. 13 and all but three of the States which have signed have ratified it. These figures, together with consistent State practice in observing the moratorium on capital punishment, are strongly indicative that Article 2 has been amended so as to prohibit the death penalty in all circumstances. Against this background, the Court does not consider that the wording of the second sentence of Article 2(1) continues to act as a bar to its interpreting the words 'inhuman or degrading treatment or punishment' in Article 3 as including the death penalty . . . [63]

Accordingly, the Chamber proceeded to find that the UK had breached Article 3 as the applicants had been exposed to psychological suffering amounting to inhuman treatment, since handing them over to the Iraqi authorities had caused them to fear execution (the criminal cases against the applicants were still pending at the time of the Strasbourg judgment).

[61] Protocol No. 13 to the Convention for the Protection of Human Rights and Fundamental Freedoms concerning the Abolition of the Death Penalty in All Circumstances, Vilnius, 3 May 2002.

[62] ECtHR 2 March 2010.

[63] *Ibid.*, at para. 120.

Al-Saadoon and Mufdhi is the authoritative view of the Court on the death penalty when assessed from the perspective of contemporary values.[64]

The second example of the Court responding to increasing human rights standards involved the reversal of the original Court's interpretation of limited trade union rights under Article 11 of the ECHR. In the early judgments in *Swedish Engine Drivers' Union* v. *Sweden* and *Schmidt and Dahlstrom* v. *Sweden* the Court held that the right of trade unions to engage in collective bargaining with employers, on behalf of the unions' members, was not an element of the 'right to form and join trade unions' guaranteed by Article 11 of the ECHR.[65] However, in the more recent case of *Demir and Baykara* v. *Turkey*,[66] the President and a member of a trade union representing local government workers argued that the domestic judicial quashing of a collective agreement signed between the union and a local council violated Article 11. The unanimous Grand Chamber considered that the essential rights of trade unions and their members found within Article 11 are:

> subject to evolution depending on particular developments in labour relations. In this connection it is appropriate to remember that the Convention is a living instrument which must be interpreted in the light of present-day conditions, and in accordance with developments in international law, so as to reflect the increasingly high standard being required in the area of the protection of human rights . . .[67]

Taking account of relevant International Labour Organization Conventions,[68] the European Social Charter,[69] the European Union's Charter of Fundamental Rights,[70] the practice of the 'vast majority' of Member States in recognising the right of civil servants to engage in collective bargaining,[71] and new Turkish legislation empowering collective bargaining by civil servants' unions, the Grand Chamber held that:

> [i]n the light of these developments, the Court considers that its case–law to the effect that the right to bargain collectively and to enter into collective agreements does not constitute an inherent element of Article 11 . . . should be reconsidered, so as to take account of the perceptible evolution in such matters, in both international law and domestic legal systems . . .

[64] The Grand Chamber refused to reconsider the Chamber's judgment under Art. 43: screening panel decision of 18 October 2010.

[65] Both ECtHR 6 February 1976.

[66] ECtHR (GC) 12 November 2008.

[67] *Ibid.*, at para. 146.

[68] Including Convention No. 151 (1978).

[69] Art. 6(2).

[70] Art. 28.

[71] See note 66 at para. 151.

> Consequently, the Court considers that, having regard to the developments in labour law, both international and national, and to the practice of Contracting States in such matters, the right to bargain collectively with the employer has, in principle, become one of the essential elements of the 'right to form and to join trade unions for the protection of [one's] interests' set forth in Article 11 of the Convention . . .[72]

Furthermore, the Grand Chamber went on to find that Turkey had violated the applicants' rights under that Article.

Demir and Baykara is thus a very powerful demonstration of the impact of enhanced human rights standards on the Court's interpretation of the Convention. The multiplicity of sources underpinning the Court's conclusion as to what constitute contemporary labour relations standards in collective bargaining may explain why the Grand Chamber was willing to overturn the established jurisprudence.

An even more recent example of the Court reinterpreting the scope of Convention rights to reflect contemporary standards is *Bayatyan* v. *Armenia*,[73] which dealt with the sensitive topic of conscientious objection to compulsory military service. The applicant, a member of the Jehovah's Witnesses, had been convicted and imprisoned for refusing to undertake military service (he had offered to participate in civilian service, but that option was not available at that time in Armenia). He complained to Strasbourg, contending that his conviction breached his right to freedom of thought, conscience and religion guaranteed by Article 9 of the ECHR. The Chamber, subject to one dissent, followed the established approach of the former European Commission and held that Article 4(3)(b) restricts the ambit of Article 9 in regard to claims of conscientious objection.[74] Bayatyan then requested the Grand Chamber (successfully) to reconsider his case. A number of third parties were also given permission to intervene including the Quakers, the European Association of Jehovah's Christian Witnesses and Amnesty International. Before the Grand Chamber the applicant and the interveners contended that, at the present day, virtually all Member States recognised the right to conscientious objection and that United Nations' organs also endorsed such a right. Therefore, they argued that the Court should apply its living instrument doctrine to

72 *Ibid.*, at paras 153–4. 73 ECtHR (GC) 7 July 2011.

74 ECtHR 27 October 2009 and see my criticism of the Chamber's reasoning: A. Mowbray, 'European Court of Human Rights May 2009–April 2010', (2010) 16(4) *European Public Law* 495 at p. 512.

interpret Article 9 in accordance with the current standard recognising conscientious objection. The Grand Chamber noted that today amongst the Member States only Azerbaijan and Turkey have not recognised a right to conscientious objection. Furthermore, the Committee of Ministers, taking account of developments in international fora, had recommended that Member States grant conscripts the right to conscientious objection:[75]

> In the light of the foregoing and in line with the 'living instrument' approach, the Court therefore takes the view that it is not possible to confirm the case-law established by the Commission, and that Article 9 should no longer be read in conjunction with Article 4(3)(b). Consequently, the applicant's complaint is to be assessed solely under Article 9.
>
> In this respect, the Court notes that Article 9 does not explicitly refer to a right to conscientious objection. However, it considers that opposition to military service, where it is motivated by a serious and insurmountable conflict between the obligation to serve in the army and a person's conscience or his deeply and genuinely held religious or other beliefs, constitutes a conviction or belief of sufficient cogency, seriousness, cohesion and importance to attract the guarantees of Article 9 . . . Whether and to what extent objection to military service falls within the ambit of that provision must be assessed in the light of the particular circumstances of the case.[76]

The Grand Chamber went on to determine that Armenia could not justify its interference with the applicant's protected religious beliefs under Article 9(2) as, *inter alia*, his conviction was not 'necessary in a democratic society'. Judge Gyulumyan, from Armenia, dissented as she believed that:

> the role of this Court is to protect human rights which already exist in the Convention, not to create new rights. One can argue that the evolutive approach to the Convention permits the Court to broaden the rights protected. However, this in my view is not permitted when the Convention itself leaves the recognition of particular rights to the discretion of the Contracting Parties.[77]

We may observe that the majority of the Grand Chamber in *Bayatyan*, like the Grand Chamber in *Demir and Baykara*, could rely on an extensive range of evidence that relevant human rights standards had broadened since the drafting of the Convention, whilst Judge Gyulumyan's attitude

[75] Recommendation CM/Rec(2010)4. [76] See note 73 at paras 109–10.
[77] *Ibid.*, Dissenting Opinion of Judge Gyulumyan at para. 2.

towards conscientious objection was a reflection of state practice when the Convention was agreed.

4. The Court's jurisprudential tools for expanding the application of the Convention

It has not been the primary purpose of this chapter to examine the tools and techniques developed by the Court to underpin its extension of the rights and freedoms elaborated in the text of the Convention. I and other contributors have focused on this aspect of the Court's jurisprudence in previous publications.[78] Nevertheless, it is significant to note that the case law examined in this chapter disclosed the Court utilising several of its well established jurisprudential tools. The living instrument doctrine was first articulated back in the 1970s by the original Court in the context of the legality under the Convention of the use of corporal punishment in the criminal justice system.[79] It requires Convention rights and freedoms to be interpreted in the light of contemporary conditions and was a key component in the Court's reasoning in *Demir and Baykara* v. *Turkey* and *Bayatyan* v. *Armenia.* In both of those judgments the Grand Chamber expressly invoked the living instrument doctrine as a legal basis to justify overruling long-established interpretations of the Convention that were not in accordance with modern standards regarding trade union rights and conscientious objection to compulsory military service.

Another jurisprudential tool used in a number of the above cases was the Court's consideration of whether a European consensus existed for an expansive interpretation of a particular Convention right or freedom. Where a clear majority of Member States' practice, either in *de facto* behaviour or via legal regulation, was consistent with a wider interpretation of a Convention right or freedom the Court was more likely to endorse such an expansion of the Convention's guarantees. For example, as we saw in *Al-Saadoon and Mufdhi* v. *UK*, the Court finally recognised that the consensus amongst Member States regarding the abolition/non-use of the death penalty had become so overwhelming that it was now

[78] See for examples J.H. Gerards, 'Fundamental rights and other interests: should it really make a difference?' in E. Brems (ed.), *Conflicts Between Fundamental Rights* (Antwerp: Intersentia, 2008), 655–90 and A. Mowbray, *The Development of Positive Obligations under the ECHR by the European Court of Human Rights* (Oxford: Hart, 2004) and 'The Creativity of the European Court of Human Rights', (2005) 5(1) *Human Rights Law Review* 57.

[79] *Tyrer* v. *United Kingdom*, judgment of 25 April 1978.

permissible for the Court to hold that such a punishment violates Article 3 of the Convention. However, where the Court is unable to find the existence of a European consensus then it will tend to adopt a more literal interpretation of the Convention, as it did regarding the right to marry in *Schalk and Kopf* v. *Austria*. The European consensus tool can, of course, be used alongside the living instrument doctrine as the dominant (for example in *Bayatyan*) or one of a multitude (as in *Demir and Baykara*) of mechanisms for establishing the contemporary context in which the wording of the Convention should be interpreted.

Other chapters in this collection disclose further jurisprudential tools developed by the Court that facilitate the expansion of Convention rights and freedoms. For instance, Eva Brems examines how the Court has found (created) implied procedural rights within the text of substantive rights.[80] This process involved both the concept of implied rights enshrined within the Convention and the Court's well established doctrine that Convention rights and freedoms must be interpreted in a way that ensures they are of 'practical and effective' use to individuals, not merely worthless rhetoric. Laurens Lavrysen also offers a novel theoretical analysis of implied positive obligations, a key mechanism for the expansion of Convention rights and freedoms, that seeks to address the Court's reluctance to develop a general theory of this type of obligation.[81]

5. Conclusions

As we have discerned there were considerable differences of views amongst the drafters on the scope of the rights and freedoms enshrined in the Convention. Furthermore, the ensuing decades have witnessed unforeseeable evolutions in technology, social relations and human rights standards and practices. Consequently, we should not be surprised to discover, as the above case law has demonstrated, that the Court generally interprets and applies the Convention in accordance with contemporary needs. However, where states have signalled their intention to revise the breadth of a Convention right by the process of negotiating and ratifying additional protocols (for example regarding the death penalty), or where a particular Convention right was drafted with a clearly limited ambit and no subsequent enhancement of that right has conclusively emerged in the relevant practice of the Member States (e.g. sanctioning marriages between same-sex couples), then the Court has been cautious not to

[80] See Chapter 7 below. [81] See Chapter 8 below.

interpret the Convention contrary to the will of the states. The Court has thus navigated a challenging traverse between the ravines of unjustifiable judicial activism and restraint. Generally, an expansive stance towards the interpretation of Convention rights and freedoms has been followed by the Court subject to the occasional dissenting judgment, such as that of Judge Gyulumyan in *Bayatyan*. However, the Brighton Declaration has been viewed as an expression of the desire of the Member States to curtail the discretion of the Court.[82] Therefore, the coming years may witness a rebalancing of power between national authorities and the Strasbourg judiciary.

[82] Brighton Declaration: High-Level Conference on the Future of the European Court of Human Rights, 20 April 2012. See also L.R. Helfer, 'The Burdens and Benefits of Brighton', 1(1) *ESIL Reflections* 1: http://esil-sedi.eu/node/138.

3

The scope and balancing of rights

Diagnostic or constitutive?

GEORGE LETSAS

1. Constitutive v. diagnostic questions

One recurrent problem in much contemporary literature on rights is the failure to distinguish between constitutive and diagnostic questions. Constitutive questions are questions about what makes it the case that the world is such and such. For example, what makes it the case that someone suffers from cancer? What makes it the case that it will snow tomorrow? Diagnostic questions by contrast are questions about how we come to *find out* that the world is such and such. How do we find out whether someone has cancer? How do we find out whether it will snow tomorrow? Constitutive questions are questions about how the world is. Diagnostic questions are questions about how we form *beliefs* about the world and how we go about acquiring knowledge about it.

For example, a constitutive question about cancer is a question about the genetic make-up of the disease, which roughly consists in unregulated cell growth. Unregulated cell growth is part of what constitutes cancer. A diagnostic question about cancer, by contrast, is a question about how we go about ascertaining whether someone has cancer. This can take the form of performing various tests, such as MRI, X-rays, blood tests or looking for relevant symptoms such as pain or swelling. Such tests do not constitute cancer, even when they are positive; they merely indicate the presence or absence of cancerous cells. Likewise, a constitutive question about snow is a question about the physics and chemistry of snow, which roughly consists in precipitation of atmospheric water vapour in the form of crystalline water ice. A diagnostic question about snow, by contrast,

I am grateful to audiences at the University of Ghent conference 'The Scope of Fundamental Rights' in March 2012 and the New York University Jean Monnet Centre Workshop in April 2012 for their comments and suggestions. I would also like to thank Joanna Tzoulaki for extremely helpful discussion on proxies and surrogate end-points.

is a meteorological question about the tests we use (e.g. thermometers, barometers, satellites) to predict whether the atmosphere in a particular region will precipitate into crystalline water ice at a given time.

The results of diagnostic tests should be distinguished from the property the presence of which they seek to detect. It would be a category mistake to conflate cancerous cells with the X-ray film showing a malignant tumour, or to conflate a thermometer indication with fever. Destroying the X-ray or the thermometer will not make the cancer or the fever disappear. Diagnostic tests do not normally affect whether the property they seek to detect exists or not. A thermometer, unlike a thermostat, does not regulate temperature; it simply indicates it. Likewise, an X-ray does not affect whether the body cells that it scans are cancerous, except of course if one is exposed to large amounts of radiation.[1] Diagnostic tests are epistemic tools we design to help us form true beliefs about the world; they give us reasons to believe that the world is such and such. But what essentially matters of course is not whether someone (or everyone) has good grounds to *believe* that the world is such and such, but rather whether the world *in fact* is such and such. For example, what matters is not whether someone has good reasons to believe he is healthy, but rather whether he in fact has any cancerous cells. Being epistemic tools that humans design and use, diagnostic tests are fallible. They can produce false negatives and false positives. For example, a blood test may fail to indicate the presence of HIV (false negative);[2] and an ultrasound scan may falsely indicate the presence of ovarian cancer (false positive).[3] So it is important not to conflate constitutive questions with diagnostic questions because it is important not to conflate how the world is with what someone believes about it. A person will not be healthy just because a test produced a false negative, nor will that person be ill, just because a test produced a false positive.

Sometimes diagnostic tests do not seek to detect directly the property that constitutes the entity under study. Rather, they are designed to detect some other property (the 'proxy') that typically correlates with the constitutive property. These tests are indirectly diagnostic. For example, decreasing atmospheric pressure typically correlates with rain; tumours

[1] Even in that case, though, the cells just scanned would not, yet, be cancerous.

[2] The new 'take-home' HIV test, approved by the US Food and Drug administration, produces one in twelve false negatives. See www.nytimes.com/2012/07/04/health/oraquick-at-home-hiv-test-wins-fda-approval.html.

[3] See www.nytimes.com/2012/09/11/health/research/ovarian-cancer-tests-are-ineffective-medical-panel-says.html.

typically correlate with cancerous cells. The proxies (e.g. low pressure; tumours) correlate with properties that are constitutive elements of some entity (rain; cancer) the presence of which we are seeking to establish or predict. By contrast, direct diagnostic tests (e.g. a biopsy) are designed to detect directly the properties that are constitutive of the relevant disease.

The use of indirect diagnostic tests may be appropriate for many reasons. Sometimes it is easier to spot the presence of the proxy than the presence of the constitutive property in which we are interested. For example, the percentage of alcohol in one's breath can be used as a proxy for the percentage of alcohol in one's blood, which is a constitutive element of the state of being drunk. It is easier (e.g. quicker and less invasive) for the police to breathalyse drivers than to take a blood sample from them. This gives the police a reason to prioritize the use of breathalysers over blood testing as a means for detecting drunk drivers. The law uses the high percentage of alcohol in one's breath as a presumption that the driver was over the limit. But this does not mean that the percentage of alcohol in one's breath is a constitutive element of the state of being drunk. That is why, in several jurisdictions,[4] the law gives suspected drunk drivers the right to request a blood test, upon failing a breathalyser test. The former is a more accurate test precisely because it is the high percentage of alcohol in one's blood, not one's mouth, that makes one drunk (and hence unfit to drive).

Apart from being more convenient, safer or easier to administer, the use of indirect diagnostic tests – such as breathalysers – may have other public benefits. They can be cheaper, enabling the government to help a greater number of people (e.g. to reduce road accidents caused by drink and driving), or to prevent greater harm (e.g. to reduce fatal accidents). In other cases, the use of indirect diagnostic tests may be justified when it is extremely difficult or even impossible to establish the presence of some relevant property or to establish it promptly. Medical researchers or drug companies often use proxies (called 'surrogate end-points') for medical events they seek to target (called 'clinical end-points'). For example, blood pressure is used as a proxy for stroke, cholesterol levels as a proxy for myocardial infarctions and CD4 cell count as a proxy for AIDS-related mortality.[5] Governments authorise drugs that have been shown to control

[4] For instance in the US states of Florida, Oregon, New Jersey and North Carolina. In the United Kingdom, this right was abolished in 2009; see www.guardian.co.uk/society/2009/mar/15/drink-driving-blood-test-breathalyser.

[5] See H.C. Bucher, G.H. Guyatt, D.J. Cook and A. Holbrook, 'Users' guides to the medical literature XIX. Applying clinical trial results. A. How to use an article measuring the effect

the proxy (e.g. cholesterol) in an attempt to prevent the event with which the proxy correlates (e.g. heart attacks), even if there is yet no reliable evidence that the drug will succeed in doing so. The reason is that it takes several years and many patients to study the effects of the drug on the clinical end-point, whereas it might take only a few months and a small number of patients to study the effects of the drug on the surrogate end-point.[6] Moreover, apart from being expensive and time-consuming, studies on the clinical end-point will be of no benefit to those who, in the meantime, will suffer the studied medical event and die. Until studies on the clinical end-point are concluded, it is not possible to know with certainty whether some drug indeed saves lives. The fact that a drug controls the surrogate end-point gives us reason to believe that it will also control the clinical end-point and hence may justify authorising it.[7]

The distinction between constitutive questions and diagnostic questions is one that applies to fundamental rights, too. We can, first, ask constitutive questions about rights: what makes it the case that Jones has a fundamental right to burn the national flag in the middle of Times Square? In virtue of what is Jones entitled to do so? And we can also ask diagnostic questions about rights: how should one go about deciding whether Jones has a right to burn the national flag? What is the best way to acquire knowledge about whether there is such a right? In designing legal institutions with the task of adjudicating on fundamental rights, our main concern is of a diagnostic nature: we want to make sure that the way courts go about deciding whether someone's rights have been violated maximises correct results and minimises false ones (positives or negatives). The courts' task in other words is a diagnostic one: their aim to find out whether a fundamental right has been violated. And their method of reasoning is the equivalent of a diagnostic test: its success is to be measured by its accuracy rate, i.e. how often it produces false negatives

of an intervention on surrogate end points', (1999) 282(8) *Journal of the American Medical Association* 771–8.

6 See B.M. Psaty, N.S. Weiss, C.D. Furberg *et al.*, 'Surrogate end points, health outcomes, and the drug-approval process for the treatment of risk factors for cardiovascular disease', (1999) 282(8) *Journal of the American Medical Association* 786–90.

7 The use of surrogate end-points is not uncontroversial. See T. Fleming and D. David, 'Surrogate end points in clinical trials: Are we being misled?', (1996) 125(7) *Annals of Internal Medicine* 605–13; C. Gluud and K. Krogsgaard, 'Would you trust a surrogate respondent?', (1997) 349 *Lancet* 665–6; P.C. Gøtzsche, A.L.V. Torri and L. Rossetti, 'Beware of surrogate outcome measures', (1996) 12 *International Journal of Technology Assessment in Health Care* 238–46.

and false positives. For, just like any diagnostic test, nothing the courts do or say affects whether someone's right has *in fact* been violated. A court may fail to spot a violation or declare one when no violation took place, but it cannot change whether or not there was *in fact* a violation. It follows therefore that the reasoning that courts use when they adjudicate on fundamental rights is a diagnostic tool and not necessarily a theory of what rights people have. Just as a barometer does not tell us what snow is but merely indicates whether snow is likely to fall, so judicial tests about fundamental rights do not tell us what a right is, they merely indicate whether a right has been violated. Moreover, just as a medical test can be indirect, seeking to detect proxies that do not themselves constitute a disease, so judicial review may be seeking to detect properties that do not themselves constitute a violation of rights, but are rather proxies for a violation.

It seems to me that the failure to grasp the distinction between constitutive and diagnostic questions bedevils much theoretical work on rights in Europe. According to what we might call the 'orthodox' view in Europe, the test that courts use to adjudicate on fundamental rights amounts to the structure in which these rights consist. Let us first have a brief look at the judicial test (commonly referred to as 'judicial review'). Let's take the European Court of Human Rights, for example. When deciding a case, the Court asks first whether the liberty with which some state measure interfered falls within the scope of a right protected under the European Convention on Human Rights (the 'scope' test). Second, it asks whether the interference was prescribed by law (the 'legality' test) and whether it was in pursuit of a legitimate aim (the 'legitimacy' test). Finally, the Court asks whether the interference was necessary in a democratic society (the 'proportionality' test). The final stage is commonly referred to as the test of proportionality *lato sensu*. In Germany and elsewhere in Europe the test of proportionality is subdivided into three questions: is the impugned measure rationally connected to the pursuit of a legitimate aim ('suitability' test)? Is the measure necessary for the pursuit of that aim ('necessity' test)? Is the seriousness of the interference with the applicant's right proportionate to the benefits gained in pursuit of the legitimate aim in question (proportionality in the narrow sense, or 'balancing')?

Now, many scholars take this three-part test that European courts use in adjudicating on rights (i.e. scope, proportionality and balancing) and treat it as a theory of what rights *are*. So for example Gerards and Senden argue that the European Court's test, as outlined above, amounts to the 'structure' of fundamental rights and complain that the Court often offends this structure by skipping the test of scope, i.e. that part of the test which asks whether the liberty that was restricted falls within the scope of the ECHR right.[8] And Robert Alexy, whose theoretical work on proportionality is a standard reference in the literature, takes the principle of proportionality to be constitutive of what rights people have.[9] According to Alexy, proportionality is an optimisation principle and rights are inherently conditioned by the need to optimise the realisation of all relevant values. If an interference with the applicant's liberty is minor and the gains to the collective good are huge, then the applicant has no right. Likewise, if an interference with the applicant's liberty is serious and the gains to the collective good are minor, then his or her right has been violated. It seems to me that the orthodox view conflates a component of a diagnostic test (the proportionality test) with a constitutive element of rights (their moral nature).[10]

Interestingly, critics of the judicial test of proportionality also fail to distinguish between what rights are (the constitutive question) and how courts go about diagnosing whether there has been a human rights violation (the diagnostic question). So they argue, for instance, that the proportionality test is necessarily the enemy of rights because it is incompatible with the anti-utilitarian nature of rights.[11] In so arguing, they too treat the Court's judicial test as a conception of rights and find it wanting at that. This seems to me too quick a criticism. We first have to ask what is problematic about the use of the Court's test.

So what problem is raised by conflating constitutive with diagnostic questions about judicial review? And is there a problem independently of whether judicial review, *qua* diagnostic test, produces correct results?

One obvious problem is the risk of failing to grasp the truth about the nature of rights. Just because courts follow a certain structure in adjudicating about rights, this does not mean that the rights we have

[8] See J. Gerards and H. Senden, 'The structure of fundamental rights and the European Court of Human Rights', (2009) 7 *International Journal of Constitutional Law* 619.

[9] See R. Alexy, *A Theory of Constitutional Rights* (Oxford University Press, 2002); R. Alexy, 'Constitutional rights, balancing and rationality', (2003) 16 *Ratio Juris* 131; see also M. Kumm, 'Institutionalizing Socratic contestation, the rationalist human rights paradigm, legitimate authority and the point of judicial review', (2007) 1 *European Journal of Legal Studies* (December).

[10] I speak loosely of the moral *nature* of rights, simply to denote that human rights are objective moral standards the truth of which does not depend on agreement. I do not mean to imply any strong 'natural law' position about their meta-ethical grounding.

[11] See e.g. S. Tsakyrakis, 'Proportionality: an assault on human rights?', (2009) 7 *International Journal of Constitutional Law* 468.

consist in that very same structure (scope–proportionality–balancing). For example, as a matter of the moral truth about rights, it would be a mistake to think that our right to freedom of expression is to be balanced against the (alleged) right of others not to be offended.[12] So it does not follow from the fact that European courts use a test that consists in balancing the right of freedom of expression against other rights, that the right to free speech itself is in fact conditioned by the (alleged) right of others not to be offended.[13]

However, the problem of misunderstanding the truth about the nature of rights would be a purely academic one if it had no practical consequences. To be sure, it is a loss if judges and lawyers have a distorted understanding of the moral nature of rights. What also matters, however, as with any diagnostic test, is whether the test that courts use produces the right kind of results. We do not simply want our judges to have the best philosophical understanding of rights; we also want them – more importantly – to spot as many rights violations as possible (true positives) and to refrain as much as possible from blocking state measures when no right has been violated (false positives).[14] So the accuracy rate of the judicial test used, i.e. the ratio between correct diagnoses (positive or negative) and false diagnoses (positive or negative), is crucial. In fact, the accuracy rate is the most important criterion for assessing the merits of any test, including judicial tests about fundamental rights. We would condemn a judicial test that led to false diagnoses more often than not, no matter how close it brought judges' understanding of rights to the moral truth about rights.

That is not to say of course that the accuracy rate of a judicial test about fundamental rights is unconnected to the truth about the nature of those rights. Flipping a coin is a way to decide cases but is unlikely to have a high accuracy rate because it is totally unconnected to the nature of rights (or to any other legal issue, for that matter). The more a test is tailored

[12] Most liberal philosophers of rights take this view. See the discussion in G. Letsas, 'Is there a right not to be offended in one's religious beliefs?' in L. Zucca (ed.), *Law, State and Religion in the new Europe: Debates and Dilemmas* (Cambridge University Press, 2011).

[13] Any more than it would follow from the fact that a doctor looks at various symptoms (pain, swelling, etc.) that indicate the presence of a disease, that the disease itself consists in having those symptoms. One may have the disease without some or all of the symptoms associated with it.

[14] Unjustifiably inflating the scope of fundamental rights is not without cost: giving a right to an individual entails depriving the government of a means to promote vital public goals. Granting rights is never cost-free and the idea that false positives are unproblematic obscures this important collective dimension of rights adjudication.

in the light of the constitutive elements of fundamental rights, the more accurate it will be. Yet no diagnostic test is 100 per cent accurate and often no single test is sufficient to prevent false negatives and false positives. In an ideal world, courts could begin by studying the moral nature of rights (perhaps taking advanced courses in moral and political philosophy) and then develop a series of elaborate tests that are most likely to capture all the necessary elements of rights. However, just as with medical tests, there are several pragmatic reasons why the tests actually used in most cases are imperfect and may miss out on several constitutive elements of rights.

To begin with, resources are limited. Given the high number of cases with which courts have to deal and the limited time they usually have, it is more efficient to use a test that will produce correct results in the majority of cases. A General Practitioner (GP – physician) does not prescribe all the diagnostic tests that exist for a disease, which might be costly and time-consuming, but rather looks first for symptoms. Likewise, courts do not ask all the possible questions there are about the nature of rights, but rather look for indicators that there has been a rights violation. For example, if an important interest of the applicant has been interfered with (the 'scope test'), then it is more likely that there has been a violation. So it makes sense to treat the fact of interference with important interests as a symptom (rather than a cause) of a rights violation, thus triggering the need for further inquiry.

Second, the more complex and elaborate the judicial test is, the more difficult it will be for judges to administer it. It might be better to have a simple test that most judges can use easily, regardless of their knowledge about the moral nature of rights, than to expect them to use successfully a series of elaborate tests that require detailed and advanced knowledge about rights.

Third, the richness and complexity of the constitutive elements of human rights (just like those of the elements of human diseases) make it highly impractical for a court to ask *all* the questions that might be relevant about rights. The number of facts that might be relevant for whether a right has been violated is so high (let alone their combination), that it may be impossible to have a complete checklist of all the facts for which the judge has to look. And even if such a long checklist could be produced, other practical difficulties would persist: the judge would need substantial amounts of time to go through the checklist in each and every case. But judges do not have the time to produce such a complete checklist, nor to check whether all the facts that might be relevant for indicating a right have obtained in a particular case. Judges need some structure to make their inquiry more efficient, some way of *limiting* the number of facts they will look at. They need in other words some *clue* about what the right might be and which facts are relevant.

In sum, the judge's position is directly analogous to that of GPs, who look for *symptoms* in order to limit the number of diseases for which they will check the patient. Likewise, human rights judges need to have some structure in order to get a clue about which facts might be relevant in each case. Some of this structure is provided by how rights are worded in relevant treaties and constitutions and by matters of procedure (such as standing, admissibility, etc.). For example in the case of the ECHR, the text of the Convention splits up the rights in different actions or activities (private life, correspondence, association, religious practices) and mentions some very abstract considerations that might be pertinent (public safety, national security, economic well-being, etc.). Also, the procedure before Strasbourg provides some structure too: the applicants have to mention the facts that they think constitute a violation and to invoke particular articles of the Convention. But not much should be read into these contingencies. How the rights are divided and worded in the ECHR is just *one* possible way of imposing a structure on the judge's task of looking for relevant facts. Other jurisdictions do it differently. For example some rights in the US Constitution have no express limitation clauses:

> Congress shall make no law respecting an establishment of religion, or prohibiting the free exercise thereof; or abridging the freedom of speech, or of the press; or the right of the people peaceably to assemble, and to petition the Government for a redress of grievances.

The wording of these provisions has not prevented US courts from correctly upholding restrictions on speech. Defamation for example is prohibited in the USA, just as it is prohibited elsewhere.

What all judicial tests about fundamental rights do is to provide a structure through which courts look for (a) which facts might be relevant, (b) whether they obtain in the present case and (c) what weight is to be assigned to them. Again though, the test a court uses is no more than a diagnostic tool that is neither infallible nor unique. There may be other tests that can be equally accurate. A court should be flexible, not losing sight of the fact that a method of review is *not* a theory of what rights we have. And just as any medical examination may produce a false negative (e.g. the MRI did not show the tumour), so a court's method of review may produce a false negative (i.e. no rights violation where there was one) and a false positive (a rights violation where there was none). Since no diagnostic test is 100 per cent accurate nor provides a unique, epistemic access to what rights we have, courts should be aware of the weaknesses of the tests they use and of what these tests might miss out.

Having in mind the distinction between constitutive and diagnostic questions about rights, I will now move on to assess the accuracy rate of the test that the European courts use. In order to do this, I shall first provide a rough account of the constitutive elements of fundamental rights and then check whether the test that European courts use is likely to miss any of them. My argument is that, although it handles many cases really well, the European test is not perfect and it may miss some very important constitutive elements of rights, producing false negatives and false positives. This is not to say that the test European courts use should be abandoned, as some have argued. Rather, my proposal is that the test be seen as no more than what it is: an imperfect diagnostic tool and not a theory of what rights we have. One cure for its imperfections is to apply it flexibly, having in mind the false diagnoses that it is prone to produce.

2. Constitutive elements of fundamental rights

Let me start by highlighting eleven general characteristics of all rights (be they *human* rights or other rights), that will help us to get a better grasp of the nature of rights and of what a diagnostic test should ideally be able to capture.

First, rights are reasons for action. They are not reasons for the right-holder. Rather, they are reasons for *others*, for not interfering with the right-holder in certain ways. For example, my right to freedom of political speech does not give *me* a reason to say something nor, for that matter, a reason to remain silent. It gives *the government* a reason not to censor my speech, should I choose to express any political views. Call this the 'reason-givingness of rights'.

Second, certain rights are *pro tanto*. A *pro tanto* right is a weighty reason why others should not interfere with the right-holder in certain ways. But the weight need not be absolute. It can be outweighed by different, more weighty considerations (including other rights), permitting action that infringes the right.[15] When this is the case, one acts unjustifiably in so far as (*pro tanto*) the right in question is concerned, yet justifiably *all things considered*, i.e. on the balance of reasons. For example, if I promise to

[15] S. Kagan, *The Limits of Morality* (Oxford: Clarendon Press, 1989), p. 17.

meet you for lunch, you have a *pro tanto* right that I be there. But your promissory right may be outweighed by the more weighty consideration that there has been an accident and I needed to drive someone to hospital. In this case, you had a *pro tanto* right that I was justified in infringing, because (all things considered) the balance of reasons required me not to keep my promise. When *pro tanto* rights are justifiably overridden they always leave behind a residue of obligation: one has a duty to feel regret, to apologise and possibly to make amends, because one has acted against a *pro tanto* reason. As Raz says, a reason that is defeated nevertheless is 'somehow still there, it somehow survives'.[16] Acting against reason is always regrettable but it is, as John Gardner says, 'a key defining aspect of the human predicament'.[17]

Third, not all restrictions on people's liberty are infringements of their *pro tanto* rights. This is because there is no such thing as a general right to liberty.[18] For example, the government can make a street one-way, restricting people's liberty to drive both ways along it, without interfering with anyone's rights.[19] It does not follow from the fact that someone's *liberty* has been restricted, that a *pro tanto* right of that person has been infringed. Call this the 'normative inertness of liberty'.

Fourth, and relatedly, some 'rights' are *prima facie* – they *appear* to be rights, i.e. to ground reasons not to interfere with the right-holder's liberty, but in the circumstances, they are not.[20] Once the circumstances surrounding the situation of the alleged right-holder are known, it transpires that there was actually no right and hence no reason *not* to have interfered with someone's liberty. Suppose you are told that someone had been arrested and imprisoned for something he said. You are then told that he shouted 'fire' in a crowded theatre; and then it turns out that he was a member of the audience, that there was no fire in the theatre, that he knew that there was no fire, and that he intended to cause harm to the public. In these circumstances, his 'right' to shout 'fire' in a crowded theatre was *prima facie*, which is to say that it wasn't really a right *at all*:

16 J. Raz, *Practical Reason and Norms* (Oxford University Press, 1999), p. 27 n 6.

17 J. Gardner, *Offences and Defences* (Oxford University Press, 2007), p. 81.

18 R. Dworkin, *Taking Rights Seriously* (Cambridge, MA: Harvard University Press, 1977), Ch. 12.

19 Dworkin's example, *ibid.*

20 The term '*prima facie* rights' was coined by W.D. Ross, *The Right and the Good* (Oxford University Press, 1930), who however used it in a different sense, to denote what Kagan calls *pro tanto* right. See Kagan, *Limits of Morality*, note 15 above.

he was not justified in shouting 'fire' and the government was justified in arresting and imprisoning him. By doing so, the government did not act against reason and it had nothing to regret or to apologise for. Unlike *pro tanto* rights, the infringement of *prima facie* 'rights' leaves no residue of obligation, no reason to feel regret. The distinction between *pro tanto* and *prima facie* rights matters a lot.

Fifth, balancing is only possible between real *pro tanto* rights and other real *pro tanto* considerations (be they rights or other normative considerations such as aims). A 'right' which is *prima facie*, i.e. not a real one, cannot be balanced because it does not have any genuine weight. Only real *pro tanto* considerations (rights, duties, aims) can be balanced against one another. Like thin air, pseudo-reasons and pseudo-rights cannot be balanced because they have no real weight. Pondering over considerations that might or might not be constitutive of a right is sometimes called 'epistemic' balancing, but this is a misnomer. A consideration that in the end is irrelevant is *not* put on the scale.

Sixth, on any non-utilitarian account of them, rights are not subject to a cost–benefit analysis comparing the average utility produced by protecting the right with the average utility produced by restricting it. For example, whether I have a right to express my political views does not depend on whether preventing me from expressing my views maximises average utility. If it did, then there would be no right to express views that most people find even mildly unpleasant. Though rights can be balanced against other moral concerns (including other rights), taking into account relevant consequences, such balancing cannot be one of cost–benefit analysis. To engage in cost–benefit analysis is to deny that any rights exist. Call this the 'anti-utilitarian' character of rights.

Seventh, the right to take some action (under a certain description) can be a *prima facie* right in some circumstances and a *pro tanto* right in others. Consider the same example again: suppose you are told that someone had been arrested and imprisoned for something she said. Then you are told that she shouted 'fire' in a crowded theatre. But now the facts are different. It turns out that the person was an actor, that shouting 'fire' was part of the script of the play, that she did not intend to cause harm, and that it was reasonable and foreseeable that the audience would not be misled. The police nevertheless arrested her, since her action fitted an over-inclusive criminal offence. Unlike the previous case, the person here had a *pro tanto* right to shout 'fire' in a crowded theatre: the government had no reason to interfere with her rights. The performance of the same action (shouting 'fire') can be a *pro tanto* right in one case and a *prima facie* right in another. So the kind of action that others interfere with does not fully determine whether there is a *pro tanto* right to take that action. Call this the 'normative under-determinacy of action'.

Relatedly, whether the right to take some action is *pro tanto* (having real weight) or *prima facie* (no right, only the appearance of one) may depend on the circumstances in which it was taken (e.g. was there really a fire? did the person reasonably think there was one? etc.). The rights that people have may depend on the facts that have obtained in the circumstances and not on the description of the right-holder's action. This is because reasons are based on facts,[21] and rights are reasons. Call this the 'fact-dependence of rights'. The fact-dependence of rights entails that their scope is not fixed. An action or activity that is protected in one case might not be protected in another.

Eighth, one can specify in advance (i.e. as a matter of theory) all the facts and circumstances that ground a *pro tanto* right. For example, we can specify the *pro tanto* right to shout 'fire' in a crowded theatre, and distinguish it from the *prima facie* right, by listing a set of conditions that have to obtain (conjunctively or disjunctively): that there is an actual fire, that one reasonably believes that there is a fire, that one does not intend to cause harm, and so on and so forth. Admittedly, this could be a very long list. In theory, we can provide a similar list for the considerations that can be weighty enough to override a *pro tanto* right. For example, it may be that the pressing need to deter people from shouting fire (there have been too many incidents and too many deaths) justifies extending criminal prohibition even to cases where someone reasonably thought there was a fire.

Ninth, rights may exclude certain facts from *ever* grounding a reason to interfere with someone's liberty. For example, the fact that the majority of the population is prejudiced against one's sexual preferences, race or religion is *never* a reason for the government to restrict one's liberty or deprive one of opportunities. In fact, the government has a positive *duty* not to allow this fact, under any circumstances, to influence people's liberties and opportunities. In cases where there is known to be societal prejudice against a group, the government has a duty to examine whether, in the circumstances of each case, there was a justified basis on which to restrict

[21] J. Gardner and T. Macklem, 'Reasons' in J. Coleman and S. Shapiro (eds), *Oxford Handbook of Jurisprudence and Philosophy of Law* (Oxford University Press, 2002), pp. 440–75.

liberty. Call this the 'reason-blocking feature' of certain rights.[22] These rights are best formulated as a 'that' clause: persons have a right that their interests do not suffer solely on the basis that the majority is prejudiced against their way of life. In order to determine whether a reason-blocking right has been infringed, we have to look at the circumstances of each case, and at whether there was some justified basis (i.e. other than the impermissible one of majoritarian prejudice) for restricting liberty.

Tenth, a *pro tanto* right may be unjustifiably infringed without setting back the interests of the right-holder. Consider the following case. A policeman enters my flat without a judicial warrant and without suspecting any criminal conduct. She goes through my personal belongings and reads my diary, but puts everything back and leaves no trace of any interference. As soon as she leaves my flat, she is run over by a truck and nobody (including me) ever finds out. My right to privacy has been violated here, even though I suffered no loss and no distress. If the example sounds too extreme, consider the tort of trespass. If you trespass on my land, you violate my legal right to property, even where I suffer no loss or distress (or even where I gain from it – say you trespassed to water my plants). It is not a necessary condition for a right to X to have been infringed, that the right-holder suffered loss, or a setback to his interest in X.

Eleventh, not all rights-infringements consist in a physical restriction of the liberty of an individual or the threat of such restriction. First, they may consist in omissions. For example, the principle of easy rescue imposes a duty (co-relative to a right) to save others from imminent threat to life so long as one is aware of the threat and it is easy for one to do so.[23] Second, a right-infringement may consist in an *attitude of disrespect*. For example, if I refuse to shake your hand motivated by prejudice against a characteristic of yours, I express disrespect to your status as a human being and thereby infringe your rights.[24] This is so even if you do not care much that I expressed this attitude of disrespect.

[22] See G. Letsas, *A Theory of Interpretation of the European Convention on Human Rights* (Oxford University Press, 2009), Ch. 5.

[23] L. Murphy, 'Beneficence, law, and liberty: the case of required rescue', (2001) 89 *Georgetown Law Journal* 605.

[24] In what was taken to be a disgraceful incident, Liverpool's Luis Suárez refused to shake the hand of Manchester United's Patrice Evra before kickoff in February 2012. Suárez had just returned from an eight-match ban imposed against him for calling Evra racist names. See www.nytimes.com/2012/02/12/sports/soccer/liverpools-luis-suarez-refuses-to-shake-the-hand-of-uniteds-patrice-evra.html.

3. Three test cases

Let us now consider some examples in the light of the constitutive elements of rights identified above. Consider the following test cases:

1. Smith knowingly makes an untrue statement that is defamatory of Jones and is forced by the courts to pay damages. Jones's reputation was already very bad, however, for good reasons, and the damage that Smith's statement caused to his reputation was really minor.
2. The police have reason to believe that someone has crucial information about an imminent terrorist attack that would cost hundreds of lives. They obtain a judicial warrant and tap his phone. They listen to a conversation that he has with his wife, Mary, which contains sensitive information about her personal life. Shortly after, the police manage to arrest the terrorists and avert the danger of an attack.
3. Betty, a lesbian, wishes to adopt a child. The law permits single-parent adoption and Betty meets all the criteria. The authorities refuse her, however, motivated by their prejudice against Betty's sexual preferences. In their decision, they cite the interests of the child as the basis for refusing, concealing their real motives. Soon after, Betty becomes pregnant and has a child, which she always preferred to an adoption.

There is an important difference between these three cases. Smith has no right. Mary has a right but her right has *justifiably* been infringed. Betty too has a right but her right has *unjustifiably* been infringed. The test European human rights courts use in order to decide cases (scope, proportionality and balancing) should be able to capture the subtle, yet important, differences between the three cases.

Consider Smith's case first. Is there a *pro tanto* right to utter a statement that one knows is untrue and that one knows will damage someone's reputation? Clearly not. There is no right to defame. It is not that Smith has some abstract right to free speech here but that the right is outweighed by another consideration. If that were true, then we would have to feel regret for punishing Smith, to apologise to him and perhaps to try to relieve his pain and suffering. But clearly we don't. In the circumstances of this case Smith's right to free speech is a *prima facie* 'right', which is to say that it is not a right *at all*. So no real balancing takes place here. Once all the facts are known, it turns out that there is no real right, only the appearance of one, and hence no balancing to be done.

Now contrast Smith's case to Mary's. The police interfered with her personal communication with a view to protecting public safety. They had a reasonable basis for thinking that intercepting her husband's calls would lead them to information that could save hundreds of lives, and in fact it did. Yet Mary was not herself a criminal suspect nor did she commit any criminal offences. She was engaged in a conversation that she reasonably considered to be private and she revealed sensitive information about her private life. Clearly she had a *pro tanto* right that others should not intercept her private communication and get hold of this information. On the other hand, the need to prevent the killing of hundreds of people is a very weighty consideration. Surely it outweighs Mary's right not to have her private communication intercepted. So, all things considered, the police were justified in infringing Mary's right. On the balance of reasons, they acted justifiably. Unlike the case of Smith, a real balancing took place here: Mary's *pro tanto* right to private life was balanced against the value of the life of others (public safety). But since her right was *pro tanto*, and not *prima facie*, there is something to regret here. The police infringed a real right and they have resulting duties: they ought to apologise to Mary, make sure that they do not make public what they know about her private life and possibly compensate her.

Now consider the case of Betty. Betty meets all the criteria for an adoptive parent. Her sexuality would not interfere at all with her ability to be an adoptive parent, nor would the adopted child suffer in any case because of Betty's sexuality; yet the authorities refused her, motivated by sheer prejudice. In doing so, they violated a *reason-blocking* right of Betty's, namely her right that the government does not deprive her of a liberty or an opportunity on the sole basis that the majority is prejudiced against her way of life. For Betty meets all the criteria for an adoptive parent *and* in the circumstances no other consideration exists to justify refusing adoption to her. So just like Smith's case, no real balancing is taking place here. When all the facts are known (Betty's ability to be an ideal parent, no risk of harm to the interests of the adopted child, authorities' refusal out of pure prejudice), it becomes evident that, in the circumstances, Betty had a real *pro tanto* right, which was unjustifiably infringed.

Of course, if facts were different and there was substantial risk of harm to the interests of the adopted child (say because of the lack of a male referent in her household), then some balancing might have been appropriate. But this would not be a case of balancing a reason-blocking right, because that right would no longer be applicable: it would no longer be true that the *sole* basis for denying adoption was the societal prejudice against Betty's sexuality. There would now be a permissible basis, that of the best interests of the child. So the process of determining whether a reason-blocking right has been infringed, is *not* a process of balancing anything. It is a process of looking at the relevant facts with a view to establishing whether majoritarian prejudices were the sole basis for depriving a person of a liberty (or an opportunity) or whether, in the circumstances, there was some other, permissible, basis.

Note moreover that it is irrelevant whether Betty's interests have suffered a setback as a result of the infringement of her right. In the example, things for Betty turned out for the better: she gave birth to a child, which is what she always preferred. Not only did she not suffer detriment; she is actually better off than having adopted. Nonetheless, her reason-blocking right was still infringed.

To recap: in Smith's case we concluded that there was no real right (and hence no violation of one), so there was no need to do any balancing. In Mary's case we concluded that there was a real right but that, on balance, it had been outweighed and hence justifiably infringed. And in Betty's case we concluded that a real right was unjustifiably infringed, without the need to do any balancing. Can the judicial test that European courts use capture the differences between these three cases? And if not, is the test likely to lead the courts astray and produce false diagnoses? The next section looks at the case law of the European Court of Human Rights with a view to illustrating its strengths and weaknesses.

4. Strasbourg's diagnostic test and its shortcomings

Strasbourg's main diagnostic test, i.e. its method of judicial review, is familiar. I shall briefly mention again its main stages.

The Court would ask the following questions:

1. Do the facts that the applicant invokes fall within the scope of a Convention right?
2. Was there an interference with the applicant's right?
3. Was the interference prescribed by law?
4. Was the interference in pursuit of a legitimate aim?
5. Was the interference necessary in a democratic society?

Let's now apply this test to each of the three test cases.

4.1 Mary

Strasbourg's diagnostic test handles cases like Mary's well. If Mary were to submit her complaint before the European Court of Human Rights, the Court would reason as follows:

1. Telephone conversations fall within the ambit of the right to private life and correspondence under Article 8 ECHR.[25]
2. Mary's right was interfered with because her conversation was intercepted by the police.
3. The interference was prescribed by law and authorised according to domestic procedures.
4. The interference was in pursuit of a legitimate aim, namely public safety.
5. The interference was necessary in a democratic society because there was a pressing social need to prevent a terrorist attack.

The test performs well because it captures all the relevant facts in Mary's case. She did have a *pro tanto* right that her telephone conversation not be intercepted and that right was justifiably outweighed by the need to save people's lives. The fifth stage (the balancing stage) would give the Court the opportunity to balance the weight of Mary's *pro tanto* right against the risk of harm to the lives of others. As we saw, doing so would be necessary in order to establish whether Mary's human rights had been unjustifiably infringed. In the circumstances, her *pro tanto* right to privacy is overridden by a stronger *pro tanto* reason to prevent real and present danger to the life and bodily integrity of others.

4.2 Smith

Strasbourg's diagnostic test does not fare as well in cases like Smith's and Betty's, however. Let's begin with Smith. The Court would first have to ask whether expressing a defamatory statement falls within the scope of freedom of expression under Article 10 ECHR. It clearly does, in the sense that it is a form of speech. As to whether there was an interference with Smith's freedom of expression, this would again be clear: the applicant was made to pay damages for something he said. Assuming that the tort of defamation was prescribed by law, the Court would then ask whether the

[25] See e.g. ECtHR *Klass and Others* v. *Germany*, 6 September 1978, Application No. 5029/71; ECtHR *Malone* v. *United Kingdom*, 2 August 1984, Application No. 8691/79.

interference was in pursuit of a legitimate aim. Again, the answer is clear, in that the tort of defamation protects the reputation of others, which is listed as a legitimate aim in para. 2 of Article 10 ECHR. But things would become problematic at the fifth stage. There, the Court would have to ask whether the interference with Smith's right of free speech was proportionate to the aim being pursued (protecting the reputation of others). The Court would have to perform a balancing test. Yet, as we saw, there is *nothing* to balance in Smith's case, because Smith has no *pro tanto* right knowingly to make an untrue statement that damages someone's reputation. His 'right' is only *prima facie*. It is not that the Court has to assess the weight of Smith's liberty to say defamatory things, and likewise the weight of others not to be defamed, and balance the two. Unlike Mary's case, the fifth stage in Smith's case is redundant.

It is here that the Strasbourg test may produce a false diagnosis: for the Court will not stop at the fourth stage. It will continue to examine whether the restriction is proportionate to the aim pursued and to perform some kind of balancing. But what kind of balancing is possible here, given that there is no genuine right? What will the Court be measuring? What might happen in these cases is cost–benefit analysis. The Court will end up comparing two elements: (i) the cost of the interference to the applicant and (ii) the benefit to others of having this interference. For example, in this case this would lead the Court to compare Smith's cost (e.g. the amount of compensation he had to pay) with Jones's benefit (e.g. how much his reputation had been damaged, and how far this was restored by forcing Smith to pay damages). Doing this kind of cost–benefit analysis might well favour Smith and hence mislead the Court into upholding what in reality is an *appearance* of a right. As explained in section 2 of this chapter, however, this type of cost–benefit analysis is inappropriate. The balancing of rights is *not* a cost–benefit analysis. Balancing is the weighing of *pro tanto* reasons, not the weighing of average utility and of interpersonal losses and gains. Recall that the existence of a loss is not a necessary condition for a right to have been violated. What loss one suffered may be irrelevant to whether there has been a violation.

So this is one significant weakness of Strasbourg's diagnostic test. In cases of *prima facie* rights, the Court may reach the fifth stage (at which no balancing is appropriate in the circumstances) and be led to perform a cost–benefit analysis instead, which might well lead to the upholding of a pseudo-right. Let us look at some real examples in which the Court's diagnostic test led it astray.

The first is the Chamber judgment of *Hatton* v. *United Kingdom*,[26] where the Court found that Heathrow Airport's night-flight scheme amounted to a violation of the applicant's right to family life. From the point of view of the morality of rights, there is no such thing as a *pro tanto* right to sleep well at night, free from the noise interference that it was reasonable to expect will affect properties near airports.[27] In comparing the harm to the sleep of the applicants to the benefit of more night-time flights to the economy, the chamber judgment performed a cost–benefit analysis that resulted in upholding a pseudo-right. The result was a false positive.

The second case is that of *IA* v. *Turkey*,[28] which concerned the fine imposed on a publishing company in Turkey for publishing a novel that contained blasphemous remarks about the Prophet Muhammad.[29] The Public Prosecutor charged the director of the publishing company with the offence of blasphemy against 'God, the Religion, the Prophet and the Holy Book', under Article 175 of the Criminal Code. He relied on an expert opinion that had been prepared, at his request, by the dean of the theology faculty of Marmara University. The Court of First Instance, having received a second expert opinion from a committee of professors, convicted the applicant and sentenced him to two years' imprisonment and a fine. It commuted the prison sentence to a fine, so that the applicant was ultimately ordered to pay a total fine of 3,291,000 Turkish lira (equivalent at the time to $16 US). The European Court of Human Rights upheld the conviction as a proportionate limitation to freedom of expression. It found that the case concerned not only comments that offend or shock, or a 'provocative' opinion (which are generally protected), but also 'an abusive attack on the Prophet of Islam'. Given that 'believers may legitimately feel themselves to be the object of unwarranted and offensive attacks', the Court held that there was a 'pressing social need' to restrict the publication of the book. It found that the $16 fine was a

[26] ECtHR 2 October 2001 (Chamber), Application No. 36022/97.

[27] For ease of exposition, I bracket some possible factors that might make a night-flight scheme a violation of human rights, such as the case of *de facto* expropriation: if the government decides to build a new airport next to my house, and as a result my property loses most of its market value, then I have a valid claim under the right to property. None of this was the case in *Hatton*, however.

[28] ECtHR 13 September 2005, Application no. 42571/98.

[29] The book contained the following passage: 'Some of these words were, moreover, inspired in a surge of exultation, in Aisha's arms . . . God's messenger broke his fast through sexual intercourse, after dinner and before prayer. Muhammad did not forbid sexual intercourse with a dead person or a live animal.'

proportionate restriction of the applicant's freedom of expression. Here, the Court's diagnostic test produced a false negative. This is because the Court here balanced a real, *pro tanto* right to publish on religious matters, against a *prima facie*, pseudo-right not to be offended by blasphemous publications. The result was another false diagnosis, again the product of inappropriate cost–benefit analysis: the Court measured how much the applicant was inconvenienced ($16 fine) against the amount of utility that the prohibition of blasphemy produces. It naturally concluded that the latter outweighed the former, failing to uphold a *pro tanto* right.

I should stress at this point, however, that it is not the case that each time the Court takes a pseudo-right to the fifth stage (balancing or proportionality *stricto sensu*), it will *necessarily* reach a wrong result. The Court might 'appear' to be doing balancing but instead cite all the facts that make it the case that no *pro tanto* right existed in the circumstances (be it the applicant's right or those of others with which the applicant's right comes into conflict). In the case of Smith for example the Court could say something like the following: 'the fact that the applicant knew the statement was untrue and that he knew it would damage someone's reputation means that the interference with his freedom of expression was proportionate and necessary in a democratic society'. Such reasoning would be neither cost–benefit analysis, nor (real) balancing. Rather, it would be a substantive analysis of why Smith's circumstances do not substantiate a *pro tanto* right to defame, an analysis suppressed under the heading of 'balancing'. Nothing in the logic of the test would prevent the Court from doing this. In fact, the Court often engages in substantive reasoning at the stage of 'balancing' without weighing any two elements (i.e. either rights v. legitimate aims or conflicts of rights cases).

A good example is the case of *S and Marper* v. *United Kingdom*.[30] The UK had a policy of collecting and storing the DNA of people charged with a criminal offence. The aim of this policy was to prevent future crimes and there was no doubt that this is a legitimate aim under Article 8 ECHR (right to private life). The applicants, however, complained that storing the DNA of people who were subsequently acquitted (or whose charges were dropped) violates their right to private life. The European Court upheld the complaint, finding a violation on the grounds that the policy of not removing the DNA of those who are acquitted was disproportionate. Let us assume, for the sake of argument, that *S and Marper* was decided correctly. The Court's reasoning, however, had little

[30] ECtHR 4 December 2008, Applications No. 30562/04 and 30566/04.

to do with whether keeping the DNA of people who are subsequently acquitted is proportionate to the aim of preventing crime. And this is not a surprise because there is no doubt that it is proportionate: the more people whose details are in the police DNA database, the more likely it is to deter crime. In so far as we are trying to assess the weight of the restriction on the applicant's right *vis-à-vis* the benefit to the public of applying such a restriction, there was nothing disproportionate in *S and Marper*: there is no harm, caused simply by virtue of details of one's DNA being stored somewhere, whereas there is considerable benefit to be gained in preventing crime. Moreover, it cannot be said that the harm the applicants suffered consists in the risk of the police abusing the DNA database (planting evidence, etc.), because that risk applies equally to everybody in the database, including those who – unlike the applicants – have been convicted. In finding a violation in *S and Marper* the Court did not really balance the weight of anything. It simply pointed to an important distinction – upon which it based its judgment – between the group of those who have been acquitted (or whose charges have been dropped) and the group of those who have been convicted. This distinction has nothing to do with how each group's right fares in relation to the aim of preventing crime. The Court pointed to the unfairness of failing to distinguish between those who have been convicted and those who have not. And it took this unfairness, rightly, to be constitutive of a *pro tanto* right that the applicants had, a right that should not be subject to cost–benefit analysis. Moreover, the unfairness of failing to distinguish between these two groups has nothing whatsoever to do with notions of balancing and proportionality, no matter how broadly we understand them. What the Court did in *S and Marper* was to engage in substantive reasoning about which facts constitute a *pro tanto* right, and to present it as some form of proportionality and balancing reasoning. It is the substantive reasoning that here produced a true positive, and not the court's standard diagnostic test. The lesson of *S and Marper* is that proportionality and balancing are not necessary diagnostic tools in each and every case. It is possible for the Court to go through the motions of its standard test (scope–proportionality–balancing) and, instead of resorting to a cost–benefit analysis, to look at the substance of the complaint and whether the facts of the case substantiate a *pro tanto* moral right. Whether cases like *S and Marper* outnumber cases like *IA* is an empirical question to which I have no answer. What matters however is that Strasbourg's test, though on its face unsuitable for hypothetical cases like Smith above and real cases like *S and Marper*, can still produce correct results so long as the Court uses it flexibly, applying it only in name when appropriate.

4.3 Betty

Now let's see how Strasbourg's diagnostic test handles Betty's case. Betty's case is modelled on two actual cases, those of *Fretté* v. *France* and *EB* v. *France*.[31] So let us look at how the Court did deal with these two cases. One of the thorny issues that arose was that the Court had previously held that adoption does not fall within the scope of the right to family life under Article 8 ECHR. In two early cases, the first decided in the mid-1970s and the second in the late-1990s, the former European Commission on Human Rights declared inadmissible applications that complained that national adoption laws violate the ECHR, without examining the merits of the complaint. In the first case, *X* v. *Belgium and the Netherlands*,[32] the applicant – an unmarried man – complained that Dutch law did not allow him to adopt an abandoned child whom he had looked after for several years. In the second case, *Di Lazzaro* v. *Italy*,[33] the applicant – also unmarried – complained that at the time Italian adoption law did not permit unmarried persons to adopt save in limited circumstances; unlike Mr X, Ms Di Lazarro had no established relationship or bonds with a particular child, and was simply fighting for recognition of her eligibility, as a single person, to apply for adoption. In both cases, the Commission held that the application was incompatible *ratione materiae* with the provisions of the ECHR on the ground that the right to adopt is not among the rights guaranteed by the Convention and cannot be 'read into' either the right to respect for private and family life (Article 8 ECHR) or the right to marry and found a family (Article 12 ECHR). The Commission reached this conclusion on two bases; first, a textualist argument that the right to adopt is not enumerated in the Convention and second, an intentionalist argument that the provisions of the Convention cannot be given a scope that the Contracting Parties expressly intended to exclude. It noted, in passing, that the Convention 'does not oblige states to grant a person the status of adoptive parent or adopted child' but that interfering with an existing relationship between an adoptive parent and

31 *Fretté*: ECtHR 26 February 2002, Application No. 36515/97. *EB*: ECtHR 22 January 2008, Application No. 43546/02.

32 European Commission of Human Rights (ECommHR) 10 July 1975, Application No. 6482/74.

33 ECommHR 10 July 1997, Application No. 31924/96.

an adoptive child might engage the responsibility of a state under Article 8 ECHR.

In its 2002 Chamber judgment in *Fretté* v. *France*, the European Court of Human Rights held, by the narrowest of margins that the decision of the French authorities to deny authorisation to adopt a child to a single person,[34] based primarily on his sexual orientation (homosexual), did not violate the right not to be discriminated against under Article 14 ECHR, taken in conjunction with the right to private life under Article 8 ECHR. Three judges voted against the ruling of a violation, on the basis that the case does not fall within the ambit of Article 8 ECHR. The other four judges thought that the case fell within the ambit of that article, with one judge voting that the interference with the applicant's right was justified and three voting that it was not.[35] The scope of Article 8 ECHR was pivotal in finding no violation in *Fretté*.

Fretté is a case that exposes a weakness in the first stage of Strasbourg's diagnostic test. The weakness is usually shown in discrimination cases, which relate to reason-blocking rights. Let me explain. We saw earlier that the same action/activity (shouting 'fire!' in a crowded theatre) might be a *pro tanto* right under certain circumstances and a *prima facie* right under others. If one uses an action (e.g. 'applying for adoption') as the sole determinant of whether someone has a right, then one is bound to make an error, because sometimes there will be a right to that action and in others there will not. Strasbourg would often throw cases out at the first stage of the test (the stage of scope), because they were cases in which there is manifestly no right. But rather than explaining why the alleged right is *prima facie*, the Court would simply say that it does not fall within the ambit of the Convention. This is what happened in *Di Lazzaro* v. *Italy* where arguably there was no violation of the applicant's right.[36] But using the scope of the Convention rights as a basis for dismissing a case leads the Court into trouble when the circumstances are different. In

[34] French law (Art. 343–1 of the Civil Code) permits any single person over the age of 23 to apply for authorisation to adopt.

[35] I explain the particularities of the voting in *Fretté*, which amounted to a form of judicial paradox, in G. Letsas, 'No human right to adopt?', (2008) 1 *UCL Human Rights Review* 134–53.

[36] There was no violation of a right because there simply is no *pro tanto* right that the state provide interested individuals with an adoptive child or facilitate adoption. The same does not apply, however, in the case of *X* v. *Belgium and Netherlands*, where there was already a bond between the applicant and the child. In the latter case, there might be a *pro tanto* right that the state confer the legal status of adoption on the relationship. I discuss this in Letsas, 'No human right to adopt?', note 35 above.

the case of *Fretté*, the applicant's claim was not that a single person had the right to adopt. Rather, his complaint was a reason-blocking one: the applicant asserted a right that the government should not deprive him of the opportunity to adopt, on the sole basis that the majority is prejudiced against his way of life. In other words, the right that the applicant asserted in *Fretté* was not the same right as the one asserted in *Di Lazzaro*: the former was a *pro tanto*, reason-blocking right; the latter was a *prima facie*, pseudo-right. Nonetheless, by using the scope of Article 8 ECHR as a criterion ('applying for adoption'), the Court rejected both applications without further examination of their merits, even though in *Fretté* there had in fact been a human rights violation.

It seems to me that *Fretté* teaches us a valuable lesson: not much turns on the first stage of Strasbourg's test (also called the definitional stage). The same liberty or activity can be a real, *pro tanto*, right in one case and a *prima facie*, pseudo-right in another. Just as it is important for the Court not to allow unwarranted consideration of pseudo-rights, so it is equally crucial (perhaps more so) not to exclude consideration of real, *pro tanto*, rights. A mechanical application of the first stage of Strasbourg's test, using the type of activity in question as a proxy for whether there is a real rights issue, would have exactly this effect: first, it would allow too many *prima facie* rights to be considered – perhaps even upheld, as in the Chamber judgment in *Hatton*; and second, it would preclude the examination of many *pro tanto* rights (as in *Fretté*). It seems to me therefore that Strasbourg should not be criticised for not paying much attention to the first stage of the test and for changing what falls within the scope of a Convention right, depending on the circumstances of each case.[37] Gerards is right that such a flexible approach to the first stage of the test leads to uncertainty. Yet uncertainty is a small price to pay if the Court's approach leads, more often than not, to correct results. As I argued in section 4.2 of this chapter, what determines whether a diagnostic tool is sound is its accuracy rate.

Two cases in which the Court's flexible approach to the issue of scope lead to correct results are worth mentioning. The first is the case that corrected the error in *Fretté*. In *EB* v. *France*, which was decided by the Grand Chamber in January 2008, the applicant, a lesbian, was refused authorisation to adopt by the French authorities. Unlike in *Fretté*, the Court took a separate vote on whether the case falls within the ambit of Article 8 ECHR and held unanimously that the application was admissible.

[37] This criticism is made by Gerards and Senden, note 8 above.

When it turned to the merits, the Court found that the applicant had been refused authorisation to adopt on two grounds: first, because of the lack of a paternal referent in the applicant's household and second, because the applicant's homosexual partner expressed no commitment to the adoption plans. Although the European Court held that these two grounds are legitimate in principle, it found that, *in the circumstances of the case*, the first ground had been used as a pretext and that the applicant's homosexuality had served, implicitly, as a decisive factor leading to the decision of the French authorities to refuse her authorisation to adopt.

The second case was that of *Sidabras and Dziautas* v. *Lithuania*.[38] The Court held, rightly, that dismissal and ban from access to employment for a period of ten years fell within the ambit of the right to private life, integrating elements of the right to work into the right to private life. On its face, it seems counter-intuitive to say that employment is part of one's private life. There is, moreover, no general, *pro tanto* right to be given employment or not to be dismissed. But since employment (just like adoption) can raise issues of what I called reason-blocking rights, the Court does well to have a flexible approach on what the scope of Article 8 ECHR covers. As I argued in section 4 above, the 'scope of a right' is simply part of the diagnostic method that the Court uses to structure the way it will go about looking for relevant facts. The 'scope' is a proxy for finding out whether a real right exists, not part of what a right is.

5. Conclusion

The test that courts use to determine whether there has been a human rights violation are diagnostic; they are not meant to tell us what a right consists in. Rather, they are mechanisms for helping the courts to ask the right questions in order to find out whether a right exists and whether it was justifiably infringed. Like any diagnostic test, they have weaknesses and limitations. They can produce false negatives and false positives. In this chapter I have sought to show the shortcomings of the test that European courts use in adjudicating on fundamental rights. Perhaps the greatest shortcoming is the false negatives produced by 'balancing' (proportionality *stricto sensu*) pseudo-rights in the form of cost–benefit analysis. By contrast, the shortcomings of the 'scope' test are relatively inconsequential. To be sure, like anyone whose job is to diagnose, European courts should be aware of the limitations of the tests they use and

[38] ECtHR 27 July 2004, Applications No. 55480/00 and 59330/00.

be flexible in applying them. What matters is the substantive reasoning that goes into the various stages of the judicial test, rather than its formalistic, rule-like application. Academics should be less critical of such flexibility and should abandon the orthodox view, which conflates what rights we have with how courts go about deciding cases. Judicial tests are mere mechanisms for helping the courts do their job properly. As Roscoe Pound put it more than a century ago, speaking about the doctrine of equity: '[a] mechanism is bound in nature to act mechanically, and not according to the requirements of a particular case'.[39]

[39] R. Pound, 'The decadence of equity', (1905) 5 *Columbia Law Review* 20.

4

Interpreting the protection guaranteed by two-stage rights in the European Convention on Human Rights

The case for wide interpretation

GERHARD VAN DER SCHYFF

1. Focusing on interpretation

How should the guarantees in the European Convention on Human Rights (ECHR) be interpreted? With regard to what may be termed two-stage rights, or rights whose protection may be limited, legal reasoning tends to focus on how limits to the afforded protection should be defined under the second stage of adjudicative analysis. A consequence of this focus is often to brush aside the first stage of adjudication, which is determining the extent of the guarantee provided by a right. While many studies have devoted attention to how limitation methodology can be enhanced, this chapter aims to critically explore how protection is to be established in the first place.[1] Apart from the fact that this question is ripe for further exploration, a considered approach to the interpretation of a right is also crucial in the event the right is limited. This is because there exists a necessary interplay between the exercises of interpreting and limiting protection that needs to be understood for both these exercises to be conducted properly.

In addressing the question of interpreting the protective scope of two-stage rights in the ECHR, this chapter will advocate that a generous or wide interpretation should be followed. First, though, what is meant by

[1] For example, on the quality of limitation exercises, see E. Brems, 'Human rights: minimum and maximum perspectives', (2009) 9 *Human Rights Law Review* 349; S. Sottiaux and G. van der Schyff, 'Methods of international human rights adjudication: towards a more structured decision-making process for the European Court of Human Rights', (2008) 31 *Hastings International and Comparative Law Review* 115.

the term two-stage rights will be explained more closely and they will be distinguished from one-stage rights.

2. Scope and limit

Key to the analysis of any right is the distinction between the concepts 'scope' and 'limit'. The bearer of a right can only lay claim to that right's protection if a given set of facts apply, once it becomes clear that a particular action or inaction is indeed protected by that right. The first step in the application of a right is therefore to determine its protective ambit or scope. As soon as the scope of a right is engaged, it deploys its protection.

The next logical question relates to the conditions for such protection. What, if anything, can happen to the protection granted? The central question here relates to the relationship between the scope of a right and the possibility that such scope might be limited. It is conceivable, and indeed the case in various instruments, that some rights are illimitable in the sense that every interference with a scope is taken to be a violation of that right. This is the case with Articles 3 and 4 of the ECHR, respectively the rights not to be tortured and treated inhumanly and the prohibition on slave or forced labour. Such constructs are referred to as one-stage rights, since determining the scope of these rights is always equivalent to their definitive application because no legal possibility exists to restrict the afforded protection.[2] In contrast, limitable rights are referred to as two-stage rights, because once a right's protective scope is established the possibility remains that such protection might justifiably be limited. Whereas every interference with a one-stage right is a violation, this is not necessarily the case for two-stage rights. Most rights in the ECHR evidence a two-stage character either expressly or by implication. For example, Articles 8 to 11 each have a specific limitation provision, while some rights without comparable provisions, such as the right to free elections in Article 3 Protocol 1, may be interfered with provided the

[2] See further J. Gerards and H. Senden, 'The structure of fundamental rights and the European Court of Human Rights', (2009) 7 *International Journal of Constitutional Law* 619, 622–5; D.L. Faigman, 'Reconciling individual rights and government interests: Madisonian principles *versus* Supreme Court practice', (1992) 78 *Virginia Law Review* 1521, 1526–39; G. van der Schyff, *Limitation of Rights. A Study of the European Convention and the South African Bill of Rights* (Nijmegen: Wolf Legal Publishers, 2005), pp. 11–14.

'essence' of the right is preserved.[3] Other rights, such as that to liberty in Article 5 and to a fair trial in Article 6, may also be described as two-stage rights to the extent that they can be divided into a scope and a limit.[4]

Identifying rights and classifying them as having either one or two stages is but the beginning, as one needs to consider how these various rights should be interpreted. Since the one-stage type does not allow the imposing of limits on the scopes of rights, this model is sustained by a careful and narrow interpretation of the protection given, to ensure its absolute nature.[5] Otherwise one-stage rights would become inoperable, as wide interpretations of what they cover would lead to constant violations of their now diluted guarantees. To avoid trivialising a one-stage right such as Article 3 in this way, the European Court of Human Rights (Court, Strasbourg Court) requires that conduct must feature a 'minimum level of severity' and sets a 'high threshold' in this regard before the right is interfered with and consequently violated.[6] In relation to Article 3, arguments have also been made for setting the threshold even higher in some cases before recognising inhuman treatment in the meaning of that article, in order to safeguard the proper application of the right.[7] In this regard, Marc Bossuyt argues that the Strasbourg Court should be reluctant to find that an EU Member State had indirectly violated Article 3 by transferring a person seeking asylum under EU law to another Member State that then violates Article 3.[8]

Leaving aside the exact nature of the threshold though, it is important to note that what amounts to torture or inhuman or degrading treatment

[3] See, for example, ECtHR, *Mathieu-Mohin and Clerfayt* v. *Belgium*, 2 March 1987, para. 52, regarding Art. 3 Prot. 1 ECHR; van der Schyff, *Limitation of Rights*, note 2 above, pp. 14–22.

[4] See, for example, ECtHR, *Cordova* v. *Italy*, 30 January 2003, where an interference with Art. 6 (para. 53) was identified, which called for justification (para. 57).

[5] Van der Schyff, *Limitation of Rights*, note 2 above, pp. 19–20.

[6] ECtHR (GC), *Gäfgen* v. *Germany*, 1 June 2010, para. 88; ECtHR, *Budina* v. *Russia*, 18 June 2009.

[7] See further M. Bossuyt, *Strasbourg et les demandeurs d'asile: des juges sur un terrain glissant* (Brussels: Bruylant, 2010), pp. 127–8. Bossuyt notes the increased frequency with which violations of Art. 3 are found. Contrast M.K. Addo and N. Grief, 'Does Article 3 of the European Convention on Human Rights enshrine absolute rights?', (1998) 9 *European Journal of International Law* 510, who argue that the thresholds set under Art. 3 should generally be lowered to extend its protection.

[8] For example M. Bossuyt, 'Belgium condemned for inhuman or degrading treatment due to violations by Greece of EU asylum law', (2011) 11 *European Human Rights Law Review* 582.

is essentially a contextual question that can never be answered definitively. The application of the rule formulated in Article 3, which prohibits certain conduct, is essentially the product of a balancing exercise and is therefore dependent on the parameters of such exercises, as explained in *Selmouni* v. *France* and as further explored by Stijn Smet in his chapter in this volume.[9] Although Article 3 may never be limited, the definition of its scope may change. Essentially, with one-stage rights, compensation for the lack of a limitation provision is enabled by a careful construction of the scope of protection.

Although the wisdom of employing one-stage rights as a way of protecting important interests can be questioned, it seems correct to interpret the scopes of such rights in an exclusive rather than an inclusive manner to ensure the viable application of the rights. The effect would then be to restrict the range of conduct and interests that fall under the protection of one-stage rights to only what is pressing and necessary to avoid excessive and unwarranted application of such rights, since this cannot be corrected by means of a limitation exercise.

Abandoning one-stage rights, the South African 'final' Constitution of 1996 decided not to copy the 'interim' Constitution of 1993 in guaranteeing one-stage rights, as it was argued that a scope can always be influenced by other rights and constitutional provisions.[10] The constitutional drafters realised that guaranteeing a one-stage right cannot avoid balancing taking place in setting the parameters of protection and opted instead for a general provision (section 36 of the Constitution) to govern the limitation of the entire bill of rights.

While a narrow interpretation might be appropriate in applying one-stage rights the same cannot be said of two-stage rights. The scopes of these rights must be given a wide interpretation as a matter of principle, as argued below.

[9] ECtHR (GC), *Selmouni* v. *France*, 28 July 1999, para. 100, where it was explained that 'the "minimum severity" required for the application of Article 3, in the nature of things, [is] relative; it depends on all the circumstances of the case, such as the duration of the treatment, its physical or mental effects and, in some cases, the sex, age and state of health of the victim, etc.'. Also para. 99: 'the Court reiterates that, in respect of a person deprived of his liberty, recourse to physical force which has not been made strictly necessary by his own conduct diminishes human dignity and is in principle an infringement of the right set forth in Article 3'.

[10] L. du Plessis and H. Corder, *Understanding South Africa's Transitional Bill of Rights* (Cape Town: Juta, 1994), p. 126.

3. Wide interpretation advocated

Article 1 of the ECHR makes it clear that the Convention rights must be secured to everyone in the jurisdiction of the member states. As emphasised by the Court in *Wemhoff* and the erstwhile Commission in *Golder*, the Convention is a law-making instrument and not a treaty based on reciprocity between states, which means that its provisions must not be interpreted restrictively.[11] Scholars such as Evert Alkema argue in this regard that avoiding a narrow interpretation of protection is the foremost rule of interpretation applicable to the Convention.[12]

The optimal way of achieving these goals with two-stage rights is to give a wide interpretation to their scope by extending protection to as many forms of conduct and interests as possible, both in range and depth. In explaining what wide interpretation should entail, the theory of Robert Alexy is particularly helpful in arguing that everything suggested by the relevant constitutional principle must be included in the scope.[13] Principles are understood as optimisation requirements, which means that such norms must be satisfied to the greatest legal and factual degree possible, while the requirements of rules are always either met or not.[14] This means that everything that exhibits at least one characteristic connected to the principle underpinning a right must be taken to form part of its protected conduct and interests.[15] Formal interpretations must be followed by leaving aside value judgements as to the intent, nature and quality of the elements contending for protection. Early on, the Court illustrated this point very well in *Handyside* v. *United Kingdom* by explaining that freedom of expression includes not just information or ideas that are received favourably or regarded with indifference, but also expressions that offend, shock or disturb the state or any sector of its population.[16]

[11] ECtHR, *Wemhoff* v. *Germany*, 27 June 1968, para. 8 of the Law; ECommHR, *Golder* v. *The United Kingdom*, 1 June 1973, Application no. 4451/70, para. 57.

[12] E.A. Alkema, *Studies over Europese grondrechten* (Deventer: Kluwer, 1978), pp. 19–18.

[13] R. Alexy, *A Theory of Constitutional Rights* (Oxford University Press, 2002), p. 210.

[14] *Ibid.*, pp. 47–8.

[15] *Ibid.* One could also say that everything that falls within the 'semantic leeway' of a word must be protected. See further R. Alexy, 'Die logische Analyse juristischer Entscheidungen', (1980) 14 *Archiv für Rechts- und Sozialphilosophie* 181, 186.

[16] ECtHR, *Handyside* v. *United Kingdom*, 7 December 1976, para. 49. Interpreting freedom of expression in a content-neutral fashion also finds support in Canadian jurisprudence: see *R.* v. *Keegstra* [1990] 3 SCR 697, 828.

Although the Strasbourg Court has not always been consistent in giving wide interpretations to rights, it can be remarked that in general it has moved to wider interpretations over time.[17] While the scope of a right is sometimes cut down during the definitional stage, thereby excluding elements from the right's ambit, examples abound of cases where a principle is protected as such and not evaluated in the light of facts particular to a specific case. For example, in *Niemietz* v. *Germany* a wide interpretation was accorded to the right to private life in Article 8, so that professional and business activities are included, and not just 'private' activities in the strict sense of the word.[18] This was justified by the Court in its explanation that the purpose of the right was to protect the individual from arbitrary interference by the state.[19] In other words, instead of narrowing down the reach of the right, a generous interpretation was given that reflected its principled purpose.

While ideally wide interpretations should be adopted as a matter of course, logical exceptions to this interpretative rule would include textual formulations or the undisputed and binding intention of constitution-makers in mandating a restricted interpretation in clear terms. A good example of this is Article 11(1) of the Convention, which only protects 'peaceful assembly', meaning that assemblies that violate the peace are not protected by the provision.

4. Wide interpretation questioned

Wide interpretations are not without criticism, though. In the nineteenth century, Karl Marx maligned as a 'trick' the granting of what he called 'full liberty, of laying down the finest principles' only for such protection to be limited.[20] Comparable doubts have been expressed, depicting the limitation of rights as deeply disturbing because an illusion of unlimited applicability is created only to be dashed by the justification of a limitation.[21] Such criticism can be taken to mean that the protective

[17] Van der Schyff, *Limitation of Rights*, note 2 above, pp. 54–74.

[18] ECtHR, *Niemietz* v. *Germany*, 16 December 1992. Similarly ECtHR, *Stübing* v. *Germany*, 12 April 2012, para. 55, where Art. 8(1) was interpreted broadly to include under 'private life' sexual relations between siblings.

[19] *Ibid.*, para. 31.

[20] K. Marx, 'The Constitution of the French Republic adopted on 4 November 1848' in K. Marx and F. Engels, *Collected Works*, 47 vols, (London: Lawrence & Wishart, 1978), vol. X, p. 567.

[21] Alexy, *Constitutional Rights*, note 13 above, p. 212.

scope of rights should be given a narrow interpretation in order to reduce the need for limitation, or even that two-stage rights should be abandoned in favour of one-stage rights to eliminate limitation entirely. Other authors have also come out against wide interpretations of two-stage rights. Stu Woolman and Henk Botha, in the context of the South African Bill of Rights, recognise that protection under a right can be extended to interests that notionally fall within its ambit but prefer that a narrow conception is adopted of what a right was intended to protect.[22] This argument resembles one adopted by some scholars in Canada; P.W. Hogg, for instance, makes the point that conduct 'not worthy of constitutional protection', such as prostitution, should be excluded during the first stage of applying a right.[23] Compare also the arguments developed by Gerards (in her chapter in this volume) that scopes of Convention rights should at times be narrowed down by careful delineation. These positions should be supported to the extent that there exist undeniable markers that a right must be interpreted restrictively in some cases, leaving a court no discretion. However, both authors must be contradicted where a scope could very well have been given a wide interpretation, but instead a value-laden approach to interpretation is favoured that takes note of competing values in deciding what is to be included in the scope of protection.[24] This unsatisfactory approach also enjoys judicial followers, such as the South African Constitutional Court on occasion:

> The two-stage approach requires, as the first step, a definition of the scope of the relevant right. At this stage already, in defining the rights to privacy, it is necessary to recognise that the content of the right is crystallized by mutual limitation. Its scope is already delimited by the rights of the community as a whole (including its members).[25]

[22] S. Woolman and H. Botha, 'Limitations' in S. Woolman and M. Bishop (eds), *Constitutional Law of South Africa*, 2nd edn (Cape Town: Juta, 2006), p. 34-i, pp. 34–17. See also S. Woolman, 'Limitation' in M. Chaskalson, J. Kentridge, J. Klaaren, G. Marcus, D. Spitz and S. Woolman (eds), *Constitutional Law of South Africa*, Revision Service 5 (Cape Town: Juta, 1999), pp. 12–17.

[23] P.W. Hogg, *Constitutional Law of Canada*, 3rd edn (Ontario: Thomson Carswell, 2007), p. 953.

[24] Similarly, G. Carpenter, 'Right to physical safety as a constitutionally protected human right' in G. Carpenter (ed.), *Suprema Lex: Essays on the Constitution Presented to Marinus Wiechers/Suprema Lex. Opstelle oor die Grondwet Aangebied aan Marinus Wiechers* (Durban: Butterworths, 1998), p. 144, considers the presence of a conflicting right as a reason to interpret a right narrowly.

[25] *Bernstein* v. *Bester NO*, 1996 (2) SA 751 (CC), 1996 (4) BCLR 449 (CC), para. 79.

And, in the words of Sachs J of the same court, the over-extension of protection must be avoided by subjecting the 'definitional ambit' of a right to 'considered evaluation'.[26] This reminds us of the phrase to be found in a number of Strasbourg decisions, explaining that not every act motivated by religion can indeed count on protection under the right to freedom of religion in Article 9 ECHR, while it is not immediately clear from the text what these exceptions are, precisely.[27] However, attempts aimed at somehow restricting the principle protected by a right during the first stage of analysis, thereby decreasing the scope's extent and the possibility of interference, do not convince.

Issue can primarily be taken with how narrow interpretations come about, apart from the fact that such interpretations can be said to hinder the Convention's purpose of securing the guaranteed rights to everyone under its jurisdiction, as explained already. Narrow scopes are constructed by balancing competing interests against each other in deciding which interests are meritorious enough to warrant protection and which not. In conducting such an exercise 'the courts will have to develop principles on how it must be done, and it seems doubtful whether such guidelines could eventually be any different from those contained in limitation provisions'.[28]

Therefore, if a court decides that certain forms of political speech do not enjoy constitutional protection because such protection would undermine democratic discourse to the extent of undermining the right to freedom of expression itself, the court could just as well have argued the necessity of limiting such speech in order to preserve and strengthen a democratic society. Consider the emotive case of *Pretty* v. *United Kingdom*, where the merits of a blanket criminal ban on assisted suicide had to be decided. The Court considered the merits as part of its limitation analysis, having accepted that the choice of how someone wants to end their life falls within the ambit of Article 8(1) ECHR.[29] It is difficult to see how the Court could have narrowed the ambit of the right in a way different to how it evaluated the limitation of the applicant's human dignity and freedom in deciding the manner of her own

[26] *Ferreira* v. *Levin NO; Vryenhoek* v. *Powell NO*, 1996 (1) SA 984 (CC), 1996 (1) BCLR 1 (CC), para. 254 fn. 16.

[27] For example ECtHR, *Kosteski* v. *Former Yugoslav Republic of Macedonia*, 13 April 2006, para. 37.

[28] I.M. Rautenbach, 'General introduction to the Bill of Rights' in L. Palminha (ed.), *Bill of Rights Compendium* (Durban: Butterworths, 2002), p. 1A-33.

[29] ECtHR, *Pretty* v. *United Kingdom*, 29 April 2002, paras 67 and 78.

death. Aharon Barak makes a similar argument and draws the following conclusion:

> I believe that the scope of the right does not change when it is in conflict with other constitutional values – such as society's interests (national security, public order) or other conflicting rights. The clash between conflicting interests or values should not be expressed in the scope of the right, but rather in the manner the right is exercised and realized, and it is in this domain that proportionality plays a central role.[30]

Simply put, the limitation exercise should not be disguised as an interpretation exercise. Nonetheless, the 'benefit' of allowing the scope to be narrowed by contextual interpretation might be that a right is limited on fewer occasions, but this only happens because the field of interests protected is smaller and not because the right is necessarily protected 'better'. The bearer of a 'strong' right of this type must later discover that the right might not be as useful as it first appeared. In such instances wide interpretations are more transparent, since it has to be explained to someone how and why their right has been limited, which is mostly a more detailed and less implicit exercise than categorically denying protection during the interpretative stage.[31] A clear application of the two-stage model, aided by the wide interpretation of the first stage, gives the benefit of clarity in applying rights.

5. Constitutionalisation of disputes

Advocating a wide interpretation as a matter of course is more than simply transparency or a stylistic preference, though, as this interpretative method subjects disputes to constitutional argumentation and safeguards. In the context of American constitutional law, David L. Faigman has lamented the introduction of contextual factors to the first stage of analysis as this opens the door to importing 'government interest analysis' in interpreting the very scope of a right, thereby weakening its counter-majoritarian nature and strengthening the case of the state.[32] This, Faigman argues, runs contrary to the Madisonian spirit of the US Constitution as it allows the reach of the Constitution to be dictated by

[30] A. Barak, 'Proportionality and principled balancing', (2010) 4 *Law and Ethics of Human Rights* article 1, 5. See also A. Barak, *Proportionality: Constitutional Rights and their Limitations* (Cambridge University Press, 2012), pp. 75–82.

[31] See also van der Schyff, *Limitation of Rights*, note 2 above, p. 34.

[32] Faigman, 'Reconciling individual rights', note 2 above, 1579.

the will of the majority in constructing the very meaning of a right.[33] Translated to the ECHR this could arguably mean that the Convention's range of application should be broadened by including issues that would otherwise have fallen solely within a state's jurisdiction. That constitutionalisation through wide scope is a worthy goal is evidenced in ECHR jurisprudence in respect of relationships where someone enjoys a 'special relationship' with the state.

Traditionally, the rule has been formulated that, in general terms, disputes relating to the recruitment and careers, and termination of the service, of civil servants are outside the scope of Article 6(1) ECHR on the right of access to a court and a fair trial.[34] This is because Article 6(1) speaks of 'civil rights and obligations', while in many legal systems civil servant issues are governed by public law and not private law. Article 6(1) therefore seems to contain a textual marker that requires a narrow interpretation of its scope. However, this marker is more apparent than real, since the distinction between public and private law is essentially a national question that does not prevent the Strasbourg Court from interpreting the phrase 'civil rights and obligations' autonomously. This realisation in *Pellegrin* v. *France* has allowed the Court to interpret the ambit of the right more freely.[35]

As a consequence the exclusionary rule has been qualified in various judgments. In *Pellegrin* its application was limited to relationships where civil servants exercise a portion of the state's sovereign power and that are based on a special bond of trust and loyalty towards the state.[36] The application of this new rule ameliorated the affects of the original rule by subjecting more relationships to ECHR scrutiny, but it still failed to cover the police and armed forces as a matter of course. The minority in *Pellegrin* argued forcefully against continuing to exclude some civil servant relationships from the scope of Article 6 on the ground that rights must be construed broadly as a matter of principle.[37] Failing to do so could result in arbitrary action and unjustified unequal treatment of people, the judges found.

We should certainly agree with the minority opinion. It would have been much better to extend to everyone a fundamental safeguard such as access to a court and then take into account factors that might limit the application of the principle to a particular set of facts. The effect

33 *Ibid.*, 1528. 34 ECtHR, *Massa* v. *Italy*, 24 August 1993, para. 26.
35 ECtHR (GC), *Pellegrin* v. *France*, 8 December 1999, para. 62. 36 *Ibid.*, para. 65.
37 See the joint dissenting opinion by Tulkens, Fischbach, Casadevall and Thomassen JJ.

would then have been that an entire category of people would not have been denied outright protection, and that justice could be tailored to a particular situation instead of making sweeping and rather blunt exclusions from protection. Illustrating the danger of a general exclusion the minority questioned whether a bond of trust and loyalty could really justify denying someone the right to a judicial decision within a reasonable time, or why such a bond should justify stripping someone of elementary procedural safeguards on disputes relating to salaries and payments. Essentially, a wide interpretation would have better served the pursuit of equality by treating people equally until a justified distinction could be made, instead of simply excluding some groups of people from any protection.[38]

Recognising the problem with the *Pellegrin* decision, in *Vilho Eskelinen* v. *Finland* the Grand Chamber narrowed the class of those excluded from Article 6 to those cases where national law expressly denies some litigants access to a court and where this is based on objective grounds in the state's interest.[39] This route was adopted as the previous formulation was found to exclude too many cases from scrutiny and result in differences in the treatment of civil servants that were difficult to justify. Still, the excluding of categories from protection as a matter of course, however closely defined those categories might be, can be questioned on the grounds that the arguments advanced for excluding a category fit better in an analysis of the reasons for limiting a principle. The current test supported by the Court does not answer the question where the line should be drawn between interpretation of a right and justification of an interference with such protection, but amounts in part to a balancing of interests that in effect pre-empts what should have been a limitation analysis.

These decisions also lead to a certain tension with cases concerned with the special relationship between prisoners and the state. For example, in *Golder* v. *United Kingdom* the Court rejected the UK government's view that detained persons do not fall under the scope of Article 8(1) ECHR where the state prevents them from initiating correspondence.[40]

[38] Compare *Niemietz* v. *Germany*, note 18 above, para. 29, where Art. 8(1) was interpreted widely in the interest of equality, i.e. protecting similar interests equally instead of arbitrarily excluding a given interest from a right's scope.

[39] ECtHR (GC), *Vilho Eskelinen and others* v. *Finland*, 19 April 2007, para. 62.

[40] ECtHR, *Golder* v. *United Kingdom*, 21 February 1975, para. 43, on the possibility that the 1964 Prison Rules could strip the applicant of protection: 'it would be wrong to conclude . . . , that this text is inapplicable [Art. 8(1)]. Impeding someone from even initiating correspondence constitutes the most far-reaching form of "interference" . . . (art. 8–2)

In other words, someone's special relationship with the state, when they are lawfully detained, does not exclude them from first-stage protection under Article 8(1). The Court even went further and stressed that any interference with such protection has to be justified under the applicable limitation provision and must not be treated as an acceptable by-product of the detention, which would not call for proper limitation analysis under the second stage. Now, if a prisoner's special relationship with the state does not allow exclusion from the right to enter into correspondence, this raises the question why the Convention is interpreted to exclude civil servants from access to a court under Article 6 because of their special relationship?

The fact that someone finds themselves in a special relationship with the state cannot be used as a ground on which to exclude protection, but should be treated as a second-stage limitation consideration in the interest of applying two-stage rights. This should be done in the interest of applying all two-stage rights uniformly and ultimately to prevent the equal treatment of people being jeopardised.

Moreover, endeavouring to protect a principle as purely possible, instead of formulating rules of protection, better opens the way to interpreting the Convention as a living instrument. The benefit of a wide conception is that it recognises that rights are essentially principles, thereby creating a foundation for debate about the extent to which a right may be exercised in a given circumstance. This is to be preferred to creating rules, the application of which is not as clear-cut or equitable as a cursory glance might suppose. While one-stage rights by definition do not allow wide interpretations, two-stage rights do, and must be interpreted accordingly.

6. Deluge of cases

Fears are often expressed that courts will be faced by a deluge of cases were they not to follow narrow interpretations.[41] This argument might be particularly compelling in respect of the European Court of Human Rights. Given its vast jurisdiction and near-impossible case load one could argue that less protection at the first stage would ultimately mean

with the exercise of the "right to respect for correspondence"; it is inconceivable that that should fall outside the scope of Article 8 . . . '.

[41] For example R.J. Sharpe, 'The impact of a bill of rights on the role of the judiciary: a Canadian perspective' in P. Alston (ed.), *Promoting Human Rights through Bills of Rights. Comparative Perspectives* (Oxford University Press, 1999), p. 431 and p. 441. See also Alexy, *Constitutional Rights*, note 13 above, p. 216.

fewer cases calling for adjudication and so benefit the efficient administration of justice; compare Gerards' views elsewhere in this volume.[42] This approach should be discouraged, as it would not only undermine the Convention's central purpose of securing people's rights, but it would also invite the problems regarding the quality of protection highlighted in discussing the need for constitutionalisation. For instance, a blunt categorical denial of protection could easily disadvantage an entire group of claimants in an arbitrary fashion by not recognising any relevant factors that might plead in favour of some of them under the second stage of the analysis.

But apart from these reasons, case load might not reduce if narrow interpretations are adopted. Under such interpretations litigants can still argue that a matter should fall under a right, thereby simply shifting the enquiry from controversy about limiting protection to extending protection. Instead of arguing that an interference with the right to freedom of expression was justified, the argument would now be made that a particular form of expression should be included in the right's ambit or that a particular form of expression does not fit the definition applied by the Court. The recent case of *Rujak* v. *Croatia* proves the point.[43] In this case the applicant's claim that his criminal conviction interfered with his right to freedom of expression under Article 10 ECHR was ruled to be inadmissible, since the Court argued that the expression amounted to 'insults' that did not warrant any protection.[44] Although this might seem clear-cut, especially in the case at hand, it might not prove as straightforward to implement the hard rule formulated by the Court in future cases, thereby opening the avenue to contest what amounts to the exclusionary rule decreed in the decision. The argument that restricting what amounts to the scope of a right simply shifts the argumentation from the limitation stage of the analysis to the interpretative stage also becomes clear when we look at positive obligations arising from the ECHR.

Traditionally, the Court has been reluctant to interpret rights as also including positive obligations on states in addition to the general duty to refrain from actively interfering with rights. Generally, the mere existence of a positive obligation is made subject to a balancing exercise between the interests of the community and the individual. This was explained as follows in *Appleby* v. *United Kingdom*:

[42] On the Court's case load, see S. Greer, 'What's wrong with the European Convention on Human Rights?', (2008) 30 *Human Rights Quarterly* 680.

[43] ECtHR, *Rujak* v. *Croatia*, 2 October 2012.

[44] *Ibid.*, paras 29–30.

> In determining whether or not a positive obligation exists, regard must be had to the fair balance that has to be struck between the general interest of the community and the interests of the individual, the search for which is inherent throughout the Convention. The scope of this obligation will inevitably vary, having regard to the diversity of situations obtaining in Contracting States and the choices which must be made in terms of priorities and resources.[45]

The case concerned people who were prohibited from canvassing in an area that amounted to a privatised town centre.[46] The prohibition came not from the state, but from the owners of the area, which led the applicants to complain that their right to freedom of expression had been violated as the state had neglected its corresponding duty to protect their right to express themselves from private intrusion. Essentially, the Court had to determine whether the state indeed has a duty to protect the applicant's freedom of expression in private spaces, such as the one at hand. It held that a 'freedom of forum' does not form part of the protective scope of freedom of expression, which means that the bearer of the right does not have a choice as to where to exercise their right. A consequence of this was that no automatic right exists to enter private property (or even public property) for the purpose of expressing oneself. The Court qualified this by explaining that, where the absence of such a right of entry threatens to extinguish the essence of the right to freedom of expression, a positive obligation could arise to regulate the enjoyment of property rights.[47] On the facts it was held, however, that as the applicants had other avenues for conveying their views, the essence of the right to freedom of expression had not been impaired and consequently no duty had arisen for the state to act in defence of their right. The Court's approach can be criticised.

Instead of conducting a balancing exercise to determine whether the scope of protection includes a duty on the state to protect freedom of expression in a specific forum, the scope should have been interpreted to include a general duty on the state to protect the right from public and private interference, irrespective of the forum chosen for the expression. A comparable view is also canvassed by Laurens Lavryssen in his chapter in this volume. Applied to *Appleby* this approach would mean that, by not having prevented the interference with the applicants' expression, the state interfered with the applicants' right to freedom of expression, which would in turn have called for justification under the second, or

[45] ECtHR, *Appleby and others* v. *United Kingdom*, 6 May 2003, para. 40.
[46] *Ibid.*, para. 36. [47] *Ibid.*, para. 47.

limitation, stage of the enquiry. The fact that a private forum was chosen, or the possibility of alternative fora being available to the applicants in which to convey their message, could then have served as reasons to find that the state had not interfered unjustifiably with the right to freedom of expression. The benefit of this approach sits in the fact that it does not equate the content of the scope to the result of an ad hoc balancing exercise, but leaves the facts of the case to be scrutinised in determining whether a particular interference with the scope widely interpreted is a justified limitation.

More encouraging than *Appleby* seems to be the decision in *Mosley* v. *United Kingdom* regarding the right to private life under Article 8 ECHR.[48] In this case the applicant argued that the state should have enabled him to apply for an injunction by requiring that he be notified prior to publication of a newspaper article that interfered with his private life.[49] The government responded that a positive obligation 'could' arise under Article 8, but that a 'high threshold' had to be crossed before such a duty was recognised, which was not the case here.[50] In the alternative the government argued that if in fact a duty had arisen, it could lay claim to a wide margin of appreciation which would allow it not to require notification in cases such as that brought by the applicant.[51] In other words, if a duty indeed formed part of the scope of Article 8 irrespective of its pleas for a narrow interpretation, the government still enjoyed the possibility to limit exercise of this element of the right.

In deciding the matter, the Court took little notice of the arguments for narrowing the scope of Article 8 put forward by the government. For example, the Court simply stated that Article 8 contains 'certain positive obligations'.[52] In support of this contention it referred to the well known decision in *Marckx* v. *Belgium*; but in that case the Court had been careful to explain that positive obligations 'may' arise under some circumstances, while in *Mosley* the very existence of obligations was considered to form part of the scope without any need for further justification.[53] Also, the obligations resting on the state were not clearly defined as one might expect if we were to take the bench as having delimited the right's scope through interpretation. The Court actually

48 ECtHR, *Mosley* v. *United Kingdom*, 10 May 2011. 49 *Ibid.*, para. 79.

50 *Ibid.*, para. 85. As one of three examples of crossing the threshold, the government mentioned state inaction in recognising the status of transsexuals.

51 *Ibid.*, para. 86. 52 *Ibid.*, para. 106.

53 ECtHR, *Marckx* v. *Belgium*, 13 June 1979, para. 32.

alluded to a wide interpretation of Article 8 in this regard, by stressing that the duty to adopt positive measures exists 'even' in the sphere of relations between individuals.[54] The apparent general nature of the duty inherent in Article 8 is stressed to greater effect later in the judgment when the Court summarises its interpretation of the right's scope:

> As noted above . . . , it is clear that a positive obligation arises under Article 8 in order to ensure the effective protection of the right to respect for private life. The question for consideration in the present case is whether the specific measure called for by the applicant, namely a legally binding pre-notification rule, is required in order to discharge that obligation.[55]

This broadly defined duty allowed the Court to turn its attention to testing whether pre-notification of publication was called for in satisfying the general obligation, which it found not to be the case. One could argue that the emphasis in the case did not fall on conducting a balancing exercise to determine whether the scope of the right includes the specific duty claimed by the applicant, as this seems to have been covered in principle, thereby leaving the Court to decide whether by not adopting the measure in question the state had neglected its general duty under Article 8(1) to protect the right. Arguably, the scope of the right was given a wide interpretation, while shortcomings in satisfying the scope were treated as interferences to be justified by means of typical limitation analysis, such as considering the width of any applicable margin of appreciation left to states. This resembles the approach suggested by Wildhaber J in his minority opinion in *Stjerna* v. *Finland*, and supported by Laurens Lavryssen elsewhere in this volume, that positive obligations should be treated in a two-stage manner in much the same way as negative obligations.[56]

Comparing the approach in *Mosley* with that in *Appleby*, it becomes clear that by narrowing the scope of protection one does not avoid balancing and hence the possibility of a judicial dispute that must be decided by a court. Instead, the balancing exercise is simply shifted from the second

[54] *Mosley* v. *United Kingdom*, note 48 above, para. 106. [55] *Ibid.*, para. 118.

[56] ECtHR, *Stjerna* v. *Finland*, 25 November 1994: 'it would therefore be preferable to construe the notion of "interference" so as to cover facts capable of breaching an obligation incumbent on the State under Article 8 para. 1 (art. 8–1), whether negative or positive. Whenever a so-called positive obligation arises the Court should examine, as in the event of a so-called negative obligation, whether there has been an interference with the right to respect for private and family life under paragraph 1 of Article 8 (art. 8–1), and whether such interference was "in accordance with the law", pursued legitimate aims and was "necessary in a democratic society" within the meaning of paragraph 2 (art. 8–2).' See likewise Gerards and Senden, 'The structure of fundamental rights', note 2 above, p. 651.

to the first stage of the enquiry. Both the *Appleby* and *Mosley* cases would undoubtedly have led to litigation regardless of when the balancing exercise was conducted, thus putting into question the argument that wide interpretations of the protective scope of rights would lead to a deluge of cases.

Even if narrow interpretations would lead to fewer cases, however, the logistical problems encountered by the Strasbourg Court should not be remedied by narrow interpretation, since this would entail turning a structural problem into a substantive problem. Instead of following narrow interpretations, the quality of the Court's adjudication might be maintained by focusing on administering 'constitutional justice' instead of trying to provide an answer in each case, or 'individual justice' as it is sometimes called.[57] In other words, the Court must set European benchmarks which the Member States must meet while not turning the Court into an appellate body for every dispute, as is increasingly the case and which endangers its capacity to function properly. The goal of constitutional justice can be achieved in various ways, such as introducing case selection similar to that employed by the United States Supreme Court, so that only the most spurgent or doctrinally important cases reach Strasbourg. The introduction of pilot judgments by the Strasbourg Court goes some way to realising constitutional justice by focusing on how systemic problems in a Member State should be addressed to avoid repeat claims and adjourning similar cases pending before it in order to allow the Member State concerned to address the source of the violation, thereby ensuring national redress first and foremost.[58]

In essence, states have to be made aware that, although the Court might be the highest judicial authority on the Convention, it is not the sole dispenser of the justice it guarantees, as the Member States have the primary duty to secure the Convention's standards by acting in conformity with the Court's jurisprudence. Achieving this goal is something more

[57] Greer, 'What's wrong with the ECHR?', note 42 above, 684; S. Greer, *The European Convention on Human Rights* (Cambridge University Press, 2006), pp. 165–89. See also J. Gerards, 'Judicial deliberations in the European Court of Human Rights' in N. Huls, M. Adams and J. Bomhoff (eds), *The Legitimacy of Highest Courts' Rulings. Judicial Deliberations and Beyond* (The Hague: TMC Asser, 2009), p. 407, pp. 417–18; M. O'Boyle, 'The future of the European Court of Human Rights', (2011) 12 *German Law Journal* 1862, 1870–5.

[58] For example ECtHR (GC), *Broniowski* v. *Poland*, 22 June 2004. See also P. Leach, H. Hardman and S. Stephenson, 'Can the European Court's pilot judgment procedure help resolve systemic human rights violations? *Burdov* and the failure to implement domestic court decisions in Russia', (2010) 10 *Human Rights Law Review* 346.

than opting for narrow interpretations of rights' scope and hoping for the best.

7. Conclusion

The argument has been made that, in the interest of transparency and sound adjudication, the protective scope of two-stage rights in the ECHR must be given a wide interpretation. From this it cannot be deduced that as a necessary consequence wide scopes will leave states with less room for manoeuvre in how they choose to govern their societies, however. In other words, a wide scope does not automatically result in more concrete protection for the bearers of rights. This is because how far a state may go in limiting a right's scope must ultimately be decided as part of the limitation exercise under the second stage of a right.

In general, this means that a strict interpretation must be followed that treats limits to rights as the exception and not the norm.[59] However, a wide margin of appreciation can still be granted to states in the interest of subsidiarity that can limit the protection which the bearer of a right can ultimately rely on.[60] This means that wide application does not have to follow from a wide interpretation of Convention rights, since a margin can still be granted to states leaving the extent of a limitation to their discretion, provided that the general parameters of the Convention are still respected. *Handyside* v. *United Kingdom* is an early example, showing that although the Court adopted a wide interpretation of what amounted to freedom of expression the respondent state was granted a wide margin of appreciation which allowed it to limit the applicant's Article 10 ECHR right to publish material considered not suitable for minors.[61]

However, what does follow from the acceptance of wide scope is the need to give a wide interpretation to what amounts to interference with

[59] ECtHR, *Silver* v. *United Kingdom*, 25 March 1983, para. 97. See van der Schyff, *Limitation of Rights*, note 2 above, pp. 169–72.

[60] For example ECtHR (GC), *Leyla Şahin* v. *Turkey*, 10 November 2005, paras 108–11.

[61] *Handyside* v. *United Kingdom*, note 16 above, para. 49. Compare *Pretty* v. *United Kingdom*, note 29 above, para. 67, in which although Art. 8(1) ECHR was interpreted to include the decision how one chooses to die, the state was allowed a margin of appreciation to limit that choice by enforcing a blanket ban on assisted suicides. Also, although in *Stübing* v. *Germany*, note 18 above, paras 55, 66, Art. 8(1) ECHR was given a wide interpretation to include sexual relations between siblings, the margin of appreciation left to the state allows it to criminalise incest, thereby limiting the wide protection afforded under the first stage.

the scope of a right.[62] Were this not given the desired application of the two-stage model could still fail, since the protection offered by a right is not deployed regardless of the fact that a wide range of interests might be protected. Consequently, a wide interpretation of protection supposes a wide approach to identifying interferences, instead of requiring a particular substantive threshold before triggering limitation analysis.

Finally, it would be a mistake to conclude that in cases of a wide margin of appreciation exactly the same effect is achieved regardless of whether the scope of a right is given a narrow or a wide interpretation. This is because a narrow interpretation would essentially leave the applicant the now difficult task of proving that their right had in fact been interfered with, while a wide interpretation would intensify the onus on the Member State to justify why it had interfered with the applicant's right in the first place. The benefit of a wide interpretation of a right's scope is that Member States are thus placed on their guard in consciously having to respect people's rights, while the bearers of rights can freely exercise those rights under the Convention. In principle, therefore, Member States of the Council of Europe have to account for their actions to their inhabitants and ultimately the Strasbourg Court, and not the other way round.

62 Alexy, *Constitutional Rights*, note 13 above, p. 199 and p. 212; van der Schyff, *Limitation of Rights*, note 2 above, pp. 41–43.

5

The scope of ECHR rights and institutional concerns

The relationship between proliferation of rights and the case load of the ECtHR

JANNEKE GERARDS

1. Introduction

Debates on the scope of fundamental rights usually concentrate on substantive and conceptual issues and issues of legitimacy. The fear is often expressed that the widening of the scope of fundamental rights by national and international courts causes rights inflation and a lowering of standards of protection.[1] Sometimes, it is also contended that the very concept of fundamental rights is undermined if ever more individual interests are gathered within its scope.[2] The borderline between 'real' fundamental rights and 'normal' interests, then, is becoming a rather vague one, which makes it more difficult to defend the protection of fundamental rights at a much higher level, and by different institutions, than that of other interests.[3] And finally, the very fact that 'classic' fundamental rights have come to cover many socio-economic features (such as social security rights) and have extended to typically 'national' policy fields (such as immigration and asylum) prompts the question whether a supranational

[1] For example C. Wellman, *The Proliferation of Rights. Moral Progress or Empty Rhetoric?* (Boulder, CO: Westview Press, 1999); M.A. Glendon, *Rights Talk. The Impoverishment of Political Discourse* (New York: The Free Press, 1991), in particular p. 171; M. Cranston, 'Human rights, real and supposed' in D. Raphael (ed.), *Political Theory and the Rights of Man* (London: Macmillan, 1967), 43–53, p. 52.

[2] Cf. Ph. Alston, 'A third generation of solidarity rights: progressive development or obfuscation of international human rights law?', (1982) 29 *Netherlands International Law Review* 307, p. 315.

[3] See in particular J.H. Gerards, 'Fundamental rights and other interests – should it really make a difference?' in E. Brems (ed.), *Conflicts between Fundamental Rights* (Antwerp: Intersentia, 2008), 655–90.

court such as the European Court of Human Rights (ECtHR or Court) may legitimately correct national decisions in policy fields like those of social security, national security or immigration law.[4]

These substantive, conceptual and legitimacy issues are obviously relevant for the ECtHR. In determining the scope of the various Convention rights, the Court certainly should take notice of the relevant discourse. For the ECtHR, however, another aspect of the debates surrounding the scope of rights is of equally great importance, namely the institutional aspect. It is well known that the current institutional position of the Court is a precarious one, especially since there is a concrete risk that the Court may collapse under the sheer number of complaints that it has to deal with.[5] Many such complaints may be brought by applicants who hope that their claim is recognised as relating to a Convention right, a hope that might be inspired by a lenient stance by the Court in other cases. Moreover, the Court's position is threatened by the criticism that it interferes too greatly with national business and national policy decisions, even in cases that do not evidently concern 'real' fundamental rights.[6]

[4] Particularly critical in this respect is Marc Bossuyt; see e.g. M. Bossuyt, 'Should the Strasbourg Court exercise more self-restraint? On the extension of the jurisdiction of the European Court o Human Rights to social security regulations', (2007) 28 *Human Rights Law Journal* 321, p. 330; M. Bossuyt, 'Judges on thin ice: the European Court of Human Rights and the treatment of asylum seekers', (2010) *Inter-American and European Human Rights Journal* 47. On this problem, see also R. Kay, 'The European Convention on Human Rights and the authority of law', (1993) 8 *Connecticut Journal of International Law* 221.

[5] On this, see e.g. 'Report of the Group of Wise Persons to the Committee of Ministers', 10 November 2006, SAGES(2006) 06 EN Def., para. 28 ('If nothing is done to resolve the problem, the system is in danger of collapsing'); J.A. Frowein, 'The interaction between national protection of human rights and the ECtHR' in R. Wolfrum and U. Deutsch (eds), *The European Court of Human Rights Overwhelmed by Applications: Problems and Possible Solutions* (Berlin/Heidelberg: Springer, 2008), 51–4, p. 52 ('the days can be calculated when the system becomes inoperable'); and P. Mahoney, 'New challenges for the European Court of Human Rights resulting from the expanding case load and membership', (2002) 21 *Penn State International Law Review* 101, p. 104.

[6] This criticism is particularly fierce in the UK; for an overview and a reply, see N. Bratza, 'The relationship between the UK courts and Strasbourg', (2011) 5 *European Human Rights Law Review* 505 and J.P. Costa, 'On the legitimacy of the European Court of Human Rights' judgments', (2011) 7 *European Constitutional Law Review* 173; see also M. Pinto-Duschinsky, *Bringing Rights Back Home. Making Human Rights compatible with Parliamentary Democracy in the UK* (London: Policy Exchange, 2011). In the Netherlands, too, there has been heavy criticism, which relates partly to the perceivably intrusive character of the Court's judgments. For a short overview, see e.g. J.H. Gerards, 'The pilot judgment procedure before the European Court of Human Rights as an instrument for dialogue' in

Thus, there seems to be a connection between the institutional concerns about the effectiveness of the ECHR system and the scope of the Convention. At least, it is sometimes *assumed* that there is such a connection.[7] It is not very clear, though, whether such a relationship really exists, and even less so whether the institutional concerns can be met by changing the Court's attitude to defining the scope of the rights laid down in the Convention. This chapter therefore aims to explore the relationship between the scope of the Convention and the institutional position of the ECtHR, to discover whether changing the Court's approach to interpreting the Convention may have beneficial effects for its position and its case load. The argument made is that such a relationship indeed exists, yet it is not so much direct and quantitative as indirect and qualitative. Institutional concerns are mainly justified because the Court admits an increasing number of individual complaints that require a complex assessment of national policies and an evaluation of intricate legal issues. Moreover, the number of individual applications may have grown as a result of the relative lack of clarity provided by the Court on the precise scope of application of certain Convention rights. This argument is further elaborated in section 2 of this chapter. Section 3 discusses a few approaches that might help the Court to deal with the challenges created by the growing scope of the Convention. The chapter concludes with a short résumé in section 4.

2. The connection between the scope of rights and institutional concerns

2.1 Introduction: the assumption of a connection between scope of rights and case load

To be able to understand the actual effects of the widening of the scope of the Convention on the case load of the ECtHR, it is essential to explore the factors determining the growing influx of applications. One might be inclined to suppose that there is a connection between the widening of the Convention's scope and the growing case load if a significant

M. Claes and P. Popelier (eds), *Constitutional Conversations* (Antwerp: Intersentia, 2012), pp. 371–97; see also http://ssrn.com/abstract=1924806.

7 See in particular Bossuyt, 'Should the Court exercise more self-restraint?', note 4 above, p. 331 ('by extending its jurisdiction, the Court already runs the risk of attracting an ever increasing number of cases without having the means to deal with them in an appropriate manner').

number of applications do not clearly relate to the classic core of the Convention rights, but rather to rights that have been recently recognised and can be considered to be more 'peripheral' in character. After all, it is sometimes argued that the Court itself is responsible for its growing case load because it has accepted so many new elements of rights under the scope of the Convention, such as social security interests.[8] These elements do not always relate to particularly important fundamental rights issues, but they do invite a large number of new applications to be brought. Of course, this argument needs further explanation. To do so, this section first discusses the distinction between 'core' and 'peripheral' fundamental rights cases, paying attention to the definition of the scope of rights as well as to the nature and seriousness of the interference with such rights (section 2.2). Subsequently, section 2.3 shows that there is no demonstrable, quantitative connection between the increase of the scope of the Convention and the increase in the Court's case load. In section 2.4, however, it is argued that there might be a more qualitative connection and that some institutional concerns may be related to the extension of the Convention to cover even 'peripheral' fundamental rights cases.

2.2 Defining 'core' and 'peripheral' fundamental rights cases

The argument that there is a connection between the increasing case load and the ever-extending scope of the Convention presupposes some kind of definition of a 'core' and a 'periphery' of the Convention. Although it is difficult to provide an unambiguous and general definition, some factors may be of help to make the distinction.[9] First, it may be recalled that the Convention originally aimed to protect classic civil and political rights and freedoms against government interference.[10] Furthermore, all rights laid down in the Convention relate to such fundamental notions as human dignity, personal autonomy, physical and mental integrity, pluralism, legal certainty, the rule of law and democracy.[11] The Court

8 See above, section 1.

9 An interesting and important overview of relevant factors has been provided by Nickel (J.W. Nickel, *Making Sense of Human Rights*, 2nd edn (Malden: Blackwell, 2007), pp. 70ff) and Beitz (C.R. Beitz, *The Idea of Human Rights* (Oxford University Press, 2009), p. 109).

10 See, for greater detail, Alastair Mowbray's chapter in this volume.

11 See further on this C. Gearty, *Principles of Human Rights Adjudication* (Oxford University Press, 2004), pp. 60ff and, more generally on the foundations of fundamental rights

itself has always stressed that such fundamental notions constitute the overall objectives of the Convention and that the Convention rights should be interpreted in the light of such 'meta'-principles.[12] And finally, the Court has often mentioned that the general opinion within the Council of Europe may be relevant in determining what rights are covered by the Convention.[13] If the states tend to agree that a certain individual interest can be considered to be part of a 'fundamental right', so that a 'common core' of agreement or an 'overlapping consensus' can be said to exist,[14] the Court may recognise it as being protected by the Convention.[15]

By combining these factors, it is possible to arrive at some definition of the core of each of the rights protected by the Convention. It is obvious, for example, that press freedom belongs in the very core of the freedom of expression.[16] It is a classic right that protects against government interference, it is closely related to notions of personal autonomy, pluralism and democracy, and it is widely recognised as being a fundamental right. In contrast, the right to give birth at home might have some connection to the right to respect for one's private life, but it can hardly be considered to be a core right. Its effective protection requires positive state intervention,

protection, G. Beck, 'The idea of human rights between value pluralism and conceptual vagueness', (2007) 25 *Penn State International Law Review* 615, p. 627.

12 For some examples, see ECtHR, *Pretty* v. *United Kingdom*, 29 April 2002, Application no. 2346/02, para. 65 (human dignity as basis for interpretation); ECtHR, *Jehovah's Witnesses of Moscow* v. *Russia*, 10 June 2010, Application no. 302/02, para. 135 (personal autonomy as basis for interpretation); ECtHR (GC), *United Communist Party of Turkey and others* v. *Turkey*, 30 January 1998, Application no. 19392/92, para. 45 (democracy); ECtHR (GC), *Gorzelik* v. *Poland*, 17 February 2004, Application no. 44158/98, para. 92 (pluralism).

13 This is long-standing case law, but the Court recently brought the most important of the lines within it together in ECtHR (GC), *Demir and Baykara* v. *Turkey*, 12 November 2008, Application no. 34503/97. For a recent overview of both case law and relevant literature, see H.C.K. Senden, *Interpretation of Fundamental Rights in a Multilevel Legal System. An analysis of the European Court of Human Rights and the Court of Justice of the EU* (Antwerp: Intersentia, 2011).

14 On the theoretical foundations of this, see e.g. Beitz, *The Idea of Human Rights*, note 9 above, pp. 74–9; see also A.A. An-Na'im, 'Toward a cross-cultural approach to defining international standards of human rights' in A.A. An-Na'im (ed.), *Human Rights in Cross-Cultural Perspective: A Quest for Consensus* (Philadelphia: University of Pennsylvania Press, 1991), pp. 19ff.

15 Next to the case of *Demir and Baykara* mentioned at note 13, a good example is the classic case of ECtHR (GC), *Christine Goodwin* v. *United Kingdom*, 11 July 2002, Application no. 28957/95.

16 This is well established in the Court's case law; see ECtHR, *Sunday Times (no. 1)* v. *United Kingdom*, 26 April 1979, Application no. 6538/74, para. 65; and (more recently) ECtHR, *Manole and others* v. *Moldova*, 17 September 2009, Application no. 13936/02.

rather than abstention from interference; the right does relate to personal autonomy, but less directly than, for example, the decision to have a child at all;[17] and there appears to be little European consensus on whether the right can be said to have the 'character' of a fundamental right. Thus, even if is accepted that the right to give birth at home is protected by the Convention, as the Court has done,[18] at the most this can be termed a 'peripheral' Convention right.

It is important to note, however, that it is not just the interpretation of the various Convention provisions that determines which cases come within the scope of the Convention. Of equal relevance to the applicability of the Convention are the seriousness and character of an interference.[19] Even if a 'peripheral' interest is at stake, such as the interest to enter a dancehall, the case can still be a 'core' Convention case if the exercise of the right is limited on discriminatory or racist grounds.[20] By contrast, interferences with highly important human rights (such as privacy) can be 'peripheral' if these rights are only marginally affected.[21] Accordingly, to be able to say that a case is a 'core' or a 'peripheral' Convention case, the right or interest at stake must always be examined in combination with the nature and seriousness of the interference.

2.3 Disproving a quantitative connection

If it could be proved that a growing number of cases relate to peripheral fundamental rights issues, it would be possible to demonstrate a causal connection between widening of scope and case load.[22] The argument made in this respect might take the following form. It may be recalled,

[17] This right is also recognised expressly as part of the right to respect for one's private life; see ECtHR (GC), *SH and others* v. *Austria*, 3 November 2011, Application no. 57813/00, paras 80 and 82.

[18] ECtHR, *Ternovszky* v. *Hungary*, 14 December 2010, Application no. 67545/09.

[19] On this inter-relationship, see further R. Alexy, *A Theory of Constitutional Rights*, trans. J. Rivers (Oxford: Oxford University Press, 2002), at pp. 102ff.

[20] In more detail, see J.H. Gerards, *Judicial Review in Equal Treatment Cases* (Leiden/Boston: Martinus Nijhoff Publishers, 2005), at pp. 95–6.

[21] For some examples, see below, section 3 – the Court itself has solved this by defining a 'minimum level of severity' that has to be exceeded before a case will be admissible.

[22] See also E. Myjer, *Straatsburg zit er niet voor zweetvoeten. Over de nog immer toenemende werkdruk van het Europees Hof voor de Rechten van de Mens, over het Veertiende Protocol en over mensenrechten waar ze thuishoren* [Strasbourg is not meant for 'sweaty feet': the ever-growing workload of the European Court of Human Rights, the Fourteenth Protocol and where human rights belong] (Nijmegen: Wolf Legal Publishers, 2004), p. 17, explaining that every new line drawn by the Court attracts new applications.

for example, that the Court has accepted that not providing a prisoner with false teeth,[23] or with glasses,[24] or placing a non-smoking prisoner with health problems in a cell with prisoners who smoke,[25] exceeded the 'minimum level of severity' set for applicability of the prohibition of inhuman treatment under Article 3 of the Convention. According to the argument discussed here, it can reasonably be anticipated that other prisoners who find themselves in a similar position will see in such precedents procedural possibilities to have their rights and interests protected. Since the Council of Europe covers a geographical area with 800 million inhabitants, it may be imagined that quite a large number of potential new applications by prisoners would result from this type of judgment. Of course, there is always the requirement of first exhausting domestic remedies, and it may be hoped that the Convention is by now sufficiently embedded in national legal systems to ensure that the relevant rights are duly protected on the national level.[26] Nevertheless, if states fail to act on a judgment, or if applicants remain unsuccessful in having their rights protected by national courts, ECtHR judgments in which the scope of the Convention is widened may indeed prompt an increase in applications involving similar sets of facts.

To establish whether such a connection between widening the scope of the Convention (or, rather, lowering the threshold for its applicability) and the Court's growing case load is really present, it would be necessary to undertake an empirical study of the Court's case law. It would be necessary to draw up lists of aspects of rights that are part of the core of the Convention, and of rights that can be regarded as peripheral. For all such lists, it would be necessary to determine how many complaints are brought under each of the headings, as well as to establish whether the number of complaints increases as soon as a new aspect of a fundamental right is recognised. Such an empirical analysis is long overdue, but undertaking the necessary research is far beyond the scope of this chapter. The practical difficulties involved in carrying out such a project would be numerous. It would be almost impossible to arrive at a list of core and peripheral rights that is so objective and so little debatable as to

[23] ECtHR, *VD* v. *Romania*, 16 February 2010, Application no. 7078/02, para. 95; ECtHR, *Fane Ciobanu* v. *Romania*, 11 October 2011, Application no. 27240/03.

[24] ECtHR, *Slyusarev* v. *Russia*, 20 April 2010, Application no. 60333/00, para. 42.

[25] ECtHR, *Elefteriades* v. *Romania*, 25 January 2011, Application no. 38427/05, para. 48.

[26] See further L.R. Helfer, 'Redesigning the European Court of Human Rights: embeddedness as a deep structural principle of the European human rights regime', (2008) 19 *European Journal of International Law* 125.

constitute a good basis for any empirical study. The actual study would be complicated, too, by the fact that by far the most applications (currently about 95 per cent) are declared inadmissible, either because of failure to meet the procedural admissibility criteria, or because they are manifestly ill-founded.[27] Since the admissibility decisions in most of these cases are not published,[28] it would hardly be possible to verify the particular aspect of the substantive right on which the application concentrated.[29] This would make it extremely difficult to determine which complaints concern core rights, and which merely relate to the Convention's periphery.

As a consequence of the lack of relevant statistical data, it is hard to say whether there really is a connection between the growing scope of the Convention and the numbers of applications relating to newly recognised rights (or to relatively minor interferences with established rights). It is hardly thinkable, however, that the actual case load faced by the Court is directly related to the Court's recognition of peripheral issues as being covered by the Convention. In 2010, a report for the Parliamentary Assembly of the Council of Europe disclosed that by far the most applications find their origin in a limited, yet important number of problems of structure and of serious fundamental rights in some of the states.[30] In several states, for example, individuals have to wait for years for a court to decide their case, which can lead to financial damage and uncertainty.[31] Some of the former communist states are still confronted with difficulties relating to the transition to a free and democratic system of government. These states have found great difficulty in striking the right balance in cases about returning nationalised property or

[27] In 2010, for example, 41,183 applications were heard by the Court, of which 38,576 were declared inadmissible, which is about 93 per cent. See *Analysis of statistics 2010* (Strasbourg: European Court of Human Rights, 2011) at http://echr.coe.int/Documents/Stats_analysis_2010_ENG.pdf. At the time of writing, these data were not yet available for 2011, although more recent data are now available.

[28] This goes for the cases decided by a single judge, which constitute a very large portion of all cases heard by the Court: in 2010, 22,260 out of the 41,183 applications heard by the Court were decided by a single judge (about 54 per cent).

[29] On this difficulty, see also H. Keller, A. Fischer and D. Kühne, 'Debating the future of the European Court of Human Rights after the Interlaken Conference: two innovative proposals', (2010) 21 *European Journal of International Law* 1025, p. 1028.

[30] Ch. Pourgourides, *Implementation of Judgments of the European Court of Human Rights*, 20 December 2010, Doc. 12455. For a further overview of facts and figures, see Keller, Fischer and Kühne, *ibid.*, pp. 1026–9.

[31] Most notably in Italy, but also in Greece, Poland and Romania – see Pourgourides, *ibid.*, paras 34–8 (Greece), paras 48–52 (Italy), paras 76–80 (Poland), paras 98–101 (Romania).

in executing domestic judgments.[32] Some states, like Russia, Moldova and the Ukraine, also have structural problems concerning the protection of human rights in prisons and ill-treatment by law-enforcement officials.[33] This means that a small number of the 47 Member States are responsible for a large number of all applications and that most of these applications concern a relatively limited number of Convention rights.[34] The rights at stake in this type of case have long been recognised by the Court as constituting part of the core of the Convention.[35] Therefore, the growth in the Court's case load over the last decade can hardly be attributed to the novel or peripheral character of such rights, making it difficult to accept that there really is a close causal relationship between

[32] *Ibid.*, paras 94–7 (Romania).

[33] *Ibid.*, paras 62–3 (Moldova, non-enforcement); 66–8 (Moldova, ill treatment by the police); 69–71 (Moldova, conditions of detention); 112–44 (Russia, non-enforcement); 118–21 (Russia, poor detention conditions); 122–5 (Russia, ill treatment by the police); 153–58 (Ukraine, non-enforcement); 168–69 (ill treatment).

[34] See also L. Caflisch, 'The reform of the European Court of Human Rights: Protocol No. 14 and beyond', (2006) 6 *Human Rights Law Review* 403, at p. 404. The situation is also clear from an overview of statistical information provided by the Council of Europe: *Statistics on judgments by State, Statistics 1959–2010*, available at www.echr.coe.int/Documents/Stats_violation_1959_2010_ENG.pdf. This overview discloses, for example, that of the applications brought against Italy, 57 per cent concern the length of proceedings; 15 per cent concern protection of property; 12 per cent the right to a fair trial; and 7 per cent the right to family life and privacy. Only 9 per cent relate to 'other rights'. Similar figures can be given for the other 'frequent offenders'. Given that many complaints about 'widening of scope' probably relate to 'other rights', it seems likely that by far the most complaints do not flow directly from the recognition of 'new', peripheral rights and obligations under the Convention. Again, however, it is difficult to base any hard and fast conclusions on these statistical data alone, as they do not provide any details on the various aspects of the Convention rights that have allegedly been violated – applications on Article 1, Protocol no. 1 may concern highly sophisticated social security issues as well as hard-core and evident cases of expropriation without compensation.

[35] These are all relatively evident cases that do not require much novel application of the Convention or the Court's well established case law – cf. Helfer, 'Redesigning the ECtHR', note 26 above, p. 129, speaking of 'cookie-cutter' complaints. This is not to say that all of these complaints always relate to very important individual interests. In fact, recently many complaints about fair trial have been declared inadmissible by the Court for lack of 'significant advantage', based on Article 35(3)(b) of the Convention. In these cases, however, the Court mostly concludes that the complaint relates to a topic on which there is well established case law (meaning that deciding on the merits would not add very much from a perspective of ECHR interpretation), and concerns unimportant personal or financial interests (see for one example out of many ECtHR, *Ladygin* v. *Russia*, 30 August 2011, Application no. 35365/05). This means that the complaint may still relate to a core right (such as access to court), even though it is declared inadmissible because deciding the case would not add value for the applicant, nor for the Court.

the growing case load and the growing scope of the various Convention rights.[36]

2.4 *The qualitative connection: institutional concerns and the scope of rights*

In all probability, therefore, there is no direct connection between the growing case load of the Court, the lowering of the threshold for applicability of the Convention and the widening of the scope of Convention rights. However, there is good reason to suppose that there *is* a relationship between these developments and the increasing concerns about the Court's long-term effectiveness. This relationship is not so much quantitative, however, as qualitative. To explain this, it must be recalled, first, that the Court has recognised many 'new' individual interests as being covered by the Convention, especially over the past decade. Article 8 of the Convention, according to recent case law, covers the rights to legal recognition of gender reassignment,[37] to assisted suicide,[38] to abortion,[39] to have access to IVF facilities and,[40] as mentioned before, to give birth at home.[41] As regards the right to property, the Court has recognised that non-contributory social security benefits come within the ambit of Article 1 of Protocol No. 1.[42] By now, it is well established that, as soon as a state has voluntarily chosen to establish a social security system, that system must meet the requirements of the Convention (more particularly the requirement for non-discrimination).[43] Moreover, over time the

[36] Indeed, Rapporteur Bemelmans-Videc recently stated in a report to the Parliamentary Assembly that if the major and systematic problems in the six problem states were resolved, the Court would be able to spend much more time on its principal task as the judicial guardian of human rights in all of Europe – thereby implying that the cases that are of real fundamental rights interest or that are controversial constitute only a limited number of the cases currently brought before the Court. See M.L. Bemelmans-Videc, 'Guaranteeing the authority and effectiveness of the European Convention on Human Rights', Report to the Parliamentary Assembly of 3 January 2012, Doc. 12811, pp. 5–6.

[37] *Goodwin* v. *UK*, note 15 above.

[38] ECtHR, *Haas* v. *Switzerland*, 20 February 2011, Application no. 31322/07.

[39] ECtHR (GC), *A, B and C* v. *Ireland*, 16 December 2010, Application no. 25579/05.

[40] *SH and others* v. *Austria*, note 17 above.

[41] *Ternovszky* v. *Hungary*, note 18 above.

[42] ECtHR (GC), 6 July 2005 (dec.), Applications no. 65731/01 and 65900/01.

[43] See e.g. ECtHR (GC), *Carson and others* v. *United Kingdom*, 16 March 2010, Application no. 42184/05, para. 74 and see M. Cousins, *The European Convention on Human Rights and Social Security Law* (Antwerp: Intersentia, 2008), p. 21. In later cases the Court has held that the Convention is not only applicable in social security cases concerning a difference in treatment, but also in cases that have to be decided on the basis of Article 1 of Protocol

'minimum level of severity' threshold for applicability of Article 3 of the Convention has gradually been lowered and new types of situation have been included in the protection offered by the article.[44] Also, many Convention provisions now appear to have some horizontal effect – Article 10 was held to be applicable in a case concerning a contractual prohibition on tenants mounting a satellite dish,[45] Article 8 can be invoked to protect individual employees against camera supervision by their employer,[46] and Articles 8 and 9 may protect persons working for an organisation based on religious principles against unfair dismissal.[47] And finally, as is well known, the Court has recognised a large number of positive obligations on states as part of the various Convention rights, ranging from the obligation to prevent human trafficking,[48] or loss of life in natural disasters,[49] to procedural obligations to investigate suspicious deaths,[50] and to hear all parties in cases concerning childcare regulations,[51] or appointment of a guardian.[52]

Many of these issues obviously concern core aspects of the Convention, and clearly the recognition of such issues as being covered by the Convention increases the overall level of protection for fundamental rights. Indeed, it is certainly not the objective of this chapter to criticise the Court's choice to recognise a growing number of positive obligations

No. 1 taken on its own; see e.g. ECtHR, *Goudswaard-Van der Lans* v. *The Netherlands*, 22 September 2005 (dec.), Application no. 75255/01.

44 See, e.g. ECtHR (GC), *MSS* v. *Belgium and Greece*, 21 January 2011, Application no. 30696/09, paras 249–64. Moreover, the Court has consciously accepted that the threshold has been lowered. By doing so, it aims to respond in an adequate manner to changing views on the qualification of certain types of behaviour and to changing (international and national) human rights standards: '. . . it follows that certain acts previously falling outside the scope of Article 3 might in future attain the required level of severity', as the Court held in *Hénaf* v. *France*, 27 November 2003, Application no. 65436/01, para. 55.

45 ECtHR, *Khurshid Mustafa and Tarzibachi* v. *Sweden*, 16 December 2008, Application no. 23883/06.

46 ECtHR, *Köpke* v. *Germany*, 5 October 2010 (dec.), Application no. 420/07.

47 See e.g. ECtHR, *Schüth* v. *Germany*, 23 September 2010, Application no. 1620/03.

48 ECtHR, *Rantsev* v. *Cyprus and Russia*, 7 January 2010, Application no. 25965/04.

49 ECtHR, *Budayeva and others* v. *Russia*, 20 March 2008, Application no. 15339/02.

50 See ECtHR, *McCann* v. *United Kingdom*, 27 September 1995, Application no. 18984/91, para. 161 and, more recently, e.g. ECtHR (GC), *Ramsahai and others* v. *The Netherlands*, 15 May 2007, Application no. 52391/99.

51 To mention just one example: see ECtHR, *Venema* v. *The Netherlands*, 17 December 2002, Application no. 35731/97.

52 See e.g. ECtHR, *X and Y* v. *Croatia*, 3 November 2011, Application no. 5193/09. For an overview of these obligations, see also the chapters of Eva Brems and Maris Burbergs in the current volume.

and new fundamental rights. Nevertheless, it must be acknowledged that many of the newly recognised rights and obligations have the inherent result of obliging the Court to get involved in highly complex and difficult matters of national law and policy. Of course, the Court has always had to deal with 'hard' and politically sensitive cases and it has always had to strike difficult balances between conflicting interests. Most of the Court's early cases were no less difficult than the cases it presently has to decide (think of the *Belgian Linguistics case*,[53] *Dudgeon*,[54] or *James and others*[55]). What is important, though, is that the sheer number of such 'hard cases' has considerably increased as a result of the developments in the Court's case law and the Court's willingness to recognise new elements of rights as covered by the Convention. To evaluate whether childcare proceedings comply with the many procedural obligations under the Convention the Court needs to obtain a sound understanding of the national legal system, as well as of the procedural intricacies of the specific case at hand. To review the reasonableness of a prohibition of assisted suicide or abortion, the Court needs to take a position in debates on insoluble ethical dilemmas. And to determine whether a classification contained in a national social security system constitutes a prohibited form of discrimination under the Convention, the Court may need to familiarise itself with the historical and legal backgrounds of the system, the specific context that might explain the choice of a particular classification, and possibly the technical ins and outs of the regulatory system as a whole, as well as any compensatory measures that may have been introduced.

Over time, the Court has developed instruments to help it decide this type of case. For example, granting a wide margin of appreciation to states means that it does not need to get deeply involved in national ethical or policy debates and can limit itself to determining whether an interference was manifestly unreasonable.[56] Moreover, it is clear that the Court usually adopts a 'minimalist' approach, deciding cases based on all circumstances of the case and supported by 'shallow' reasoning rather than deep, moral arguments.[57] This provides the Court with much flexibility and helps it to

[53] ECtHR, 23 July 1968, Applications no. 1474/62, etc.

[54] ECtHR (GC), *Dudgeon* v. *United Kingdom*, 22 October 1981, Application no. 7525/76.

[55] ECtHR, *James and others* v. *United Kingdom*, 21 February 1986, Application no. 8793/79.

[56] On the advantages of using this doctrine, see e.g. J.H. Gerards, 'Pluralism, deference and the margin of appreciation doctrine', (2011) 17 *European Law Journal* 80.

[57] See further on this J.H. Gerards, 'Judicial minimalism and "dependency": interpretation of the European Convention in a pluralist Europe' in M. van Roosmalen *et al.* (eds), *Fundamental Rights and Principles* (Antwerp: Intersentia, 2013), 73–92; see also H-M. ten

avoid politically sensitive decisions.[58] Nevertheless, it remains true that, in all of these cases, the Court has to give a decision on contentious legal, political, social, economic or ethical matters.

This is not to say that the Court lacks the legitimacy and the quality to rule on this type of case – quite the contrary. From an institutional perspective it is important to note, however, that deciding such cases is demanding and burdensome. In particular, since most of these cases need to be decided by Chambers of seven judges and there often will be a need for (comparative) research by the Registry, they take up much of the time and resources that are available to the Court.[59] Moreover, under the pressure of time and case overload, it will be increasingly difficult to give each of these cases the attention it needs. Some of the dissenting opinions in cases such as those mentioned above disclose doubts within the Court as to its ability to understand national legal intricacies or policy debates sufficiently well to justify arriving at a different balance or outcome than has been reached at the national level.[60]

The Court makes a great effort to hand down well reasoned judgments based on a thorough understanding of national law. Thus far, the quality of its judgments has been high and inconsistencies in the case law limited.

Napel and F. Theissen, 'The European Court of Human Rights' jurisprudence on religious symbols in public institutions in comparative perspective: maximum protection of the freedom of religion through judicial minimalism?' in S. Ferrari and R. Christofori (eds), *Law and Religion in the 21st Century. Relations between States and Religious Communities* (Farnham: Ashgate, 2010), pp. 313–22.

58 A good illustration is the Grand Chamber's judgment in the case of *Lautsi* v. *Italy* – a case about the obligatory presence of crucifixes in public elementary schools in Italy – where it overturned a deeply reasoned Chamber judgment that had favoured a particularly secularist approach, instead handing down a narrowly and shallowly reasoned judgment that hardly contained any arguments from principle on the role of religion in the state and that offered much room for the religious traditions in the various Member States – see ECtHR (GC), *Lautsi* v. *Italy*, 18 March 2011 and see further on this D. McGoldrick, 'Religion in the European public square and in European public life – crucifixes in the classroom?', (2011) 3 *Human Rights Law Review* 451 and J-M. Piret, 'Limitations of supranational jurisdiction, judicial restraint and the nature of treaty law' in J. Temperman (ed.), *The Lautsi Papers: Multidisciplinary Reflections on Religious Symbols in the Public School Classroom* (Leiden/Boston: Martinus Nijhoff Publishers, 2012), pp. 59–89.

59 It must be admitted that, following the priority policy it announced in 2011, the Court has granted this type of case a relatively low priority (four on a scale of six, one being the most important). Thus, the time taken to decide these cases will not be found at the expense of other, more urgent human rights cases. Nevertheless, all of these cases must be assessed and evaluated at one point and this certainly may add to the overall burden of the Court.

60 See in particular the dissenting opinion of Judge Ziemele in ECtHR (GC), *Andrejeva* v. *Latvia*, 18 February 2009, Application no. 55707/00.

Nevertheless, it might be difficult for the Court to continue to achieve such a high level of judicial decision-making in the long run. Although examples of failures are few and far between, the growing number of difficult and delicate cases might increase the chances of inaccuracy in the application of national law and of misconceived valuation of national debates. If the Court wishes to avoid mistakes, as is clearly desirable, the problem remains that the process of preparing sound judgments in such cases is costly and may prolong the procedure before the Court.

Naturally, it is fully reasonable for the Court to resort to such time-consuming and costly assessments in cases concerning core aspects of rights or cases concerning important interpretative questions. Yet it is equally clear that the desirability of recognising new aspects of Convention rights or new obligations on the states, such as obligations in relation to social security or assisted reproduction, can be questioned if the rights and interests concerned are rather peripheral in character.[61] Concerns about the long-term effectiveness of the Convention system and the ability of the Court to deal with the substance of any resulting complaints must be consciously balanced against the gain in protection for fundamental rights. It is at this point that institutional concerns and the scope of the Convention are closely related.

3. Are there any solutions?

3.1 Introduction

Some critics of the Court have stressed that the Court itself shares responsibility for the problems resulting from its enormous case load by accepting ever more individual interests as being covered by the Convention.[62] The analysis in section 2 aimed to demonstrate that this criticism is largely misconceived. By far the most complaints result from the failure of national authorities to protect fundamental rights in an effective manner, as a consequence of which many individuals need to access the Court to obtain redress. Reduction of the Court's case load cannot be

[61] For a further definition of what kinds of right and interest can be considered 'peripheral', see above – many examples might relate to social security law, environmental law and policy, planning policy and property law, minor flaws in national civil and administrative procedure, or highly sophisticated elements of the right to privacy, such as the right to assisted reproduction for prisoners.

[62] In particular Bossuyt, 'Should the Court exercise more self-restraint?', note 4 above, p. 330.

achieved, therefore, by simply cutting back the scope of protection of the Convention.[63] It was also noted, however, that the growing scope of the Convention might result in institutional concerns of a different nature, which relate to the time and resources taken up by many of the cases concerning newly recognised rights and obligations. It is vitally important that the Court is aware of this when having to answer a novel question of interpretation, or when deciding whether to recognise new positive obligations.

3.2 Looking ahead

First of all, the Court should consciously consider the need to protect yet another aspect of a fundamental right. The core rights approach mentioned above may be of help to the Court in this respect. When deciding whether to stretch a Convention right to a new or slightly different set of facts, the Court should be mindful both of how close the relevant interest may be to the fundamental principles underlying the Convention,[64] and of the strength of consensus in Europe on the qualification of a certain interest *as a fundamental right.*[65] In applying such yardsticks, the Court should also keep in mind the difficulties that might attend having to decide on a potentially large number of cases similar to the one placed before it. Perhaps, if the Court had tried to imagine how difficult it would be to decide on a myriad of complex social security complaints, it would have decided *Stec* differently. Of course, it was necessary for the Court in

[63] Rather, reduction must be achieved by improving effective fundamental rights protection on the national level, as has often been repeated by scholars as well as by the Council of Europe institutions; for a recent overview, see Bemelmans-Videc, 'Guaranteeing authority and effectiveness', note 36 above.

[64] Cf. O. de Schutter and F. Tulkens, 'Rights in conflict: the European Court of Human Rights as a pragmatic institution' in Brems, *Conflicts between Fundamental Rights*, note 3 above, pp. 169ff. See also J.H. Gerards, 'The prism of fundamental rights', (2012) 2 *European Constitutional Law Review* 173. An interesting and useful approach using these factors has been proposed by Nickel, *Making Sense of Human Rights*, note 9 above, pp. 70ff.

[65] Cf. the dissenting opinion of Judge Matscher in *König* v. *Germany*, stating that an autonomous reading of ECHR notions should be based on a 'common denominator . . . since it is legitimate to suppose . . . that such is the meaning which the Contracting States wished these provisions to have' (ECtHR, *König* v. *Germany*, 28 June 1978, Application no. 6232/73). Cf. also P. Mahoney, 'The comparative method in judgments of the European Court of Human Rights: reference back to national law' in G. Canivet *et al.* (eds), *Comparative Law Before the Courts* (London: British Institute of International and Comparative Law, 2004), 135ff, p. 138. For a theoretical underpinning of this approach, see An-Na'im, 'Toward a cross-cultural approach', note 14 above, p. 22, stating that consensus may be found by means of 'cross-cultural dialogue'.

Stec to give a clear decision on how far Article 1 of Protocol No. 1 should apply to social security benefits, but there seems to have been no pressing need to extend the scope of this provision to all social security benefits that national authorities voluntarily opt to provide. Although it is always easier to criticise such a judgment with hindsight, the Court may turn the *Stec* experience to its benefit in future high-impact cases by showing more awareness of the potential consequences of its own work, as well as to the centrality of the right that is at stake.

3.3 Clarifying the scope of the Convention

The institutional concerns mentioned in section 2.4 might be alleviated if the Court provided more clarity on the precise scope of the various Convention rights.[66] A case in point is *Salduz*, in which the Court recognised that Article 6 §1 requires 'that, as a rule, access to a lawyer should be provided as from the first interrogation of a suspect by the police'.[67] Unfortunately, the Court did not indicate clearly the stage of the police interrogation at which such access must be provided and what the requirement of 'access' actually entails. Consequently, the judgment has caused great confusion and controversy in many legal systems.[68] Should the judgment be understood to mean that a lawyer must be present *during* the police interrogation, or is it sufficient that suspects can discuss their case with a lawyer before the interrogation itself takes place?[69]

It is understandable that the Court cannot determine the precise scope of a newly recognised right in great detail in a single judgment, since it will be able to foresee neither all consequences nor all possible occasions for its

[66] See also S. Greer, 'What's wrong with the European Convention on Human Rights?', (2008) 30 *Human Rights Quarterly* 680, p. 696 and L. Wildhaber, 'A constitutional future for the European Court of Human Rights?', (2002) 23 *Human Rights Law Journal* 161, p. 164.

[67] ECtHR (GC), *Salduz* v. *Turkey*, 27 November 2008, Application no. 36391/02, para. 55.

[68] On the impact of *Salduz* in various states, see E. Myjer, 'One *Salduz* a year is enough. 20 associative thoughts on Judge Rozakis, judicial activism and the *Salduz* judgment' in D. Spielmann *et al.* (eds), *La Convention européenne des droits de l'homme, un instrument vivant* [The European Convention on Human Rights, a living instrument] *Mélanges en l'honneur de* [Essays in honour of] *Christos L. Rozakis* (Brussels: Bruylant, 2011), pp. 419–30, p. 421.

[69] On the judgment's lack of clarity, which makes a good response on the national level rather difficult, see e.g. Ch. Brants, 'The reluctant Dutch response to *Salduz*', (2011) 15 *Edinburgh Law Review* 298 and A. Beijer, 'False confessions during police interrogations and measures to prevent them', (2010) 18 *European Journal of Crime, Criminal Law and Criminal Justice* 311; Myjer, 'One *Salduz* a year is enough', note 68 above, pp. 424–5.

application. Moreover, as Sunstein has explained for constitutional courts, it may be undesirable for a court to give very detailed and deeply reasoned judgments.[70] The better approach might be to provide a 'shallow' or 'narrow' judgment.[71] After having probed the political and legal responses to this initial judgment, the Court might gradually deepen the foundations of its general findings, or extend a narrow judgment to other sets of facts. Indeed, as mentioned before, this is an approach that at present is clearly favoured by the Court – much of its case law can be characterised as strongly case-based (and accordingly 'narrow') and based on superficial ('shallow') arguments and general principles derived from previous case law rather than principled, moral and substantive arguments.[72]

Usually, this can be considered a very appropriate and desirable approach for a court such as the ECtHR. Nevertheless, the judgment in *Salduz* makes it clear that the Court's position will sometimes require a different approach. In the ECHR system, handing down a rather vague, shallowly and narrowly reasoned, yet far-reaching judgment may unleash an enormous amount of litigation on the national level, resulting in even more applications to the Court.[73] Indeed, many cases since *Salduz* have

[70] See e.g. C.R. Sunstein, 'Beyond judicial minimalism', Harvard University Law School Public Law & Legal Theory Research Paper No. 08–40 (2008), http://ssrn.com/abstract=1274200.

[71] 'Shallow' judgments leave open the foundational principles of a certain decision, looking for agreement on a practical level (*ibid.*, p. 4); 'narrow' judgments are limited to the facts of one specific case, without saying much about their applicability in future, similar cases (*ibid.*, p. 13).

[72] Cf. Gerards, 'The prism of fundamental rights', note 64 above.

[73] Other examples may be given of this. For the UK, for instance, the case of *Al-Khawaja and Tahery* v. *United Kingdom* is a case in point. Before the Grand Chamber, the UK government complained that the outcome reached by the Chamber fit poorly with procedural traditions in UK criminal law, about the lack of clarity of the interpretation provided and the difficulties involved in following it up, as well as about the shortage of reasoning underlying the outcome (see ECtHR (GC), *Al-Khawaja and Tahery* v. *United Kingdom*, 15 December 2011, Applications no. 26766/05 and 22228/06, para. 229). The Grand Chamber provided more clarity as to the underlying reasoning, but only after the UK Supreme Court had refused to act on the Chamber judgment (UK Supreme Court, judgment of 9 December 2009, *R* v. *Horncastle and others* [2009] UKSC 14, *per* Lord Phillips, para. 11: '[t]here will . . . be rare occasions where this court has concerns as to whether a decision of the Strasbourg Court sufficiently appreciates or accommodates particular aspects of our domestic process. In such circumstances it is open to this court to decline to follow the Strasbourg decision, giving reasons for adopting this course. This is likely to give the Strasbourg Court the opportunity to reconsider the particular aspect of the decision that is in issue, so that there takes place what may prove to be a valuable dialogue between this court and the Strasbourg Court. This is such a case'). Although this may be regarded as a good example of judicial dialogue, much trouble and criticism

been decided at state level, and many measures have been taken.[74] It will probably not be long before numerous applicants start to flow from various Member States, asking the Court for clarification or confirmation.

When an important new question of interpretation presents itself, the lesson to be learnt from the *Salduz* saga may be that the Court cannot always resort to shallow reasoning or limit its judgment to the concrete circumstances of the individual application.[75] Instead, in these cases the Court should play a more 'constitutional' role.[76] It should carefully select a case that appears to be relatively representative of a set of cases concerning novel questions of law or fact and that can provide a clear precedent.[77] Consequently, the Court (preferably in its Grand Chamber setting) should decide such a case in sufficient detail, phrasing and delimiting the right in as concrete a manner as possible. Moreover, it should do so only after careful consideration of possible future questions and issues. Interventions by third parties and non-governmental organisations might help the Court to estimate the possible results of recognising a given right. In particular, as was recommended by the Committee of Wise Persons in 2006, the Court might invite all States Parties to intervene and express their opinion on certain possible interpretations.[78] Such involvement might ease the Court's task of arriving at a clear and workable interpretation that can relatively easily be applied.[79] If the Grand Chamber has decided that a certain set of facts does not come within the scope of the Convention, single judges and committees of the Court can subsequently decide that

might have been avoided if the Court had realised that this case concerned a controversial issue and ought to have been decided by the Grand Chamber at once, leaving room for more input by third parties and exchange of arguments, and provided translucent argumentation of the outcome.

[74] For a convenient overview, see the '*Salduz* watch' tag at the website of the Legal Aid Reformers' Network: www.legalaidreform.org/police-station-legal-advice/salduz-watch; see also Myjer, 'One *Salduz* a year is enough', note 68 above, p. 427.

[75] Indeed, Sunstein has mentioned that some cases, such as fundamental rights cases in which legal certainty is of great importance, should not be decided shallowly or narrowly, but deserve more elaborate reasoning in depth. In particular, fundamental rights must sometimes be formulated in more detail; see Sunstein, 'Beyond judicial minimalism', note 70 above, p. 16.

[76] The desirability of such an approach has also been stressed by other scholars. See e.g. Greer, 'What's wrong with the ECHR?', note 66 above, p. 686.

[77] Possibly the priority rules of the Court should be changed to reflect this.

[78] 'Interim Report of the Group of Wise Persons to the Committee of Ministers', 116th session of the Committee of Ministers, 18–19 May 2006, CM(2006)88, 10 May 2006, para. 51.

[79] See D. Nicol, 'Lessons from Luxembourg: federalisation and the Court of Human Rights', (2001) 26 *European Law Review – Human Rights Survey* HR/7.

similar complaints are inadmissible *ratione materiae* (Article 34).[80] As a result, there will mostly be no need to burden a Chamber with deciding such cases on their merits. Instead, such cases must be dealt with on the national level, which accords with the principle of subsidiarity.[81]

3.4 Setting clear thresholds for Convention applicability

The Court might find a further solution to the problems analysed in section 2.4 by defining translucent criteria for determining the applicability of the Convention, which relate to the scope of the Convention rights as well as to the severity of an interference with such rights. The Court has already recognised some limitations in this respect. As mentioned above, for example, Article 3 of the Convention only applies once ill-treatment has exceeded a minimum level of severity.[82] The Court has devised a similar standard in relation to Article 8.[83] These standards, however, still have the disadvantage of being rather fluid, vague and unpredictable.[84] Litigation may be inevitable to determine whether the threshold level of severity has been crossed in a given case. Given the present case load of the Court, such additional litigation is undesirable and should be avoided.

80 See further ECtHR, *Practical Guide on Admissibility Criteria* (Strasbourg: Council of Europe/European Court of Human Rights, 2011), para. 207:

> [t]he compatibility *ratione materiae* with the Convention of an application or complaint derives from the Court's substantive jurisdiction. For a complaint to be compatible *ratione materiae* with the Convention, the right relied on by the applicant must be protected by the Convention and the Protocols thereto that have come into force. For example, applications are inadmissible where they concern the right to be issued with a driving licence . . . , the right to self-determination . . . , and the right of foreign nationals to enter and reside in a Contracting State . . . , since those rights do not, as such, feature among the rights and freedoms guaranteed by the Convention.

81 Cf. Bemelmans-Videc, who has argued that the potential for limiting the number of applications brought to Strasbourg can be increased once the authorities in the various states are sufficiently aware of the standards stemming from the Court's case law – see Bemelmans-Videc, 'Guaranteeing authority and effectiveness', note 36 above, p. 15. See further Helfer, 'Redesigning the ECtHR', note 26 above, pp. 125–59 and Keller, Fischer and Kühne, 'Debating the future of the ECtHR', note 29 above, arguing that it is essential to stimulate careful incorporation of the Court's case law in national law to avoid new cases coming to the Court.

82 See further Chapter 13 by Stijn Smet in this volume.

83 See e.g. ECtHR, *Atanasov* v. *Bulgaria*, 2 December 2010, Application no. 12853/03, para. 75.

84 Cf. Stijn Smet in Chapter 13 in the current volume.

From this perspective it would be preferable for the Court to set more concrete standards. Although this might seem rather difficult to achieve, the Court's case law demonstrates that it is not impossible. A good example of relatively clear standards can be found in the case law on environmental damage and nuisance. Although the general threshold in these cases is one of a minimum level of severity, in several cases the Court has clarified the criteria that have to be met before a complaint can be considered admissible. Amongst other factors, there has to be identifiable damage to the individual's health,[85] there must be a causal connection between the nuisance or environmental harm and the individual damage,[86] the state must or should have been aware that the hazard or the nuisance was affecting the applicant's private life,[87] and applicants must not be responsible for the damage themselves.[88] The great advantage of such substantive criteria, which define both scope and the seriousness of an interference with a particular right, lies in their predictability and clarity: they enable prospective applicants (and their legal representatives) to estimate their chances of success fairly.[89] This might produce the result that fewer clearly unmeritorious applications are brought before the Court and that the Court does not have to investigate the reasonableness of the decisions made by the national authorities in each of these cases.

Thus, creating clear and detailed substantive standards to determine the applicability of certain rights might reduce the claims that are made

[85] *Atanasov* v. *Bulgaria*, note 83 above, para. 76.

[86] ECtHR, *Grimkovskaya* v. *Ukraine*, 21 July 2011, Application no. 38182/03, para. 60.

[87] ECtHR, *Dubetska and others* v. *Ukraine*, 10 February 2011, Application no. 30499/03, para. 108.

[88] Cf. ECtHR, *Fadeyeva* v. *Russia*, 9 June 2005, Application no. 55723/00, para. 120 and ECtHR, *Zammit Maempel* v. *Malta*, 22 November 2011, Application no. 24202/10, para. 72. These factors might be even more valuable if the Court would consistently use them as elements of the threshold for admissibility, rather than as factors relevant to deciding whether the state has struck a 'fair balance' between all interests concerned. Moreover, at present the Court sometimes applies the criteria in a rather lenient manner, widening the scope of Art. 8 even further; for example, see ECtHR, *Mileva and others* v. *Bulgaria*, 25 November 2010, Applications no. 43449/02 and 21475/04. From an institutional perspective, such lenient application can be criticised, especially since protection of non-core interests can also be provided at the national level.

[89] Currently the Court does not seem to apply the criteria mentioned above very consistently and strictly – in the case of *Di Sarno*, for example, the Court did not find the criterion of demonstrable medical impact to be relevant, without explaining the reasons for that (see ECtHR, *Di Sarno* v. *Italy*, 10 January 2012, Application no. 30765/08). The usefulness of the criteria in reducing the number of applications could be enhanced by applying them more consistently to create greater awareness among potential applicants and their legal representatives of the chances of success in Strasbourg.

on the Court's resources and time. Given the fact that at present the Court hardly pays attention to the issue of definition and delineation of rights, much may be gained here.[90]

4. Conclusion

It has been stated and restated that the ECHR system for protecting fundamental rights is in danger of collapsing as a result of the ever-increasing case load of the Court. The aim of this chapter was to demonstrate that the Court's gradual widening of the scope of the Convention cannot be regarded as one of the direct causes of the case load problem. Nevertheless, widening the Convention's scope raises some institutional concerns of its own. The recognition of socio-economic rights as part of the Convention rights, the acknowledgement of the Court's competence to decide highly delicate ethical questions, and the application of the doctrine of positive obligations, have saddled the Court with the responsibility to decide a great many complex and delicate cases. It is not so much the sheer number of these cases that is worrisome, but the demand they make on the Court's resources. The Court does not visibly pay heed to this in its judgments. Instead, perhaps understandably, it prefers to limit itself to what would be an appropriate and desirable interpretation of the Convention from the perspective of effective protection of fundamental rights.

This chapter has put forward the argument that it is vital for the Court to show more consciousness of the institutional consequences of its interpretations. The number of 'hard cases' that take so much time and effort to be decided might be reduced if the Court took more care to distinguish 'peripheral' cases from 'core' fundamental rights issues, and concentrated on the latter category. Moreover, much would be gained if the Court delineated new rights and obligations as carefully and precisely as possible and if it formulated detailed and substantive standards for the applicability of specific Convention rights. The result of this might be that legal practitioners in Member States could more readily estimate their chances of success before the Court, which consequently might be burdened less often with unmeritorious, but difficult and time-consuming cases.

As mentioned before, such changes will not suffice to reduce the Court's overall workload, nor will they satisfy the critics of the Court who believe

[90] See further J.H. Gerards and H.C.K. Senden, 'The structure of fundamental rights and the European Court of Human Rights', (2009) 7 *International Journal of Constitutional Law* 619.

that it should not deal with socio-economic cases anyway, or should limit itself to cases concerning government interference with classic fundamental rights. Nevertheless, some profit might be gained in the shape of a reduction of applications and by increasing the capacity of the Court to decide on all of its cases in an adequate manner. Perhaps the result will prove to be limited, and it might only emerge over the long run, but every little bit counts if the Court is to be saved.

PART 2

Scope and more – developments in the case law of the ECtHR

6

Defining the scope of economic and social guarantees in the case law of the ECtHR

INGRID LEIJTEN

1. Introduction

The case law of the European Court of Human Rights (the Court; the ECtHR) shows a great variety of fundamental rights issues. Whereas the European Convention on Human Rights (the Convention; the ECHR) enumerates rights we would traditionally call 'civil' and 'political', or 'classical' rights, the interests the Court deals with today cannot always be labelled as such, or not exclusively as such.[1] A quick look at the cases adjudicated in Strasbourg reveals that these not infrequently concern social welfare,[2] health care,[3] or the

[1] See J.H. Gerards, 'Fundamental rights and other interests – should it really make a difference?' in E. Brems (ed.), *Conflicts Between Fundamental Rights* (Antwerp: Intersentia, 2008), 655–90, pp. 659–67. On social rights in the jurisprudence of the ECtHR see also, e.g., E. Brems, 'Indirect protection of social rights by the European Court of Human Rights' in D. Barak-Erez and A.M. Gross (eds), *Exploring Social Rights: Between Theory and Practice* (Oxford: Hart, 2007), 135–67; L. Clements and A Simmons, 'European Court of Human Rights: sympathetic unease' in M. Langford (ed.), *Social Rights Jurisprudence: Emerging Trends in International and Comparative Law* (Cambridge University Press, 2008), 409–27; C. O'Cinneide, 'A modest proposal: destitution, state responsibility and the European Convention on Human Rights', (2008) 5 *European Human Rights Law Review* 583; E. Palmer, 'Protecting socio-economic rights through the European Convention on Human Rights: trends and developments in the European Court of Human Rights', (2009) 2 *Erasmus Law Review* 397.

[2] Think for example of discrimination in the award of welfare benefits; see, e.g., ECtHR (GC), *Stec and others* v. *United Kingdom*, 6 July 2005 (dec.), Applications no. 65731/01 and 5900/01. For an overview see the Court's factsheet *Social Welfare* of December 2010, to be found at www.echr.coe.int/ECHR/EN/Header/Press/Information+sheets/Factsheets/. For the 'socialisation' of the Convention through the principle of non-discrimination, see Oddný Mjöll Arnardóttir's chapter in this volume.

[3] For an example under Art. 3 see ECtHR, *D* v. *United Kingdom*, 2 May 1997, Application no. 30240/96 (dealing with the deportation of a person suffering from AIDS) and, with a different outcome, ECtHR (GC), *N* v. *United Kingdom*, 27 May 2008, Application no.

environment.[4] Nowadays, the Court concerns itself with issues that range from social security,[5] via housing policy,[6] to aircraft noise,[7] building permits,[8] and waste collection.[9]

Issues concerning economic and social rights are generally classed as 'second-generation' rights,[10] rather than classical 'first-generation' rights.[11] Whilst first-generation rights place a negative duty on states to

26565/05. See for an overview the Court's factsheet on health of February 2012, to be found at www.echr.coe.int/ECHR/EN/Header/Press/Information+sheets/Factsheets/.

4 See for an overview the Court's factsheet on environment-related cases in the Court's case law, to be found at www.echr.coe.int/ECHR/EN/Header/Press/Information+sheets/Factsheets/.

5 In the case of *Stec and others* v. *United Kingdom*, note 2 above, the Court recognised that social security claims are generally protected by the Convention. Later cases have confirmed this, and have shown that various aspects of national social security systems can be reviewed under Art. 1 of Protocol No. 1. See e.g. ECtHR, *Luczak* v. *Poland*, 27 March 2007, Application no. 77782/01; ECtHR, *Carson and others* v. *United Kingdom*, 4 November 2008, (GC) 16 March 2010, Application no. 42184/05; ECtHR (GC), *Andrejeva* v. *Latvia*, 18 February 2009, Application no. 55707/00; ECtHR, *Moskal* v. *Poland*, 15 September 2009, Application no. 10373/05; ECtHR, *Andrle* v. *The Czech Republic*, 17 February 2011, Application no. 6268/08.

6 See, e.g., ECtHR, *Marzari* v. *Italy*, 4 May 1999, Application no. 36448/97; ECtHR, *Bah* v. *United Kingdom*, 27 September 2011, Application no. 56328/07.

7 ECtHR, *Hatton and others* v. *United Kingdom*, 2 October 2001, (GC) 8 July 2003, Application no. 36022/97. On this case see also G. Letsas, *A Theory of Interpretation of the European Convention on Human Rights* (Oxford University Press, 2007), pp. 127–8.

8 ECtHR, *SCEA Ferme de Fresnoy* v. *France*, 1 December 2005, Application no. 61093/00. Here, the Court noted that

> the easement relating to adjacent property did not deprive the applicant company of its possessions but subjected their use to certain restrictions, such as the need to obtain prior authorisation before any new construction or demolition. The interference with the applicant company's right to the peaceful enjoyment of its possessions can thus be regarded as a measure to control the use of property within the meaning of the second paragraph of Article 1 of Protocol No. 1.

9 ECtHR, *Di Sarno* v. *Italy*, 10 January 2012, Application no. 30765/08 (where the Court found a violation concerning the state of emergency in relation to waste collection, treatment and disposal in the Campania region in Italy).

10 In the following, I will mostly use 'economic and social rights' rather than 'economic, social and cultural rights' or any other term. This does not mean, however, that I speak only of 'strictly' economic and social rights. Rather, this term is used to refer to a broad category of rights that cover social assistance, health, housing, the environment, etc.

11 See generally, on these different 'generations', C. Tomuschat, *Human Rights. Between Idealism and Realism* (Oxford University Press, 2003), p. 24. Second-generation rights are generally guarantees of an economic, social and cultural kind. Third-generation rights ('collective' or 'solidarity' rights) concern for example the right to a clean environment, development and peace. See, e.g., P. Alston, 'A third generation of solidarity rights: progressive development or obfuscation of international human rights law?', (1982) 29 *Netherlands International Law Review* 307, p. 309.

refrain from interfering with the free sphere surrounding individuals,[12] second-generation rights require active engagement by the state. The International Covenant on Economic, Social, and Cultural Rights (ICESCR),[13] for example, mentions the rights of everyone 'to social security, including social insurance' (Article 9), 'to the enjoyment of the highest attainable standard of physical and mental health' (Article 12), and 'to an adequate standard of living for himself and his family, including adequate food, clothing and housing' (Article 11). As well as the provisions laid down in the ICESCR, those that can be found in the European Social Charter (ESC) are explicitly directed at the state,[14] stating that '[t]he States Parties to the present Covenant recognize' or 'undertake' certain things. Accordingly, these states need to regulate and/or take other appropriate measures in order to fulfil their obligations under the Covenant and the Charter.

Various authors, however, agree that, at most, the distinction between civil and political, and economic and social, rights is a relative one.[15] Many classical rights depend for their fulfilment upon (socio-economic) participation or support by the state. The often broadly and vaguely formulated norms invite the recognition of aspects that would not automatically be

[12] In the words of Kymlicka and Norman: 'democratic constitutions have traditionally protected civil and political rights (e.g., freedom of speech and association, freedom to vote). These are "negative rights" in the sense that they prohibit the state from doing certain things *to* you.' W. Kymlicka and W.J. Norman, *The Social Charter Debate: Should Social Justice be Constitutionalised?, Network Analyses: Analysis No. 2, January 1992* (Ottawa: Network on the Constitution, 1992). See also A.C. Pereira-Menaut, 'Against positive rights', (1998) 22 *Valparaiso University Law Review* 359.

[13] Opened for signature 16 December 1966, 993 UNTS 3 (entered into force 3 January 1976), GA Res. 2200 (XXI), UN Doc. A/6316.

[14] European Social Charter, adopted in 1961 (CETS No. 35, 18 October 1961) and revised in 1996 (CETS No. 163, 3 May 1996).

[15] Cf. C. Fabre, 'Constitutionalizing social rights', (1998) 6 *Journal of Political Philosophy* 263, pp. 267ff; I. Koch, 'The justiciability of indivisible rights', (2003) 72 *Nordic Journal of International Law* 3, pp. 6–9; I. Koch, 'Economic, social and cultural rights as components in civil and political rights: a hermeneutic perspective', (2006) 10 *International Journal of Human Rights* 405, pp. 408ff; Clements and Simmons, 'ECtHR: sympathetic unease', note 1 above, p. 409. See, more generally on the justiciability of socio-economic rights, C. Fabre, *Social Rights under the Constitution: Government and the Decent Life* (Oxford University Press, 2000); D. Bilchitz, *Poverty and Human Rights: The Justification and Enforcement of Socio-Economic Rights* (Oxford University Press, 2007); S. Fredman, *Human Rights Transformed: Positive Rights and Positive Duties* (Oxford University Press, 2008); S. Liebenberg, *Socio-Economic Rights: Adjudication Under a Transformative Constitution* (Claremont, South Africa: Juta Law, 2010); V. Mantouvalou, 'In support of legalisation' in C. Gearty and V. Mantouvalou, *Debating Social Rights* (Oxford: Hart Publishing, 2011); P. O'Connell, *Vindicating Socio-Economic Rights: International Standards and Comparative Experiences* (London: Routledge, 2012).

considered to fall within the sphere of 'first-generation' rights such as those protected by the ECHR.

In line with this, the Strasbourg Court has argued that there cannot be a clear distinction between civil and political rights on one hand, and economic and social rights on the other. For instance, in the case of *Airey* v. *Ireland* – a case dealing with the costs of litigation – the Court noted that

> [w]hilst the Convention sets forth what are essentially civil and political rights, many of them have implications of a social or economic nature. The . . . mere fact that an interpretation of the Convention may extend into the sphere of social and economic rights should not be a decisive factor against such an interpretation; there is no water-tight division separating that sphere from the field covered by the Convention.[16]

Indeed, a clear conceptual distinction between the various kinds of rights cannot be drawn, and a corresponding division between negative and positive demands fails to hold water in practice.[17] Nevertheless, tasks and obligations of an economic, social, or environmental kind are hardly ever cost-free and cannot always be performed merely by refraining from something. Also, even when such tasks and obligations require no extra costs or action, they are usually intimately linked with a state's (short-term) policy and budgetary choices, and subject to political controversy.[18] Moreover, in the context of the ECtHR it is important to note that the

[16] ECtHR, *Airey* v. *Ireland*, 9 October 1979, Application no. 6289/73, para. 26. See also, e.g., *Stec and others* v. *United Kingdom*, note 2 above, para. 52 (concerning entitlement to a pension).

[17] See, e.g., Fabre, *Social Rights under the Constitution*, note 15 above, pp. 267ff. In this regard, it is also important to pay attention to the idea of indivisibility, as discussed in section 4 of this chapter. See on the determination of positive obligations the chapter of Laurens Lavrysen in this volume.

[18] Because social rights are related to resource allocation, many hold that they should not be conceived of as rights in the first place. See, e.g. D. Barak-Erez and A.M. Gross, 'Introduction: do we need social rights? Questions in the era of globalisation, privatisation, and the diminished welfare state' in Barak-Erez and Gross, *Exploring Social Rights*, note 1 above. Y. Shany, 'Stuck in a moment in time: the international justiciability of economic, social and cultural rights' in *ibid.*, 77–106, p. 78, notes that 'it has been alleged, that even if clear legal standards could be developed, their enforcement would have sweeping redistributive implications, which courts or quasi-judicial committees cannot fully grasp and are, anyway, not competent to decide upon. Instead, decisions on the pace and degree in which [economic and social rights] should be implemented in a given society should, according to this view, remain in the hands of domestic politicians.' Conversely, amongst authors who do think of economic and social rights as (justiciable) *rights* it is argued that, although the differences are relative, it is still too soon to let go of the dichotomies between the different sets of rights, because socio-economic rights generally demand

supranational character of this court further complicates interference with economic and social policies.[19]

It can be said that when rights are evolving in a more socio-economic direction the Court needs to be especially 'mindful of the limits of its legitimate intervention in national resource allocation policy'.[20] Moreover, it is important for a state to become aware of what are its exact responsibilities under the ECHR in order to overcome the need for supranational interference in the first place. How far does the scope of specific ECHR rights reach and which 'non-classical' guarantees do they include? Precisely which obligations of a more economic, social, or environmental character need to be fulfilled in order to ensure the Convention's right to respect for private and family life (Article 8 ECHR) or the protection of property (Article 1 of Protocol No. 1 ECHR)? For states that have to deal with the outcomes of ECHR adjudication, it is important to get adequate and sufficiently clear answers to questions like these.

Clarity on the exact reach of Convention rights and accompanying duties is to the benefit of states, individuals, and the effectiveness of the Council of Europe's fundamental rights system.[21] Therefore, one could expect the Court to be precise in defining the scope of the Convention rights and to inform states of what is expected in the socio-economic fields not traditionally falling within the scope of the Convention.

In practice, however, this is not happening. The Court is clear only about what the Convention does *not* provide for. More than once it

greater resources and are more imprecise. Cf. Koch, 'Justiciability of indivisible rights', note 15 above, p. 25; Koch, 'A hermeneutic perspective', note 15 above, p. 407.

19 See, for information on the subsidiary role of the Court and a general picture of the specific 'problematic' of the ECtHR, J.H. Gerards, 'Judicial deliberations in the European Court of Human Rights' in N. Huls, M. Adams and J. Bomhoff (eds), *The Legitimacy of Highest Courts' Rulings* (The Hague: T.M.C. Asser Press, 2009), 407–436, pp. 409–18. See, on several institutional concerns relating to the expansion of the Court's case law, the chapter of Janneke Gerards in this volume.

20 Palmer, 'Protecting socio-economic rights', note 1 above, p. 398 (focusing on the positive obligations the Court has recognised under Arts 2, 3 and 8 ECHR, and on the indirect protection offered under Arts 6 and 14 of the Convention).

21 Indeed, even though the Court's judgments are only legally binding on the state that is a party to the case (see Art. 46 ECHR), it is recognised that in practice the impact of the Strasbourg case law reaches beyond individual applications and has an important influence on future cases and hence individuals' reasons for filing an application and states' efforts to comply with the Convention. See Gerards, 'Judicial deliberations', note 19 above, pp. 409–10.

has reiterated that the Convention does *not* include rights to a clean environment,[22] to housing,[23] to acquire property,[24] or to a pension of a certain amount.[25] In *Pancenko* v. *Latvia*, the Court recalled that

> the Convention does not guarantee, as such, socio-economic rights, including the right to charge-free dwelling, the right to work, the right to free medical assistance, or the right to claim financial assistance from a State to maintain a certain level of living.[26]

While 'full' social and economic rights are generally laid down in other fundamental rights documents, the Court excludes them from the scope of the ECHR rights. Yet it is evident that the Court *de facto* does review cases regarding environmental issues, housing, and social security.[27] Its judgments remain rather vague, however, as to whether and to what extent such social and economic interests actually constitute enforceable rights under the ECHR. Likewise, the Court does not provide clarity as to the exact requirements a state must meet to comply with the Convention. If 'the right to be provided with housing', 'nature preservation', etc. do not need to be respected *in full*, what then is the precise level of protection that the states are expected to provide? Or, put differently, what socio-economic guarantees *can* be regarded as falling within the scope of the Convention?

A closer look at the case law of the Court reveals that instead of defining the 'economic and social scope' of Convention rights like Article 8 and Article 1 of the First Protocol (hereafter: P1), the Court tends to avoid determining the exact rights and duties involved. Either it 'skips' making

[22] For example ECtHR, *Kyrtatos* v. *Greece*, 22 May 2003, Application no. 41666/98, para. 52; ECtHR, *Fadeyeva* v. *Russia*, 9 June 2005, Application no. 55723/00, para. 68: 'Article 8 has been relied on in various cases involving environmental concern, yet it is not violated every time that environmental deterioration occurs: no right to nature preservation is as such included among the rights and freedoms guaranteed by the Convention'.

[23] For example ECtHR (GC), *Chapman* v. *United Kingdom*, 18 January 2001, Application no. 27238/95, para. 99 ('[i]t is important to recall that Article 8 does not in terms recognise a right to be provided with a home'); *Bah* v. *United Kingdom*, note 6 above, para. 40.

[24] For example, ECtHR, *Van der Mussele* v. *Belgium*, 23 November 1983, Application no. 8919/80, para. 48, and recently ECtHR, *Lakicević and others* v. *Montenegro and Serbia*, 13 December 2011, Applications no. 27458/06, 37205/06, 37297/06 and 33604/07, para. 59.

[25] For example ECtHR, *Kjartan Ásmundsson* v. *Iceland*, 12 October 2004, Application no. 60669/00, para. 39, and recently ECtHR, *Maggio and others* v. *Italy*, 31 May 2011, Applications no. 46286/09, 53851/08, 53727/08, 54486/08 and 56001/08, para. 55.

[26] ECtHR, *Pancenko* v. *Latvia*, 28 October 1999 (dec.), Application no. 40772/98.

[27] See, for an argument of how the principle of non-discrimination adds to this, the chapter by Oddný Mjöll Arnardóttir in this volume.

a decision on whether or not the interest invoked actually falls within the reach of a Convention right, or it simply 'assumes' that this is the case, on an ad hoc basis.[28] It is imaginable that the Court does so in order to provide for protection of fundamental rights in individual cases while trying to avoid imposing far-reaching Convention obligations. Socio-economic fields like social security are sensitive, after all, for the reasons mentioned above: socio-economic rights require certain budgetary and policy choices to be made and any new obligations have to be reconciled with existing rules and policies. For that reason the Court will be very careful and reluctant to interfere in a too obvious way with national decision-making in these areas. However, providing no exact definition of Convention guarantees may result in uncertainty about the exact meaning of the Convention, which can have the effect of curtailing the willingness of Member States to fulfil their obligations under it.

This chapter focuses on the problem of a lack of a clear definition of the scope of requirements of an economic and social kind, which, according to the Court's case law, are nevertheless implied by the Convention. Section 2 aims to illuminate the various ways in which the Court avoids defining the scope of socio-economic rights and obligations and thereby creates uncertainty – even though regularly reviewing cases on housing, health, and environmental matters. This raises the question whether and how in these cases the Court could deal with the problem of defining scope in a different manner. As is shown in section 3, the structure of fundamental rights norms generally directs the Court towards drawing a clear distinction between determining the scope of a right and reviewing the justifications advanced for limiting it.[29] This 'bifurcated approach' allows the Court to determine the content of the right at stake at the first stage of its examination of a complaint, then take state interests into account at the second stage, when it reviews the justification put forward.

28 At least two different 'constructions' can be identified with the help of which the Court avoids or ignores the question of the scope of a right. Often, it holds that, in cases concerning positive obligations, an overall test needs to be applied to determine whether a fair balance has been struck between the interests of the individual and the general interest – without first clearly defining what rights fall within the reach of the Convention. Also, the Court sometimes ignores the definition of scope and instead 'proceeds on the assumption' that a certain Convention Article is applicable. These constructions will both be further elaborated in section 2.

29 See generally J.H. Gerards and H. Senden, 'The structure of fundamental rights and the European Court of Human Rights', (2009) 7 *International Journal of Constitutional Law* 619–653, in which the authors emphasise the importance of the distinction between the definition of scope and the review of justification in the context of the ECHR.

It is argued that this method is not always workable or desirable when it comes to guarantees of an economic and social nature. In section 4, therefore, a different perspective on defining the scope of rights will be explored. In the context of the debate on 'second-generation' economic and social fundamental rights, e.g., the rights laid down in the ICESCR and ESC, it is recognised that the 'full' rights cannot always be realised. Hence, in line with the requirement for 'progressive realisation' of these rights, efforts have been made to define the pragmatic, or 'usable' content of these rights with the help of the concept of 'minimum core obligations'. It is this concept that can offer inspiration for taking an alternative view on the issue at stake here, and that can show the (im)possibilities and chances for framing the task of defining ECHR rights in a different manner.

2. Economic and social aspects of the Court's case law: avoiding the definition question

Through the (implicit) recognition of economic and social aspects of the case law of the Court, the reach of various ECHR rights has increased, but has also become less clear. Now that the ECHR either directly or indirectly enters the field of economic and social rights, the outer borders of its guarantees have become difficult to determine – the distinction between ECHR rights and other interests has become a blurry one.[30]

Neither should this come as a surprise, nor is it by definition undesirable. After all, the Court aims at the practical and effective protection of individual fundamental rights, while it also has to give due consideration to national prerogatives and to the national sensitivities at play in the forty-seven Council of Europe Member States. Especially in the field of socio-economic entitlements these states have reached different arrangements, based on different funding methods and subject to different eligibility criteria (nationality, age, sex or other factors).[31] In offering economic and social guarantees, the Court's role is not an unambiguous

[30] Cf. J.H. Gerards, 'The prism of fundamental rights', (2012) 8 *European Constitutional Law Review* 173 (analysing the incremental method used by the Court and comparing fundamental rights to a prism: fundamental rights are clearly recognisable on first viewing, but turn out to cover a great many interests and values that, like inseparable colours, cannot easily be determined). See also Gerards, 'Fundamental rights and other interests', note 1 above.

[31] Palmer, 'Protecting socio-economic rights', note 1 above, p. 401.

one.[32] Though recognised as an important goal of the welfare state that is omnipresent in modern Europe, furtherance of welfare goals remains something that is generally regarded as belonging primarily to the prerogatives of national (democratic) decision-making. Today, moreover, criticisms directed at the Court concerning its expansionist tactics,[33] as well as the economic crisis that is making government spending an even more delicate issue, do not provide a strong footing for the straightforward advancement of economic and social goals through Strasbourg case law.[34]

It is said that the Court's socio-economic case law signals an incremental approach that fails to address the question of the scope of the applicable rights and duties in a consistent and structured manner.[35] In line with this, the Court often circumvents the question of scope by means of two different strategies.[36]

First, the Court regularly avoids giving a definition and instead 'proceeds on the assumption' that the interest at stake concerns a right protected by the Convention. In the recent case of *Valkov and others* v. *Bulgaria*, for example, the ECtHR reviewed the applications lodged by nine Bulgarian nationals who claimed that the statutory cap on their pensions breached their rights under the ECHR.[37] Rather than determining whether the pensions claimed constituted 'possessions' within the scope of Article 1 P1, the Court simply assumed that the article was applicable.[38]

[32] It can be argued that the ECtHR is not competent *per se* to have the final say on such issues. However, this ambiguity also has to do with the fact that, since 1998, a mechanism has existed within the Council of Europe for adjudicating the social rights in place: the collective complaints procedure under the European Social Charter. See Brems, 'Indirect protection of social rights', note 1 above, p. 164.

[33] See e.g. M. Bossuyt, 'Should the Strasbourg Court exercise more self-restraint? On the extension of the jurisdiction of the European Court of Human Rights to social security regulations', (2007) 28 *Human Rights Law Journal* 321, but also consider the political debates on the ECtHR that are ongoing in various Member States such as the UK and the Netherlands. See also the chapter by Janneke Gerards in this volume.

[34] Cf. Koch, 'Justiciability of indivisible rights', note 15 above, p. 25.

[35] See e.g. Palmer, 'Protecting socio-economic rights', note 1 above (arguing that the Court is still influenced by the positive–negative dichotomy and continues to undermine the development of a principled approach to the protection of socio-economic rights).

[36] Note that these ways of avoiding the scope question are not exclusively visible in the case law on economic and social guarantees. Cf. Gerards and Senden, 'The structure of fundamental rights', note 29 above, pp. 630–6.

[37] ECtHR, *Valkov and others* v. *Bulgaria*, 25 October 2011, Applications no. 2033/04, 19125/04, 19475/04, 19490/04, 19495/04, 19497/04, 24729/04, 171/05 and 2041/05.

[38] *Ibid.*, paras 87 and 113. See also ECtHR, *Sali* v. *Sweden*, 10 January 2006 (dec.), Application no. 67071/01; *Maggio and others* v. *Italy*, note 25 above.

The parties involved were sent home with a forty-page judgment containing extensive discussions of the Bulgarian pension system – leading to the conclusion that there had not been a violation – but without knowing whether truly a Convention right or obligation had been at stake in the first place.[39]

The Court took a similar approach in the case of *Sentges and others* v. *The Netherlands*, which concerned a severely disabled boy's request for a robotic arm.[40] Understandably, it is difficult for the Court to determine whether, in general, a right to be provided with such things falls within the reach of Article 8 ECHR. Probably for that reason, it chose to avoid the question of definition, stating that

> [e]ven assuming that in the present case . . . a special link [between the situation and the applicants' private life] . . . exists . . . regard must be had to the fair balance that has to be struck between the competing interests of the individual and of the community as a whole and to the wide margin of appreciation enjoyed by States in this respect in determining the steps to be taken to ensure compliance with the Convention.[41]

Perhaps this construction seems harmless in light of the fact that in matters of economic and social policy a violation is not often found and a wide margin of appreciation is usually granted.[42] Consider for example the Court's decision in the case of *Mólka* v. *Poland*,[43] concerning a man in a wheelchair who was unable to access a polling station. In this judgment the Court stated that it

> does not rule out the possibility that, in circumstances such as those in the present case, a sufficient link would exist to attract the protection of

[39] Of course, not just Bulgaria and the individuals involved are left in doubt: the same goes for other states and individuals coping with similar circumstances who might want to bring their case to Strasbourg. See, e.g. Gerards and Senden, 'The structure of fundamental rights', note 29 above, p. 637.

[40] ECtHR, *Sentges* v. *The Netherlands*, 8 July 2003 (dec.), Application no. 27677/02.

[41] *Ibid.*; paragraphs not numbered.

[42] See, e.g., ECtHR, *James and others* v. *United Kingdom*, 21 February 1986, Application no. 8793/79, para. 46:

> [T]he decision to enact laws expropriating property will commonly involve consideration of political, economic and social issues on which opinions within a democratic society may reasonably differ widely. The Court, finding it natural that the margin of appreciation available to the legislature in implementing social and economic policies should be a wide one, will respect the legislature's judgment as to what is 'in the public interest' unless that judgment be manifestly without reasonable foundation.

[43] ECtHR, 11 April 2006 (dec.), Application no. 56550/00.

> Article 8. However, the Court does not find it necessary finally to determine the applicability of the Article in the present case since, for the reasons which follow, the application is in any event inadmissible on other grounds.[44]

It is generally recognised that it is difficult to provide a clear answer to the scope question, especially when positive obligations are concerned.[45] It must nevertheless be asked what is it that allows the Court to assume that a 'possession' is at stake? And what information is gained by the acknowledgement that a 'sufficient link' with a Convention Article *could* exist in similar circumstances?

The second way in which the Court avoids clear definition of social and economic rights and guarantees is related to the first one: whenever positive state action is required to protect guarantees of fundamental rights, or in Convention terms, if the Court has to determine whether there are positive obligations on a state to protect a right in an effective manner, it tends to mix the definition of scope with the review of the justification. In those instances, it holds that

> regard must be had to the fair balance that has to be struck between the general interest of the community and the interests of the individual... In striking this balance the aims mentioned in the second paragraph... may be of a certain relevance.[46]

In practice, this often means that the Court does not define the scope of the right at stake, but instead engages in an overall evaluation of whether the state fulfilled its (undefined) obligations.[47] At most, in these

[44] A similar approach can be found in ECtHR (GC), *Draon* v. *France*, 6 October 2005, Application no. 1513/03, para. 111. See also, concerning Art. 2 ECHR and health care, ECtHR (GC), *Cyprus* v. *Turkey*, 10 May 2001, Application no. 25781/94, para. 219; ECtHR, *Nitecki* v. *Poland*, 21 March 2003 (dec.), Application no. 65653/01.

[45] See also Laurens Lavrysen's chapter in this volume.

[46] See e.g. ECtHR, *Rees* v. *United Kingdom*, 17 October 1986, Application no. 9532/81, para. 37.

[47] Cf. also *Hatton and others* v. *United Kingdom* (GC), note 7 above, para. 98; ECtHR, *Giacomelli* v. *Italy*, 2 November 2006, Application no. 59909/00, para. 78. In both cases the Court emphasised that, whether or not the case should have been judged in the light of positive duties on a state, or in the light of an interference with Art. 8, the focus is on the fair balance that has or has not been struck. It then goes into any justification given by the state without further clarifying this right's applicability. It is important to stress that, in this chapter, the view is taken that defining (positive or negative) obligations is a matter of scope determination, since the recognition of obligations mirrors the recognition of *prima facie* rights. See, for a different point of view, the chapter by Laurens Lavrysen in this volume.

instances, case-specific information on the content of rights and duties can be inferred from a Court judgment. Taking account of the specific circumstances of a case, including the interests brought forward by the state, the Court sometimes identifies an obligation and determines whether it was fulfilled or not. General information on the reach of the Convention provision as such, however, is mostly lacking.

In general, it can be said that the Court can only exercise its power of review once it has determined that the interest invoked comes within the scope of the Convention, which means that substance has to be given to what the Convention requires.[48] It is for that reason that it is sometimes argued that the Court should take better care in defining the scope of Convention rights before embarking on review of justification. More particularly, however, given the complicated, multilevel setting in which the Court is operating, it is clear that a lack of clarity can obstruct the effectiveness of Strasbourg's case law.[49] Hence, if it is accepted that it is important for the Court to determine the scope of Convention rights and duties, and that its current practice in cases of a more social and economic kind discloses that it is not sufficiently doing so, the question is how the situation can be improved. Before answering this question it is important, however, to first examine how the determination of scope is usually perceived in the context of the ECHR.

3. Determining the scope of rights in line with the structure of fundamental rights

When it comes to defining the scope of fundamental rights, the structure of fundamental rights is generally said to be of crucial importance. Fundamental rights are sometimes understood as 'trumps',[50] or 'firewalls',[51]

[48] This concerns the structure of fundamental rights, which will be explored further in section 3 of this chapter.

[49] See e.g. L.R. Helfer, 'Consensus, coherence and the European Convention on Human Rights', (1993) 26 *Cornell International Law Journal* 133–165, p. 137. Gerards and Senden note that 'the Court will have to hand down clear judgments that are understandable for the national authorities and provide convincing interpretations of the text of the Convention' ('The structure of fundamental rights', note 29 above, p. 638).

[50] R. Dworkin, 'Rights as trumps' in J. Waldron (ed.) *Theories of Rights* (Oxford University Press, 1984), 153–167.

[51] J. Habermas, *Between Facts and Norms. Contributions to a Discourse Theory of Law and Democracy* (Cambridge, MA: MIT Press, 1996), p. 254. See also Rawls's priority of the right over the good: J. Rawls, *Political Liberalism* (New York: Columbia University Press, 1993), p. 173.

yet many authors convincingly argue that it is neither desirable nor feasible to conceptualise fundamental rights as 'absolutes'.[52] Because of the existence of a broad variety of often conflicting (fundamental and other) interests, fundamental rights cannot always be realised.[53] They cannot invariably take precedence over other (general) interests, and hence they can and should sometimes be limited.

The possibility of limitation is closely connected with the twofold structure of fundamental rights. First, there is the *prima facie* right,[54] e.g. the right to respect for private and family life, home and correspondence (Article 8 ECHR). Second, there is a possibility for limitation or justification, sometimes made explicit by reference to a number of express conditions or standards of review.[55] For example, a limitation of Article 8 is justified when this is 'in accordance with the law and . . . necessary in a democratic society in the interests of national security, public safety', etc. This two-part or binary structure of ECHR rights suggests that, when it is confronted with an individual complaint, the Court should first establish whether the interest invoked falls within the reach of the right as spelled out in the first paragraph. Only if that is the case, should it continue and examine whether the interference was justified in line with the second paragraph.[56]

52 This might however be different for the so-called non-derogable rights. However, the existence of truly 'absolute' rights is sometimes questioned (e.g. M. Kumm, 'Constitutional rights as principles: on the structure and domain of constitutional justice', (2004) 3 *International Journal of Constitutional Law* 574, p. 592. And see, e.g., Sir John Laws, 'The limitations of human rights', (1998) *Summer Public Law* 254, p. 255, who argues that

> [a] society whose values are defined by reference to individual rights is by that very fact already impoverished. Its culture says nothing about individual duty – nothing about *virtue* . . . Self-discipline, self-restraint, to say nothing of self-sacrifice, are at best regarded as optional extras and at worst (and the worst is too often the reality) as old-fashioned ideas worth nothing more but a scoff and a gibe.

53 Also, on their own fundamental rights do not suffice to achieve the aims of a society, e.g. dealing with conflicts in an appropriate manner. See G. van der Schyff, *Limitation of Rights. A Study of the European Convention and the South African Bill of Rights* (Nijmegen: Wolf Legal Publishers, 2005), p. 8.

54 On the characterisation of rights norms as *prima facie* rights see R. Alexy, *A Theory of Constitutional Rights*, trans. J. Rivers (Oxford University Press, 2002), p. 196. A *prima facie* right is a right endowed on individuals before considering any limit that might have been set on it in practice.

55 See also, for an extensive discussion on the twofold structure of ECHR rights, Van der Schyff, *Limitation of Rights*, note 53 above, Ch. 3.

56 See, e.g., Gerards and Senden, 'The structure of fundamental rights', note 29 above.

Not only does their structure illustrate that the determination of scope is only a first, and separate, step in dealing with a fundamental right; it also sheds light on *how* the scope of a right should be defined. While limitations of fundamental rights can be justified by the need to protect important, countervailing (state) interests or rights, the question of scope precedes this exercise and should not be influenced by the state's aims and choices. For example, questions such as whether the utterance that caused an individual's criminal conviction is protected by freedom of expression (Article 10 ECHR), or whether a claim to an early retirement pension can be counted among the 'possessions' that are covered by Article 1 P1, should be answered without taking into account information on any possible justification, i.e. state interests, policies and resources. One important reason for this, which has been set out particularly convincingly by Faigman, is that fundamental rights are directed in particular at protecting vulnerable minorities against the state. Whilst 'majority interests' might impart a presumptive validity to limitations of rights by the state, these should not determine what individual interests deserve the special safeguards offered to fundamental rights, as this could make the protection of minorities illusory.[57] As argued by Faigman, it should therefore be ensured that the definition of fundamental rights follows from these rights *per se*.[58] According to this argument, courts should determine the scope of rights autonomously, without reference to the (national) majority's understanding of the reach of fundamental rights protection.

In Europe, a related but different argument is often made, which leads to the similar conclusion that it is important to state the exact right at stake in an independent fashion. Alexy famously grounds the importance of distinguishing definition of scope from review of justification on his view that fundamental rights have both a rule-like and a principle-like character.[59] Rules are either valid or not, whereas principles can be understood as 'optimisation requirements'.[60] *Prima facie* rights, i.e. rights

[57] Cf. R.A. Dahl, *A Preface to Democratic Theory* (Chicago: The University of Chicago Press, 1956), p. 24.

[58] D.L. Faigman, 'Reconciling individual rights and government interests: Madisonian principles *versus* Supreme Court practice', (1996) 78 *Virginia Law Review* 1521, p. 1529: 'When defining the Constitution, the guiding values come from the diverse constitutional authorities demarcating the contours of individual liberty . . . '.

[59] Alexy, *Theory of Constitutional Rights*, note 54 above, pp. 84–6.

[60] 'Principles are *optimization requirements*, characterized by the fact that they can be satisfied to varying degrees, and that the appropriate degree of satisfaction depends not on what

as they are stated without or before taking into account the possibility of limitations,[61] have a rule-like character. They can be applied in a judicial context through mere subsumption, without there being any need to balance these rules against other norms.[62] Alexy stresses that rights should generally be interpreted in a broad manner, and that a court should thus allow for the unequivocal inclusion of a broad range of interests.[63] However, fundamental rights can be limited because of their 'relative', non-absolute nature; moreover, they often contain (written) limitation clauses. In Alexy's view, therefore, it is impossible to apply fundamental rights as if they were rules. The 'principle-aspect', i.e. the aspect that explicitly requires that (listed) competing interests be taken into account, implies that fundamental rights can only be 'optimised'. State interests and other relevant interests have to be taken into account when examining whether a right has been violated.[64] Thus the difference that exists between the way a court should treat the 'threshold question' (i.e. the 'rule' part), and how it should proceed in reviewing the justification advanced (i.e. the 'optimisation' part, taking into consideration that it deals with competing principles) makes it crucial not to blend the different and consecutive phases of fundamental rights adjudication.

Thus, there appear to be strong arguments in favour of a binary approach towards fundamental rights, with the definition of a right clearly preceding the assessment of any possible justification. What we often see happening in cases concerning economic and social issues, however, is that the phases are mixed and the distinction is blurred. As has been demonstrated in section 2 above, the Court regularly 'assumes' that a *prima facie* fundamental rights 'rule' is applicable, without clarifying and defining this rule and without providing further explanation of the rule's scope or meaning. Moreover, the separate stages of fundamental rights adjudication are often expressly blended when the Court starts balancing the various interests in order to define the (positive) obligations at issue. Gerards and Senden have suggested in this regard that '[m]uch would be gained if the Court took more seriously the bifurcated approach toward fundamental rights'.[65] This is easier said than done, however. Especially

is factually possible but also on what is legally possible. The scope of the legally possible is determined by opposing principles and rules.' *Ibid.*, pp. 47–8.

61 Cf. the 'first paragraphs' of Arts 8–11 ECHR.

62 Alexy, *Theory of Constitutional Rights*, note 54 above, p. 85.

63 *Ibid.*, pp. 210–17. 64 *Ibid.*

65 Gerards and Senden, 'The structure of fundamental rights', note 29 above, p. 652.

in cases concerning socio-economic policy, welfare benefits, and the like, it is not merely unwillingness or sloppiness that leads the Court to fail to define the exact rights and duties involved. It has already been argued that avoiding broad socio-economic interpretations is understandable in the light of the Court's special position, which implies that it must protect individual fundamental rights in a practical and effective manner while showing sufficient awareness of national sensitivities.[66] Understandably, the Court is hesitant to recognise new, far-reaching guarantees,[67] especially when this boils down to incorporating *prima facie* economic and social fundamental rights and, thereby, increases Strasbourg's influence over certain socio-economic areas.[68] When it does extend such recognition, this can easily be regarded as 'activism' and, accordingly, evoke criticism and doubts as to whether the Court acted legitimately in including these areas in the scope of its review.[69]

Moreover, even when the Court would like to state the obligations at stake precisely, in the way suggested by the bifurcated structure of fundamental rights, it would run into inherent difficulties. For is socio-economic content determinable without taking into account the competing interests that played a role in the specific circumstances? And can (positive) obligations be defined without showing due deference to the state, its resources and its short- and long-term policy goals? It seems that the ideal character of a right's definition – as an 'independent rule' – in fact discourages the Court from addressing this issue in the first place. It should not come as a surprise that this court is unwilling to hand down a very inclusive definition of scope when the socio-economic issue at stake does not 'naturally' fall within the wording of the Convention Article that was invoked, and moreover without showing due regard to the interests of the state involved.

66 See, e.g., Helfer, 'Consensus, coherence and the ECHR', note 49 above, p. 173.

67 Think of a right to housing, a clean environment or a pension of a particular amount.

68 This might be too much even when it is just the identification of *prima facie* rights, that can justifiably be limited, especially in the field of social and economic rights. Increasing a right's scope does not mean that it becomes easier for a state to violate that right, but that potential for violating it is created. Thus, solely by increasing the scope, the Court might be perceived as increasing its influence in an undesirable manner.

69 In *Stec and others* v. *United Kingdom*, note 2 above, the Court brought virtually all social security benefits within the ambit of the Convention, regardless of whether these are contributory or not. This has led to a line of cases characterised by sensitive issues and broad margins of appreciation that hardly allow the applicants any chances of success. This development does indeed evoke criticism; see, e.g., Bossuyt, 'Should the Strasbourg Court exercise more self-restraint?', note 33 above.

Hence, regardless of whether the bifurcated approach laid out above in theory presents the ideal way of dealing with the scope of rights, it must be acknowledged that it is sometimes almost impossible to give content to fundamental rights in the way their structure suggests, i.e. on the basis of the right itself and independently of majority concerns. Particularly when it comes to defining socio-economic guarantees in a sensitive international context, it might therefore be interesting to look at the issue in a slightly different fashion. How is the question of scope perceived in the debate about second-generation economic and social fundamental rights, and what lessons learned there could also be valuable in the Strasbourg context?

4. Framing the issue in a different fashion: defining minimum core obligations

The particular way of looking at how to determine the scope of rights that is explored in this section is intimately related with the debate on the economic and social rights laid down in the ICESCR. To provide a good basis for finding possible sources of inspiration for improvement of the ECtHR's practice, this section first presents some information on the ICESCR. It explains why the notion of 'minimum core obligations' presents a perspective that contains interesting insights on the definition of the scope of fundamental rights, then goes on to investigate the possible relevance in the Strasbourg context.

Since its adoption by the General Assembly of the United Nations in 1966, the International Covenant on Economic, Social, and Cultural Rights and the rights incorporated therein have proven anything but easy to understand.[70] At the UN level it was held that, regardless of the distinction between 'civil and political' and 'economic and social' rights documents,[71] '[t]he international community must treat human rights globally in a fair and equal manner, on the same footing, and with the same emphasis'.[72] Nevertheless, the specific character of economic, social

[70] ICESCR, note 13 above. See generally, e.g., P. Alston, 'Out of the abyss: the challenges confronting the new UN Committee on Economic, Social and Cultural Rights', (1987) 9 *Human Rights Quarterly* 332.

[71] The former were laid down in the International Covenant on Civil and Political Rights (ICCPR), and the latter in the ICESCR.

[72] Vienna Declaration, para. 5, adopted by the 1993 second World Conference on Human Rights in Vienna. One can speak in this regard of the 'indivisibility', or interdependence, of fundamental rights: see further below.

and cultural rights has not made it easy to truly give these rights the same 'standing' as classical rights. As was noted before, treaty instruments protecting economic and social fundamental rights are generally directed at the state, rather than providing enforceable rights to the individual. They require states to recognise, and to undertake certain steps in order to effectuate, broadly stated rights.[73]

One of the particularities of the ICESCR can be found in Article 2(1) of the Covenant, which requires that

> [e]ach State Party to the present Covenant undertakes to take steps, individually and through international assistance and co-operation, especially economic and technical, *to the maximum of its available resources*, with a view to *achieving progressively the full realization* of the rights recognized in the present Covenant by all appropriate means, including particularly the adoption of legislative measures.[74]

In other words, the extent to which ICESCR rights must be guaranteed is not necessarily always the same, but is subject to the resources available. Moreover, the standard of implementation adopted in the Covenant is 'progressive realisation', which means that the rights can be realised in phases, rather than fully and instantly respected at the moment the Covenant is ratified.[75] If we imagine that a state might lack sufficient resources, requiring progressive realisation of economic and social rights seems a necessary approach.

Nevertheless, the concept of 'progressive realisation' has further complicated both understanding and monitoring of the rights laid down in the ICESCR.[76] On one hand, the concept takes into account the practical

[73] Think of the rights of everyone to 'social security, including social insurance', 'the enjoyment of the highest attainable standard of physical and mental health' and 'an adequate standard of living for himself and his family, including adequate food, clothing and housing' that were introduced above (Arts 9, 12 and 11 ICESCR, note 13 above, respectively).

[74] Article 2(1) ICESCR, note 13 above (emphasis added).

[75] It has been recognised by the (UN) Committee on Economic, Social and Cultural Rights (CESCR), however, that there are several obligations that need to be respected immediately, as for example the guarantee that action will be taken without discrimination. See para. 1 of General Comment No. 3, 'The Nature of States Parties Obligations', 5th Sess. (1990), CESCR, reprinted in *Compilation of General Comments and General Recommendations*, UN Doc. HRI/GEN/1/Rev.1 (1991) (hereafter General Comment No. 3). To be found at www.unhchr.ch/tbs/doc.nsf/0/ca12c3a4ea8d6c53c1256d500056e56f/$FILE/G0441302.pdf.

[76] A.R. Chapman and S. Russell, 'Introduction' in Chapman and Russell (eds), *Core Obligations: Building a Framework for Economic, Social and Cultural Rights* (Antwerp, Oxford, New York: Intersentia, 2002), p. 4.

reality that the obligations under the ICESCR might prove so onerous that not every state will be able to comply with them fully and directly. The encouragement to ensure compliance in a progressive manner ideally results in best efforts being made, even where completely satisfying the demands of the ICESCR is not (yet) possible. On the other hand, the requirement for progressive realisation 'provides a loophole large enough in practical terms to nullify the Covenant's guarantees: the possibility that States will claim lack of resources as the reason they have not met their obligations'.[77] Indeed, particularly in light of the 'availability of resources' phrasing, the obligation can become 'empty' in practice.[78]

As the available resources differ from state to state, an element of distinction is recognised that renders obligations neither uniform nor universal. The lack of an objective and clear definition of the relevant obligations may obscure the evaluation of compliance with the Covenant, as well as result in states perceiving a lack of clarity as to the expected level of protection.[79] It is a challenge *per se* to identify effective approaches for implementation of ICESCR rights. The United Nations Committee on Economic, Social and Cultural Rights (CESCR), the body tasked with monitoring the implementation of the ICESCR, can supervise countries on the basis of regular reports by its State Parties. But supervising whether states comply with the requirement for 'progressive realisation' presents some methodological difficulties. It is far from easy, for example, to determine how to calculate a state's maximum available resources.[80] Moreover, even if there were plenty of data it would remain hard to determine what moving towards full implementation would actually entail. Does this mean that a state can spend its available resources on whatever it thinks

[77] *Ibid.*, p. 5. According to Steiner *et al.* (H.J. Steiner, P. Alston and R. Goodman, *International Human Rights in Context. Law Politics, Morals*, 3rd edn (Oxford University Press, 2008), p. 275) '[g]overnments can present themselves as defenders of [economic and social rights] without international imposition of any precise constraints on their policies and behaviour'.

[78] Steiner *et al.*, *ibid.*, p. 275.

[79] A.R. Chapman, 'A "violations approach" for monitoring the International Covenant on Economic, Social and Cultural Rights', (1996) 18 *Human Rights Quarterly* 23.

[80] Chapman and Russell, 'Introduction', note 76 above, p. 5: 'this necessitates the development of a multiplicity of performance standards for each enumerated right in relationship to the varied social development and resource contexts of specific countries'. See also Chapman, 'Violations approach', note 79 above, pp. 29ff; R.E. Robertson, 'Measuring state compliance with the obligation to devote the "maximum available resources" to realizing economic, social and cultural rights', (1994) 16 *Human Rights Quarterly* 693 (introducing a methodology for measuring state compliance with the obligation to devote the maximum available resources).

is relevant in light of the rights enumerated in the Covenant, so long as this can be considered a step towards full realisation? Or should there be stricter standards?

In order to give more content to (for example) the right to health (Article 12(1) ICESCR),[81] social security (Article 9 ICESCR)[82] and education (Article 13(1) ICESCR),[83] some elements or aspects of these rights have been highlighted that must be respected immediately because of their 'core' importance. As Bilchitz puts it, 'the notion of progressive realization must thus be read to include as a base-line the provision of minimum essential levels of a right which the State is then required to build upon'.[84] In its General Comment No. 3, 'The Nature of States Parties Obligations', dating from 1990,[85] the Committee states the following:

> On the basis of the extensive experience gained by the Committee, as well as by the body that preceded it, over a period of more than a decade of examining States parties' reports the Committee is of the view that a minimum core obligation to ensure the satisfaction of, at the very least, minimum essential levels of each of the rights is incumbent upon every State party. Thus, for example, a State party in which any significant number of individuals is deprived of essential foodstuffs, of essential primary health care, of basic shelter and housing, or of the most basic forms of education is, *prima facie*, failing to discharge its obligations under the Covenant. If the Covenant were to be read in such a way as not to establish such a minimum core obligation, it would be largely deprived of its *raison d'être*. By the same token, it must be noted that any assessment as to whether a State has discharged its minimum core obligation must also take account of resource constraints applying within the country concerned. Article 2(1) obligates each State party to take the necessary steps 'to the maximum of its available resources'. In order for a State party to be able

[81] 'The States Parties to the present Covenant recognize the right of everyone to the enjoyment of the highest attainable standard of physical and mental health.'

[82] 'The State Parties to the Present Covenant recognize the right of everyone to social security, including social insurance.'

[83] 'The States Parties to the present Covenant recognize the right of everyone to education. They agree that education shall be directed to the full development of the human personality and the sense of its dignity, and shall strengthen the respect for human rights and fundamental freedoms. They further agree that education shall enable all persons to participate effectively in a free society, promote understanding, tolerance and friendship among all nations and all racial, ethnic or religious groups, and further the activities of the United Nations for the maintenance of peace.'

[84] D. Bilchitz, 'Towards a reasonable approach to the minimum core: laying the foundations for future socio-economic rights jurisprudence', (2003) 19 *South African Journal of Human Rights* 1, p. 12. See also, e.g., Robertson, 'Measuring state compliance', note 80, pp. 701ff.

[85] General Comment No. 3, note 75 above.

> to attribute its failure to meet at least its minimum core obligations to a lack of available resources it must demonstrate that every effort has been made to use all resources that are at its disposition in an effort to satisfy, as a matter of priority, those minimum obligations.[86]

Recognising that there is a 'minimum core obligation' inherent in the rights laid down in the ICESCR, the Committee has tried to give hands and feet to these rights. In later general comments, it has fleshed out its first remark concerning these obligations, stating, for example, that the right to housing requires that due priority be given to social groups living in unfavourable conditions,[87] that the right to food implies '[t]he availability of food in a quantity and quality sufficient to satisfy the dietary needs of individuals',[88] and that a core obligation coming with the right to health is to provide for 'essential drugs, as from time to time defined under the WHO Action Programme on Essential Drugs'.[89]

The identification of the most important aspects of economic and social rights seems to be based on an acknowledgement of the idea that fundamental rights have a core that cannot be limited.[90] However, the Committee's approach might just as well be understood as a way of defining the scope of rights.[91] After all, the minimum core obligations doctrine rests on the fact that the 'full' rights as stated in the Covenant cannot be realised immediately and entirely. The Covenant states desirable goals, but when it comes down to supervising and monitoring these, they cannot be taken as a workable starting-point. Rather than ignoring this and trying to make sense of whether a state has fulfilled its obligations at least to the extent necessary and possible given its resources, the scope of these rights is 'narrowed' and a core area is recognised. Thus, minimum core

86 *Ibid.*, para. 10.

87 General Comment No. 4, 'The Right to Adequate Housing', 6th Sess. (1991), CESCR, reprinted in *Compilation*, note 75 above, para. 11. To be found at www.unhchr.ch/tbs/doc.nsf/0/ca12c3a4ea8d6c53c1256d500056e56f/$FILE/G0441302.pdf.

88 General Comment No. 12, 'The Right to Adequate Food', 20th Sess. (1999), CESCR, para. 8. See http://daccess-dds-ny.un.org/doc/UNDOC/GEN/G99/420/12/PDF/G9942012.pdf.

89 General Comment No. 14, 'The Right to the Highest Attainable Standard of Health', 22nd Sess. (2000) CESCR, para. 43(d). See http://daccess-dds-ny.un.org/doc/UNDOC/GEN/G00/439/34/PDF/G0043934.pdf.

90 Think for example of the German *Wesensgehaltgarantie*. Art. 19(2) of the German Basic Law lays down the requirement that '[i]n no case may the core content of a constitutional right be infringed' ('[i]n keinem Falle darf ein Grundrecht in seinem Wesensgehalt angetastet werden').

91 After all, the 'cores' that are highlighted do not provide a concrete boundary, in the sense that they cannot be infringed upon. Rather, they restate the *prima facie* right at stake.

obligations constitute the 'narrow' scope of economic and social goals – the scope of rights so far as they can be monitored and taken as a point of departure for increasing fundamental socio-economic protection.[92]

This understanding of the notion of minimum core obligations can be related to the definition of scope in the ECtHR's socio-economic case law. The problem identified there can be perceived in more or less the same way, even though the background is a different one. In the Strasbourg context, just as in the Covenant's, recognition of 'full' economic and social rights is not desirable and practical considerations make it impossible to rely on these rights in their entirety. As was set out in section 2 of this chapter above, the ECtHR is reticent when it faces an issue concerning socio-economic obligations and has often 'solved' such issues by refraining from giving a definition of the rights and guarantees that are applicable. Interestingly, the CESCR has come up with another solution, the minimum core obligation, which focuses on aspects of rights, rather than on broad guarantees. The minimum core provides clarity as to the concrete (core) content of what is *prima facie* guaranteed and can hence help to move forward implementation of the relevant elements of socio-economic rights.

It is anything but easy to answer the question whether it would be helpful for the Strasbourg Court to use a 'minimum core approach'. Perhaps, however, it is interesting for the Court to realise that it is possible to separate certain 'core' elements of economic and social rights, instead of focusing on the civil and political character of ECHR norms and giving in to legitimate concerns that bar the incorporation of 'full' economic and social rights. A minimum core approach would mean that the socio-economic requirements and positive obligations that are recognised in the Court's case law are regarded as elements of broader, or 'full', economic and social rights, rather than solely as indeterminable aspects of particular ECHR rights. For example, when dealing with a matter concerning health care, the question becomes more than whether the Court can recognise a general right to health care under Article 3 ECHR (prohibiting inhuman or degrading treatment). Instead, it should be asked what core aspects of a broad right to health – which the Convention does not grant – can be

92 It must be noted that, albeit a link exists between minimum core obligations and the ICESCR, the concept also features in the South African socio-economic rights discussion. Even though thus far the South African Constitutional Court has refrained from defining core obligations, this debate shows that the minimum core is not just a monitoring device, but can also be used in the adjudication of individual fundamental rights cases. See, e.g., Bilchitz, 'Towards a reasonable approach', note 84 above.

linked to Article 3 ECHR and hence be identified and recognised as ECHR guarantees. Thus far the ECtHR has (understandably) refrained from guaranteeing full socio-economic rights. However, instead of leaving it at that and refraining from giving a definition of the rights and obligations that are nevertheless at stake, using the minimum core concept would allow the Court to address the question of definition more openly and frankly. For example, it would not have to recognise a right to housing for all, but could incorporate a core aspect of such a right, e.g. the obligation on states to implement a programme that aims at providing shelter, especially for vulnerable groups and individuals. With the help of the notion of minimum core obligations the Court could expressly identify those elements of broad economic and social rights that are required in light of the aims of the Convention. Not only would this be in line with the idea of indivisibility of human rights,[93] but it would also provide more clarity on what the ECHR requires.

However, the fact that elements of rights can be delineated is only the first advantage of taking on a minimum core obligations approach. The demarcation of minimum core obligations allows for the necessary definition of applicable rights, without incorporating broad and unworkable or undesirable rights. But, next to that, the idea is also enlightening if we look at *how* a minimum core (or indeed, the 'narrow scope') of a right is defined. According to the general, bifurcated approach the Court should define scope without taking into account state interests, through an independent investigation of what the right requires. Thereby it should look at the right itself and determine what that right implies in terms of individual guarantees and state obligations. As analysed in section 3 of this chapter, however, this has presented stumbling-blocks to the Court when it is dealing with socio-economic issues. These are of a sensitive national, political character and it appears very difficult and potentially open to criticism for a supranational court to state socio-economic rights and obligations without having regard to national budgetary and policy considerations. The minimum core approach can provide a solution to this problem, at least to a certain extent. Of course it can also be argued, with regard to the determination of economic and social core rights, that these should be inspired solely by an idea of what is implied by the right itself.[94] Nevertheless, because of the specific nature of these rights, it is

[93] In the context of the ECtHR see, e.g., Koch, 'Justiciability of indivisible rights', note 15 above, and Koch, 'A hermeneutic perspective', note 15 above.

[94] See, e.g., Bilchitz, 'Towards a reasonable approach', note 84 above, p. 20.

also put forward that the definition of core obligations leaves some room for the majority or state concerns that are generally supposed to be left out when following the traditional civil and political rights approach. At least indirectly, context, available resources and state preferences and policies can play a role in the demarcation of (the extent of) workable and acceptable core elements. This does not really mean that minimum core obligations are by definition case-dependent and accordingly also state-specific. In the ICESCR monitoring process it has proved desirable to work with obligations that can be applied in a general manner.[95] This has resulted in various approaches to determining minimum core obligations that help to achieve the aims of general applicability and to take into account the fact that states do not allow very much (judicial) interference with their socio-economic policies.[96] After all, the minimum core was 'invented' to make social and economic rights workable and practically viable, and to ensure compliance. Ignoring entirely the potential concerns of states could hence run counter to what minimum cores aimed at.

In this regard it is interesting to look at the 'consensus approach' that has been proposed for defining minimum core obligations.[97] Under this approach, the core content is 'the right's agreed-upon nucleus'. It is presented as a 'wider agreement',[98] a 'synthesis of jurisprudence'[99] or as what states have been doing so far.[100] The consensus approach does not

[95] This is sometimes criticised, for it can have the result of lowering expectations. After all, if requirements take into account state resources but at the same time have to be generally applicable, no more can be required than what is possible in the state with the fewest resources and/or possibilities. Under the Convention, however, the 'weakest link' problem and the corresponding low level of protection do not necessarily occur. After all, the Convention does not aim at progressively realising 'full' economic and social rights. Hence, when defining generally applicable obligations while giving due account both to context and to national prerogatives and budgetary concerns, the obligations recognised might not entail very much, but may be just what can realistically be demanded given the various challenges Strasbourg faces and its necessary efforts at acting according to what Member States permit.

[96] See K.G. Young, 'The minimum core of economic and social rights: a concept in search of content', (2008) 33 *Yale Journal of International Law* 113–175.

[97] *Ibid.*, pp. 140ff.

[98] S. Russell, 'Minimum state obligations: international dimensions' in D. Brand and S. Russell (eds), *Exploring the Core Content of Economic and Social Rights: South African and International Perspectives* (Pretoria, South Africa: Protea Book House, 2002), p. 11.

[99] S. Leckie, 'The human right to adequate housing' in A. Eide, C. Krause and A. Rosas (eds), *Economic, Social and Cultural Rights: A Textbook*, 2nd edn (Dordrecht: Martinus Nijhoff Publishers, 2001), 149ff, p. 155.

[100] See, e.g., General Comment No. 3, note 75 above, at para. 10, where the Committee refers to the extensive experience it gained and the examining of States Parties' reports in relation to the recognition of minimum core obligations.

focus on what should normatively be required, but on already existing consensus featuring in, for example, state conduct and jurisprudence.[101] As the starting-point for determining workable core obligations it focuses on the socio-economic protection states conceive as essential, i.e. on what the various states have been able to (or are trying to) provide for, such as in the area of environmental protection. In this way questions about normative content and possible criticism of court over-activity can be avoided.[102]

Whereas purely normative cores would follow from the right itself, the Court could thus also use 'external' sources to determine what a core obligation should entail, as the CESCR does. Next to consensus among Member States, such external sources could include expert opinions – as is the case whenever the CESCR relies on WHO norms to delineate one of the core aspects of the right to health.[103] In a similar fashion, the Court could rely on internationally accepted norms to define aspects of health care that fall under Articles 3 or 8 ECHR. Doing this accords with the idea that fundamental rights should be indivisible, as well as with the value the ECtHR often attaches to consensus and/or other external sources. It would allow the Court to be clear on the scope of rights while its interpretation was (partly) backed by what states actually do and want to achieve. Focusing on social realities offers promising improvements to the effectiveness of economic and social requirements in the complex, political, multilevel setting in which the Court functions. After all, in the Strasbourg context it can be argued that it is more likely that states will embrace widely accepted 'minimum core obligations' than an undefined set of socio-economic requirements that cannot 'literally' be found in the Convention.

Much more can be said about the debate over economic and social fundamental rights and minimum core obligations, and its possible value in the Strasbourg context. The aim of this chapter, however, is merely to frame the issue of defining such rights and obligations in a different fashion. By now, it has become clear that a degree of overlap can be perceived between the Court's dilemma whether to answer the question of scope where this is a sensitive matter or simply a very difficult thing to do, and

[101] See, e.g., *ibid.* where the Committee refers to the 'extensive experience gained by the Committee . . . examining States parties' reports'.

[102] L. Bolivar and E. Gonzalez, 'Defining the content of ESC rights-problems and prospects' in *Circle of Rights: Economic Cultural and Social Rights Activism: A Training Resource* (International Human Rights Internship Program & Asian Forum for Human Rights and Development, 2000), 151ff, p. 156.

[103] General Comment No. 14, note 89 above, para. 43(d).

the CESCR's problem in defining workable rights that can be monitored effectively. The solution the CESCR proposed (defining minimum core obligations) sheds a new light on the way the ECtHR could deal with the dilemma. The CESCR's approach acknowledges that, instead of stressing 'full' rights, it is possible and often even necessary to determine a few core obligations that must be met first and foremost. Doing this gives socio-economic rights a 'narrow scope' that appears more workable and hence is more likely to be accepted and implemented by States Parties. Moreover, it was shown that, in the field of economic and social rights, state concerns are sometimes allowed to play a role in the definition of minimum core obligations. Additionally, the CESCR determines cores of rights partly on the basis of consensus or other external sources. This makes more viable the determination of concrete requirements in an international or supranational context. Potentially, thus, the idea of minimum cores could help the Court to do away with its hesitant attitude to the definition of socio-economic guarantees while ensuring the continued acceptance of its case law by the Member States.

5. Conclusion

The aim of this chapter was to present the dilemma of defining the scope of ECHR rights when the issues at stake are closely related to economic and social fundamental rights. Moreover, it aimed to introduce an alternative perspective on defining the scope of rights in which the relevant requirements should be clear to states and individuals, and workable at the same time.

Section 2 of this chapter analysed the Court's case law dealing with economic, social, and environmental issues. It was demonstrated that in socio-economic cases the Court is often hesitant to define the rights and duties at stake clearly. It either refrains from giving a definition of the (positive) obligations involved, or it simply 'assumes' that the interest at stake falls within the scope of the rights protected by the Convention. This might be understandable in light of the fact that, given its sensitive subsidiary role, the Court feels that it should be careful in recognising generally applicable economic and social requirements. At the same time, however, it means that Member States and (potential) applicants cannot clearly see what, exactly, the ECHR requires.

Section 3 looked at how the determination of scope is usually perceived in the context of fundamental rights. The structure of fundamental rights, it was shown, directs the Court to first determine the *prima facie* right at stake, preferably in a broad manner, before reviewing the justifications advanced by the state. In line with the idea that fundamental rights can and should sometimes be limited, this second step allows state and other interests to be balanced against the interests of the individual. In order to ensure real protection for fundamental rights, however, defining the *prima facie* right should be done autonomously, without reference to state concerns and other (general) interests.

Nevertheless, and not just because the Court does not want to confront Member States with broad economic and social rights, but also because socio-economic obligations simply seem hard to define without giving due regard to the resources and policies of states, an alternative perspective on the scope of rights was presented. Section 4 focused on the notion of 'minimum core obligations' as it is used in the context of the ICESCR. ICESCR rights must be 'progressively realised'. In order to make this requirement workable, the CESCR has shifted its focus from broadly stated rights that are impossible to comply with entirely, to particular core elements. Unlike the process in which scope is defined under the bifurcated approach, determining the 'narrow scope' of economic and social rights through the recognition of minimum core obligations can allow states' considerations (indirectly) to be taken into account via the weight that is given to consensus and existing, authoritative interpretations of what should be considered essential.

The doctrine of minimum core obligations can be related to the dilemma the Court faces when having to determine the scope of rights. It can help the ECtHR to frame this dilemma in a different fashion. Although the full range of consequences that would follow any transplanting of the CESCR's approach to Strasbourg needs further exploration, the doctrine of minimum core obligations with its focus on core elements of economic and social rights offers the Court an interesting way of viewing its difficult task. Rather than refraining from an independent and far-reaching interpretation of the civil and political ECHR norms, the Court could aim at recognising aspects of socio-economic rights that could be considered essential, both under the Convention and more generally. When framing the issue in this way, moreover, it could take into account certain facts and interests that are generally perceived as unimportant or irrelevant. Core elements can be determined in line with and backed by states' choices and possibilities in the field of socio-economic rights.

Understanding the issue of determining the scope of rights in this way shows clearly that giving content to sensitive rights is not impossible.

Often, now, the Court mixes interpretation with review of justification, thereby taking into account majority concerns, but without providing a clear demarcation of the scope of a right. The minimum core obligation approach shows that when state considerations are given appropriate weight it is not unthinkable that a separate determination of the scope of a right can take place – on the contrary. It is worthwhile to further explore what this would mean in the context of the ECtHR, and whether this different perspective might indeed offer possibilities thus far unknown.

7

Procedural protection

An examination of procedural safeguards read into substantive Convention rights

EVA BREMS

1. Procedural scope

Discussing the 'scope' of ECHR rights means asking what exactly a particular ECHR provision protects, or what kinds of injustice that provision shields rights-holders from. Among these is the injustice that consists of a lack of remedies when violations of other Convention rights occur (Article 13 ECHR) and the injustice that consists of unfairness in the course of a judicial procedure, or with respect to access to that procedure or the implementation of a judicial decision (Article 6 ECHR). Additionally, explicit procedural guarantees are found in Article 5 ECHR relating to arrest and detention, and in ECHR Protocol Number 7 relating to the expulsion of aliens (Article 1), the right of appeal in criminal cases (Article 2), compensation for wrongful conviction (Article 3) and the right not to be tried or punished twice (Article 4).

These procedural provisions, and Article 6 ECHR in particular, take up the lion's share of the Court's time and resources. The Court's overview of its judgments up to 2011 lists 45.01 per cent of its judgments under Article 6 ECHR and a further 8.1 per cent under Article 13 ECHR.[1]

Despite this major focus of the ECHR system on procedural protection, the explicit procedural guarantees of the ECHR and its protocols do not apply to all judicial procedures,[2] nor to administrative remedies, let alone to decision-making procedures. Nonetheless, a broader look at international human rights standards reveals that a right to fair treatment by administrative bodies has gained recognition internationally. In

1 Available at www.echr.coe.int/Documents/Overview_2011_ENG.pdf, p. 5.

2 See Chapter 14 by Paul Lemmens on Article 6 ECHR.

particular, Article 41 of the Charter of Fundamental Rights of the European Union states in its first and second paragraphs:

> 1. Every person has the right to have his or her affairs handled impartially, fairly and within a reasonable time by the institutions and bodies of the Union.
> 2. This right includes:
>
>   the right of every person to be heard, before any individual measure which would affect him or her adversely is taken;
>
>   the right of every person to have access to his or her file, while respecting the legitimate interests of confidentiality and of professional and business secrecy;
>
>   the obligation of the administration to give reasons for its decisions.

Despite the absence of a comparable provision in the ECHR system, it would be wrong to assume that beyond the ECHR articles enumerated above procedural fairness falls outside the Convention's scope of protection. In numerous fields of its case law, the Court has in fact added a procedural layer to the scope of substantive Convention rights, by deriving state obligations of a procedural nature from substantive ECHR provisions. This development has taken place under most Convention rights, with varying degrees of detail and consistency. It is most prominent under Article 8 ECHR and Article 1 of the First Additional Protocol (Article 1 P1), as well as Articles 2 and 3 ECHR. The Court has also highlighted procedural dimensions of state obligations in Articles 4, 9, 10, 11 and 12 ECHR, as well as in Article 3 of the First Additional Protocol and Articles 2 and 4 of the Fourth Additional Protocol. The present chapter analyses this development and its impact.

These procedural obligations may apply *ex ante* as well as *ex post facto*. Among the *ex ante* obligations are those that apply to the procedure that led to the individual decision allegedly violating the Convention (e.g. rules mandating that persons must be heard before a decision is taken). *Ex ante* obligations may also require procedural guarantees as part of the general normative framework governing the matter that gave rise to an alleged human rights violation (e.g. rules providing for internal monitoring), or that concern the procedure leading up to the adoption of this normative framework (e.g. the consultation of studies or expertise before making rules). *Ex post* obligations may concern the need for and the quality of an investigation into an alleged human rights violation or the availability and quality of remedies for those who claim to have suffered a human rights violation.

Procedural obligations under substantive provisions can be both positive and negative obligations on states. In many cases, a procedural obligation mandates the state to do something – for example, establish a procedure – yet there are also instances in which the procedural shortcoming is caused by something a state authority did – for example, organising a body in a manner that falls short of impartiality standards, or setting unfair rules of procedure. In practice, the distinction between positive and negative obligations is often blurred.[3] As the procedural obligations with which this chapter is concerned are embedded in substantive provisions, and to the extent that alleged procedural shortcomings often occur in conjunction with alleged substantive shortcomings, it is not surprising to find that in treating procedural obligations as positive or negative obligations the Court tends to follow its characterisation of the substantive obligations under the provision that applies to the case at hand. As the preceding paragraph makes clear, positive procedural obligations may be intended to prevent human rights violations in general, by providing an adequate normative framework; to prevent violations in specific cases; and to oblige states to react appropriately to credible allegations of human rights violations. Within a framework of negative obligations, it is interesting to find that procedural shortcomings may be identified either as a violation of the legality requirement or as a factor (negatively) affecting the Court's assessment of the proportionality of an infringement in relation to its aim.

Indeed, the Court has often ruled that reference to the need for an interference to have a basis in the law in Articles 8, 9, 10, 11 and 1 P1 ECHR requires control over the quality of domestic legislation from a rule of law angle, verifying that the law does afford sufficient protection against arbitrary interference by public authorities. This may require such guarantees as the availability of a procedure to make a right effective,[4] effective procedural deadlines,[5] clearly stipulated modalities to the exercise of invasive public power,[6] judicial supervision,[7] or access to adversarial proceedings before an independent body.[8] Further, the Court also adopts another approach, in which it considers the absence of sufficient procedural guarantees to be a factor that upsets the 'fair balance' between

[3] See Chapter 8 by Laurens Lavrysen.

[4] ECtHR (GC), *Kuric and others* v. *Slovenia*, 26 June 2012, para. 344 (Art. 8).

[5] ECtHR, *Aliyev and others* v. *Azerbaijan*, 18 December 2008, para. 42 (Art. 11).

[6] ECtHR (GC), *Bykov* v. *Russia*, 10 March 2009, paras 78–81 (Art. 8).

[7] ECtHR (GC), *Rotaru* v. *Romania*, 4 May 2000, para. 59 (Art. 8).

[8] ECtHR, *Forminster Enterprises Ltd* v. *Czech Republic*, 9 October 2008, para. 69 (Art. 1 Protocol 1 – hereafter P1).

a Convention right and a public or private interest so far as to justify a proportionate restriction of the right.[9] One line of reasoning considers that a right has been violated when it is established that the domestic decision-making procedure was defective, in the sense that no domestic assessment of proportionality has taken place.[10] Why the Court chooses to verify the availability of procedural guarantees in some cases under the legality criterion and in others under the necessity criterion, is not clear.

In what follows, the reach of procedural obligations under substantive Convention rights will be clarified, distinguishing between the requirement that a procedure be available (section 2) and more specific requirements concerning guarantees that have to be included in existing procedures or in those that the Court requires to be set in place (section 3). After this overview, an attempt will be made to analyse the impact of the 'proceduralisation of substantive rights' (section 4).[11]

For the case references in this chapter, the choice has been made to give one reference for each claim, rather than collecting as many references as possible. In choosing a supporting case, priority has been given to Grand Chamber judgments over chamber judgments, and within each category, to the most recent judgment.

2. Right to a procedure

Arguably the most important procedural right is the right to a procedure. This applies in particular to *ex post* procedures, i.e. investigations into alleged human rights violations (section 2.1 of this chapter) and the availability of remedies for those who claim to have suffered a human rights violation (section 2.2). In addition, the Court has occasionally stipulated the need for a domestic evaluation or supervision procedure (section 2.3), and has in some cases granted a right to a procedure that gives access to protection of a contested fundamental right rather than directly granting that right (section 2.4).

[9] See e.g. ECtHR, *Sovtransavto Holding* v. *Ukraine*, 25 July 2002, para. 98 (Art. 1 P1); ECtHR, *Vordur Olafsson* v. *Iceland*, 27 April 2010, paras 81–3 (Art. 11).

[10] ECtHR (GC), *Dickson* v. *United Kingdom*, 4 December 2007, para. 85 (Art. 8).

[11] J. Christoffersen, *Fair Balance: Proportionality, Subsidiarity and Primarity in the European Convention on Human Rights* (Leiden/Boston: Martinus Nijhoff Publishers, 2009), p. 455.

2.1 Right to an investigation

2.1.1 Under Article 2 ECHR

The Court routinely distinguishes between this article's 'substantive aspect' and its 'procedural aspect'. The latter concerns positive state obligations to investigate problematic deaths. In addition to numerous and detailed provisions that concern the quality of such an investigation (see section 3 below), the primary obligation in this context is that:

> there should be some form of effective official investigation when individuals have been killed as a result of the use of force by,[12] *inter alios*, agents of the State . . . The essential purpose of such an investigation is to secure the effective implementation of the domestic laws safeguarding the right to life and, in those cases involving State agents or bodies, to ensure their accountability for deaths occurring under their responsibility.[13]

The same obligation arises 'where individuals, last seen in the custody of agents of the State, subsequently disappeared in a life-threatening context'.[14] Moreover, under Article 2 states are obliged to set up an effective judicial system for establishing the cause of death where an individual dies while under the care and responsibility of health professionals as well as any responsibility on the part of the latter.[15]

The Court has stated that this procedural obligation 'has evolved into a separate and autonomous duty'.[16] Compliance with this procedural obligation can be the subject of a separate vote on admissibility, and a breach of the procedural obligation under Article 2 ECHR can be alleged regardless of any complaint relating to the substantive aspect of the same article.[17] The procedural obligation is detachable from the substantive obligation, in the sense that it can bind the state even when the death to which an investigation refers took place before the Convention became binding on the state concerned.[18]

This obligation is read into the obligation to protect the right to life under the first paragraph of Article 2 ECHR, in conjunction with states' general duty under Article 1 ECHR to 'secure to everyone within their

[12] The same obligation has been extended to other situations in which lives have been lost in a situation potentially engaging the responsibility of the state: ECtHR (GC), *Öneryildiz* v. *Turkey*, 30 November 2004, para. 91.

[13] ECtHR (GC), *Al-Skeini and others* v. *United Kingdom*, 7 July 2011, para. 163.

[14] ECtHR (GC), *Varnava and others* v. *Turkey*, 18 September 2009, para. 181.

[15] ECtHR (GC), *Šilih* v. *Slovenia*, 9 April 2009, para. 155.

[16] *Ibid.*, para. 159. [17] *Ibid.*, para. 158. [18] *Ibid.*, para. 159.

jurisdiction the rights and freedoms defined in [the] Convention'.[19] This reading of Article 2 ECHR is motivated by a concern that human rights should be protected effectively,[20] with the Court arguing that

> [t]he general legal prohibition of arbitrary killing by agents of the State would be ineffective in practice if there existed no procedure for reviewing the lawfulness of the use of lethal force by State authorities.[21]

It is therefore self-evident that the Court is not satisfied with the mere existence of legal provisions establishing a framework for investigation, and that it will require the framework to operate effectively in practice.[22]

The Court accepts that such an investigation can take various forms depending on the circumstances. It does not have to be a judicial investigation.[23] In all cases, these proceedings should be geared to holding the perpetrator(s) accountable – the award of damages to the victim(s) is not sufficient. Moreover, when intentional killing is alleged, the investigation should be initiated by the authorities of their own motion once the matter has come to their attention.[24] Generally, then, civil proceedings will not be considered adequate as they tend not to be initiated by the authorities nor to involve the identification and punishment of the perpetrator(s).[25]

2.1.2 Under Article 3 ECHR

A parallel procedural obligation to investigate exists 'where an individual raises an arguable claim that he has suffered treatment infringing Article 3 at the hands of the police or other similar agents of the state'.[26] As under Article 2, the 'procedural limb' of Article 3 ECHR is motivated by a concern for the practical effectiveness of the provision and by the need to avoid impunity.[27] In this respect, reference was made to the Council of Europe's Guidelines of 30 March 2011 on eradicating impunity for serious

19 *Al-Skeini*, note 13 above, para. 163.

20 In medical negligence cases a public health concern is added to this:

> Knowledge of the facts and of possible errors committed in the course of medical care [is] essential to enable the institutions concerned and medical staff to remedy the potential deficiencies and prevent similar errors. The prompt examination of such cases is therefore important for the safety of users of all health services.

(*Šilih*, note 15 above, para. 196.)

21 *Al-Skeini*, note 13 above, para. 163.

22 *Šilih*, note 15 above, para. 195.

23 ECtHR (GC), *Giuliani and Gaggio* v. *Italy*, 24 March 2011, para. 298. Medical negligence cases form an exception here; cf. note 20 above.

24 *Šilih*, note 15 above, para. 156.

25 *Al-Skeini*, note 13 above, para. 165.

26 ECtHR (GC), *El Masri* v. *FYROM*, 13 December 2012, para. 182.

27 *Ibid.*

human rights violations, stating that 'impunity must be fought as a matter of justice for the victims, as a deterrent to prevent new violations and to uphold the rule of law and public trust in the justice system'.[28] However, while the obligation to investigate under Article 2 ECHR is systematically examined under that provision alone, where Article 3 ECHR is concerned the Court hesitates between a similar approach (Article 3 alone) and one that builds on Article 13 ECHR in combination with Article 3. This will be further examined in section 4.1.1 of this chapter.

2.1.3 Other ECHR provisions

Article 4 ECHR This article prohibits slavery, servitude and forced or compulsory labour and is applicable to human trafficking. Like Articles 2 and 3 ECHR, it imposes a procedural obligation to investigate where there is a credible suspicion that an individual's rights under the article have been violated.[29]

Article 5 ECHR The disappearance of an individual is examined under Article 2 ECHR when it takes place in circumstances that make the death of that individual plausible. In other cases, a disappearance is examined under Article 5 ECHR. In such cases, the obligation to conduct an effective investigation is examined under that article.[30]

Article 8 ECHR The obligation to investigate alleged breaches of an individual's physical integrity by state agents extends beyond Article 3 to infringements of physical integrity falling under Article 8 ECHR.[31] In addition, there are other scenarios where lack of an (effective) investigation might give rise to finding a violation of Article 8 ECHR. In particular, this has been ruled where personal information has been disclosed without consent.[32]

Articles 10 and 11 ECHR The obligation to investigate violent incidents targeting expressions, assemblies or associations may be examined under the provisions protecting these political freedoms rather than those protecting life and physical integrity. For example, the lack of an effective investigation into a campaign of violence against a newspaper, aimed at

[28] *Ibid.*, para. 192. [29] ECtHR, *CN* v. *United Kingdom*, 13 November 2012, para. 69.

[30] *El-Masri*, note 26 above, para. 233.

[31] ECtHR, *MC* v. *Bulgaria*, 4 December 2003, paras 152–3; *CN*, note 29 above, para. 103.

[32] ECtHR, *Craxi (no. 2)* v. *Italy*, 17 July 2003, paras 74–5.

and leading to the silencing of that newspaper, has been found to violate Article 10 ECHR.[33] Similarly, the absence of an investigation into an attack on the headquarters of a political party contributed to the finding of a violation of Article 11 ECHR.[34]

Article 14 ECHR Whenever there is a suspicion that a violent act (falling under Article 2 or 3 ECHR) was motivated by racism, a procedural obligation arises under Article 14 in combination with Article 2 and/or 3 to investigate this possible motive.[35] The Court obliges states, in the investigation of incidents involving the use of force, to distinguish both in their legal systems and in practice between cases of excessive use of force and of racist killing.[36]

Article 3 P1 ECHR The Court has found that if domestic courts that are called upon to decide an arguable claim concerning election irregularities fail to take reasonable steps to investigate the alleged irregularities, this failure violates the state's positive obligation under Article 3 P1.[37]

Summing up The obligation to investigate appears to exist as part of a state's positive obligations under a substantive ECHR provision whenever the alleged substantive violation involves violence. In addition, the Court has found a similar obligation in some other cases (disclosure of personal information, election irregularities) for which no clear pattern emerges.

2.2 Right to a remedy

As part of the procedural aspect of Article 2 ECHR, the Court has also examined the possibility that relatives of a deceased might obtain compensation for wrongful death, where the applicant did not found this claim on Article 13.[38]

[33] ECtHR, *Özgür Gündem* v. *Turkey*, 16 March 2000, paras 45–6.
[34] ECtHR, *Ouranio Toxo and others* v. *Greece*, 20 October 2005, para. 43.
[35] ECtHR (GC), *Nachova and others* v. *Bulgaria*, 6 July 2005, para. 160. However, the Court indicated in para. 161 that Art. 2 ECHR, taken alone, imposes the same obligation to investigate.
[36] *Ibid.*, para. 160. [37] ECtHR, *Namat Aliyev* v. *Azerbaijan*, 8 April 2010, para. 88.
[38] ECtHR (GC), *Mastromatteo* v. *Italy*, 24 October 2002, para. 88.

However, the right to a remedy under a substantive provision has most often been affirmed concerning decisions by public authorities that restrict individual rights. In general terms, the Court has repeatedly ruled that

> the concepts of lawfulness and the rule of law in a democratic society require that measures affecting fundamental human rights must be subject to some form of adversarial proceedings before an independent body competent to review the reasons for the decision and relevant evidence.[39]

In some cases, the Court specifies that this remedy has to be a judicial one. The Court has so ruled in cases of eviction,[40] and environmental impact of planning decisions,[41] among other issues.

The right to judicial review has also been recognised in cases in which the infringement of a fundamental right is caused by a private entity, such as dismissal on account of one's political affiliation,[42] and property disputes among private parties.[43]

Occasionally, the Court has stated detailed requirements concerning the type of procedure that should be available. For example, when the protection of journalistic sources is at stake, it has specified that the review should occur prior to the handing over of material,[44] and has specified the powers the review body should have as well as some of the criteria it should use.[45]

In the field of democratic elections, the Court has ruled that 'the existence of a domestic system for effective examination of individual complaints and appeals in matters concerning electoral rights is one of the essential guarantees of free and fair elections',[46] and referred to the Venice Commission's Code of Good Practice in Electoral Matters for a description of an effective system of electoral appeals.[47]

[39] ECtHR, *Kaushal and others* v. *Bulgaria*, 2 September 2010, para. 29.

[40] ECtHR, *Yordanova and others* v. *Bulgaria*, 24 April 2012, para. 118.

[41] ECtHR, *Flamenbaum and others* v. *France*, 13 December 2012, para. 138.

[42] ECtHR, *Redfearn* v. *United Kingdom*, 6 November 2012, paras 55–7.

[43] ECtHR (GC), *Kotov* v. *Russia*, 3 April 2012, paras 113–14.

[44] ECtHR (GC), *Sanoma Uitgevers bv* v. *The Netherlands*, 14 September 2010, para. 90 (under the legality requirement).

[45] *Ibid.*, para. 92. [46] *Namat Aliyev*, note 37 above, para. 81.

[47] ECtHR, *Petkov and others* v. *Bulgaria*, 11 June 2009, para. 63. Venice Commission Code available at http://www.venice.coe.int/webforms/documents/CDL-AD(2002)023rev.aspx.

2.3 Evaluation/supervision procedure

Occasionally, the Court has stated that the positive obligations on the state in a particular area require it to set up not only appropriate regulations and mechanisms for the protection of fundamental rights in that context, but also a system for monitoring such mechanisms.

In particular, as regards the regulation of hazardous activities, the Court held that rules governing the licensing, setting-up, operation, security and supervision of the activity must mandate practical measures protecting against life-threatening risks, and that

> the relevant regulations must also provide for appropriate procedures, taking into account the technical aspects of the activity in question, for identifying shortcomings in the processes concerned and any errors committed by those responsible at different levels.[48]

Similarly, in the area of secret surveillance, the Court has found violations relating to

> (a) the lack of *ex post facto* review by an independent body of the implementation of surveillance measures or of whether the material obtained through such measures would be destroyed within the statutory time–limit if the surveillance had proved fruitless; . . .
> (b) the lack of an independent body to oversee and report on the functioning of the system of secret surveillance; and
> (c) the lack of independent control over the use of material falling outside the scope of the original application for the use of covert surveillance measures.[49]

In a related field, the Court has stated that it is mandatory to have control mechanisms in place in psychiatric institutions. On account of their obligation to secure their citizens' rights to physical and moral integrity, states have a positive obligation to instal mechanisms for supervision and control of private psychiatric institutions.[50]

2.4 Procedure as right/right as procedure

In a number of cases, instead of explicitly deriving a new substantive (sub-) right from a Convention provision, the Court has formulated a right to

[48] *Öneryildiz*, note 12 above, para. 90.
[49] ECtHR, *Savovi* v. *Bulgaria*, 27 November 2012, para. 57.
[50] ECtHR, *Storck* v. *Germany*, 16 June 2005, para. 150.

a procedure that would enable the applicant to enjoy such a right. The Court thus makes a procedural detour away from recognising a new right.

For example, under Article 8 ECHR, the Court has recognised the right of access to information about the health risks of hazardous activities via the right to a procedure that enables applicants to seek such information.[51] The Court adopted a similar approach to govern access to personal files held by public authorities. The state has to provide a procedure that enables interested parties to have access to information, and the possibility to correct any erroneous entries.[52]

In a recent case the Court stated in a more general manner that the state's positive obligation under Article 8 ECHR can imply the provision of an effective and accessible procedure to protect the right to private life.[53] In the same case – concerning the right to conscientious objection to military service or, more specifically, the right of access to a procedure that would determine whether one is entitled to conscientious objector status – the Court stated that the same reasoning applies to Article 9 ECHR.[54]

While the cases mentioned above oblige states to provide procedures that enable the enjoyment of rights that had not previously been substantively guaranteed under domestic law, the Court has also found violations of the same procedural obligation in cases in which a right is substantively protected under domestic law, yet cannot be enjoyed for lack of effective procedures that give access to it.[55]

However, the opposite situation also occurs, in which the Court extends its protection to matters of substance without obliging states to provide certain procedures. In particular, the Court ruled that the imposition of an irreducible life sentence may violate Article 3 ECHR, so that 'the existence of a system providing for consideration of the possibility of release is a factor to be taken into account when assessing the compatibility of a particular life sentence with Article 3'.[56] Yet at the same time, it stated that 'the Convention does not confer, in general, . . . a right to have a sentence reconsidered by a national authority, judicial or administrative, with a view to its remission or termination'.[57]

[51] ECtHR (GC), *Roche* v. *United Kingdom*, 19 October 2005, para. 167.

[52] ECtHR, *Joanna Szulc* v. *Poland*, 13 November 2012, paras 85–7.

[53] ECtHR, *Savda* v. *Turkey*, 12 June 2012, para. 98.

[54] *Ibid.*, paras 98–9.

[55] ECtHR (GC), *A, B and C* v. *Ireland*, 16 December 2010, para. 267 (third applicant had an arguable claim of access to abortion under domestic law, but no access to a procedure through which she could make that claim).

[56] ECtHR (GC), *Kafkaris* v. *Cyprus*, 12 February 2008, para. 99.

[57] *Ibid.*

3. Procedural quality control

Since the existence of a procedure cannot by itself offer any guarantees, the Court has regularly gone into the requirements of a fair procedure.

3.1 Effectiveness

Effectiveness is a prominent requirement in the investigation procedures described above (in section 2.1). To be effective the investigation must be

> capable of leading to a determination of whether the force used was or was not justified in the circumstances and to the identification and punishment of those responsible. This is not an obligation of result, but of means. The authorities must take the reasonable steps available to them.[58]

In this context, the Court scrutinises the efforts that have been undertaken to secure evidence, such as eye-witness testimonies, forensic evidence and autopsies. Any deficiency in the investigation that undermines its ability to establish cause of or responsibility for death, may lead to the finding of a violation.[59]

Effectiveness can be related to most other procedural guarantees, as well as to the scope of the procedure:

> the investigation should also be broad enough to permit the investigating authorities to take into consideration not only the actions of the State agents who directly used lethal force but also all the surrounding circumstances, including such matters as the planning and control of the operations in question, where this is necessary in order to determine whether the State complied with its obligation under Article 2 to protect life.[60]

In a recent case concerning extraordinary renditions that had attracted worldwide attention and triggered several international inquiries, the Court added another rationale for an effective investigation, i.e. the impact of a defective investigation on the right to the truth. It stated that not only the applicant and his family, but other victims of similar crimes and also the general public, have a right to know what happened.[61]

In general, rules governing situations that might infringe Convention rights, to be effective procedures must limit the risk of such infringement as far as possible. For example, in the area of secret surveillance and covert intelligence-gathering, the Court requires

[58] *Al-Skeini*, note 13 above, para. 166. [59] *Ibid.*
[60] *Ibid.*, para. 163. [61] *El Masri*, note 26 above, para. 191.

> clear, detailed rules governing the scope and application of measures, as well as minimum safeguards concerning, *inter alia*, duration, storage, usage, access of third parties, procedures for preserving the integrity and confidentiality of data and procedures for its destruction, thus providing sufficient guarantees against the risk of abuse and arbitrariness.[62]

In a procedure by which a individual seeks protection of his or her rights, excess formalism may counteract effectiveness. For example, the Court has ruled that the automatic and mechanical application of a five-day time limit for submitting an application for asylum must be considered at odds with Article 3 ECHR.[63]

3.2 Independence/impartiality

The requirement for independence has been stated for different types of *ex post* procedures, both investigative procedures and remedies. With respect to the latter, the requirement is made explicit in particular when it is left open whether the remedy should be before a court or not. In such cases, a remedy before a non-judicial body is accepted, provided that this body is independent and impartial.[64]

Yet even the issue of judicial impartiality has been raised under a substantive provision: the Court held that the failure to give consideration to an applicant's fears that a judge might not be impartial constituted a grave procedural omission, and contributed to the finding of a violation of Article 10 ECHR.[65]

In some scenarios, the Court has described what the independence/impartiality requirement implies. For example, an investigation into alleged unlawful killing by state agents should be carried out by persons who are independent from those implicated in the events, hierarchically, institutionally and in practice.[66] For the Court, 'what is at stake here is nothing less than public confidence in the State's monopoly on the use of force'.[67]

62 ECtHR (GC), *S and Marper* v. *United Kingdom*, 4 December 2008, para. 99.
63 ECtHR, *Jabari* v. *Turkey*, 11 July 2000, para. 40.
64 For example, with respect to the protection of journalistic sources: *Sanoma Uitgevers bv*, note 44 above, para. 109.
65 ECtHR, *Kudeshkina* v. *Russia*, 26 February 2009, para. 97.
66 *Al-Skeini*, note 13 above, para. 167.
67 *Giuliano and Gaggio*, note 23 above, para. 300.

3.3 Participation

When the participation of interested persons in a procedure is required, this is with a view to guaranteeing that their interests are taken into account.

Participation has been a consistent and prominent feature in cases about access and custody rights. In such cases, the Court examines, as part of the proportionality assessment, whether the applicants (generally the parents) have been properly involved in the decision-making process and whether that process provided them with the requisite protection of their interests.[68] This implies amongst other things an obligation on the authorities to make available to the parents, on their own motion, the relevant information on the basis of which a decision has been taken.[69] Moreover, in these cases the Court has not only emphasised the centrality of the 'best interests of the child', but also the participation of children in the procedure.[70]

Furthermore, a general appreciation of the fairness of a decision-making process, based on the statement that 'the decision-making process leading to measures of interference must be fair and such as to afford due respect for the interests of the individual as safeguarded by Article 8', has spread from 'family life' cases to other cases under Article 8, dealing with issues such as planning and the environment,[71] deprivation of legal capacity,[72] data registration,[73] registration of ethnic identity,[74] and access to abortion.[75] In the last context, the Court specified that 'the relevant procedure should guarantee to a pregnant woman at least the possibility to be heard in person and to have her views considered'.[76]

Participation in a procedure in order to defend one's point of view is considered also under other provisions when the fairness of a decision-making procedure is assessed, such as under Article 1 P1.[77]

68 ECtHR (GC), *K and T* v. *Finland*, 12 July 2001, para. 173.
69 ECtHR (GC), *TP and KM* v. *United Kingdom*, 10 May 2001, paras 80–2.
70 ECtHR, *Saviny* v. *Ukraine*, 18 December 2008, para. 51.
71 ECtHR (GC), *Hatton and others* v. *United Kingdom*, 8 July 2003, para. 99.
72 ECtHR, *Salontaji-Drobnjak* v. *Serbia*, 13 October 2009, para. 143.
73 ECtHR, *Turek* v. *Slovakia*, 14 February 2006, para. 111.
74 ECtHR, *Ciubotaru* v. *Moldova*, 27 April 2010, para. 51.
75 ECtHR, *RR* v. *Poland*, 26 May 2011, para. 191.
76 ECtHR, *P and S* v. *Poland*, 30 October 2012, para. 99.
77 ECtHR, *Megadat.com srl* v. *Moldova*, 8 April 2008, para. 73.

In medical decision-making, the Court requires a procedure that guarantees the informed consent of the patient.[78]

In an investigation into a death that might constitute a violation of Article 2 ECHR, the Court requires the involvement of the victim's next-of-kin in the procedure to the extent necessary to safeguard their legitimate interests.[79] Under Article 3 ECHR, the victim should be able to participate in the investigation.[80]

3.4 Timeliness/promptness

Promptness and reasonable expedition are required for investigations into alleged violations of Articles 2 and 3. The European Court has stated that this is 'essential in maintaining public confidence in [the authorities'] adherence to the rule of law and in preventing any appearance of collusion in or tolerance of unlawful acts'.[81]

In child custody cases, the Court has included the length of the local authority's decision-making process and of any related judicial proceedings in its Article 8 ECHR assessment. In such cases, this is motivated by the close link with the substance of the case:

> in cases of this kind there is always the danger that any procedural delay will result in the *de facto* determination of the issue submitted to the court before it has held its hearing. And an effective respect for family life requires that future relations between parent and child be determined solely in the light of all relevant considerations and not by the mere effluxion of time.[82]

Similar considerations apply to the termination of pregnancy, where the Court has held that the procedures in place should ensure that decisions are taken in good time, since time is of critical importance.[83]

Moreover, even when an unreasonably lengthy procedure does not affect the enjoyment of a Convention right as such, it may result in the infringement of a Convention right in the concrete circumstances of a case. For example, even though the Convention does not encompass a right to divorce, the unreasonable length of divorce proceedings can constitute a violation both of the right to marry (Article 12 ECHR) and

[78] ECtHR, *VC* v. *Slovakia*, 8 November 2011, para. 112 (under Art. 3 ECHR); ECtHR, *Csoma* v. *Romania*, 15 January 2013, para. 42 (under Art. 8 ECHR).

[79] *Al-Skeini*, note 13 above, para. 167.

[80] *El Masri*, note 26 above, para. 185.

[81] *Al-Skeini*, note 13 above, para. 167.

[82] ECtHR (GC), *W* v. *United Kingdom*, 8 July 1987, para. 65.

[83] *P and S*, note 76 above, para. 111.

of the right to a fair trial (Article 6 ECHR) as they affect an applicant who wishes to remarry.[84]

3.5 Motivation of decision

With respect to investigative procedures, the Court has stated that the investigation's conclusions must be based on thorough, objective and impartial analysis of all relevant elements.[85]

When decisions by public authorities restricting Convention rights are at stake, absence of motivation may reveal arbitrariness. In eviction cases, the Court goes so far as to derive from the absence of motivation a presumption of violation:

> Where the national authorities, in their decisions ordering and upholding the applicant's eviction, have not given any explanation or put forward any arguments demonstrating that the applicant's eviction was necessary, the Court may draw the inference that the State's legitimate interest in being able to control its property should come second to the applicant's right to respect for his home.[86]

Moreover, scant motivation may prevent the individual who is affected by the decision from defending him or herself in the course of the decision-making procedure or when challenging it afterwards.[87]

For a name-change procedure, the Court has stated that, despite a wide margin of appreciation, it can accept the necessity in a democratic society of a decision to refuse a change of name only where the decision-making body justifies its refusal with relevant and sufficient reasons.[88] For procedures pertaining to access to abortion, the Court has held that the competent body or person should issue written grounds for its decision.[89]

3.6 Assessment of relevant information and expertise

The Court has repeatedly required that decisions of or actions by public authorities that impact upon fundamental rights must not be taken lightly, and that all relevant information necessary to properly consider a decision or course of action should be available and should be taken into account.

[84] ECtHR, *VK* v. *Croatia*, 27 November 2012, paras 105–7.
[85] *Giuliano and Gaggio*, note 23 above, para. 302.
[86] *Yordanova*, note 40 above, para. 118.
[87] ECtHR, *Lombardi Vallauri* v. *Italy*, 20 October 2009, paras 52 and 54.
[88] ECtHR, *Golemanova* v. *Bulgaria*, 17 February 2011, para. 39.
[89] *P and S*, note 76 above, para. 99.

This requirement is particularly prominent in cases concerning planning decisions with significant environmental impact. In these cases, the Court splits its Article 8 ECHR reasoning into a substantive part and a procedural part. In the latter, the Court will examine (among other things) which studies have been undertaken or consulted, arguing that

> a governmental decision-making process concerning complex issues of environmental and economic policy . . . must necessarily involve appropriate investigations and studies in order to allow them to strike a fair balance between the various conflicting interests at stake.[90]

Similar concerns are expressed in different areas of case law.

Concerning the planning of an arrest operation – and in particular the potential need to use firearms – the Court has stated that the 'absolute minimum' information to be analysed concerns 'the nature of the offence committed by the person to be arrested and the degree of danger – if any – posed by that person'.[91] The Court examines this at the level of the decision taken in the case at hand, as well as at the level of the relevant regulations, which ought to make the use of firearms depend on an assessment of the surrounding circumstances, and to require an evaluation of the nature of the offence and of the threat.[92]

In assessing an asylum decision, the Court has emphasised that the personal circumstances of each applicant must have been carefully considered in the light of a substantial body of material concerning the current situation in the country in question and the position of the relevant community within it.[93]

With respect to deprivation of an individual's legal capacity, the Court states:

> Any deprivation or limitation of legal capacity must be based on sufficiently reliable and conclusive evidence. An expert medical report should explain what kind of actions the applicant is unable to understand or control and what the consequences of his illness are for his social life, health, pecuniary interests, and so on. The degree of the applicant's incapacity should be addressed in sufficient detail by the medical reports.[94]

[90] *Hatton*, note 71 above, para. 128.
[91] *Nachova*, note 35 above, para. 103.
[92] *Ibid.*, para. 104.
[93] ECtHR, *Vilvarajah and others* v. *United Kingdom*, 30 October 1991, para. 114.
[94] ECtHR, *Sykora* v. *Czech Republic*, 22 November 2012, para. 103.

3.7 Accounting for relevant specificities

At the interface between procedural and substantive control, the Court examines whether the domestic authorities carefully considered all of the interests at stake in a case. In addition, the Court requires these authorities to explicitly take into account certain relevant factors concerning particular categories of applicant. These concern in particular minority status and vulnerability. Both are intertwined where Roma applicants are concerned.

The Grand Chamber has emphasised that

> the vulnerable position of Roma/Gypsies means that special consideration should be given to their needs and their different lifestyle, both in the relevant regulatory framework and in reaching decisions in particular cases.[95]

The chamber judgment in *Yordanova*, which concerned collective eviction of Roma, went even further in emphasising the weight of this requirement and its concrete implications:

> In general, the underprivileged status of the applicants' group must be a weighty factor in considering approaches to dealing with their unlawful settlement and, if their removal is necessary, in deciding on its timing, modalities and, if possible, arrangements for alternative shelter.[96]

3.8 Other procedural guarantees

3.8.1 Public character of investigation

To maintain public confidence, the procedural obligations under Articles 2 and 3 ECHR require sufficient public scrutiny of the investigation or its results 'to secure accountability in practice as well as in theory'.[97]

3.8.2 Overall fairness of decision-making procedure

Under Article 8 ECHR, the overall assessment of the fairness of a decision-making procedure may involve many dimensions of fairness, including matters of proof and evidence. For example, in finding a violation of Article 8 of the Convention the Court has given weight to the fact that the state had placed too heavy a burden of proof on the applicant.[98]

[95] ECtHR (GC), *Aksu* v. *Turkey*, 15 March 2012, para. 75.

[96] *Yordanova*, note 40 above, para. 133.

[97] *Al-Skeini*, note 13 above, para. 167.

[98] *Ciubotaru*, note 74 above, para. 51, referring to ECtHR, *I* v. *Finland*, 27 July 2008, para. 44.

In another case, the Court found fault with the failure to communicate witness declarations and an inspection report to the applicant.[99]

3.8.3 Procedural guarantees in general rules (and their application)

Likewise, the overall assessment of the existence of safeguards against arbitrariness in general rules or established practice (either under the legality requirement or the proportionality requirement) encompasses a wide range of factors, depending on the issue at hand. For example, with respect to a house search, the Court will examine

> whether the search was based on a warrant issued by a judge and based on reasonable suspicion, whether the scope of the warrant was reasonably limited and – where the search of a lawyer's office was concerned – whether the search was carried out in the presence of an independent observer in order to ensure that materials subject to professional secrecy were not removed.[100]

Procedural shortcomings can be situated in the general rules themselves or in their (deficient) application in the case at hand.

Other guarantees that may be required at the level of general rules, include time limits and transparency and accountability mechanisms.[101]

3.8.4 Procedural guarantees in court

When the alleged violation is the result of a judicial procedure, as in the case of a conviction for defamation, fair trial requirements in the classical sense may impact on the Court's assessment of a substantive violation. The Court has stated in this respect that

> the procedural guarantees afforded to the defendants in defamation proceedings are among the factors to be taken into account in assessing the proportionality of the interference under Article 10. In particular, it is important that the defendant is afforded a realistic chance to prove that the factual basis for his allegations was true. A lack of procedural fairness and equality may give rise to a breach of Article 10.[102]

[99] ECtHR, *Özpinar* v. *Turkey*, 19 October 2010, para. 77.

[100] ECtHR, *Wieser & Bicos Beteiligungen GmbH* v. *Austria*, 16 October 2007, para. 57.

[101] Time limits: ECtHR, *Tebieti Muhafize Cemiyyetti and Israfilov* v. *Azerbaijan*, 8 October 2009, para. 64. Transparency and accountability mechanisms: *Olafsson*, note 9 above, para. 82.

[102] ECtHR, *Andrushko* v. *Russia*, 14 October 2010, para. 53.

Sometimes in such cases the Court refers to its finding of procedural defects under Article 6 ECHR and states that this 'serves to compound' its finding of a lack of proportionality with respect to the substantive right.[103] However, procedural shortcomings may in themselves constitute a violation of Article 10 ECHR, as in a case in which applicants had to confront a powerful multinational corporation without legal aid, resulting in inequality of arms and procedural unfairness that violated both Articles 6 and 10 ECHR.[104]

3.9 'Inhuman' procedural shortcomings

In some disappearance cases, violations of the procedural obligations under Article 2 ECHR may give rise to an autonomous violation of Article 3 ECHR *vis-à-vis* the relatives of the disappeared person. Such is the case

> where the failure of the authorities to respond to the quest for information by the relatives or the obstacles placed in their way, leaving them to bear the brunt of the efforts to uncover any facts, may be regarded as disclosing a flagrant, continuous and callous disregard of an obligation to account for the whereabouts and fate of a missing person.[105]

4. Implications

The above overview of the 'procedural scope' of substantive rights is by no means exhaustive. However, it does sketch a clear trend, the implications of which will be examined in this final section, successively focusing on the relationship with the 'real' procedural ECHR provisions (section 4.1 below), the relationship between the substantive and procedural scopes of the same provision (section 4.2), and the margin of appreciation (section 4.3).

4.1 Relationship to procedural provisions

4.1.1 Article 13

The right to an effective investigation has been examined under substantive provisions (especially Articles 2 and 3 ECHR) as described above,

[103] ECtHR, *Igor Kabanov* v. *Russia*, 3 February 2011, para. 57.
[104] ECtHR, *Steel and Morris* v. *United Kingdom*, 15 February 2005, para. 95.
[105] *Varnava*, note 14 above, para. 200.

but also under Article 13 ECHR in combination with the relevant substantive provision. Sometimes both approaches occur in the same case and the Court seems to consider them as complementary. In other cases the Court's language suggests that they are interchangeable.[106] With several recent Grand Chamber judgments explicitly (though not necessarily clearly) distinguishing between the two approaches, it has to be assumed that the Court intends to cover different types of harm from each angle.[107] In general, it may be said that, under the substantive provision, the emphasis is on an effective investigation of whether or not a violation of the substantive Article occurred, identification of the perpetrator and holding him or her accountable. Under Article 13, on the other hand, the emphasis is on remedies from the perspective of the applicant. However, the procedural obligations under substantive provisions have been interpreted so as to include the question of how the applicants should be involved in the proceedings, as well as issues such as compensation (cf. section 2.2 above). Likewise, the idea of an effective remedy under Article 13 ECHR has been interpreted as including 'a thorough and effective investigation capable of leading to the identification and punishment of those responsible'.[108] Hence, the overlap is considerable, even if it is not complete. For example, the Court held in *Öneryildiz* that a violation of a procedural obligation under Article 2 ECHR does not automatically result in a violation of Article 13 ECHR:

> What is important is the impact the State's failure to comply with its procedural obligation under Article 2 had on the deceased's family's access to other available and effective remedies for establishing liability on the part of State officials or bodies for acts or omissions entailing the breach of their rights under Article 2 and, as appropriate, obtaining compensation.[109]

The impression that procedural obligations under substantive provisions have colonised Article 13 ECHR's territory also applies beyond the right to an investigation, as the Court has found under substantive provisions what has been termed a 'right to a remedy' (section 2.2 above), which in fact is the core business of Article 13. It is not surprising, therefore, to find the Court ruling after finding a violation of this type that 'no separate issue arises under Article 13'.[110] Yet cases do occur in which the Court finds a violation of Article 13 ECHR after rejecting allegations of

[106] Christoffersen, *Fair Balance*, note 11 above, pp. 503–7.

[107] For example *El Masri*, note 26 above, para. 256.

[108] *Ibid.*, para. 255.

[109] *Öneryildiz*, note 12 above, para. 148.

[110] For example *A, B and C*, note 55 above, para. 274.

a procedural violation under the substantive provision, or the other way round.[111]

4.1.2 Article 6

Some overlap with Article 6 ECHR exists as well, to the extent that the procedural obligations found under substantive provisions concern judicial proceedings that fall within the scope of Article 6, and concern procedural deficiencies that are covered by Article 6, such as the length of proceedings, equality of arms or the impartiality of the bench.

In this manner, the remaining restrictions on the scope for application of Article 6 ECHR may be circumvented to some extent.[112] In fact, not only is there no restriction on the judicial procedures the fairness of which may be examined under the procedural aspect of substantive provisions, such examination is by no means restricted to judicial procedures, as explained earlier. However it should be noted that under substantive provisions a procedural shortcoming is not necessarily conclusive for the finding of a violation; in many cases it is one among several factors that contribute to such a finding. This is related to the different rationales for the two types of provision: procedural provisions protect against procedural harm as a goal in itself, whereas under substantive provisions procedural protection is instrumental for the protection of substantive human rights (cf. below, section 4.2).

4.2 Relationship to substantive guarantees

Christoffersen argues that 'proceduralisation' of substantive rights is valuable only to the extent that it aims to increase process efficacy, rather than merely add process value. The term 'process value' refers to the independent value of legal procedures, whereas the term 'process efficacy' indicates procedural rights and obligations that 'have the purpose and effect

[111] L. Lavrysen, 'Protection by the law' in E. Brems and Y. Haeck (eds), *Human Rights and Civil Rights in the 21st Century* (Heidelberg: Springer, 2013), footnote 254, notes that in *Hatton*, note 71 above, the Court found the remedy of judicial '*Wednesbury* unreasonableness' review insufficient for the purposes of Art. 13 ECHR (paras 141–2), whereas it did not find a procedural violation of Art. 8 ECHR (paras 128–9). On the other hand, in the case of *Redfearn*, note 42 above (para. 62) the Court found a 'procedural' violation of Art. 11 ECHR, while rejecting the complaint under Art. 13 ECHR, because this provision 'does not require the law to provide an effective remedy where the alleged violation arises from primary legislation'.

[112] See Chapter 14 by Paul Lemmens.

of improving the process in order to achieve good results'.[113] From the above analysis it appears that efficacy in protecting the substantive right at issue has indeed been the central motive advanced by the European Court of Human Rights whenever it envisaged developing procedural rights and obligations. While the procedural obligations are autonomous in the sense that procedural shortcomings may be the sole basis for finding a violation of a substantive right, they are at the same time instrumental, in the sense that the identification and scope of procedural obligations are designed to improve protection of the substantive right. This may mean that certain procedures are considered necessary to prevent violations of the substantive right or to remedy such violations. Procedural shortcomings in the investigation of alleged violations may be the reason why the Court cannot conclusively determine whether or not a substantive violation has taken place. These are arguably the cases in which the finding of a procedural violation has most value for the applicant, who otherwise might be left empty-handed.

Yet procedural development can also weaken substantive human rights protection,[114] when the procedural dimension is not added to substantive scrutiny but rather tends to replace it. Several authors have criticised the Court for seemingly avoiding difficult issues 'by focusing on procedural safeguards instead of substantive issues'.[115] In this respect, it might not be problematic for the Court to draw negative substantive inferences from the non-observance of procedural obligations, but the situation is very different when it draws positive substantive inferences from the observance of procedural obligations.[116] After all, it is far from unthinkable that, after consulting all relevant expertise and hearing all interested parties in a fair procedure, domestic authorities might nevertheless take a decision that violates human rights. I have argued elsewhere that procedural justice should not be conceived of as a substitute for distributive justice.[117] Hence I submit that the absence of a substantive violation can never be based to decisive effect on procedural arguments.

113 Christoffersen, *Fair Balance*, note 11 above, p. 462. 114 *Ibid.*, p. 455.

115 *Ibid.*, p. 460, where he mentions Mowbray and van Drooghenbroeck.

116 For example, Gerards states that, when a measure has been carefully prepared and considered at the domestic level, often the Court will rather easily assume that it is justified: J.H. Gerards, 'The prism of fundamental rights', (2012) 8 *European Constitutional Law Review* 173–202.

117 E. Brems and L. Lavrysen, 'Procedural justice in human rights adjudication: the European Court of Human Rights', (2013) 35 *Human Rights Quarterly* 176–200.

4.3 Relationship to margin of appreciation

In some cases,[118] procedural scrutiny functions as a check on state discretion in settings where the domestic margin of appreciation is wide. Nonetheless, in some other cases, the Court has ruled that a wide margin of appreciation could only be granted if the domestic decision-making process includes sufficient procedural guarantees. The statement that '(t)he extent of the State's margin of appreciation depends on the quality of the decision-making-process' was made in cases concerning deprivation of legal capacity and environmental pollution.[119] Moreover, the Court's concern with procedural guarantees is not restricted to settings with a wide margin of appreciation.[120]

I have argued elsewhere that when the Court grants a wide margin of appreciation, it should take particular care to include in this assessment an appreciation of domestic procedures.[121] The minimal scrutiny that is exercised when the Court grants the widest possible margin of appreciation should still include a screening for procedural shortcomings. At the same time, the Court should consider making the grant of a wide margin of appreciation depend, as a rule, on the absence of serious procedural deficiencies, as it has already done in occasional cases. A finding of deficient procedural safeguards should automatically lead to a narrow margin of appreciation, thereby increasing the intensity of the Court's scrutiny and leaving less room for domestic authorities to restrict human rights.

5. Conclusion

In many instances the Court has added a procedural layer to the protection of substantive ECHR provisions. The main driver for this development appears to be the wish to make the guarantees of human rights more effective. Yet while this development is explicit and consistent in some areas of case law, it remains inconsistent and less-than-transparent in

[118] See *ibid.*, referring amongst others to ECtHR (inadm.), *Noack* v. *Germany*, 25 May 2005 and ECtHR (GC), *Leyla Şahin* v. *Turkey*, 10 November 2005, para. 120.

[119] Deprivation of legal capacity: ECtHR, *Shtukaturov* v. *Russia*, 27 March 2008, para. 89. Environmental pollution: ECtHR, *Giacomelli* v. *Italy*, 2 November 2006, para. 84.

[120] A clear case of a strong emphasis on procedural justice with a narrow margin of appreciation is *Lombardi Vallauri*, note 87 above, paras 45–9.

[121] Brems and Lavrysen, 'Procedural justice', note 117 above.

others. Moreover, caution should be taken to hold the focus of procedural protection on complementing and optimising, rather than substituting substantive protection. Thoughtful use of margins of appreciation may be an instrument to this effect.

8

The scope of rights and the scope of obligations

Positive obligations

LAURENS LAVRYSEN

1. Introduction

In the traditional view, civil and political rights merely consist of 'negative obligations' prohibiting state action that 'interferes' with a certain right. However, in its famous *Marckx* judgment, the European Court of Human Rights (the Court) held that

> the object of [Article 8 ECHR] is 'essentially' that of protecting the individual against arbitrary interference by the public authorities . . . Nevertheless it does not merely compel the State to abstain from such interference: in addition to this primarily negative undertaking, there may be positive obligations inherent in an effective 'respect' for family life.[1]

This kind of 'positive obligation' requires state action to actively 'protect' or 'fulfil' a Convention right.

Since *Marckx*, the Court has found positive obligations under almost every Convention right.[2] The existence of these positive obligations is generally based either on the need to guarantee the 'effective' protection of a Convention right or on Article 1 ECHR, which requires states to 'secure' the enjoyment of the Convention rights to everyone within their jurisdiction.[3] Despite the widespread application of the doctrine

My research has been funded by the Research Foundation Flanders (FWO) within the framework of the European Research Council-funded project 'Strengthening the European Court of Human Rights: More Accountability through Better Legal Reasoning'.

1 ECtHR, *Marckx* v. *Belgium*, 13 June 1979, para. 31.

2 See A. Mowbray, *The Development of Positive Obligations under the European Convention on Human Rights by the European Court of Human Rights* (Oxford: Hart Publishing, 2004).

3 F. Sudre, 'Les "obligations positives" dans la jurisprudence européenne des droits de l'homme' in P. Mahoney, F. Matscher, H. Petzold and L. Wildhaber (eds), *Protection des Droits de l'Homme: la Perspective Européenne* [Protecting Human Rights: The European Perspective] (Cologne: Carl Heymanns Verlag, 2000), pp. 1362–3.

of positive obligations, the Court itself has stated that it 'does not have to develop a general theory of the positive obligations which may flow from the Convention'.[4] This has resulted in a case-by-case approach that teaches us little about the nature and the correct application of positive obligations.

This chapter argues that the Court should take a more structured approach. Taking into account the bifurcated nature of human rights (section 2.1 of this chapter), it proposes to apply a symmetrical approach to positive and negative obligations (section 2.2). The chapter then examines the link between the scope of a Convention right (section 2.3) and the scope of positive obligations stemming from that right, i.e. the extent to which this Convention right entitles an individual to state action (section 2.4). While the former notion belongs to the first stage of the analysis, the latter pertains to the second. Finally, the chapter argues in favour of keeping the scope 'clean': elements from the second stage of the analysis – in particular proportionality (section 3.1) and legality (section 3.2) – should not be introduced during the first stage.

It should be noted that, while some Convention rights explicitly contain positive obligations (e.g. the procedural guarantees of detainees under Article 5 ECHR), this chapter is only concerned with 'implied' positive obligations that have been 'read' into the Convention.

2. Structure of human rights

2.1 Bifurcation scope – limit

Gerards and Senden convincingly argue that the bifurcation between the scope of a right and the review of justification (or limit) is an important aspect of the structure of fundamental rights.[5] This flows from their non-absolute nature,[6] or principle-like character, which is most clearly illustrated by rights that contain express limitation clauses, such as Articles 8–11 ECHR.[7] Following Alexy, a fundamental right can be considered as

4 ECtHR, *Plattform 'Ärzte für das Leben'* v. *Austria*, 21 June 1988, para. 31.

5 J. Gerards and H. Senden, 'The structure of fundamental rights and the European Court of Human Rights', (2009) 7 *International Journal of Constitutional Law* 619–53.

6 With the exception of non-derogable rights, e.g. the prohibition of torture (Art. 3 ECHR).

7 The two-stage nature of ECHR rights, however, is not confined to rights that are guaranteed subject to such an express possibility of limitation (G. van der Schyff, *Limitation of Rights* (Nijmegen: Wolf Legal Publishers, 2005), p. 16).

having both a rule-like and a principle-like character.[8] In his view, principles are 'optimization requirements relative to what is legally and factually possible'.[9] According to Alexy, this principled character inevitably necessitates a test of proportionality in order to establish whether these legal and factual considerations take precedence over the protected right or not.[10]

Thus he distinguishes between a *first stage* in which we ask what is *prima facie* protected by the fundamental right, and a *second stage* that asks what is *definitively* protected after taking into account the possibility of limitations.[11] This distinction is crucial in distributing the burden of proof, as the individual has to adduce reasons in favour of *prima facie* protection in the first stage, while the state has to adduce counter-reasons for granting *definitive* protection in the second stage.[12] In Alexy's words, 'constitutional protection always depends on a relationship between a reason for constitutional protection and some relevant contrary reason'.[13]

While this theory builds on the jurisprudence of the German Constitutional Court, it 'has been widely recognised as a theory that helps to shed light on human and constitutional rights practice more generally'[14] and the rights entrenched in the ECHR more specifically.[15] The strength of Alexy's model is that it allows all the relevant considerations to be taken into account, while allowing a fair distribution of the burden of proof. This makes it an adequate model for examining both negative and positive obligations.[16] In the latter case, the individual must establish whether a situation enters the scope of a Convention right in the first stage, while the state has to provide justification for its inaction to protect this right in the second stage. However, as Gerards and Senden show, the Court does not always take the bifurcated nature of human rights seriously in positive obligation cases.[17]

8 R. Alexy, *A Theory of Constitutional Rights* (Oxford University Press, 2002), pp. 84–6. The rule-like element relates to the fact that the norm itself 'is applicable without needing to be balanced by any other norm, and cases can be subsumed under it' (p. 85).

9 *Ibid.*, p. 67. 10 *Ibid.*, pp. 66–9.

11 *Ibid.*, pp. 196–200. The concepts of a 'first' and a 'second stage' are drawn from van der Schyff's two-stage-model (van der Schyff, note 7 above, p. 11). See also van der Schyff's chapter in this volume.

12 Gerards and Senden, note 5 above, pp. 641–4. 13 Alexy, note 8 above, p. 209.

14 M. Kumm, 'Political liberalism and the structure of rights: on the place and limits of the proportionality requirement' in G. Pavlakos (ed.), *Law, Rights and Discourse – The Legal Philosophy of Robert Alexy* (Oxford: Hart Publishing, 2007), p. 136.

15 S. Greer, ''Balancing' and the European Court of Human Rights: a contribution to the Habermas–Alexy debate', (2004) 63 *Cambridge Law Journal* 433.

16 Cf. Leijten's chapter in this volume, considering 'socio-economic' positive obligations.

17 Gerards and Senden, note 5 above, pp. 634–6.

2.2 The symmetrical model

While the Court applies a clear, bifurcated approach to negative obligation cases – by examining whether there has been an 'interference' with a Convention right (first stage) and whether that interference could pass the legality, legitimacy and proportionality tests (second stage) – in positive obligation cases the Court often merges the first and second stages into a single, unstructured, test,[18] in which it examines whether, all things considered, a state's inaction had not upset a 'fair balance'. In an opinion concurring with the judgment in *Stjerna* – in which the Court found that refusal to alter a man's surname did not violate Article 8 ECHR – this was criticised by Judge Luzius Wildhaber, who argued that

> it would . . . be preferable to construe the notion of 'interference' so as to cover facts capable of breaching an obligation incumbent on the State under Article 8 paragraph 1, whether negative or positive. Whenever a so-called positive obligation arises the Court should examine, as in the event of a so-called negative obligation, whether there has been an interference with the right to respect for private and family life under paragraph 1 of Article 8, and whether such interference was 'in accordance with the law', pursued legitimate aims and was 'necessary in a democratic society' within the meaning of paragraph 2.[19]

There are strong arguments in favour of Wildhaber's proposal to apply the same analytical framework to examinations both of negative and of positive obligations (the 'symmetrical model'). To begin with, the first stage of the analysis concerns the reasons in favour of human rights protection.[20] Therefore, the focus of this analysis should lie on the *perspective of the (alleged) victim* of a human rights violation, which relates to the *actual experience of a situation* in which human rights are violated, rather than on the question who is responsible for this situation (private actors by actions or state authorities by actions or omissions). While the perspectives of those responsible (and their interests) are important in

[18] *Ibid.*, with references to ECtHR (GC), *Hatton and others* v. *United Kingdom*, 8 July 2003, and ECtHR (GC), *Christine Goodwin* v. *United Kingdom*, 11 July 2002.

[19] ECtHR, *Stjerna* v. *Finland*, 25 November 1994, concurring opinion Judge Wildhaber. Similarly Sudre, note 3 above, pp. 1372–5. Gerards also argues in favour of a symmetrical approach to negative and positive obligations: J. Gerards, 'The prism of fundamental rights', (2012) 8 *European Consitutional Law Review*, pp. 194–5. For a good example of a symmetrical approach to positive obligations, see ECtHR, *Shofman* v. *Russia*, 24 November 2005. Also see ECtHR, *Mosley* v. *United Kingdom*, 10 May 2011, as discussed in van der Schyff's chapter in this volume.

[20] Alexy, note 8 above, p. 206.

the second stage of the analysis, it does not make sense to take them into account at the first stage. Second, the Court has repeatedly acknowledged that 'the boundaries between the State's positive and negative obligations . . . do not lend themselves to precise definition'.[21] In case of doubt, the Court usually states that it is not necessary to decide whether a case should be examined as one concerning a positive or a negative obligation, because 'the applicable principles are nonetheless similar'.[22] In practice, this merely means that the Court applies a similar 'fair balance' test and allows the state 'a certain margin of appreciation',[23] instead of the stricter justification required,[24] and narrower margin of appreciation generally applied,[25] when dealing with negative obligations. Only by applying a symmetrical approach to positive obligation cases can the Court truly live up to its statement that the applicable principles are similar and avoid providing the applicant less protection in cases of doubt. Third, as Sudre argues, it does not make sense to maintain on one hand that positive obligations are 'inherently' part of the content of a right,[26] and to apply, on the other hand, a different legal approach.[27]

In the sections that follow, I will elaborate on what the analysis under the symmetrical model should look like, taking into account the particularities of positive obligations (sections 2.3 and 2.4). Subsequently, I will discuss how the lack of a clear understanding of the bifurcated nature of the human rights analysis leads the Court and academic scholars to introduce second-stage elements into the first stage of the examination (section 3).

2.3 The scope of a Convention right

2.3.1 Protected interest/infringement

In the first stage of this analysis, I will use the concept of a 'protected interest/infringement scope'. In line with Alexy, such an understanding

[21] For a recent example, ECtHR (GC), *SH and others* v. *Austria*, 3 November 2011, para. 87. Sometimes the choice to examine a case from the angle of positive rather than negative obligations and vice versa appears to be totally arbitrary: see Sudre, note 3 above, p. 1374.

[22] For example ECtHR (GC), *Dickson* v. *United Kingdom*, 4 December 2007, paras 70–71.

[23] For example ECtHR (GC), *Odièvre* v. *France*, 13 February 2003, para. 40.

[24] Sudre shows that the current approach to positive obligations lacks the rigour with which negative obligations are controlled and is often reduced to a simple test of 'reasonability' (Sudre, note 3 above, p. 1373).

[25] For example ECtHR, *Women on Waves and others* v. *Portugal*, 3 February 2009, para. 40.

[26] For example *Marckx*, note 1 above, para. 30.

[27] Sudre, note 3 above, p. 1374.

equates the scope of a human rights norm with everything that is *prima facie* protected by it.[28] The *prima facie* protection depends on two factors: (1) whether the contested action or inaction constitutes part of the 'protected conduct and interests of a right' and (2) whether there has been an 'infringement' of the 'protected conduct and interests'.[29]

According to van der Schyff, 'protected conduct and interests' relate to 'a field or range of values that may not be intruded upon either by an event or non-event that would impair the exercise of such guaranteed values, unless such an intrusion is justified'.[30] The justification for such intrusion occurs in the second stage. Van der Schyff defines an 'interference' in its turn as 'a state of affairs, be it occasioned by an action or in-action which causes the exercise of the protected conduct and interests of a right to be impaired or hindered'.[31] The identification of an 'interference' 'must result in a factual inquiry in order to determine whether an action or in-action had any effect on the protected conduct and interests of a right'.[32]

In line with van der Schyff, it can be argued that it makes perfect sense to apply this understanding of an 'interference' in positive obligation cases, since it covers the notion of inaction. In order to avoid confusion – as 'interference' is typically used in the context of negative obligations – I will use the broader term 'infringement' to label the 'disturbance' of a human right that is caused by either action or inaction by the state.[33]

An important issue is what this factual inquiry should resemble. Confusingly, Van der Schyff states that 'an [infringement] would . . . arise with the protection of a right, were a state not to discharge such positive obligations'.[34] This is chronologically wrong: whether there is a *definitive* positive obligation – and thus the need to actually 'discharge' it – depends on the second stage of the analysis, so it cannot be a precondition to the question whether an 'infringement' has occurred, which belongs to the first stage. The quoted fragment also seems to suggest that it is necessary for the applicant to identify a particular measure that could remedy the situation; but this cannot be required as the choice of measures to discharge a positive obligation will generally fall within the authorities'

[28] Alexy, note 8 above, p. 199.

[29] Van der Schyff, note 7 above, p. 29; Alexy, note 8 above, p. 198.

[30] Van der Schyff, note 7 above, p. 31. [31] *Ibid.*, p. 41.

[32] *Ibid.*, p. 42. Similarly Sudre, note 3 above, p. 1374.

[33] According to Alexy, '[t]he concept of infringement is a general term covering obstruction, interference and removal' (Alexy, note 8 above, p. 197).

[34] Van der Schyff, note 7 above, p. 67.

margin of appreciation.[35] The mere fact that an individual can arguably claim that an action by the state could have had 'any effect' should thus be sufficient to establish that its inaction constitutes an 'infringement'.[36] As the authorities are principally better placed to assess the efficiency of particular measures as well as their alternatives – whether taking these measures could have safeguarded the individual's right – this question clearly belongs to the second stage of the analysis.

2.3.2 Wide interpretation

In the interest of legal reasoning, both the 'protected conduct and interests' and the concept of 'infringement' should be interpreted widely.[37] According to Alexy, this implies that 'everything which the relevant constitutional principles suggests should be protected falls within the scope of protection'.[38] A narrow interpretation will always be problematic in cases where people do not share the sense of certainty that there should be *prima facie* protection.[39] If the opponents of protection cannot persuade the proponents to adopt their view, they necessarily have to focus on reasons based on the rights of others or common interests that counterbalance the substantive reasons put forward by those proponents of *prima facie* protection.[40] In other words, Alexy's most convincing argument in favour of wide scope is that narrow conceptions of scope amount to 'premature balancing',[41] that do not respect the necessary structure of reason and counter-reason, however, and thereby render the relevant limiting reasons superfluous.[42] According to van der Schyff, the question whether a conduct is 'worthy of constitutional protection' should therefore be a matter for the second stage of the analysis, not the first.[43]

It is important to make it clear that this conception of scope is a formal theory that concerns the structure of fundamental rights and not a normative theory concerning the necessary level of *definitive* protection.[44] While thus necessarily wide scope leads to a high level of *prima facie* protection, it in no way prejudges the extent of *definitive* protection, which depends on the results of the second stage of the analysis.

[35] Here, see ECtHR, *Budayeva and others* v. *Russia*, 20 March 2008, para. 134.
[36] This follows the required, wide interpretation of the concept of 'infringement'.
[37] See, likewise, van der Schyff's chapter in this volume.
[38] Alexy, note 8 above, p. 210. [39] *Ibid.*, p. 214. [40] *Ibid.*
[41] Van der Schyff, note 7 above, p. 37. [42] Alexy, note 8 above, p. 206.
[43] Van der Schyff, note 7 above, p. 37. [44] Alexy, note 8 above, p. 201.

2.3.3 Application to the Court's case law

Just as for negative obligations, so in the first stage of a positive obligation case the Court should examine whether there has been an infringement of the 'protected conduct or interests' under a Convention right. As a general rule, when a factual disturbance of the 'protected conduct or interests' counts as an infringement in the context of negative obligations, a similar disturbance (of which the authorities are aware or should be aware) must amount to an infringement in the context of positive obligations. If they have infringed, the authorities are under a *prima facie* positive obligation to 'protect' or 'fulfil' the individual's right.[45]

The fact that negative and positive obligations are treated symmetrically, however, does not imply that the victim of a factual disturbance necessarily enjoys the same level of definitive protection in both cases. The extent of definitive protection – the question whether there is a *definitive* positive obligation to 'protect' or 'fulfil' – depends on the second stage of the analysis and different competing interests may apply in cases of positive and negative obligations.[46]

2.3.4 A 'knowledge' condition?

At this point it is also necessary to stress the fact that positive obligations oblige due diligence.[47] Positive obligations can only reasonably arise insofar as responsibility can be attributed to the state,[48] which requires that authorities are aware or should be aware of (the possibility of) a factual disturbance of the 'protected conduct or interests' under a right (the 'knowledge' condition).[49] In this respect, the Court's approach to Article 2 cases is illustrative. It is settled case law that Article 2 ECHR requires state authorities to take preventive operational measures to protect an individual, but only when they 'knew or ought to have known at the time of the existence of a real and immediate risk to the life'.[50] The question whether the inaction (the lack of preventive operational measures) can be justified

45 Similarly *ibid.*, p. 347. 46 See section 2.4.2 below.

47 C. Dröge, *Positive Verpflichtungen der Staaten in der Europäischen Menschenrechtskonvention* (Berlin: Springer-Verlag, 2003), p. 388.

48 J. Christoffersen, *Fair Balance: Proportionality, Subsidiarity and Primarity in the European Convention of Human Rights* (Leiden: Martinus Nijhoff, 2009), pp. 103–5.

49 According to Xenos, knowledge of the need for human rights protection is prerequisite for both positive and negative obligations to arise: D. Xenos, *The Positive Obligations of the State under the European Convention of Human Rights* (Routledge: New York, 2012), pp. 73–91.

50 For example ECtHR (GC), *Osman* v. *United Kingdom*, 28 October 1998, para. 116.

(the second stage of the analysis),[51] can only arise insofar as this 'knowledge' condition has been fulfilled. Therefore the 'knowledge' condition is inherent to the question whether an inaction constitutes an infringement and thus to the first stage of the analysis. To hold otherwise would imply that authorities would have to provide a justification in the second stage for a factual disturbance of which they could not have reasonably been aware.[52]

2.4 The second stage of the analysis

2.4.1 Legality and legitimacy

Whether a state is under a definitive positive obligation depends on the second stage of the inquiry.[53] In this stage, the Court should first examine whether the inaction (infringement) is 'in accordance with the law' (legality test). If domestic law requires state authorities to act in a certain way to safeguard an individual's rights, then the rule of law generally prohibits these authorities from remaining inactive.[54] That the Court sometimes applies such a test is well illustrated by some environmental cases in which the Court found a violation of Article 8 ECHR because state authorities had failed to enforce domestic environmental standards.[55]

[51] The relevant test in the second stage is whether the authorities 'failed to take measures within the scope of their powers which, judged reasonably, might have been expected to avoid that risk' (e.g. *ibid.*). Although the Court appears to merge the two elements into a single test, the correct view is that the first question concerns the first stage of the analysis, while the second question concerns the second stage.

[52] It is important not to overstress this 'knowledge' condition. Outside the context of preventive positive obligations – which is characterised by a sense of urgency – the 'knowledge' condition will almost always be fulfilled, since the mere fact that an individual seeks to remedy his or her situation at the domestic level should be sufficient to alert the authorities to the need for human rights protection. Similarly, Xenos, note 49 above, pp. 80–81, who stresses that the state should nonetheless be allowed a reasonable time to address a human rights complaint.

[53] Alexy, note 8 above, p. 348.

[54] See e.g. ECtHR (GC), *Broniowski* v. *Poland*, 22 June 2004, para. 184:

> The rule of law underlying the Convention and the principle of lawfulness . . . require States not only to respect and apply, in a foreseeable and consistent manner, the laws they have enacted, but also, as a corollary of this duty, to ensure the legal and practical conditions for their implementation.

[55] For example ECtHR, *Deés* v. *Hungary*, 9 November 2010, paras 22–4. Cf. ECtHR, *Fadeyeva* v. *Russia*, 9 June 2005, paras 96–8, in which the Court held that 'domestic legality should be approached not as a separate and conclusive test, but rather as one of many aspects which should be taken into account in assessing whether the State had struck a fair balance',

Subsequently, the Court needs to establish whether the authorities' inaction is based on a legitimate aim (legitimacy test). This requirement is not alien to the Court's positive obligations case law, since the Court has repeatedly held in the context of Article 8 ECHR that 'in striking the required balance the aims mentioned in the second paragraph may be of a certain relevance'.[56] Rather than merely integrating the requirement for a legitimate aim into the fair balance test, legitimacy should be examined separately, resulting in the rejection of inactions based on manifestly illegitimate considerations.[57] When the authorities' inaction fails the legality or legitimacy test, the Court should find a violation of the Convention right concerned.

2.4.2 Necessary in a democratic society

When an inaction passes the legality and legitimacy test, the Court must proceed to examine whether this inaction was 'necessary in a democratic society'. This is essentially a test of proportionality in which the Court takes into account the various competing interests.[58]

Even when the scope is determined symmetrically, it will generally be more difficult to find a violation in a positive obligation case, as not only are there competing substantive principles, such as the possible interests of the human rights violator and of society, but also competing formal principles, such as the competence of the democratically legitimated legislature and budgetary limitations.[59] Often, therefore, protection will be more extensive in cases of negative obligations because, all things being

because domestic authorities may still fulfil their positive obligations by means other than applying a particular measure provided by domestic law. In any event, enforcing total compliance by third parties with domestic law may well be outside a state's powers, so the legality test may more appropriately be considered as an 'obligation of means', requiring the domestic authorities to take 'reasonable steps' to enforce the domestic law, rather than as an 'obligation of results' (*mutatis mutandis Osman*, note 50 above, para. 116). In this sense, the application of the legality principle may differ from negative obligation cases in which *ipso facto* domestic illegality results in the finding of a violation.

56 For example *Hatton*, note 18 above, para. 98.

57 For example inactions based on racist or sexist assumptions.

58 It should be noted that the Court has developed an extensive set of procedural positive obligations; for an overview see Brems's chapter in this volume. Procedural protection also has to be proportionate to the human rights violation concerned. However, in many cases this proportionality will be assessed categorically, rather than by ad hoc balancing, e.g. the checklist of procedural obligations under Art. 2 (see ECtHR (GC), *Ramsahai and others* v. *The Netherlands*, 15 May 2007).

59 Alexy, note 8 above, p. 348. Negative obligations also cost money, however, and they restrict the options open to the legislature.

equal, the 'cost' of discharging a positive obligation (i.e. a competing formal principle) will often be higher than that attaching to a negative obligation, since the former requires state action while the latter 'simply' requires absence of state action.[60]

2.4.3 'Non-qualified' rights

While the above relates to what are called 'qualified' rights,[61] it would make sense to apply a similar approach to positive obligations under Articles 2 and 3 ECHR. While Article 3 is absolute in its negative aspect, the fact that it is not reasonable to expect from the state that it prevent any event of ill-treatment at private hands necessitates a second stage in which arguments against government action can be adduced. Similarly – beside the strictly construed exceptions of Article 2 paragraph 2 – in its negative aspect Article 2 generally prohibits killing, while a second stage is nonetheless required with respect to positive obligations. In both instances, a failure to protect should not be based on illegitimate reasons (lack of legitimacy) or result from a failure to comply with domestic law (lack of legality). Furthermore, lack of protection can only be justified in the light of competing interests (proportionality).

Specifically in the context of Article 3, Palmer has stressed that

> the scope of the positive obligation is limited by what can be reasonably expected of the State in the circumstances. Nevertheless this does not affect the absolute nature of the Article 3 right . . . [T]he absolute terms of the guarantee prohibits any qualifying conditions under which restrictions may be legitimately imposed.[62]

Palmer is correct insofar as she argues that there can be no room for the balancing of competing substantive principles in favour of ill-treatment – otherwise ill-treatment by private persons would be considered justified and thus the prohibition would not be absolute. In determining the extent of a *definitive* positive obligation, however, there is room for the balancing of formal principles (e.g. policing priorities), as well as substantive principles opposing state action (e.g. considerations of privacy). Thus,

[60] This should not be overstated, however, as often compliance with a negative obligation also comes at high cost.

[61] That is, rights containing express limitation clauses.

[62] S. Palmer, 'A wrong turning: Article 3 ECHR and proportionality', (2006) 65 *Cambridge Law Journal* 448.

although Article 3 ECHR is absolute, the positive obligation it entails is not: inevitably the obligation to protect is subject to a balancing exercise.[63]

2.4.4 Determining the 'scope' of positive obligations

If the arguments in favour of the authorities' inaction fail in the second stage of the analysis, what remains of the *prima facie* positive obligation is a *definitive* positive obligation. The exact extent of this *definitive* positive obligation will depend on the result of the legality, legitimacy and proportionality tests. This extent is what is generally meant when commentators discuss 'the scope of positive obligations'.[64]

Some criticism of positive obligations concerns their allegedly 'open-ended nature', which implies that positive obligations may potentially be applied in a wide and undefined variety of cases.[65] Although this is undoubtedly correct when applied to *prima facie* positive obligations in the first stage of the analysis, the second stage will necessarily 'filter out' numerous claims, ending up with a much more limited quantity of *definitive* positive obligations.

Another issue concerns so-called 'human rights inflation', a term that is generally used to criticise the fact that the Court is allegedly reading 'new' human rights into the ECHR, especially through the extensive 'creation' of positive obligations.[66] This criticism stems from the symmetrical nature of rights and obligations – a right for an individual corresponds to an obligation on the state and vice versa.[67] Take the example of the environmental cases: the individual's right to respect for private life or home may take on a particular significance in cases of environmental nuisance, in some of which cases results in a particular *definitive* positive obligation on the authorities to protect that right. The Court does not create an abstract 'right to a clean and quiet environment' thereby,[68] let

[63] Cf. Smet's chapter in this volume.

[64] For example Christoffersen, note 48 above, p. 107. In Christoffersen's words, 'the scope of the positive obligation is subject to balancing'. He explains this by the example of the preventive positive obligation under Art. 2 ECHR, where the scope of the positive obligation depends on the question whether the authorities took 'measures within the scope of their powers which, judged reasonably, might have been expected to avoid that risk'.

[65] Xenos, note 49 above, p. 4.

[66] For example G. Letsas, *A Theory of Interpretation of the European Convention on Human Rights* (Oxford University Press, 2007), pp. 126–30. Also see the concerns expressed by Gerards in her chapter in this volume.

[67] Alexy, note 8 above, p. 296.

[68] Discussing *Hatton*, note 18 above, Gerards and Senden deplore the fact that the Court 'did not address the more abstract question of whether a right to a clean and quiet environment

alone an abstract 'right to sleep',[69] since Article 8 ECHR only protects the right to respect for private life and the home. While the mirror of such a *definitive* positive obligation may correctly be understood as a particular right of the individual, this certainly does not entail an abstract right, as it is strictly confined to the results of the two-stage-model, taking into account the concrete elements of the case. As the Court does not create such 'new' human rights this way, the criticism of 'human rights inflation' is simply incorrect. The opponents of extensive human rights protection should instead shift their focus to how the two-stage-model could be applied in order to find violations only in a more limited range of cases.

3. Keep the scope 'clean'

As explained above, restricting the first stage of the analysis by introducing elements from the second stage should be avoided. Especially with respect to positive obligations, both scholars and the Court itself regularly fail to avoid this. This is probably the inevitable result of the lack of a clear, bifurcated approach to positive obligation cases: there is confusion as to what might constitute reasons in favour of protection and what might be counter-reasons, and therefore about the distribution of the burden of proof. I will briefly discuss some examples in which considerations of proportionality (section 3.1) and legality (section 3.2) are introduced during the first stage.

3.1 Keep proportionality out of the scope

In the *Appleby* case, the Court held that '[i]n determining whether or not a positive obligation exists, regard must be had to the fair balance that has to be struck between the general interest of the community and the interests of the individual'.[70] In this fragment, the Court merges the first and second stage into a single test, by not distinguishing between

could be read into Article 8' (Gerards and Senden, note 5 above, p. 636). In their view, the Court did little in this judgment to clarify the exact scope of Art. 8 ECHR. In the bifurcated model, however, there is no reason why failing to recognise such a right in the abstract should prevent the Court from examining environmental nuisance from the viewpoint of Art. 8.

69 S. Greer, *The European Convention on Human Rights – Achievements, Problems and Prospects* (Cambridge University Press, 2006), p. 258.

70 ECtHR, *Appleby and others* v. *United Kingdom*, 6 May 2003, para. 40.

prima facie and *definitive* positive obligations.[71] While a *definitive* positive obligation depends on a balancing exercise, this is absolutely not the case with respect to *prima facie* positive obligations, however.

In a similar vein, Christoffersen fails to distinguish the two stages clearly. In his view, '[t]he fair balance-test is . . . complicated in the context of positive obligations as it is applied at two levels; firstly to determine the proper level of protection of the right in issue, and secondly to delimit the State's responsibility'.[72] In this summary he seems to suggest that this first fair balance test, necessary to determine the proper level of protection, takes place at the first stage of the examination. It makes sense to maintain that a *definitive* positive obligation depends on the weight both of counterbalancing, substantive interests (of the individual and the community) and of counterbalancing, formal interests related to the state action needed to remedy the infringement – as these are counter-reasons for definitive protection, they should however be considered in the second stage of the analysis and not in the first.

Equally, it makes no sense to allow states a margin of appreciation in determining whether or not a positive obligation arises:[73] the question whether a *prima facie* positive obligation arises belongs to the first stage of the analysis, while 'allowing a broad margin of appreciation is reasonable only at the stage of justification, not at the stage of defining the rights protected by the Convention'.[74]

3.1.1 Reasonable accommodation

Botta is a notorious example of a case in which the Court introduced proportionality in the first stage of the analysis.[75] The applicant was a physically disabled man who complained about the lack of access to private bathing establishments during his stay at a seaside resort, owing to the absence of special access ramps for wheelchairs and specially equipped lavatories and washrooms. The Court placed a very high burden on the applicant by requiring 'a direct and immediate link between the measures sought by an applicant and the latter's private and/or family life', before a positive obligation under Article 8 ECHR would arise (paragraph 34). Nonetheless, according to the Court the applicant's complaint concerned 'interpersonal relations of such broad and indeterminate scope that there

[71] In a similar sense, see van der Schyff's chapter in this volume.

[72] Christoffersen, note 48 above, p. 106.

[73] ECtHR, *Gül* v. *Switzerland*, 19 February 1996, dissenting opinion Judge Martens, joined by Judge Russo.

[74] Gerards and Senden, note 5 above, p. 650.

[75] ECtHR, *Botta* v. *Italy*, 24 February 1998.

can be no conceivable direct link between the measures the State was urged to take in order to make good the omissions of the private bathing establishments and the applicant's private life' (paragraph 35). Accordingly, the Court found that Article 8 was not applicable.

First, it is regrettable that the Court placed so much emphasis on the need for a 'direct and immediate link' between the requested measures and the applicant's private life. In doing so it applied a very narrow approach to the concept of infringement. The Court cannot require an applicant to establish such a 'direct and immediate link': as explained above, the choice of remedying measures is a matter for the state in the second stage, while the first stage should instead focus on whether an inaction had 'any effect' on the 'protected conduct and interests' of a right. The Court should focus on the relationship between the situation and an applicant's private life, rather than on the relationship between the requested measures and his or her private life. Moreover, Xenos has argued that elements of 'directness' and/or 'immediacy' can make sense when applied to negative obligations, where these elements are 'usually established from the real consequences of that interference', but that 'the position is different when individuals claim assistance from the state due to their own personal vulnerability in order to be able to enjoy human rights'.[76]

Second, the Court could equally have argued in the second stage that, since the complaint concerned 'interpersonal relations of such a broad and indeterminate scope', the applicant's right to private life was therefore outweighed by the authorities' interests in not acting. Instead, by strongly emphasising the link between the inaction and the right, the Court implicitly balanced the applicant's 'light' interests against the authorities' 'heavy' interests, which amounted to 'premature' balancing, pre-empting the second stage of the analysis.[77]

While it may well be justified to argue that the applicant's right was outweighed by private or general interests (in the second stage),[78] the Court seemed to suggest in the first stage that this will generally be true in cases of reasonable accommodation. As a result, the Court invoked *Botta* as a precedent to easily dismiss a whole variety of reasonable accommodation claims.[79]

[76] D. Xenos, 'The human rights of the vulnerable', (2009) 13 *International Journal of Human Rights*, pp. 597–8.

[77] Cf. van der Schyff, note 7 above, p. 37.

[78] It should be noted, however, that increasing attention to the human rights of disabled persons is likely to shift the balance in the individual's direction.

[79] For example ECtHR, *Zehnalová and Zehnal* v. *Czech Republic*, 14 May 2002.

A better approach is the one followed in the Convention on the Rights of Persons with Disabilities (CRPD).[80] This Convention generally provides *prima facie* protection in cases concerning claims for 'reasonable accommodation'[81] – not only against the state, but also against third parties.[82] *Definitive* protection, however, depends on the question whether or not the duty bearer can show that the 'necessary and appropriate modification and adjustments' impose 'a disproportionate or undue burden'.[83] This amounts to a clear two-stage approach, which generally provides wide, *prima facie* protection in the first stage, but nonetheless allows relevant, counterbalancing reasons to be taken into account in the second stage. As the Court increasingly takes the CRPD into account in disability cases,[84] it would be desirable to also adopt the CRPD's two-stage approach regarding reasonable accommodation.

3.1.2 Environmental cases

Another problematic aspect of the Court's case law is discernible in some recent environmental cases. In these cases the Court has required the environmental nuisance to exceed a 'minimum level of severity' before Article 8 ECHR becomes applicable.[85] Again, the underlying idea seems to be that – unless such a 'minimum level' is reached – the private interest will generally be outweighed by competing interests, thereby pre-empting the second stage of the analysis. The 'balancist' position underlying the 'minimum level of severity' threshold is obvious in certain cases in which the Court held that '[t]here would be no arguable claim under Article 8 if the detriment complained of was negligible in comparison to the environmental hazards inherent to life in every modern city'.[86] In other words,

80 Convention on the Rights of Persons with Disabilities, 13 December 2006, UNTS vol. 2515, p. 3.

81 A *prima facie* claim for 'reasonable accommodation' arises when a person with a disability cannot enjoy or exercise all human rights and fundamental freedoms on an equal basis with others (Art. 4 CRPD).

82 The CRPD requires states to 'take all appropriate steps to ensure that reasonable accommodation is provided' (Art. 5 para. 3 CRPD). Thus states have a positive obligation to provide an effective legal framework in which individuals can request reasonable accommodation from third parties.

83 Art. 2 CRPD. The Court has applied a kind of reasonable accommodation test in the context of Art. 5 para. 2, requiring the authorities to take 'reasonable steps' to ensure that a person with a disability understands the reasons for a deprivation of liberty (ECtHR, *ZH* v. *Hungary*, 8 November 2012, para. 43).

84 For example ECtHR, *Alajos Kiss* v. *Hungary*, 20 May 2010, para. 14.

85 For example ECtHR, *Moreno Gómez* v. *Spain*, 16 November 2004, para. 58.

86 For example *Fadeyeva*, note 55 above, para. 69.

the 'preservation' of modern city life necessarily outweighs the damage to Article 8 interests in cases where environmental hazards are 'negligible'. This type of balancing exercise ideally belongs to the second rather than the first stage, however.

Furthermore, the 'minimum level of severity' is a very high threshold that is usually only applied in Article 3 cases. Such a high threshold definitively makes sense under Article 3 ECHR because that article concerns an absolute right: if a case comes within its scope, *ipso facto* there is a violation[87] – at least in negative obligation cases. A one-stage model that allows no consideration of competing interests can only be sustained by a careful and restrictive approach, resulting in a narrow interpretation of scope.[88] Transposing an Article 3 test to Article 8 therefore makes no sense whatsoever – in Article 8 cases there is no pressing need for such a narrow conception of scope, as 'lighter' private life/home interests will easily be outweighed in any case of genuinely competing interests.[89] The latter, moreover, is clear from the case law: the Court generally only finds a violation in cases concerning the most horrid forms of environmental nuisance when the authorities blatantly fail to enforce their own legislation.

In a recent case, it has applied a better approach to the scope of Article 8 ECHR. According to the Court the fact that a situation could lead to a deterioration in the quality of the life of the persons concerned, and in particular harm their right to respect for private life and home, was sufficient to warrant concluding that Article 8 was applicable.[90] The quality of life is the value underlying Article 8's application in environmental cases – therefore a (risk that) quality of life will deteriorate is a better criterion for triggering the *prima facie* protection and the need for justification than the unnecessarily high 'minimum level of severity'.

3.1.3 Religion in the workplace

A last example concerns religious accommodation in the workplace. The old Commission case *Stedman* concerned a Christian woman who worked

[87] See Smet's chapter in this volume.

[88] Van der Schyff, note 7 above, pp. 19–20, and his chapter in this volume.

[89] Cf. the chapter by Gerards in this volume. Gerards questions whether 'peripheral' interests should give rise to 'new' obligations. She therefore proposes to strengthen the 'minimum level of severity' threshold in environmental cases.

[90] ECtHR, *Di Sarno and others* v. *Italy*, 10 January 2012, para. 108. In the Court's view, the fact that there was no actual danger to the applicants' health was not decisive. Similarly *Hatton*, note 18 above, para. 118.

at a travel agency.[91] She was dismissed after refusing on religious grounds to accept new terms of employment under which she would have had to work on Sundays. She complained that this violated her right to freedom of religion. According to the Commission, there was no interference with Article 9 ECHR because 'the applicant was dismissed for failing to agree to work certain hours rather than her religious belief as such and was free to resign and did in effect resign from her employment'. This is a very narrow approach to scope: it would be very unlikely, for example, that anybody would argue that there is no interference with the right to respect for private life simply because an employee is free to resign in a case where an employer monitors the employee's private telephone conversations. Whether resignation is an alternative, and to what extent it can mitigate the infringement of a Convention right, can only be relevant as an element in the proportionality test, but it cannot define the scope of a right.[92]

3.1.4 *De minimis*

The expansion of the Court's positive obligations case law has triggered calls for internal thresholds or *de minimis* limits to the scope.[93] As shown in this section, in many cases such attempts to restrict the scope can be analysed as 'premature' balancing. The examples discussed above illustrate how arguments in favour of protection are categorically dismissed in the first stage of the analysis – based on underlying assumptions that the situation complained of is not serious enough to give rise to positive obligations – without leaving room to consider the possibility that the balance might still be upset in a particular case at hand (i.e. in the second stage).

It has been argued that the 'inflation' of human rights is partly caused by the use of analogical reasoning: if a particular situation is protected by a human right, a comparable, albeit slightly different situation will most likely also be protected, thereby continuously broadening the scope

91 ECommHR, *Stedman* v. *United Kingdom*, 9 April 1997. The Court has never had the opportunity to rule on a similar case, so this Commission decision remains the authoritative interpretation of Art. 9 ECHR.

92 Similarly S. Ouald Chaib, 'Religious accommodation in the workplace: improving the legal reasoning of the European Court of Human Rights' in K. Alidadi, M-C. Foblets and J. Vrielink, *A Test of Faith? Religious Diversity and Accommodation in the European Workplace* (Farnham: Ashgate, 2012), pp. 38–41.

93 For example the chapter by Gerards in this volume and Gerards, note 19 above, pp. 187–96.

of human rights protection.[94] However, by remedying this through the introduction of thresholds, the use of analogical reasoning might well analogously lead to a constant narrowing of the scope of human rights. If one is to take human rights protection seriously, introducing such a risk of 'human rights deflation' to the Court's case law should be avoided.

This does not imply that the Court should spend much energy ruling on 'silly' cases. It would however be better to dismiss such cases by applying admissibility criteria – by declaring them 'manifestly ill-founded' or by ruling that the applicant did not suffer a 'significant disadvantage' – rather than by categorically excluding certain areas from the scope of Convention rights. These procedural tools allow the Court's case load to be alleviated – thus taking into account legitimate institutional concerns[95] – without however discharging Member States from the obligation to themselves consider the appropriate extent of *definitive* positive obligations in future cases.

3.2 Keep legality out of the scope

In *MSS*, the Court ruled that Greece had violated Article 3 ECHR because of the circumstances in which the applicant found himself living owing to the lack of accommodation and assistance provided by the state. Bizarrely, in finding that the 'minimum level of severity' had been exceeded and the situation thus came within the scope of Article 3, the Court strongly emphasised the fact that the EU Reception Conditions Directive obliges Greece to provide asylum seekers with accommodation and decent material conditions.[96]

This approach makes no sense, however: whether a 'minimum level of severity' is reached cannot be made dependent on the question whether a positive obligation rests on the state to remedy that situation. The logical sequence is the other way round: the applicant's situation came within the scope of Article 3, therefore a *prima facie* positive obligation arose to remedy that situation. In determining the extent of *definitive* protection, Greece's obligations under EU law were of decisive importance, however. This is nothing more than the application of the legality criterion.

As explained above, in cases concerning positive obligations under Article 3, the analysis necessarily has a two-stage-character. As the rule of

[94] Gerards, note 19 above, pp. 180–82. [95] See the chapter by Gerards in this volume.

[96] ECtHR (GC), *MSS* v. *Belgium and Greece*, 21 January 2011, paras 250, 263 and concurring opinion Judge Rozakis.

law requires states to comply with their own legislation, a legality criterion makes sense in these cases, but only in the second stage of the analysis, not in the first. Otherwise it would be possible for states to determine for themselves the minimum level of human rights protection, which is contrary to the counter-majoritarian function of human rights.

4. Conclusion

The Court should take the bifurcated nature of human rights seriously by applying a two-stage-test in positive obligation cases. The bifurcated nature of human rights stems from the fact that human rights protection always depends on the relationship between a reason for such protection and a relevant reason to the contrary. The proposed two-stage-test is modelled symmetrically on the approach used to examine whether a violation of a negative obligation has occurred.

In the first stage, the Court needs to apply a 'protected interests/infringement' conception to the scope of a right: it must establish whether an inaction constitutes an infringement of the 'protected conduct and interests' under a Convention right. If it does, a *prima facie* positive obligation to protect that right arises. An infringement is demonstrated when an individual successfully argues that state inaction had 'any effect' on the 'protected conduct and interest' under a right, on condition that the authorities had been aware or ought to have been aware of the situation concerned. In the interest of legal reasoning, the concept 'protected conduct and interests' necessarily also has to be interpreted widely, in order, principally, to cover everything that the Convention provision concerned suggests should be protected.

In the second stage, the state has to justify its inaction. The extent of the *definitive* positive obligation (or the 'scope of the positive obligation') depends on the criteria of legitimacy and legality and on the need to strike a fair balance. Although traditionally legitimacy and legality tests are not applied in positive obligation cases, it is unreasonable to allow states to base their inaction on manifestly illegitimate considerations, while an inaction that breaks domestic law is fundamentally problematic from the viewpoint of the rule of law. If the state fails to comply with a *definitive* positive obligation that has been shown to exist, it violates the Convention right.

Owing to the lack of a clear, bifurcated approach to positive obligation cases, the Court regularly introduces elements from the second stage into the first stage of the analysis. This should be avoided, however, as it disturbs the distribution of the burden of proof. As illustrated in several disability and environmental cases, the Court should not be tempted by *de minimis* approaches to the scope of Convention rights, as these amount to premature balancing, pre-empting the second stage of the analysis. Equally, it should avoid introducing elements of the legality test into the first stage of the analysis. As human rights have a counter-majoritarian function, the minimum level of protection cannot be made dependent on whether a situation is protected by domestic law.

It should be stressed that the proposed model is not based upon a normative theory concerning the necessary level of human rights protection, but upon a formal theory concerning the structure of human rights. The current application of the positive obligations doctrine is clouded by uncertainty. The proposed model would bring structure into the argument and would undoubtedly be useful in creating consistency in the application of the doctrine.

9

Contested contours

The limits of freedom of expression from an abuse of rights perspective – Articles 10 and 17 ECHR

ANTOINE BUYSE

> Democracies do not become Nazi countries in one day. Evil progresses cunningly, with a minority operating, as it were, to remove the levers of control . . . It is necessary to intervene before it is too late. A conscience must exist somewhere which will sound the alarm to the minds of a nation, menaced by this progressive corruption, to war[n] them of the peril and to show them that they are progressing down a long road which leads far, sometimes even to Buchenwald or Dachau.[1]

1. Introduction

These words of Pierre-Henri Teitgen, the French lawyer and politician who was one of the driving forces behind the drafting of the European Convention on Human Rights (ECHR), reflect the awareness shortly after World War II that democracies need to defend themselves against the threat of totalitarianism. As a former resistance fighter and later as the Minister of Justice responsible for the purges of people who had collaborated with the Nazis, Teitgen might not have been surprised if he had known how very much aware the Nazis themselves were of the potential weaknesses of democracy. Joseph Goebbels, Hitler's propaganda minister, famously wrote that it was one of the best jokes of democracy that it gives its lethal enemies the tools to destroy it.[2]

This article was written as part of my VENI research project on conflict dynamics and free speech, funded by the Netherlands Organisation for Scientific Research (NWO). Case law used for this contribution was scrutinised up to August 2012.

1 Pierre-Henri Teitgen, in a speech before the Consultative Assembly of the Council of Europe in September 1949, cited in E. Bates, *The Evolution of the European Convention on Human Rights. From its Inception to the Creation of a Permanent Court of Human Rights* (Oxford University Press, 2010), p. 44.

2 'Das wird immer einer der besten Witze der Demokratie bleiben, dass sie ihren Todfeinden die Mittel selber stellte, durch die sie vernichtet wurde.' Cited in S. van Drooghenbroek,

The idea of a democracy that is able to defend itself directly touches upon a central dilemma. How does one achieve such an aim without violating fundamental rights, that other important ideal that was fostered in the late 1940s? Too much leeway for freedom of expression or the rights to freedom of association and to form political parties may endanger democracy, when such rights are used by anti-democratic or totalitarian movements. By contrast, too many restrictions on such rights run the risk of destroying freedom and human rights themselves. In the wake of the war, many European states struggled with this dilemma when they restricted or even banned the activities of anti-democratic persons or organisations.[3] The ECHR, adopted in 1950, echoed these concerns by allowing limitations to most of the rights in the Convention and by including an abuse of rights provision in Article 17. While remaining a barely used, symbolic part of the Convention for decades, recent years have seen an increasing, albeit inconsistent application of the provision. This inconsistency is most probably due to the inherent tension between human rights protection and an abuse of rights clause.

A second important dilemma, distinct but related in this context, is the choice between a categorical and a balancing approach to national and international constitutional adjudication. The former reaches decisions by drawing up categories of situations to which certain outcomes apply and thus has the advantage of offering predictability. The latter does so by weighing a broad range of relevant factors. It thereby fosters flexibility by judicial and other decision-makers, tailoring their acts and verdicts to the specifics of the situation at hand.[4] In the context of the European Convention, this problem plays out whenever a choice needs to be made between dismissing a claim by applying the abuse of rights clause, Article 17 ECHR, and assessing a situation under a right that can be limited, such as freedom of expression under Article 10 ECHR. The application of Article 17 functions as a categorical tool of judicial decision-making:

'L'article 17 de la Convention européenne des droits de l'homme est-il indispensable?', (2001) 46 *Revue trimestrielle des droits de l'homme* 541–66, p. 541.

3 S. Sottiaux, 'Anti-democratic associations: content and consequences in Article 11 adjudication', (2004) 22(4) *Netherlands Quarterly of Human Rights* 585–99, p. 585.

4 For a broader discussion of these two methods, as applied to the European Court on Human Rights, see S. Sottiaux and G. van der Schyff, 'Methods of international human rights adjudication: towards a more structured decision-making process for the European Court of Human Rights', (2008) 31 *Hastings International and Comparative Law Review* 115–56.

when a situation falls into the category 'abuse of rights', an applicant will not enjoy the protection of the Convention and an application will be declared manifestly ill-founded. Conversely, rights with limitations – freedom of expression being the key right in this sense – have generally been dealt with by the Court through constitutional balancing.[5] The material assessment of the expression at stake (is it a danger to democracy or not?) thus determines whether the issue is basically dismissed as an admissibility issue or explored further and assessed on its merits. This *categorical* choice settles whether the Court will end up using the balancing method or not – in the ECHR context an additional complication to an already complex debate.

Both dilemmas relate directly to the scope of fundamental rights, first of all in a very principled way, since the outer reaches of the scope of the freedoms of expression and association, for example, also form a circle in the sand. Whoever steps outside it can be considered an enemy of democracy and human rights, against whom the state may use harsher methods and apply further reaching limitations than in ordinary situations. Second, the dilemmas are related to scope in a very practical way. What falls within the (non-protective) scope of Article 17 automatically falls outside the shield of the Convention. From a procedural point of view, this ends a case before the European Court.

In this chapter I will assess the function of the abuse of rights clause, Article 17 ECHR, and more particularly its effects on the scope of rights. First, I will go into the genesis and character of this provision. Subsequently, I will address the relationship between this provision and other Convention articles. This will be followed by an assessment of the jurisprudence of the Court on Article 17 in relation to Article 10, since this is the right to which most abuse of rights cases are linked. As this analysis will show, the Court's case law is not entirely dyadic in that it does not clearly and systematically categorise freedom of expression cases as falling either within the Convention's protective scope (Article 10) or outside it (Article 17). In applying the abuse of rights philosophy in its material assessment under Article 10, the Court *de facto* blurs categorical and balancing aspects of judicial decision-making. The abuse of rights consideration becomes a strong but not always defining factor in a balancing exercise. Finally, the pros and cons of applying Article 17 will be addressed.

[5] *Ibid.*, at p. 133.

2. An unnoticed side entrance: the genesis of Article 17

From the outset, the European Convention on Human Rights was an instrument to which different purposes were ascribed. Most of its founding fathers regarded it as a kind of collective pact against totalitarian regimes at both extremes of the political spectrum: both recent Nazi and fascist dictatorships and contemporary communist regimes. From that perspective, the Court was set in place to function as an alarm bell in the rare cases that could be seen as footsteps on the path to totalitarianism:[6] a true conscience for Europe, as Teitgen's quote at the start of this chapter reminds us. This vision can be seen as one in which the Convention and the Court were symbolically very important, but which would rarely permit the Court to enter into the nitty-gritty of specific cases. The second purpose envisaged was much more practical. Proponents saw the Convention as having the potential to become a true European Bill of Rights. This vision, which included a much more active role for the Court, did not prevail in the beginning, but did become the dominating view of the Convention from the 1970s onwards, eventually evolving into a very active Court deciding thousands of cases a year.[7]

In both visions the protection and realisation of human rights was closely connected to democracy. This is evident from the Preamble to the Convention in which the Contracting Parties reaffirmed 'their profound belief in those fundamental freedoms which are the foundation of justice and peace in the world and are best maintained on the one hand by an effective political democracy and on the other by a common understanding and observance of the human rights upon which they depend'. Thus, the philosophy underlying the Convention was three-pronged: (1) peace and justice were key; (2) to achieve them fundamental freedoms were needed; and (3) to secure those freedoms the twin tools of human rights observance and democracy were crucial. As noted by the British Lord Steyn in the early years of the present century, the drafters realised that, in order to uphold freedom and democracy, human rights need to be limited. Individuals are not islands unto themselves but live in a community and thus the interests of the individual and of the community need to be balanced.[8] An idea that found its way into the Universal Declaration of Human Rights (UDHR) of 1948 is the concept of 'duties to the community

[6] Bates, *The Evolution of the ECHR*, note 1 above, pp. 8 and 53–4. [7] *Ibid.*, at p. 8.

[8] Lord Steyn, 'Human rights: the legacy of Mrs Roosevelt', (2002) *Public Law* 473–84, pp. 479–80.

in which alone the free and full development of his personality is possible'.[9] The final provision of the Declaration, Article 30, is an abuse of rights clause that prohibits activities aimed at the destruction of fundamental rights. The first drafts for a European Convention on Human Rights, by the European Movement, did not include such a clause.[10] However, as soon as the first debates on the Convention started within the Council of Europe, several representatives successfully called for the inclusion of an abuse of rights provision. They referred to the dangers of Nazism, fascism and communism, against which democratic societies should be able to defend themselves.[11] The provision was accepted without much debate or reflection,[12] which shows how uncontested and self-evident it seemingly was. The final text of Article 17 (carrying the heading 'Prohibition of abuse of rights') reads as follows:

> Nothing in this Convention may be interpreted as implying for any State, group or person any right to engage in any activity or perform any act aimed at the destruction of any of the rights and freedoms set forth herein or at their limitation to a greater extent than is provided for in the Convention.[13]

This wording is strongly based on Article 30 UDHR;[14] similar provisions can be found in numerous other universal and regional human rights treaties.[15] As the text shows, Article 17 ECHR is a microcosm for particular instances of what the Convention as a whole is meant to do on a larger scale: to protect democracy and to prevent totalitarianism. This ties in with the idea of a democracy able to defend itself or – from its German original – *wehrhafte Demokratie*, a concept that the Court has recognised in its case law as a legitimate aim of a rights-restrictive policy.[16]

9 Article 29 UDHR.

10 J. Vande Lanotte and Y. Haeck, *Handboek EVRM Deel 2. Artikelsgewijze Commentaar*, vol. II (Antwerp: Intersentia, 2004), p. 244.

11 H. Cannie and D. Voorhoof, 'The abuse clause and freedom of expression in the European Human Rights Convention: an added value for democracy and human rights protection?', (2011) 29(1) *Netherlands Quarterly of Human Rights* 54–83, pp. 56–7, citing the *travaux préparatoires* of the Convention.

12 Van Droogenbroeck, 'L'article 17', note 2 above, pp. 542–3.

13 It must be added that the expression of opinions is also considered to be an 'act' or 'activity' within the meaning of Article 17, as the case law overview below will show.

14 D. Keane, 'Attacking hate speech under Article 17 of the European Convention on Human Rights', (2007) 25(4) *Netherlands Quarterly of Human Rights* 641–63, p. 643.

15 For example, Article 5(1) ICCPR; Article 5(1) ICESCR; Article 29(1) American Convention on Human Rights.

16 ECtHR, *Vogt* v. *Germany*, 26 September 1995 (Application no. 17851/91) para. 51.

3. Character and meaning

Article 17 has a peculiar character in that it addresses the state (on one hand) and private groups and individuals (on the other). It is 'eine besondere Schrankenklausel', as Frowein and Peukert have dubbed it:[17] a special limitation clause. As to its first aspect, addressed to the state, the provision seems rather superfluous as a protection against state abuse. If indeed no greater limitations are allowed than those provided for in the Convention, what then is the added value of an assessment of state action under Article 17? The normal limitation clauses, such as those under Articles 8–11 then seem to apply. This is indeed the logic that the former European Commission on Human Rights and the Court itself implicitly seem to follow. If an interference with a fundamental right is justified under (for example) the freedom of association, then an additional review under the abuse of rights clause is not necessary, as thus far the Court has always found.[18] And if a violation is found under one of the other Convention provisions, the use of the abuse of rights clause does not add much either. In effect, when an applicant invokes Article 17 in addition to another Convention right, it is 'essentially an allegation of bad faith against the state', as Harris *et al.* have asserted.[19] It is indeed difficult to provide proof of such an allegation, which again serves to explain why so far the Court has never dealt with issues from that perspective.[20] Therefore, the rest of this chapter will not deal with this aspect of the abuse of rights clause.

The other aspect of Article 17, directed at individuals and groups, seems to extend rather than to limit the powers of the state. Thus, while one

17 J.A. Frowein and W. Peukert, *Europäische Menschenrechtskonvention. EMRK-Kommentar*, 3rd edn (Kehl am Rhein: Engel Verlag, 2009), p. 430.

18 See e.g. ECtHR (GC), *Refah Partisi* v. *Turkey*, 13 February 2003 (Applications no. 41340/98 and others) para. 137. See also, in this connection, Frowein and Peukert, *ibid.*, at p. 433.

19 D.J. Harris, M. O'Boyle, E.P. Bates and C.M. Buckley, *Harris, O'Boyle and Warbrick. Law of the European Convention on Human Rights*, 2nd edn (Oxford University Press, 2009), p. 652.

20 Vande Lanotte and Haeck, *Handboek EVRM*, note 10 above, pp. 248 and 264. In the *Seurot* case, for example, a schoolteacher was dismissed from his job for having published a vehemently Islamophobic article in the school's magazine. The applicant accused the French state of abuse of rights under Article 17. The Court viewed this claim with such suspicion, considering Seurot's own utterances, that it openly asked itself whether it was not rather his own expressions that would fall outside the sphere of protected freedom of expression by virtue of the abuse of rights clause – before continuing to declare the case inadmissible on other grounds: ECtHR, *Seurot* v. *France* (decision), 18 May 2004 (Application no. 57383/00).

part of the provision protects persons against state abuse, another part takes the protection of the Convention away from people 'in any activity or (who) perform any act aimed at the destruction of any of the rights and freedoms set forth herein'. This is what Vande Lanotte and Haeck have called the boomerang effect of Article 17: those who seek to destroy the human rights of others are effectively barred from successfully invoking those rights themselves.[21] There are limits to the boomerang's range, however. The Article implicitly seems to include a principle of proportionality, although as Van Dijk and Van Hoof concede, that has not really been developed in the jurisprudence.[22] What does emerge is that, even when interfering with the acts of individuals or groups that seek to destroy fundamental rights, the state cannot act outside boundaries. Indeed, one cannot imagine that a life sentence in prison for someone who once denied the Holocaust in public – a category of cases that is normally dealt with under Article 17 by the Court – could ever be considered proportionate under the European Convention. This, however, poses problems *vis-à-vis* the categorical approach to Article 17. If applying Article 17 directly leads to a complaint being ruled inadmissible, then balancing and thus a certain proportionality test seem impossible. Nevertheless, the Commission held in the early *De Becker* case that interferences should be strictly proportionate to the gravity and duration of the threat.[23] In addition, the Court held in one of the judgments in its first case, *Lawless* v. *Ireland*, that 'this provision which is negative in scope cannot be construed *a contrario* as depriving a physical person of the fundamental individual rights guaranteed by Articles 5 and 6 of the Convention'.[24] Thus, procedural rights such as the rights to liberty and to a fair trial cannot be taken away by the state under the cloak of Article 17. We will revisit this inherent tension between the need for some kind of proportionality and the categorical nature of the abuse of rights clause below.

In proceedings before the European Court the double-edged character entails scope for the Article to be invoked by either the applicant or the state – or even by both – to support their arguments.[25] We may note,

21 *Ibid.*, at p. 246.

22 P. van Dijk, F. Van Hoof *et al.*, *Theory and Practice of the European Convention on Human Rights*, 4th edn (Antwerp: Intersentia, 2006), p. 1086.

23 European Commission on Human Rights (ECommHR), *De Becker* v. *Belgium* (report), 8 January 1960 (Application no. 214/56), para. 279.

24 ECtHR, *Lawless* v. *Ireland (No. 3)*, 1 July 1961 (Application no. 332/57) para. 7.

25 Vande Lanotte and Haeck, *Handboek EVRM*, note 10 above, pp. 245–6, and Keane, 'Attacking hate speech', note 14 above, p. 643.

moreover, that Article 17 enables states to act to protect freedoms and democracy, but does not force them to do so. This is a choice for the state to make. Article 17 itself does not impose positive obligations.[26] These may flow, however, from other international treaties, such as the Convention on the Elimination of Racial Discrimination.

Paradoxically, Article 17 reflects the core of the Convention – the protection of human rights and democracy – but does not play a prominent role in case law. Some commentators, as we will see below, would even argue against any autonomous application of the provision. As Cannie and Voorhoof stress, Article 17 is 'a symbolic declaration in the light of which the whole Convention should be read and interpreted'.[27] Van Dijk and Van Hoof would not go that far, but they do affirm that the abuse of rights clause is one of the general principles of the Convention.[28] Thus, even where a case is not brought under the provisions of Article 17 but through another Convention provision, as would normally happen, Article 17 may still be used as an additional tool of interpretation – akin to the role of the ECHR's preamble for example – to assess whether the limitations the state imposes upon the enjoyment of a right are justified.[29] To what extent this plays out in practice will be addressed in section 5 of this chapter.

4. The relationship between Article 17 and other Convention provisions

Article 17 deals with extraordinary situations: those instances in which fundamental rights are threatened with destruction. This seems to go beyond singular violations or even an administrative practice that violates ordinary Convention rights. As indicated previously, here the threat comes from the enemies of democracy. This renders it of a different nature than, for example, that posed by a state that is structurally failing to clean up rubbish thereby violating the right to respect for the home and private life.[30] It is a provision for states to rely upon in situations that do pose a threat but that are not yet so severe as to lead to a state of emergency under Article 15 ECHR.[31] That provision enables states to derogate from

[26] Harris *et al.*, *Law of the ECHR*, note 19 above, p. 652.
[27] Cannie and Voorhoof, 'The abuse clause and freedom of expression', note 11 above, p. 83.
[28] Van Dijk, Van Hoof *et al.*, *Theory and Practice of the ECHR*, note 22 above, p. 1084.
[29] C. Grabenwarter and K. Pabel, *Europäische Mensenrechtskonvention. Ein Studienbuch*, 5th edn (Munich: Verlag C.H. Beck, 2012), p. 134.
[30] ECtHR, *Di Sarno and others* v. *Italy*, 10 January 2012 (Application no. 30765/08).
[31] Harris *et al.*, *Law of the ECHR*, note 19 above, p. 650.

a number of Convention rights, including the freedom of expression, in times of war or other public emergency 'threatening the life of the nation'. This gives Article 17 a place halfway between 'ordinary violations' and states of emergency. Thus, the scope of Article 17 is again important. On one hand its full and direct application seems to exclude the normal tests applied by the Court for other Convention rights. On the other hand it stops short of giving the state a free hand in limiting certain rights as would be possible when derogating from the Convention in times of emergency.

The relationship to articles other than Article 15 is complicated. Van Dijk and Van Hoof assert that the very formulation of Article 17 means 'that its violation is necessarily connected with one or more of the rights and freedoms enumerated in Section one of the Convention and its Protocols. The nature and degree of such connection may vary . . . '.[32] The articles in relation to which the abuse of rights clause seems to be most pertinent are the right to respect for private life, freedom of religion, freedom of expression, freedom of association and the right to free elections.[33] As the Court indicated in the *Lawless* judgment mentioned earlier, the procedural guarantees of the rights to liberty and a fair trial cannot be negated by the state invoking Article 17. The same holds for *notstandsfeste Rechte* such as the right to life, the prohibitions of torture and slavery and the rule *nulla poena sine lege*.[34] Article 15 rules that those cannot be derogated from even in times of emergency. *A fortiori*, neither can the protection of these rights and prohibitions be ignored in the less serious situations that fall within the scope of Article 17. In practice, most instances in which the European Court of Human Rights applies Article 17 directly or indirectly relate to freedom of expression and more rarely to freedom of association – Articles 10 and 11 respectively.[35] Accordingly, the analysis of the case law in the following section will mostly focus on freedom of expression.

5. Case law – ways of applying Article 17

The lack of prominence of Article 17 in the case law of the Convention's supervisory institutions has been called paradoxical, considering how important is the underlying idea of protecting democracy.[36] This paradox

[32] Van Dijk, Van Hoof *et al.*, *Theory and Practice of the ECHR*, note 22 above, p. 1084.

[33] Articles 8–11 and Article 1 of Protocol 1 ECHR respectively.

[34] Articles 2–4 and 7 ECHR respectively. See also Vande Lanotte and Haeck, *Handboek EVRM*, note 10 above, pp. 258 and 260.

[35] Cannie and Voorhoof, 'The abuse clause and freedom of expression', note 11 above, p. 58.

[36] Van Drooghenbroeck, 'L'article 17', note 2 above, p. 542.

may be explained by the two dilemmas of Article 17 mentioned in the introduction: the choice between categorical and balancing approaches in making decisions and the difficulty of squaring the circle of preventing destruction of the rights of many by taking human rights protection away from some. Put differently, it might easily be controversial for applicants or states to invoke the provision and equally open to criticism for the Court to apply it. Still, a small number of cases does exist in which Article 17 played a role. These cases show the difficulty of drawing convincing lines between the scope of the freedom of expression and the reach of the abuse of rights clause.

Article 17 has been applied in three different ways which help to show the different relationships between that provision and other Convention rights. These approaches are: direct application, indirect application, and discarding application of the Article entirely, even when it has been invoked by one of the parties.

5.1 Direct application

The first approach, direct application, poses the most problems since it gives precedence to a categorical approach without the possibility to balance interests and thus assess the proportionality of a state's interference. It also means that Article 17 is applied without an assessment under the relevant substantive right that is part of the complaint in Strasbourg. Direct application precludes a situation from coming within the scope of that other, connected right. This approach has been described as having a guillotine effect:[37] in effect, directly applying Article 17 kills an application. Under the system that applied before the creation of the full-time Court in 1998, the Commission decided admissibility issues. By applying Article 17 directly, it could declare the case manifestly ill-founded. The result was that such a case would not reach the Court. Consequently, the only two pre-1998 instances of direct application are Commission decisions. As if by coincidence, they represent the extreme ends of the political spectrum.

The first was the very early decision (1957) in the case of the *German Communist Party*.[38] The applicants in the case complained about the dissolution and prohibition of the party and the seizure of its assets

[37] See e.g. Vande Lanotte and Haeck, *Handboek EVRM*, note 10 above, p. 249.

[38] ECommHR, *German Communist Party* v. *Germany* (decision), 20 July 1957 (Application no. 250/57).

in what was then West Germany. The German Basic Law provided for state action against anti-democratic parties. The party's aims were the establishment of a socialist-communist system by means of a dictatorship of the proletariat. The Commission held that Article 17 had been designed to safeguard Convention rights 'by protecting the free operation of democratic institutions'.[39] The Commission concluded that recourse to dictatorship for establishing a new political system is incompatible with the ECHR, since it would entail the destruction of many of the Convention rights and freedoms. The application was declared inadmissible. For the Commission it was clear that the party could not invoke any Convention provision, least of all Articles 9, 10 and 11. One might note that the assessment was made on the basis of the stated aims of the party and thus measured by its intentions, irrespective of the real consequences or dangers of the party's actions and irrespective of the degree of interference by the German state. As in earlier history, the guillotine fell without much explicit care for context. This may be explained by implicit and at the time probably widely-held views that countries were allowed to stop the activities of communist parties, especially since such political movements had recently taken power in East Germany, Czechoslovakia and Poland. The Cold War context is thus palpable in the decision. Simultaneously, however, sizeable communist parties against which no such dissolution orders were issued existed in other Council of Europe states such as France and Italy. In any event, clearly the freedoms of expression and association here found their limits in an almost unspoken consensus that orthodox communist political activities could be seen as aimed at destroying Convention rights.

The second case of direct application followed more than two decades later. This time, extreme right-wing political activism was at stake in the application by *Glimmerveen and Hagenbeek*.[40] The applicants complained about their conviction for having possessed (with a view to spreading) political leaflets of a racist nature issued by the political party NVU (*Nederlandse Volksunie* or 'Dutch People's Union') and about the fact that the Dutch state barred them from standing in municipal elections. The leaflets referred to 'our Dutch, white people' and called for the removal of all foreigners from the Netherlands. The party's principles were described by the first applicant as in favour of an ethnically homogeneous society and

[39] *Ibid.*, p. 4.

[40] ECommHR, *Glimmerveen and Hagenbeek* v. *The Netherlands* (decision), 11 October 1979 (Applications no. 8348/78 and 8406/78).

against racial mixing. Again, the Commission applied Article 17 directly and declared the complaints inadmissible. Interestingly, it did so by referring to Article 10's notion of 'duties and responsibilities' which, according to the Commission, are even more strongly reflected in the more general Article 17. The purpose of the latter provision is 'to prevent totalitarian groups from exploiting in their own interests the principles enunciated by the Convention'.[41] It found that the racist utterances of Glimmerveen and Hagenbeek in the leaflets went against 'the text and spirit of the Convention' and could contribute to the destruction of rights.[42] The same was held for the mass removal of non-white people from the country. Again, intentions rather than real or expected consequences were the important consideration – the party had very few sympathisers.

These two decisions, in hindsight, show rare instances of the guillotine effect based on openly stated dictatorial or racist aims. The same can be said of openly racist remarks by Danish youth in a television interview programme for which a journalist was fined. Although the case at the European Court, *Jersild*, was based on an application by the journalist, the Court did mention in passing that the remarks of the youngsters 'were more than insulting to members of the targeted groups and did not enjoy the protection of Article 10'.[43] In other words, the Court alluded to the fact that it would have applied Article 17 directly if the young people themselves had complained in Strasbourg – and it did so with a reference to the Commission's *Glimmerveen* decision. In more recent times it would be more difficult to find explicit racism of this kind in the programmes of political parties. Politicians and others have become better versed in the use of terms that may negatively describe foreigners or people with a different religion without being blatantly racist. Openly anti-democratic party programmes are also rarer than during the Cold War. Moreover, unspoken consensus among European judicial decision-makers about the limits of permissible or forbidden expression might therefore be even more difficult to arrive at.

Tellingly, most of the very few judgments of the European Court in which Article 17 was directly applied concerned facts about which large societal consensus still existed: the abhorrence of Holocaust denial or revisionism. In *Garaudy* the Court had to assess a situation in which the applicant had been convicted, fined and given a suspended term of imprisonment for writing and publishing a book entitled *The Founding*

41 *Ibid.*, p. 195. 42 *Ibid.*, p. 196.

43 ECtHR, *Jersild* v. *Denmark*, 23 September 1994 (Application no. 15890/89) para. 35.

Myths of Israeli Politics which claimed that the Holocaust was a myth.[44] The Court found that denying 'the reality of clearly established historical facts, such as the Holocaust'[45] does not amount to historical research that would be protected by Article 10, since such denial has nothing to do with the quest for truth. Rather, it held that the true aim of Holocaust denial was the rehabilitation of National Socialism and in doing this denial in effect accuses Nazi victims themselves of falsifying history. As a result, it constitutes one of the worst instances of defaming Jews and of incitement to hatred. In the Court's eyes denial undermines the struggle against anti-Semitism and racism and threatens public order. It concluded that it is undisputed that the aims of Holocaust deniers are incompatible with both human rights and democracy. The applicant in this case had tried 'to deflect Article 10 of the Convention from its real purpose by using his right to freedom of expression for ends which are contrary to the text and spirit of the Convention. Such ends, if admitted, would contribute to the destruction of the rights and freedoms guaranteed by the Convention.'[46]

Garaudy was not the first Holocaust denial or revisionism case to reach Strasbourg. Earlier the Commission had dealt with several comparable applications. What is remarkable is the change in the way such applications were dealt with. As Cannie and Voorhoof note, until the late 1980s such cases were simply assessed under the freedom of expression without reference to Article 17.[47] Then, in its 1988 decision in *Kühnen*, the Commission started to apply the abuse of rights clause indirectly. The Court's direct application of Article 17 in *Garaudy* is a culmination of that development, which may be explained by an increasing awareness in the 1980s and 1990s of the pernicious nature of Holocaust denial.

In an earlier French case, *Lehideux and Isorni* – which will be dealt with more extensively below under the indirect approach – the Court had already held that 'the justification of a pro-Nazi policy' would not be given the protection of Article 10, implying that it would also use the guillotine approach for such utterances.[48] According to Oetheimer, this means that,

44 ECtHR, *Garaudy* v. *France* (decision), 24 June 2003 (Application no. 65831/01).

45 *Ibid.* 46 *Ibid.*

47 Cannie and Voorhoof, 'The abuse clause and freedom of expression', note 11 above, p. 60. They refer to ECommHR, *X* v. *Germany*, 16 July 1982 (Application no. 9235/81) and ECommHR, *T* v. *Belgium*, 14 July 1983 (Application no. 9777/82).

48 ECtHR, *Lehideux and Isorni* v. *France*, 23 September 1998 (Application no. 24662/94) para. 53.

as well as engaging in Holocaust denial, justifying any atrocity committed by the Nazis falls within the scope of Article 17.[49]

The reference to the fight against racism and anti-Semitism in *Garaudy* paved the way to direct application of Article 17 in a case that had nothing to do with Holocaust denial as such but rather with direct and open anti-Semitism and also Islamophobia: *Norwood.* Mr Norwood had been fined for displaying, in the months immediately following the terrorist attacks of 2001, a poster that depicted the burning Twin Towers and a crescent and star in a prohibition sign. The caption was 'Islam out of Britain – Protect the British People'. The Court found this to be a 'general, vehement attack' against all Muslims in the United Kingdom. Connecting a whole religious group with grave acts of terror was considered incompatible with the Convention's values, specifically 'tolerance, social peace and non-discrimination'.[50] The specifics of the context were not taken into account, although the applicant had tried to convince the Court that the poster had not provoked any violence, that the countryside where he lived did not suffer from racial or religious tensions, and that no Muslim had seen the poster. These were irrelevant to the Court – intentions rather than consequences seem to have been decisive.

In *Ivanov*, the Court used the same guillotine approach in dismissing the complaint of a newspaper publisher who had been convicted in Russia for writing a series of articles in which he depicted Jews as the cause of evil in the country. He labelled them as fascists and alleged that they had engaged in a conspiracy against the Russian nation. The Court:

> has no doubt as to the markedly anti-Semitic tenor of the applicant's views and it agrees with the assessment made by the domestic courts that he sought through his publications to incite hatred towards the Jewish people.[51]

Once again, a general and vehement attack on an ethnic group was deemed to be in contradiction with the Convention's underlying values – the same ones mentioned in the *Norwood* decision.

More than just the denial or justification of the Holocaust or other Nazi crimes falls within the scope of Article 10. In addition, the Court

[49] M. Oetheimer, 'Protecting freedom of expression: the challenge of hate speech in the European Court of Human Rights case law', (2009) 17 *Cardozo Journal of International and Comparative Law* 427–43, p. 432.

[50] ECtHR, *Norwood* v. *United Kingdom* (decision), 16 November 2004 (Application no. 23131/03).

[51] ECtHR, *Ivanov* v. *Russia* (decision), 20 February 2007 (Application no. 35222/04).

held in *Orban* – a case concerning a book about the Algerian war of independence – that expressions that clearly aim at justifying war crimes such as torture or summary executions would deflect Article 10 from its real purpose. In the case at hand, the Court concluded that this had not been the aim of the book and therefore it did not apply Article 17.

The jurisprudential guillotine has also fallen in two situations relating to the freedom of association. The first concerned a Polish group of applicants that had been barred from forming a 'National and Patriotic Association of Polish Victims of Bolshevism and Zionism'.[52] The Court held that they could not rely on Article 11 but rather that the situation came within the scope of Article 17. It had become clear from the organisation's memorandum of association that the applicants alleged that the Poles had been persecuted by the Jewish minority and that there was inequality between them. The Court found, as Poland itself had also argued, that this could be seen as reviving anti-Semitism. In addition, the applicants' racism had also become clear from the anti-Semitic tone of some of the submissions they made in Strasbourg.

The second instance, the case of *Hizb Ut-Tahrir*, shows that calls for violence and destruction of states fall outside the scope of the Convention's rights and within the scope of Article 17.[53] The case concerned an Islamic association that had been proscribed in Germany, since it had advocated the violent destruction of Israel and the killing of its citizens, and justified suicide attacks against them. The Court concluded that such calls are contrary to the Convention's values, specifically 'the peaceful settlement of international conflicts' and 'the sanctity of human life'.[54]

What transpires from the above is that, first, the Court deems Article 17 applicable in situations that relate directly to its original aim of preventing totalitarian movements from abusing the Convention. But it goes further: the article also applies to the denial of (or revisionism about) crimes committed by Nazism and fascism in World War II, pre-eminently the Holocaust, and other war crimes or crimes against humanity. Third, it covers open instances of racism, anti-Semitism and Islamophobia; and fourth, open calls to violence.[55] All these categories are problematic, however, both from the perspective of proof and from that of scope; not just

[52] ECtHR, *WP and others* v. *Poland* (decision), 2 September 2004 (Application no. 42264/98).

[53] ECtHR, *Hizb Ut-Tahrir and others* v. *Germany* (decision), 12 June 2012 (Application no. 31098/08).

[54] *Ibid.*, para. 74.

[55] See e.g. ECtHR, *Yazar and others* v. *Turkey*, 9 April 2002 (Applications no. 22723/93 and others), para. 49.

because intentions are not always clear, but also because the question of what is a clearly established historical fact is very often open to debate.

5.2 Indirect application

While direct application of Article 17 is quite rare and in the Court's own words to be effected 'only on an exceptional basis and in extreme cases',[56] the indirect approach is more common in the Court's jurisprudence. This approach has been labelled a weak or soft form of applying Article 17,[57] in which underlying values such as the protection of democracy are included in the rights and interests to be balanced under the third prong of the test of limitations of rights – the assessment whether an interference was necessay in a democratic society. Here, situations are perceived to fall within the scope of freedom of expression, for example, but Article 17 serves as a strong magnetic pole that often draws the judicial compass-needle towards the conclusion that no violation of the right has occurred. Thus, the soft form is not weak: the practical difference from direct application of Article 17 is small when one looks at outcomes.[58] Nevertheless, one could argue that, by balancing and thus opening up the option to look at the proportionality of the interference, state excesses could be tackled.

The 1988 Commission decision in *Kühnen* was the first in which it applied Article 17 indirectly. The application concerned an alleged attempt to reinstitute the NSDAP (German Nazi Party). At the national level Kühnen was sentenced to more than three years' imprisonment for having spread propaganda relating to an unconstitutional organisation. It may be that the fact that a rather severe deprivation of liberty was at stake here caused the Commission to opt for indirect application; or this may have been triggered by the fact that the domestic court had extensively argued the case. In any event, in deciding whether the interference with Kühnen's rights had been necessary in a democratic society, the Court held that his activities had run counter to one of the Convention's basic values, democracy, and more generally it added that he had been 'essentially seeking to use the freedom of information enshrined in Article 10 of the Convention as a basis for activities which are, as shown above, contrary to the text and spirit of the Convention and which, if admitted,

[56] ECtHR (GC), *Paksas* v. *Lithuania*, 6 January 2011 (Application no. 34932/04), para. 87.

[57] See respectively Vande Lanotte and Haeck, *Handboek EVRM*, note 10 above, p. 251, and van Drooghenbroeck, 'L'article 17', note 2 above, p. 551.

[58] See also, in that respect, Cannie and Voorhoof, 'The abuse clause and freedom of expression', note 11 above, pp. 67–8.

would contribute to the destruction of the rights and freedoms set forth in the Convention'.[59] The Commission concluded that the interference by the state had thus been necessary. Ever since, the Commission's application of Article 17 has been indirect.[60] Many such cases have related to Holocaust denial or revisionism.[61]

The Court applied Article 17 indirectly in *Lehideux and Isorni*,[62] a case about a book that tried to revise the role of Philippe Pétain, the head of the collaborating French Vichy regime during World War II, in a positive light. The Court found that the criminal conviction of the applicants had not been necessary and thus found a violation of Article 10. It applied a proportionality analysis, but was at pains to distinguish the case from situations of Holocaust revisionism to which Article 17 would directly apply. In its judgment, the Court did this by first stating that the role of Pétain was still controversial and that in their writings the applicants did condemn the Nazi atrocities and thus the policy but did not mention Pétain's role in collaborating and thereby contributing to the deportation of Jews. Thus, in the Court's view the case centred on a controversy about the person rather than the policy. The Court was divided over the issue: fifteen votes against six. The dissenters argued, amongst other things, that such issues should be left within France's margin of appreciation, since they concerned an issue peculiar to that country's history, which could be better decided by national than by international courts.

There is no clear system in the Court's choice whether to apply Article 17 directly or indirectly. In *Kaptan*, a case about anti-Turkish publications, the Court held that the writings advocated and glorified violence and therefore fell outside the scope of Article 10. It stated this, paradoxically, as part of its assessment of necessity under Article 10 and then concluded that the interference by the state had been necessary in a democratic society. This use of the three-step limitations test becomes all the more puzzling, since this was not a judgment but an admissibility decision in which the Court declared the complaint manifestly ill-founded.[63]

Even more extremely, in the case of *Schimanek*, the necessity test consisted of nothing more than a reference to Article 17. Schimanek was an active promoter of National Socialism and had been imprisoned for these

59 ECommHR, *Kühnen* v. *Germany*, 12 May 1988 (Application no. 12194/86).

60 Vande Lanotte and Haeck, *Handboek EVRM*, note 10 above, p. 251.

61 For a large number of references to such cases, see Cannie and Voorhoof, 'The abuse clause and freedom of expression', note 11 above, p. 60.

62 See note 48 above.

63 ECtHR, *Kaptan* v. *Switzerland* (decision), 12 April 2001 (Application no. 55641/00).

activities. The Court accepted Austria's claim that his conviction had been necessary by holding that his ideology was totalitarian and irreconcilable with human rights and democracy. It considered that without any doubt adherents of National Socialism had aims of the kind referred to in the abuse of rights provision of the ECHR. It thus concluded, without further ado – and thus in fact virtually entirely based on the national court's assessment of the facts – that Schimanek's conviction had been necessary under Article 10.[64]

Two admissibility decisions concerning the same applicant show the same lack of a systematic approach. Mr Witzsch, a Bavarian schoolteacher, had been involved in Holocaust denial and revisionism. This led the Court to dismiss his claims on the issue. It held that denying that mass killings in gas chambers had occurred and calling references to them a historical lie 'amounted to disparaging the dignity of the deceased who had a particularly cruel fate'.[65] After referring to Article 17, the Court somewhat puzzlingly stated that it:

> has previously held that the negation or revision of clearly established historical facts – such as the Holocaust – would be removed from the protection of Article 10 by Article 17 . . . Against this background, the Court finds that the public interest in the prevention of crime and disorder due to disparaging statements regarding the Holocaust, and the requirements of protecting the interests of the victims of the [N]azi regime, outweigh, in a democratic society the applicant's freedom to impart views denying the existence of gas chambers and mass murder therein.[66]

This seems incoherent because it explicitly refers to earlier case law removing Article 10 protection from Holocaust denial but then goes on to balancing rhetoric under Article 10. Is this because the applicant had claimed before the domestic courts not to have wanted to deny the Holocaust, or is it because the Court thought balancing would make its decision more convincing? Having been convicted for another act of revisionism later on, Witzsch again lodged a complaint to Strasbourg. This time the Court's patience had apparently run out. It emphasised that even if in this case Witzsch had not denied the Holocaust as such, he had

> denied an equally significant and established circumstance of the Holocaust considering it false and historically unsustainable that Hitler and the NSDAP had planned, initiated and organised the mass killing of Jews.

64 ECtHR, *Schimanek* v. *Austria* (decision), 1 February 2000 (Application no. 32307/96).
65 ECtHR, *Witzsch* v. *Germany* (decision), 20 April 1999 (Application no. 41448/98).
66 *Ibid.*

> The applicant's statement that the opinion expressed by W[67] was part of the war propaganda and after-war atrocity propaganda combined with the denial of Hitler's and the National Socialists' responsibility in the extermination of the Jews showed the applicant's disdain towards the victims of the Holocaust. The Court finds that the views expressed by the applicant ran counter to the text and the spirit of the Convention. Consequently, he cannot, in accordance with Article 17 of the Convention, rely on the provisions of Article 10 as regards his statements at issue. The fact that they were made in a private letter and not before a larger audience is irrelevant insofar.[68]

Same applicant, very similar context, even same outcome to the case, but a different application of Article 17: it fails to convince.

A final and very important reflection of indirect application of the abuse of rights clause can be seen in a case about freedom of association in political parties. In a much debated Grand Chamber judgment the Court held that the dissolution of the *Refah Partisi* (Welfare Party), Turkey's main Islamic political party at the time, had been justified under the Convention.[69] It considered that the application of Article 17 could only be decided *after* an assessment of whether the limitations imposed by the state had accorded with paragraph 2 of Article 11. In that context, it pointed out that a 'compromise between the requirements of defending democratic society and individual rights is inherent in the Convention system'.[70] This unequivocal Grand Chamber pronouncement seems to be a strong indication that the Court would prefer a balancing approach – the mention of a compromise implies this – as opposed to a categorical approach. This, in turn, would entail a broad scope for the freedoms of association and expression – since it is under those provisions that balancing is possible. In *Refah Partisi* the crux of the matter for the Court was that the party was regarded as wanting to replace a free and pluralistic democracy with a theocratic system.[71] That strikes at the heart of the original purpose of Article 17: to protect democracy and thereby fundamental rights. The Court noted that it was 'not at all improbable that totalitarian movements, organised in the form of political parties, might do away with democracy, after prospering under the democratic regime, there

67 A professor of history whose views had been published in a German weekly review.
68 ECtHR, *Witzsch* v. *Germany* (decision), 13 December 2005 (Application no. 7485/03).
69 *Refah Partisi* v. *Turkey*, note 18 above.
70 *Ibid.*, para. 96.
71 A. Nieuwenhuis, 'The concept of pluralism in the case-law of the European Court of Human Rights', (2007) 3(3) *European Constitutional Law Review* 367–84, p. 381.

being examples of this in modern European history'.[72] However, restrictions to political activities should be construed strictly. Consequently, it developed a strict test which contains three criteria:

> (i) whether there was plausible evidence that the risk to democracy, supposing it had been proved to exist, was sufficiently imminent;
> (ii) whether the acts and speeches of the leaders and members of the political party concerned were imputable to the party as a whole; and
> (iii) whether the acts and speeches imputable to the political party formed a whole which gave a clear picture of a model of society conceived and advocated by the party which was incompatible with the concept of a 'democratic society'.[73]

To all intents and purposes, although the Court does not explicitly state that it has applied Article 17 in the context of Article 11 here, the test is a clear elaboration of the abuse of rights clause applied in an indirect manner.[74] What also transpires from this, is that when assessing state interference with political parties, not just the intent matters – as in the older cases about communist or Nazi parties – but also an assessment of consequences. This is what the imminence of the risk to democracy points at.[75]

5.3 No application

Cases in which Article 17 seemed relevant but was not applied fall in two categories. First, there are cases in which applications are dismissed in admissibility decisions that do not use or mention Article 17, but that concern situations similar to those in which Article 17 has been applied. The Commission did this in a number of cases, mostly in the 1950s, 60s, and 70s, concerning persons convicted for or prevented from undertaking Nazi or fascist activities.[76] The Court has decided similarly in a case of Islamophobic speech.[77] The Grand Chamber judgment of the Court in *Refah Partisi*, although in practice an example of indirect application, is also an instance of no explicit application, strictly speaking. However, *Refah Partisi* is the odd one out. This brings us to the second category of non-application: situations in which Article 17 is brought forward by the

72 *Refah Partisi* v. *Turkey*, note 18 above, para. 99. 73 *Ibid.*, para. 104.
74 Vande Lanotte and Haeck, *Handboek EVRM*, note 10 above, p. 258.
75 Sottiaux, 'Anti-democratic associations', note 3 above, p. 599.
76 See e.g. ECommHR, *X* v. *Austria*, 1 December 1963 (Application no. 1747/62). For more references, see Vande Lanotte and Haeck, *Handboek EVRM*, note 10 above, p. 254.
77 ECtHR, *Le Pen* v. *France* (decision), 20 April 2010 (Application no. 18788/09).

state, but the Court decides that the issue falls outside the clause's scope of application. Thus, in all party dissolution cases in which Turkey invoked Article 17 apart from *Refah Partisi*, the Court dismissed the arguments.[78] The Article pops up in such cases, but they are decided by applying the usual three-pronged test. One example out of a number of similarly decided cases may illustrate this. In the case of *The United Communist Party*, a party that had been dissolved by Turkey before it had undertaken any political activities, the state argued that Article 17 should be applied since Turkey should be able to prohibit the forming of parties 'that would inevitably incite violence and enmity between the various sections of Turkish society'. But the Court found nothing in the party's constitution or programme to justify concluding that 'it relied on the Convention to engage in activity or perform acts aimed at the destruction of any of the rights and freedoms set forth in it'.[79] What would take a party's activities outside the scope of Article 10 or 11 and bring them within Article 17 ECHR's range, is recourse to violence.[80] Other examples of the Court's refusal to apply the abuse of rights clause, without further explanation, include instances of racist or xenophobic speech.[81]

6. Conclusion – pros and cons of applying Article 17

The overview of case law has shown that one of the main problems with the application of Article 17 is its high degree of unpredictability. This lack of predictability concerns the scope of the right – and consequently the connected material right at stake, for they are like two connected vessels – and it is *caused* by the two main underlying dilemmas inherent in Article 17: first, its function as a tool to restrict human rights in order to protect human rights and democracy, and second, its categorical function or guillotine effect when applied directly. The first issue calls for restraint in order to prevent alleged abuse of rights by an individual leading to actual abuse of rights by the state: an overly broad application of the abuse clause would endanger human rights protection and the rule of law

78 See also, for references to more case law in this context, K. Pabel, 'Parteiverbote auf dem europäischen Prüfstand', (2003) 63 *Zeitschrift für ausländisches öffentliches Recht und Völkerrecht* 921–44, p. 936.

79 ECtHR (GC), *United Communist Party of Turkey and others* v. *Turkey*, 30 January 1998 (Application no. 19392/92), paras 21 and 60 respectively.

80 *Ibid.*, para. 57.

81 ECtHR, *Féret* v. *Belgium*, 16 July 2009 (Application no. 15615/07).

itself.[82] The second issue means that a proportionality test is impossible if Article 17 is applied directly. These two matters help to explain why the Commission and the Court have not been consistent in their application of the Convention's abuse clause.

In principle, the underlying rationale of Article 17, to protect democracy, freedom and human rights against their enemies, is as appealing as it is crucial. The scope of each substantive ECHR right is meant to metaphorically shrink in order to exclude 'liberticidal' activities (acts aimed at destroying liberties). By applying Article 17 directly, argue the rare proponents of this approach, such as van Drooghenbroeck, democracy can be protected by a clear shield rather than by obscured and diluted case-by-case approaches. It would even allow for encroachment upon the core of rights of the enemies of freedom.[83] Also, by toning down loud racist or anti-democratic voices, the state can be seen ideally as levelling the playing field of free speech in order to give room to those attacked by such speech, such as religious or racial minorities.[84] One could add that, symbolically, the very inclusion of the abuse clause in the Convention can send a strong signal about the function of human rights and the key need to uphold democracy. However, practice shows that it is very difficult to decide which acts and activities aim at the destruction of human rights and democracy. Especially if one conceives the path towards totalitarianism as a long road, it is hard to decide at what point exactly its traveller crosses the bridge from activities that deserve protection – including criticism of democracy itself – to truly dangerous activities. It requires a deep dive beneath the surface of appearances to assess the precise context and exactly this need to evaluate a situation substantively causes the categorical approach to become entangled with a balancing approach.

Consequently, the intended simple shield has in practice turned out to be a panoply of possibilities. There are four broad categories in which the Court has deemed Article 17 to potentially apply:

(1) totalitarian/anti-democratic parties or movements;
(2) denial or revision of the Holocaust and other war crimes and crimes against humanity;
(3) open racism, anti-Semitism and Islamophobia, and
(4) open calls to violence.[85]

[82] Frowein and Peukert, *EMRK-Kommentar*, note 17 above, p. 432.
[83] Van Drooghenbroeck, 'L'article 17', note 2 above, pp. 546–50 and 563–5.
[84] Keane, 'Attacking hate speech', note 14 above, pp. 658–60.
[85] See section 5.1 of this chapter.

This broad range of possible material fields of application also represents a gradual shift from the classic cases of totalitarian threat to broader issues (such as racism) that go against the Convention's values. This shift, critics justifiably argue, is undesirable because it is overly broad in denying human rights protection and in preventing an assessment of the proportionality of state interference.[86]

The possibility of applying a proportionality test exists under most of the relevant substantive rights of the Convention, including freedom of expression. No matter how hideous or even dangerous a particular expression is, from a human rights perspective the assessment of proportionality is crucial. If states were allowed to inflict extreme punishments on the enemies of democracy, this would be just as prone to undermine that very democracy as liberticidal activities themselves. Thus, if Article 17 is to play a role it should be indirectly.[87] This connects to the other complex issue: the Court would avoid having to decide on the scope of Article 17 and constantly treading on the fault line. For example, nowadays new forms of potentially hurtful or dangerous speech, such as those related to acts of terrorism or religious intolerance – currently more prevalent than openly racist speech – are mostly dealt with by the Court under Article 10, even though there would be equally good reasons to apply Article 17 as well in those situations.[88] No longer are pernicious expressions often of the kind envisaged by the drafters of the Convention.

It could be presumed that all expressions fall within the scope of Article 10. One example may illustrate the Gordian knot, cutting which could thus be avoided. It relates to the second category of potential Article 17 applications. As shown above, the Strasbourg supervisory mechanism has mainly focused on Holocaust denial and revisionism and referred more broadly to Nazi and fascist war crimes. This is understandable, considering the European context and the original reasons for creating the European Convention. Two aspects are problematic, however. The first is that it is not easy to defend why the line should be drawn there. In general, the Court is a proponent of free debate on historical issues. Controversial viewpoints may be expressed as long as they do not spark off 'any controversy that was gratuitous or detached from

86 See generally Cannie and Voorhoof, 'The abuse clause and freedom of expression', note 11 above, and also Keane, 'Attacking hate speech', note 14 above, p. 656.

87 For example Van Dijk, Van Hoof *et al.*, *Theory and Practice of the ECHR*, note 22 above, pp. 1086–7.

88 Cannie and Voorhoof, 'The abuse clause and freedom of expression', note 11 above, pp. 73–4, and Keane, 'Attacking hate speech', note 14 above, p. 663.

the reality of contemporary thought'.[89] Holocaust denial falls outside this part of the scope of Article 10. But what about other debatable perspectives on history? The *Fatullayev* case shows that more than just holding a view that differs from prevailing state orthodoxy on a historical event is required to trigger Article 17. Azerbaijan invoked the article against a journalist who had expressed slightly revisionist views about an Azeri massacre by Armenians in the early 1990s. The Court did not accept this attempt to have the application declared inadmissible for abuse of rights. The journalist had done nothing to deny the killings as such, nor had he sought to exonerate the culprits completely, he had simply offered an alternative version of the exact circumstances.[90] To what extent Article 17 would be applied directly to the denial of massacres more recent than World War II – like the genocide in Srebrenica – remains unclear. The tension remains between applying Article 17 when the Court is of the view that a historical fact is uncontested (on one hand) and its recognition that its role does not extend to arbitrating historical issues in ongoing debates (on the other).[91]

The second problematic aspect is that another of the underlying issues, respect for the feelings of victims, has not been consistently addressed by the Court. Expressing contempt for victims of Nazism or other totalitarian regimes can amount to an abuse of rights under Article 17.[92] At the same time, in cases about the public display of symbols that could cause unease and feelings of disrespect in victims of regimes that used those symbols, the Court held that such sentiments could not be invoked to set the limits of free expression, or else the latter would be subject to 'the heckler's veto'.[93] In *Lehideux and Isorni* the Court considered that:

> [e]ven though remarks like those the applicants made are always likely to reopen the controversy and bring back memories of past sufferings, the lapse of time makes it inappropriate to deal with such remarks, forty years on, with the same severity as ten or twenty years previously. That forms

89 ECtHR, *Giniewski* v. *France*, 31 January 2006 (Application no. 64016/00), para. 50.

90 ECtHR, *Fatullayev* v. *Azerbaijan*, 22 April 2010 (Application no. 40984/07), para. 81.

91 For the latter view on its own role, see the Court's judgment in *Chauvy and others* v. *France*, 29 June 2004 (Application no. 64915/01), para. 69.

92 ECtHR, *Fáber* v. *Hungary*, 24 July 2012 (Application no. 40721/08), para. 58, with further references.

93 ECtHR, *Vajnai* v. *Hungary*, 8 July 2008 (Application no. 33629/06), para. 57 (display of the red star, used by the former communist regime) and *Fáber*, *ibid.*, para. 57 (display of the striped flag used both by Árpád and by the former fascist regime).

> part of the efforts that every country must make to debate its own history openly and dispassionately.[94]

The outer limits of this, in the Court's view, are instances of intimidation and speech that is capable of inciting violence. These categories of course yield new problems in defining the scope of rights since this depends on whether one looks at causes or effects, intentions or consequences. Indeed, the formulation of Article 17 with its wording 'aimed at the destruction' seems to put an emphasis on intentional behaviour, which fits ill with the concern for the true potential dangers, and thus consequences, for democracy.

Thus it seems both desirable – since this enables a proportionality test – and necessary – the boundaries of the scope of Article 17 are almost impossible to define convincingly – to favour the indirect over the direct application of Article 17. Since in the outcome of most cases there has generally been little or no difference between direct and indirect application,[95] Voorhoof and Cannie argue that it should be taken one step further: discarding the use of Article 17 altogether. In their view, the article should be, as mentioned above, merely a symbolic provision 'in the light of which the whole Convention should be read and interpreted'.[96] It is difficult to see how this differs in principle from the indirect approach. The proportionality test and the weighing of relevant contextual factors are also enlightened by Article 17 under that approach. However, the Court does not do this consistently at the moment, rather using Article 17 as a trump card at times, even under its Article 10 assessment. Nothing, however, precludes the Court from systematically taking all relevant contextual factors into account. Specifically, in the assessment of the existence of a 'pressing social need' (an element of the necessity test), the Court could take into account the extent to which the expression at stake is a threat to other rights or democracy. If it did so, the disadvantages of the current uses of Article 17 would be offset. In addition, in order to increase the level of predictability, it would be helpful if the Court applied 'structured balancing' in such cases. This approach, advocated by Sottiaux and van der Schyff, would indeed elucidate which specific elements of context the Court deems relevant in cases of threats to democracy. They mention the factors expounded by the Court in *Refah Partisi* under Article 11 as a

94 *Lehideux and Isorni*, note 48 above, para. 55.
95 Keane, 'Attacking hate speech', note 14 above, p. 661.
96 Cannie and Voorhoof, 'The abuse clause and freedom of expression', note 11 above, p. 83.

good example.[97] The same could be done in Article 10 cases. The Court, for example, should clarify how the role of pernicious political discourse should be taken into account in the balancing exercise.[98] In this way a better balance between flexibility and predictability could be achieved.

Obviously, the approach advanced here would not address all issues, since the problem of distinguishing intentions and possible consequences remains, but at least a balanced contextual approach becomes possible under Articles 10 and 11 if one avoids applying Article 17 directly.[99] One could thus say that in principle every expression should fall within the scope of Article 10 and thus outside that of Article 17. As this chapter has sought to explain, the contours of Article 17 are not only contested but also similar to an oil spill at sea: constantly changing. Even though the facts of life and law are constantly in flux like the sea, measures for clearer containment do not seem sufficient. Rather, it is best to clean up the oil and remain vigilant for further traces of spills in the sea. A structured balancing approach that includes a proportionality test under the substantive rights of the Convention is thus to be preferred. Only when applied consistently, but with nuance, can the alarm bell to which Teitgen referred ring with real effect.

[97] Sottiaux and van der Schyff, 'Methods of international human rights adjudication', note 4 above, pp. 154–5.

[98] This remains a very difficult issue, since negative discourse about either certain minorities or the democractic state itself might not be dangerous in the immediate short term, but weaken democracy and human rights over time. Accordingly, it could be taken into account in the proportionality analysis.

[99] See e.g. Oetheimer, 'Protecting freedom of expression', note 49 above, pp. 441–2, on ways to take the role of political discourse into account, and at 434–9, on the factors taken into account by the Court, unsystematically, in deciding cases of hate speech and incitement to violence under Article 10 ECHR. I do therefore disagree, at least in the abuse of rights context, with Croquet who argues that the over-inclusiveness of the Court in defining the scope of most rights is problematic: N. Croquet, 'The European Court of Human Rights' norm-creation and norm-limiting processes: resolving a normative tension', (2010–11) 17 *Columbia Journal of European Law* 307–73.

PART 3

360° comparison

10

Bottom-up shaping of rights

How the scope of human rights at the national level impacts upon Convention rights

EIRIK BJORGE

1. Introduction

This chapter endeavours to answer the following question: what determines whether the European Court of Human Rights (European Court; ECtHR) takes inspiration from domestic courts in its shaping of the scope of the rights under the European Convention on Human Rights (ECHR)? It will be argued that the European Court is minded in principle to accept the approach of national courts to Convention rights when it is clear from the ruling of the domestic courts in issue that they have attempted in perfect good faith to uphold those rights or to strike a fair balance between what is necessary in a democratic society and the right of the individual in issue. In other words, when the domestic courts show that, in determining the scope of the rights in issue, they have applied the Convention rights in good faith and to the very best of their ability, the European Court will go far in agreeing with the result they have reached. When, conversely, the domestic courts take a less comprehensive approach to Convention rights then the European Court will take another view of the matter.

It is to be expected that the legal reasoning of the European Court would borrow explicitly or implicitly from some of the highest jurisdictions at the national level, and that this would show, for example, in its reasoning with respect to the scope and structure of fundamental rights.[1] The present chapter examines this matter from the particular angle of the

In addition to thanking the editors and Paul Craig for their very useful comments to earlier drafts of this chapter, the author would like to thank Guy Goodwin-Gill, Dapo Akande, Ruvi Ziegler, Antonios Tzanakopolous, Thomas Lieflaender, and Lawrence Cawthorne-Hill for very valuable comments when this paper was presented at All Souls College, Oxford, on 31 October 2012.

[1] See J. Gerards and H. Senden, 'The structure of fundamental rights and the European Court of Human Rights', (2009) 7 *International Journal of Constitutional Law* 619–53.

United Kingdom. In order to amplify the argument it will nonetheless also make some references to cases against other states, and by extension the approaches taken by the courts in those states. The point is not to examine how, in their work as international judges, the judges of the European Court bring to bear the legal concepts of their home systems. It is rather to examine the judicial dialogue with the European Court into which the UK Supreme Court has entered concerning the scope of Convention rights. Nor is this chapter about UK legal concepts as such impacting upon the interpretation of ECHR provisions but rather about an interpretation of such provisions that allows for some measure of domestic idiosyncracy.

The chapter takes as its points of departure statements by perhaps the two greatest British lawyers of the last century, both of whom had the singular quality of combining in their wide-ranging legal careers not only national law and European human rights law but also public international law, showing that they were able, to use a classic formulation, to move 'freely over the boundaries, which seem to divide these fields of law and to bring out the underlying unities'.[2]

The first of these two lawyers is Sir Arnold McNair, Judge at the International Court of Justice, later Lord McNair, the first President of the European Court of Human Rights. In 1946, at a Grotius Society meeting in the Middle Temple, he expressed his worry that the common law of England as developed by many generations of English lawyers was not exerting the proper influence in building up a comprehensive system of international law. Unless in future English lawyers would devote more time and interest to the subject of international law, both as practitioners and as members of international tribunals, he feared English law would not pull its weight in establishing the rule of law between nations.[3]

Sir Thomas Bingham MR, later Lord Bingham, Senior Law Lord of the United Kingdom, in an address to his colleagues at the bar in the Middle Temple in 1992, struck the same chord that McNair had struck some fifty years earlier, arguing that 'the ability of English judges to protect human rights in this country and reconcile conflicting rights in the manner indicated is inhibited by the failure of successive governments over many years to incorporate into United Kingdom law the

[2] A.D. Denning, 'Foreword', (1952) 1 ICLQ 1, 1.

[3] A.D. McNair, 'International law in practice', (1946) 32 *Transactions of the Grotius Society* 154, pp. 164–5.

European Convention on Human Rights and Fundamental Freedoms'.[4] He furthermore made the point that incorporating the Convention into English law 'would help to reinvigorate the faith, which our eighteenth and nineteenth century forebears would not for an instant have doubted, that these were fields in which Britain was the world's teacher, not its pupil'.[5]

This point, that British law was effectively estopped from influencing the development of European law by the fact that British judges could not really rely in their judgments upon Convention law, Bingham developed further when he told the House of Commons that 'British judges have a significant contribution to make in the development of the law of human rights. It is a contribution which so far we have not been permitted to make.' To drive his point home (and tailoring its presentation to its audience as skilfully as McNair had done his) Lord Bingham quoted a seventeenth-century forebear, John Milton, who in his *Areopagitica* had made famous the exhortation that Bingham in his twentieth-century context artfully made his own: 'Let not England forget her precedence of teaching nations how to live'.[6]

This approach was very much part of conventional wisdom in the period leading up to incorporation into United Kingdom law of the ECHR. Looking back, we might now feel surprised that this was a part of the incorporation rationale. So it was, nonetheless. Witness two examples from the debate in the United Kingdom in the 1990s. First, the White Paper (government report giving information about a proposal), *Rights Brought Home: The Human Rights Bill*, explained:

> The Convention is often described as a 'living instrument' because it is interpreted by the European Court in the light of present day conditions and therefore reflects changing social attitudes and the changes in the circumstances of society. In future our judges will be able to contribute to this dynamic and evolving interpretation of the Convention.[7]

Second, one of the frustrations of non-incorporation, according to Jack Straw, the Home Secretary at the time just before incorporation, had been that the judges in the United Kingdom 'have not been able to bring their

[4] T. Bingham, 'The European Convention on Human Rights: time to incorporate', (1993) 109 LQR 390, 390; reprinted in T. Bingham, *The Business of Judging: Selected Essays and Speeches* (Oxford University Press, 2000), p. 131.

[5] *Ibid.*, p. 140.

[6] 28 HL Deb, Vol. 582, col. 1245 (3 November 1997).

[7] *Rights Brought Home: The Human Rights Bill, 1997*, Cm. 3782, para. 2.5.

intellectual skills and our great tradition of common law to bear in the development of European Convention jurisprudence'.[8]

The same has to some extent been expressed by judges from the European Court. The then Vice-President of the European Court, Françoise Tulkens, at a European gathering of judges at Strasbourg in 2010, said that the European Court 'can and must enrich its own scrutiny by reflecting on national decisions in which Convention law is analysed'.[9] In 2011 former President of the European Court Sir Nicolas Bratza expressed the view that there could indeed be lines of cases in which the national courts, in the event the British courts, were legitimately dissatisfied with the European Court's definition of the scope of a right and that, as a consequence of the national courts expressing these misgivings, the European Court would in certain cases be willing to change its course. Such a back-and-forth between the UK Supreme Court and the European Court (in the case he was discussing) over how to define a right under the ECHR went entirely with the grain of the ECHR system and could, Sir Nicolas concluded, 'only serve to cement a relationship between the two courts'.[10]

Against this background, it could reasonably be asked whether, within the context of the European Convention on Human Rights, there is much purchase in such statements or whether we ought instead to treat them more critically. In this chapter I will not venture to establish whether the incorporation of the ECHR into UK law in fact has resulted in the change that Lord Bingham implied would follow from incorporation. Rather, this chapter will ask whether the European Court, when giving shape to certain expansions or limitations of the scope of Convention rights, has taken inspiration from the British courts. The answer is 'yes'. As will be seen, the European Court has gone very far in taking into account British conceptions of rights. One element in the more recent jurisprudence of the Court that merits our interest in this regard is how explicit it has been in doing so.

8 HC Deb, Vol. 313, col. 424 (3 June 1997). Also B. Hale, '*Argentoratum locutum*: is Strasbourg or the Supreme Court supreme?', (2012) 12 *Human Rights Law Review* 65, pp. 70–71.

9 European Court of Human Rights, *Dialogue between Judges* (Council of Europe, 2010), p. 9.

10 N. Bratza, 'The relationship between the UK courts and Strasbourg', [2011] *European Human Rights Law Review* 505, p. 512.

2. UK influences in the shaping of ECHR rights

It is a well known fact that British lawyers, together especially with French ones, were instrumental in the drafting of the Convention. Famously, it was in the committee chaired by Sir David Maxwell-Fyfe, later Lord Kilmuir,[11] and Pierre-Henri Teitgen, a French professor of international law and minister of justice in de Gaulle's postwar cabinet,[12] that agreement on many of the most important issues was reached. Just how well these architects of the Convention were able to weld material from the common and the civil law is perhaps attested by the reception which Article 6 ECHR has received in English and French law. As Stirn, Fairgrieve, and Guyomar have pointed out:

> il est frappant de relever que l'article 6 de la Convention européenne est souvent présenté en France comme un produit dérivé de *common law*, certainement parce que la notion de procès équitable s'est à l'origine inspirée de celle de *natural justice*, alors qu'il est décrit au Royaume-Uni comme un levier utilisé par les juristes de droit continental pour modifier celle-ci.[13]

If these influences, both in the drafting of the rights such as they appear in the Convention text and later in the jurisprudence of the Commission and of the Court, were largely left to inference at the outset, in the last few decades they have become increasingly clear.

2.1 Courts martial: independence and impartiality in light of Article 6

Thus, for example, the issue of courts martial in the United Kingdom furnishes an apposite example of the European Court taking inspiration from UK courts in defining the scope of the rights protected by Article 6. In *Findlay* v. *United Kingdom* the European Court held that the

[11] See D.P. Maxwell-Fyfe, *Political Adventure: The Memoirs of the Earl of Kilmuir* (London: Weidenfeld & Nicholson, 1964), pp. 174–89.

[12] See L. Burgorgue-Larsen, *La Convention européenne des droits de l'homme* (Paris: LGDJ, 2012), p. 18.

[13] B. Stirn, D. Fairgrieve and M. Guyomar, *Droits et libertés en France et au Royaume-Uni* (Paris: Odile Jacob, 2006), p. 259 ('it is striking to note that Article 6 of the European Convention is often presented in France as a product deriving from the common law, no doubt because the notion of a fair trial originally took inspiration from that of natural justice, while it is decribed in the United Kingdom as a lever used by continental jurists to change the common law'). See more generally H. Muir Watt and D. Fairgrieve, *Common law et tradition civiliste* (Paris: PUF, 2006).

UK had acted in violation of Article 6(1) of the Convention when a soldier successfully challenged the court martial procedure on grounds of lack of independence and impartiality.[14] Then, in 1996, the United Kingdom court martial procedure was reformed in new legislation. Later, in 2002, in *Morris* v. *United Kingdom*,[15] the Strasbourg Court held that the new legislation also ran foul of the Convention. As, however, another case, *R* v. *Spear & Others*,[16] reached the House of Lords in 2002, before new legislation could be introduced in response to the Strasbourg Court's adverse decision in *Morris*, Lord Bingham found that, though it was for UK courts to accept the decisions of the European Court, the legislation in issue satisfied the requirements of independence and impartiality. In the wake of *Spear & Others*, a unanimous Grand Chamber of the European Court overturned their *Morris* ruling in *Cooper* v. *United Kingdom*,[17] drawing on Lord Bingham's analysis in *Spear & Others* and giving its imprimatur to his conclusions.[18]

As adumbrated above, however, in *Spear & Others* Lord Bingham crucially did not say that the House of Lords could choose not to follow the decisions of the Strasbourg Court. He rather pointed out that in point of fact they *were* following it.

2.2 Brown *v.* Stott: *the right to remain silent under Article 6*

In *Brown* v. *Stott* the Procurator Fiscal sought to use the claimant's answer that she had been driving (obtained under s 172(2)(a) of the Road Traffic Act 1988) as the basis for a prosecution for driving while drunk.[19] The Board of the Privy Council found that this 'leading' of evidence did not amount to a breach of Article 6, although the ruling by the European Court in *Saunders* might *prima facie* suggest that in fact it would.[20] The House of Lords was very critical of the way in which the European Court had defined the scope of the Article 6 rights in issue in *Saunders*.[21]

14 *Findlay* v. *United Kingdom* (1997) 24 EHRR 221.

15 ECtHR 26 February 2002; (2002) 34 EHRR 1253.

16 *R.* v. *Spear and others* [2002] UKHL 31; [2003] 1 AC.

17 ECtHR 16 December 2003, *Cooper* v. *United Kingdom*; (2004) 39 EHRR 8.

18 M. Andenas and D. Fairgrieve, '"There is a world elsewhere" – Lord Bingham and comparative law' in Andenas and Fairgrieve (eds), *Tom Bingham and the Transformation of the Law* (Oxford University Press, 2009), pp. 831–66.

19 *Brown* v. *Stott* [2003] 1 AC 681 (PC).

20 ECtHR (GC), *Saunders* v. *United Kingdom*, judgment 17 December 1996, Application No. 19187/91.

21 *Brown* v. *Stott*, note 19 above, pp. 711 (Lord Steyn) and 721 (Lord Hope).

O'Halloran concerned the absoluteness of the rights contained in Article 6: the privilege against self-incrimination and the right to remain silent. The question was whether, although the provisions contain no exceptions, these rights could be said to be legitimately abridged by reference to legitimate aims in the public interest.[22] The applicant contended before the ECtHR that the right to remain silent and the right not to incriminate oneself were absolute rights and that to apply any form of direct compulsion to require an accused person to make incriminatory statements against their will would of itself destroy the very essence of those rights. This the Court was unable to accept.[23] It held that '[w]hile the right to a fair trial under Article 6 is an unqualified right, what constitutes a fair trial cannot be the subject of a single unvarying rule but must depend on the circumstances of the particular case'.[24] In this regard the Grand Chamber of the European Court explicitly relied on the conclusions of Lord Bingham in *Brown* v. *Stott*, citing his words that '[a]ll who own or drive motor cars know that by doing so they subject themselves to a regulatory regime. This regime is imposed not because the possession and use of cars (like, for example, shotguns . . .) are recognised to have the potential to cause great injury.'

Having regard to a set of circumstances, including the special nature of the regulatory regime in issue and the limited nature of the information sought by a notice under s 172 of the Road Traffic Act 1988, the European Court considered that the essence of the applicant's right to remain silent and the privilege against self-incrimination had not been destroyed and that accordingly there had been no violation of Article 6(1). It seems clear that it was the argumentative force of Lord Bingham's judgment that swayed the European Court in defining the scope of Article 6 in respect of the right to remain silent in the same way as the House of Lords had done for traffic law.

2.3 The Horncastle *and* Al-Khawaja *saga*

Perhaps the most striking recent example, however, of the European Court borrowing from the reasoning of the UK Supreme Court is to be found

22 See N. Bamforth and L.C. Hoyano, *Human Rights Law and Principles in the United Kingdom* (Oxford University Press, 2014).

23 ECtHR (GC), *O'Halloran and Francis* v. *United Kingdom*, judgment 29 June 2007, Applications No. 15809/02 and 25624/02, para. 53.

24 *Ibid.*

in the cases *R* v. *Horncastle*[25] and the ruling by the Grand Chamber of the European Court in *Al-Khawaja and Tahery* v. *United Kingdom.*[26] In the latter case the European Court arguably went very far in taking its cues from the UK courts in defining the scope of the right guaranteed by Article 6. To explain this, it is necessary to say a few words about the background of the two cases.

The question that the Supreme Court faced in *Horncastle* was whether a conviction based 'solely or to a decisive extent' on the statement of a witness whom the defendant had no chance of cross-examining necessarily infringes on the defendant's right to a fair trial under Articles 6(1) and 6(3)(d) ECHR. The most recent Strasbourg authority on the issue was the Chamber judgment in *Al-Khawaja and Tahery* v. *United Kingdom.*[27] In the two applications jointly adjudged in this Chamber judgment, at a criminal trial statements had been admitted in evidence of a witness who was not called to testify. The Chamber held that, in both cases, the statement was the 'sole or, at least, the decisive basis' for the applicant's conviction. The Chamber then took as one starting-point the statement in *Lucà v. Italy*[28] that

> where a conviction is based solely or to a decisive degree on depositions that have been made by a person whom the accused has had no opportunity to examine or to have examined, whether during the investigation or at the trial, the rights of the defence are restricted to an extent that is incompatible with the guarantees provided by Article 6.[29]

Neither the Court of Appeal nor the Supreme Court accepted in *Horncastle* that the Strasbourg Court's ruling in *Al-Khawaja* should be determinative of the results of the appeals in the case before them. Both courts held that, in the circumstances of each of the appeals, the claimants had received a fair trial.[30] On 16 April 2009 the United Kingdom requested, under Article 43(1) of the Convention, that the Chamber decision in *Al-Khawaja* be referred to the Grand Chamber and it informed the Court that at that time the Supreme Court was about to hear *Horncastle.* On 5 June 2009 a Panel of the Grand Chamber adjourned consideration of

[25] *R* v. *Horncastle and others* [2009] UKSC 14; [2010] 2 WLR 47.

[26] ECtHR (GC), *Al-Khawaja and Tahery* v. *United Kingdom*, judgment 15 December 2011, Applications No. 26766/05 and 22228/06.

[27] *Ibid.*; (2009) 49 EHRR 1.

[28] ECtHR 27 February 2001, *Lucà* v. *Italy* (2001) 36 EHRR 807.

[29] *Ibid.*, para. 40.

[30] *Horncastle*, note 25 above; also [2009] EWCA Crim 964; [2009] WLR 173.

the request pending the Supreme Court's judgment in *Horncastle*.[31] This gave the Supreme Court a chance to have its say on the issue.

The claimants had submitted that the Supreme Court must treat *Al-Khawaja* as determining the success of their appeals. This, they argued, would be the appropriate response to the requirement of s 2(1) of the Human Rights Act 1998 (HRA) which requires a court to 'take into account' any judgment of the Strasbourg Court in determining any question to which such a judgment is relevant. It was submitted in this regard that the decision of the House of Lords in *Secretary of State for the Home Department* v. *AF (No 3)* exemplified the correct approach to a decision of the Strasbourg Court.[32] In that case their Lordships had held themselves bound to apply a clear statement of principle by the Grand Chamber covering the precise issue with which the House was faced.

A unanimous Supreme Court in *Horncastle* could not accept the claimants' submission:

> The requirement to 'take into account' the Strasbourg jurisprudence will normally result in this Court applying principles that are clearly established by the Strasbourg Court. There will, however, be rare occasions where this court has concerns as to whether a decision of the Strasbourg Court sufficiently appreciates or accommodates particular aspects of our domestic process. In such circumstances it is open to this court to decline to follow the Strasbourg decision, giving reasons for adopting this course. This is likely to give the Strasbourg Court the opportunity to reconsider the particular aspect of the decision that is in issue, so that there takes place what may prove to be a valuable dialogue between this court and the Strasbourg Court.[33]

Though this non-acceptance was a surprising move by the Supreme Court, it is not the first time one has seen signs of British judges taking issue with Strasbourg jurisprudence.[34] As was seen above the same was the case with the interplay between the House of Lords and the European Court in the matter of courts martial. As adumbrated above, however, in *R* v. *Spear & Others* Lord Bingham crucially did not say that the House of Lords could choose not to follow the decisions of the Strasbourg Court. Rather, he clarified that the House of Lords was in fact following it. *Horncastle* is

[31] *Horncastle*, note 25 above, para. 9.

[32] *Secretary of State for the Home Department* v. *AF (No 3)* [2009] UKHL; [2009] 3 WLR 74. See generally P. Craig, 'Perspectives on process: common law, statutory and political', [2010] *Public Law* 275.

[33] *Horncastle*, note 25 above, para. 11.

[34] See Andenas and Fairgrieve, '"There is a world elsewhere"', note 18 above.

different, in that it says not only that in reality English law is conforming with the precepts of Article 6 of the Convention, but also that even if this were not the case, there is effectively no reason for the Supreme Court to follow the Strasbourg jurisprudence.

The idea of a dialogue between judges was readily accepted by the Supreme Court in *Horncastle*. To the dialogue the Supreme Court submitted nine conclusions of which the Supreme Court 'hope[d] that in due course the Strasbourg Court may also take account'.[35] The Supreme Court put forth as perhaps the most salient of its conclusions that in the United Kingdom there are safeguards designed to protect a defendant against unfair prejudice as a result of the admission of hearsay evidence, seen in the context of the more general safeguards that apply to every jury trial. These include the concept that the trial judge acts as a gatekeeper and has a duty to prevent the jury from receiving evidence that will have such an adverse effect on the fairness of the proceedings that it ought not to be received. Hearsay evidence is admissible only in strictly defined circumstances, in which the judge is satisfied beyond reasonable doubt that the prosecution is not able to adduce the evidence by calling the witness.[36]

It bears mention, however, that as recently as 2008 in *R* v. *Davis*,[37] the House of Lords had held unanimously that it was a

> long-established principle of the English common law that, subject to certain exceptions and statutory qualifications, the defendant in a criminal trial should be confronted by his accusers in order that he may cross-examine them and challenge their evidence.[38]

What the Supreme Court said in *Horncastle* was really three things: in the first place, the 'sole or decisive rule' is not a good rule.[39] Second, in any case it does not follow from the Strasbourg jurisprudence.[40] And third, moreover the Supreme Court is not bound by this rule.[41] This led Lord Phillips, with whose judgment all members of the Court agreed, to conclude with the following:

[35] *Horncastle*, note 25 above, para. 47. [36] *Ibid.*, para. 38.

[37] *R* v. *Davis* [2008] UKHL 36; [2008] AC 1128.

[38] *Ibid.*, para. 5. See *Duke of Dorset* v. *Girdler* (1720) Prec Ch 531–2, 24 ER 238. Lord Bingham also cited Sir Matthew Hale, *The History of the Common Law of England*, 6th edn (1820), pp. 345–6; William Blackstone, *Commentaries on the Law of England Bk. III*, 12th edn (1794), p. 373; Jeremy Bentham, *Rationale of Judicial Evidence Vol II, Bk III* (1827), pp. 404, 408, 423.

[39] *Horncastle*, note 25 above, paras 76–94.

[40] *Ibid.*, paras 63–75. [41] *Ibid.*, paras 10–11.

> In these circumstances I have decided that it would not be right for this court to hold that the sole or decisive test should have been applied rather than the provisions of the 2003 Act, interpreted in accordance with their natural meaning. I believe that those provisions strike the right balance between the imperative that a trial must be fair and the interests of victims in particular and society in general that a criminal should not be immune from conviction where a witness, who has given critical evidence in a statement that can be shown to be reliable, dies or cannot be called to give evidence for some other reason. In so concluding I have taken careful account of the Strasbourg jurisprudence. I hope that in due course the Strasbourg Court may also take account of the reasons that have led me not to apply the sole or decisive test in this case.[42]

In an article published on the eve of the Grand Chamber's decision in *Al-Khawaja* the President of the European Court had the following to say about *Horncastle*:

> I believe that it is right and healthy that national courts should continue to feel free to criticise Strasbourg judgments where those judgments have applied principles which are unclear or inconsistent or where they have misunderstood national law or practices. But I also believe that it is important that the superior national courts should, as Lord Phillips put it in the *Horncastle* judgment, on the rare occasions when they have concerns as to whether a decision of the Strasbourg Court sufficiently appreciates or accommodates particular aspects of the domestic process, 'decline to follow the Strasbourg decision, giving reasons for adopting this course'. If, as has happened in the case of *Al-Khawaja*, Strasbourg is given the opportunity to reconsider the decision in issue, what takes place may indeed as Lord Phillips put it, 'prove to be a valuable dialogue between this court and the Strasbourg Court'. I firmly believe that such dialogue can only serve to cement a relationship between the two courts which, whatever criticisms may be levelled against the Strasbourg Court, is a sound and solid one.[43]

In its ruling the Grand Chamber ceded some ground to the Supreme Court, admitting that where a hearsay statement is the sole or decisive evidence against a defendant, its admission as evidence will not automatically result in a breach of Article 6(1). Where, however, a conviction is based solely or decisively on the evidence of absent witnesses, the court in the case must subject the proceedings to the most searching scrutiny. Because, the Grand Chamber continued (citing Lord Mance in *R* v. *Davis*), of the dangers of the admission of such evidence it would constitute a very

42 *Ibid.*, para. 108.

43 Bratza, 'Relationship between UK courts and Strasbourg', note 10 above, p. 512.

important factor to balance in the scales, and one that would require sufficient counterbalancing factors, including the existence of strong procedural safeguards.[44] The question in each case would therefore be whether there were sufficient counterbalancing factors in place, including measures that permit a fair and proper assessment of the reliability of that evidence to take place.[45]

Baroness Hale commented on the judgment of the Grand Chamber thus: 'the Grand Chamber ruled that the "sole or decisive" rule should not be applied in an inflexible manner, nor should they ignore the specificities of the particular legal system concerned. A head-on collision was thus skilfully avoided.'[46] This is obviously true in the sense that the European Court took inspiration from the approach of the Supreme Court when it came to the scope of the Article 6 rights in this case. It may be, however, that political exigencies and the pressure under which the European Court has been finding itself in the last few years, rather than the argumentative force of the *Horncastle* ruling, made the Court change its mind. At all events, given Lord Bingham's judgment in *R* v. *Davis*, it is not clear that while there may be extreme occasions on which a national court should be able to say no, this was a very good case in which to do so. One commentator, not entirely convinced of the salutary effects of *Al-Khawaja*, took the following position:

> What is genuinely bizarre was the Supreme Court's choice of subject matter. It did not go to bat on behalf of a fundamental common law principle. Instead, it went to bat against it, on behalf of the same dodgy piece of legislation that eroded the right of trial by jury and raised the maximum period of pre-charge detention from seven to 14 days.[47]

It is in any event true, as Bruno Genevois has pointed out, that the national courts are those best placed to gauge the impact of particular aspects of Strasbourg case law, and that it is therefore important that the possibility of dialogue exists,[48] so as to allow for adjustments, such as those that the Grand Chamber of the European Court allowed in *Al-Khawaja*.

[44] See generally Letsas's chapter in this book.

[45] *Al-Khawaja and Tahery*, note 26 above, para. 147 (internal references omitted).

[46] Hale, '*Argentoratum locutum*', note 8 above, p. 76.

[47] E. Metcalfe, 'Time for the UK Supreme Court to think again on hearsay', *The Guardian*, 15 December 2011.

[48] B. Genevois, 'Cour eurpopéenne des droits de l'homme et juge national : dialogue et dernier mot' in *Mélanges en l'honneur de Jean-Paul Costa* (Paris: Dalloz, 2011), pp. 281 and 291.

2.4 Countryside Alliance *in the House of Lords and in Strasbourg*

The House of Lords in *Countryside Alliance* touched upon the issue of deference to Parliament in what could be termed the shaping of the protection offered by Article 1 of the First Protocol of the ECHR.[49] This case alleged that the Hunting Act 2004, which prohibited the hunting of wild mammals with dogs, breached Article 1 of Protocol No. 1. While concluding that Article 1 was engaged, the House of Lords held that the restriction was proportionate. In so holding the House of Lords, in Craig's analysis, afforded to the legislature a wide margin of discretionary judgment on a controversial matter of social policy.[50] Lord Bingham in that regard highlighted the dangers of upsetting the democratic process if 'on a question of moral and political judgment, opponents of the Act achieve through the courts what they could not achieve in Parliament'.[51] It may, of course, be added that very few cases before the courts claiming that legislation is in breach of the ECHR will be immune to the criticism raised by Lord Bingham here. Indeed, it is difficult to see why the fact that a group had skilfully pushed the levers of parliamentary democracy ought subsequently to disadvantage their HRA bid before the courts; this might have the effect that if the group had not mobilised in respect of the issue during the legislative process then they would later have a greater chance of winning before the courts, which again would potentially discourage democratic participation.

This does not mean, however, that the result reached in the event by the House of Lords was wrong. In fact the claimants took their cause to Strasbourg, where the European Court agreed with the House of Lords over the point made by the Law Lords on how broad a margin of discretion to accord to Parliament. The European Court concluded that 'the domestic courts have given the greatest possible scrutiny to the applicants' complaints under the Convention and especially those complaints brought under Article 1 of Protocol No. 1'. This went for all the national courts that had been seized of the case. Serious reasons would therefore be required for the Court to depart from the clear findings of those courts.[52]

[49] *R (Countryside Alliance)* v. *Attorney General* [2008] 1 AC 719.

[50] P. Craig, *Administrative Law*, 7th edn (London: Sweet & Maxwell, 2012), p. 619.

[51] *Countryside Alliance*, note 49 above, para. 45.

[52] *Friend* v. *United Kingdom*; *Countryside Alliance* v. *United Kingdom* 50 EHRR SE6, para. 58. Also *R (Sinclair Collins Ltd)* v. *Secretary of State for Health* [2012] 2 WLR 304, para. 175 (Arden LJ).

3. The approach of national courts is not necessarily unitary

As the *Horncastle* saga shows, very often the domestic courts or judges of one country do not in fact all reach the same view as to the scope of a given right. Instead, as is clear from comparing Lord Bingham's judgment in *R* v. *Davis* with that of Lord Phillips in *Horncastle*, they may take views that rather are at variance with one another. What one sees is a national discourse with different strands. This is important for the discussion here, as it may have direct implications for the extent to which the European Court will feel legitimised to arrive at a result that gives to the right in issue a broader scope than the top court did.

Examples of this are not difficult to find. When in 2003 the Strasbourg Court decided finally to take seriously changes in the law of the European states and allow a state to not recognise the gender change of post-operative transsexuals, it did so in reliance on the arguments provided by the UK Court of Appeal.[53] As the European Court's former President Sir Nicolas Bratza, who presided, has recently pointed out, in this case the Court was 'emboldened to go further than it might otherwise have done in the protection of human rights by the decision and reasoning of the English Court of Appeal'.[54] It is also worth remembering, though this is perhaps more tangential to the current discussion, that the view espoused before the European Court by a government is not always the same as that of the national courts or the top national court. A prominent instance of this was *A* v. *United Kingdom* where before the Grand Chamber the UK government explicitly argued against the position of the House of Lords concerning derogation from Article 5.[55] The Strasbourg Court, on this issue, could then find against the United Kingdom by agreeing with the House of Lords. We saw this mechanism too in the views espoused by Lord Bingham and Lord Mance in the jurisprudence anterior to *Horncastle*. These views were picked up, and explicitly cited at length, by the dissenting judges in *Horncastle* v. *United Kingdom*.[56]

It is often assumed, and for good reason, that though the logic of the European Convention does focus to some extent upon the way in which national authorities go about guaranteeing the Convention rights

[53] *Bellinger* v. *Bellinger*, [2001] EWCA Civ 1140, 3 FCR 1.

[54] Bratza, 'Relationship between UK courts and Strasbourg', note 10 above.

[55] ECtHR (GC), *A* v. *United Kingdom*, judgment 19 February 2009, Application No. 3455/05, para. 190.

[56] See *Al-Khawaja and Tahery*, note 26 above, joint dissenting and partly concurring opinions of Judges Sájo and Karakas.

(for example whether the courts ask the right questions), particularly in the form of proportionality, what matters is for the national courts to reach the right result in terms of Convention rights. Such an approach – applied to the relationship between the European Court on one hand and the national authorities, including the top national court, on the other – is of course not unprecedented in the Strasbourg jurisprudence. In *Chapman* v. *United Kingdom*, for example, the European Court held that:

> [i]n particular, [the Court] must examine whether the decision-making process leading to measures of interference was fair and such as to afford due respect to the interests safeguarded to the individual by Article 8.[57]

Perhaps what the Grand Chamber of the European Court held in *Von Hannover* v. *Germany (No 2)* ought to be seen as an instance, at least in questions relating to the balancing of rights, of the European Court in effect adopting just such an approach, one which focuses upon the decision-making process of the national court more than just the 'bottom line' or the result reached. The back-story is well known and will not be rehearsed here.[58] Suffice it to say that in *Von Hannover* v. *Germany* the European Court had struck a different balance between privacy and freedom of speech than had the German courts,[59] putting a heavier thumb on the scale in favour of privacy than what followed from postwar German constitutional tradition. In the end, however, the German courts, at least to some extent, would come round to the view of the European Court. Thus the German Constitutional Court, in the case that was to become *Von Hannover (No 2)* when it reached the European Court, took a deferential stance towards what the European Court had held in the first *Von Hannover* v. *Germany*.[60] It ruled that, in the context of Article 5(2) of the Basic Law, Article 8(1) of the Convention guarantees to an individual the right to be protected by the state's courts against the publication of

[57] ECtHR 18 January 2001, *Chapman* v. *United Kingdom* (2001) 33 EHRR 399, para. 92.

[58] It is well described by K.S. Ziegler, 'The Princess and the Press: privacy after *Caroline von Hannover* v. *Germany*' in Ziegler (ed.), *Human Rights and Private Law: Privacy as Autonomy* (Oxford: Hart Publishing, 2007), p. 189; H.J. Cremer, *Human Rights and the Protection of Privacy in Tort Law: A Comparison Between English and German Law* (London: Routledge–Cavendish, 2011); S.C. Lenski, 'Human rights protection in multipolar legal relationships' in K.S. Ziegler and P.M. Huber (eds), *Current Problems in the Protection of Human Rights: Perspectives from Germany and the UK* (Oxford: Hart, 2013), p. 143.

[59] ECtHR, *Von Hannover* v. *Germany*, judgment 24 June 2004, Application No. 59320/00.

[60] 1 BvR 1602, pp. 1606 and 1626–7, BVerfGE 120, p. 180.

images taken from the individual's everyday life. Article 8(1) thus influences the constitutionally protected right to freedom of speech. This the German Court did by saying that the constitutional guarantee of the right to develop one's personality and the protection of privacy guaranteed by Article 8 ECHR are in harmony, as the former makes reference to the 'sum of the personal, social and economic relations which are constitutive of the private life of every human being'.[61] Cremer has interpreted this as the German Court 'bringing constitutional and Convention requirements in line', not least because the European jurisprudence on balancing between privacy and freedom of speech was relied on by the German court.[62] Given the importance accorded by the German courts to the *Von Hannover* line of cases, and to the issue of balancing between privacy and freedom of speech, much seemed to ride on how the Grand Chamber would settle *Von Hannover* v. *Germany (No 2)*.

The Grand Chamber took the following approach. Seeing that the German Court had 'carefully balanced the right of the publishing companies to freedom of expression against the right of the applicants to respect for their private life', while 'attaching fundamental importance' to the parameters highlighted in the European jurisprudence, as well as 'explicitly [taking] account of the Court's relevant case law',[63] the Grand Chamber found that, 'having regard to the margin of appreciation enjoyed by the national courts when balancing competing interests', the German Court was not at fault.[64] Thus the European Court changed no less than its understanding of what constitutes free speech, moving from its initial position, set out in the first *Von Hannover* case, according to which the freedom to publish celebrity news would by definition be the handmaid of celebrities' privacy interests, to a recalibrated position that took some inspiration from the initial German position according to which one cannot distinguish between important and unimportant speech. If the Grand Chamber deemed this change of position to be correct, then that must surely have been because the German court had shown willingness to change its position and because of the salutary judicial dialogue that had given way to it.

61 *Von Hannover*, note 59 above, para. 201. See Cremer, *Human Rights*, note 58 above, pp. 90–92.

62 ECtHR, *Minelli* v. *Switzerland*, judgment 14 June 2005, Application No. 14991/02; ECtHR, *Gurgenidze* v. *Georgia*, judgment 17 October 2006, Application No. 71678/01.

63 ECtHR (GC), *Von Hannover* v. *Germany (No 2)*, judgment 7 February 2012, Applications No. 40660/08 and 60641/08, para. 124.

64 *Ibid.*, para. 125.

It seems reasonable at this point to sum up what has been said in this section. What in Bruno Genevois's coinage has been called 'le dialogue des juges'[65] is at times taken to mean that national courts reassert their autonomy *vis-à-vis* the European Court.[66] Another perspective is to see the dialogic exchanges more as an effort of cooperation in good faith.[67]

As was seen above, after the European Court had handed down its judgment against Germany over the protection of privacy in *Von Hannover* v. *Germany*,[68] the German Federal Constitutional Court made considerable concessions in respect of how it balanced the protection of privacy (of celebrities) against the freedom of expression (of newspapers). It went far in putting a heavier thumb on the scales in favour of the protection of privacy than it had done hitherto. The German Court conceded that:

> [i]n balancing the conflicting legal values, taking into account the presumption, emanating from Art[icle] 5(1) of the Basic Law ... that reporting by the press aiming at a contribution to the formation of a public opinion is allowed, freedom of expression guaranteed by Art[icle] 10(1) ECHR is to be accorded special weight where reporting by the press contributes to matters of general interest.[69]

This goes some way to proving the wish of the German court to harmonise the standards applying to the rights under the Basic Law and Convention rights; the German court in this case, perhaps more than ever before in its rights jurisprudence, took seriously the influence both of Convention rights and of the European Court's interpretations of them.[70]

Andreas Voßkuhle, President of the German Constitutional Court, has said that the idea that, in constitutional terms, a national court has the

[65] B. Genevois, 'Conclusions' in *Cohn-Bendit*, Conseil d'État decision, 6 December 1978.

[66] H.J. Papier, 'Das Bundesverfassungsgericht im Kräftefeld zwischen Karlsruhe, Luxemburg und Straßburg' in H.P. Hestermeyer *et al.* (eds), *Coexistence, Cooperation and Solidarity* (Leiden: Brill, 2012), p. 2045; M. Amos, 'The dialogue between United Kingdom courts and the European Court of Human Rights', (2012) 61 ICLQ 557; N. Krisch, *Beyond Constitutionalism: The Pluralist Structure of Post-National Law* (Oxford University Press, 2010).

[67] A. Voβkuhle, 'Multilevel cooperation of the European constitutional courts: *Der Europäische Verfassungsgerichtsverbund*', (2010) 6 *European Constitutional Law Review* 175; A. Stone Sweet, 'A cosmopolitan legal order: constitutional pluralism and rights adjudication in Europe', (2012) 1 *Global Constitutionalism* 53; M. Andenas and E. Bjorge, 'National implementation of ECHR rights' in A. Follesdal, B. Peters and G. Ulfstein (eds), *Constituting Europe: The European Court of Human Rights in a National, European and Global Context* (Cambridge University Press, 2013), 181.

[68] Note 59 above. [69] *Von Hannover (No 2)*, note 63 above, para. 203.

[70] Cremer, *Human Rights*, note 58 above, p. 92.

last word does not contradict the idea of multilevel dialogue between European courts, 'so long as he who has the last word is willing to learn at the same time as he is speaking'.[71]

Seeing that the traditional German conception of freedom of speech has been that all types of speech are potentially of equal importance,[72] the European Court rightly saw this as an instance of the German court adopting Strasbourg's approach. It noted that the Federal Court of Justice had changed its approach in the wake of *Von Hannover* v. *Germany*, and that the Federal Constitutional Court, for its part, had 'not only confirmed that approach, but also undertaken a detailed analysis of the Court's case law in response to the applicants' complaints that the Federal Court of Justice had disregarded the Convention and the Court's case law'.[73] The Grand Chamber of the European Court concluded that:

> [i]n those circumstances, and having regard to the margin of appreciation enjoyed by the national courts when balancing competing interests, the Court concludes that the latter have not failed to comply with their positive obligations under Article 8 of the Convention. Accordingly, there has not been a violation of that provision.[74]

As will have been seen above, much the same could be said of *R* v. *Horncastle* and the ruling by the Grand Chamber of the European Court in *Al-Khawaja and Tahery* v. *United Kingdom*.[75] As was adumbrated in 2011 by then President Sir Nicolas Bratza, the European Court will be minded in principle to accept the approach of the national courts to ECHR rights when it is clear that the national courts have attempted in good faith to uphold Convention rights or to strike a fair balance between what is necessary in a democratic society and the right of the individual in issue.[76] This can also be seen in the examples discussed above bearing upon the Court's review of parliamentary debates, such as the *Countryside Alliance* cases.[77] The European Court felt confident in handing down an adverse judgment in *Lindheim*, where the national parliament had

[71] A. Voßkuhle, 'Menschenrechte im Europäischen Verfassungsgerichtsverbund', speech at the Berlin–Brandenburgische Akademie des Wissenschaften, 22 October 2011: 'muss einem Dialog im Europäischen Verfassungsgerichtsverbund nicht entgegenstehen, solange derjenige, der das letzte Wort spricht, beim sprechen lernt'.

[72] See the Federal Constitutional Court's first *Von Hannover* ruling: BVerfG, 1 BvR 653/96. See also Lenski, 'Multipolar legal relationships', note 58 above, p. 143.

[73] *Von Hannover (No 2)* , note 63 above, para. 125.

[74] *Ibid.*, para. 126.

[75] *Horncastle*, note 25 above. *Al-Khawaja and Tahery*, note 26 above.

[76] Bratza, 'Relationship between UK courts and Strasbourg', note 10 above.

[77] *Countryside Alliance*, note 49 above; *Friend*, note 52 above, para. 58.

taken an almost cavalier attitude to questions falling under Article 1 Protocol 1 and the striking of a 'fair balance' under that right.[78] Conversely, the Court felt confident in *not* finding a breach of the same article in *Friend* (the Strasbourg continuation of *Countryside Alliance*),[79] since all the national courts that had been seized of the case in the United Kingdom had 'given the greatest possible scrutiny to the applicants' complaints under the Convention and especially those complaints brought under Article 1 of Protocol No. 1'.[80] In the view of Sir Stephen Sedley, both a former Court of Appeal judge and an ad hoc Judge in the European Court, in the last few years that court has moved 'beyond the basic concept of the margin of appreciation towards the more profound and principled concept of subsidiarity'.[81] This is confirmed by President of the European Court, Dean Spielmann, who has maintained that:

> [p]ursuant to a recent trend in the jurisprudence of the European Court of Human Rights judicial self-restraint should prevail in the event that superior national courts have analysed in a comprehensive manner the precise nature of the impugned restriction, on the basis of the relevant Convention case law and principles drawn therefrom.[82]

4. Conclusion

The European Court now cites and relies on national courts much more than it used to do before; this goes for many courts, certainly not just the UK ones. Thus, in *M* v. *Germany*,[83] the European Court cited and relied upon the decision of the French Conseil constitutionnel in *Loi relative à la retention de sûreté et à la declaration d'irresponsabilité pour cause de trouble mentale*,[84] in finding that the German measures at issue were in breach of

[78] ECtHR, *Lindheim and others* v. *Norway*, judgment 12 June 2012, Applications No. 13221/08 and 2139/10.

[79] *Countryside Alliance*, note 49 above .

[80] *Friend*, note 52 above, para. 58.

[81] S. Sedley, Speech given at Lincoln's Inn on 13 November 2012. Also, S. Sedley, 'How to comply with Strasbourg', [2013] *London Review of Books* 22.

[82] D. Spielmann, 'Allowing the right margin: the European Court of Human Rights and the national margin of appreciation doctrine', 2011–12 *Cambridge Yearbook of European Legal Studies*, 381 at p. 411.

[83] ECtHR, *M* v. *Germany*, judgment 17 December 2009, Application No. 19359/04.

[84] Decision number 2008–562 Conseil constitutionnel; *Journal officiel* of 26 February 2008, p. 3272. See also E. Bjorge, 'National supreme courts and the development of ECHR rights', (2011) 9 *International Journal of Constitutional Law* 5, pp. 30–31; M. Andenas and E. Bjorge, 'Preventive detention', (2011) 105 *American Journal of International Law* 768.

the Convention. Similarly, in *Hirst* v. *United Kingdom*,[85] the Court cited and relied upon the way in which Canadian courts developed the right to democratic participation by prisoners in *Sauvé* v. *Attorney General of Canada*.[86] This development to some extent mirrors one observed also in national law (such as, for example, in the United Kingdom[87] and France)[88] but also more generally in international law, as evidenced by the jurisprudence of the International Court of Justice.[89] While it is certainly not wholly novel for national and international courts to rely upon the work of those who have come before them in other places and jurisdictions, this seems to happen more and more frequently.

One gets the impression from the jurisprudence analysed in this chapter that the European Court has only really been minded to take inspiration from national courts where those national courts have showed a willingness to talk the talk of fundamental rights in good faith.

It seems that the hopes of McNair and of Bingham set out at the beginning of this chapter have been realised to an astonishing degree.[90] The common law is certainly pulling its weight in European human rights law. Surely the fact that UK judges have been able to have a real say on ECHR questions through the HRA has played an important role in this regard. As has the fact that the European Court, in common with other jurisdictions, is opening up its form of judgment. But equally important have been the fact that the UK courts now take the logic of the ECHR so seriously and the good faith with which they apply Convention rights.

When it comes to influencing the Court in defining the scope of Convention rights it may even be that the jurisprudence of the UK courts is given more than its due. Surely the Court must be right in going a long way towards rooting the development of Convention rights in important legal traditions such as that of the common law. After all, the Preamble to the Convention clearly states that 'the aim of the Council of Europe is the achievement of greater unity between its members'. But the Preamble

[85] ECtHR (GC), *Hirst* v. *United Kingdom*, judgment 6 October 2005, Application No. 74025/01.

[86] *Sauvé* v. *Attorney General of Canada (No 2)* [2000] 2 CF 519.

[87] T. Bingham, *Widening Horizons: The Influence of Comparative Law and International Law on Domestic Law* (Cambridge University Press, 2010); Andenas and Fairgrieve, *Tom Bingham*, note 18 above.

[88] B. Stirn, *Vers un droit public européen* (Paris: Montchrestien, 2012).

[89] J. Crawford, *Brownlie's Principles of Public International Law*, 8th edn (Oxford University Press, 2012), p. 40.

[90] McNair, 'International law in practice', note 3 above, pp. 164–5; Bingham, 'ECHR: time to incorporate', note 3 above, p. 131.

also says that this achievement is to be achieved by 'the maintenance and further realisation of human rights and fundamental freedoms'.[91] If one goes too far in letting national courts' conceptions of how ECHR rights ought to be shaped dictate the direction of Convention jurisprudence one could end up undermining both the maintenance and the further realisation of the rights of the Convention. Then the exercise of getting national courts on one's side by citing them and letting their conception of rights shape those of the ECHR could end up not being worth the candle.

[91] See E. Bjorge, *The Evolutionary Interpretation of Treaties* (Oxford University Press, 2014).

11

Old and new human rights in Europe

The scope of EU rights *versus* that of ECHR rights

XAVIER GROUSSOT AND EDUARDO GILL-PEDRO

> The thesis, often put forward in the literature, that there is a tension or even conflict between Luxembourg and Strasbourg case law is somewhat exaggerated. Harmony rather than conflicts is a much more likely scenario.[1]

With the entry into force of the Lisbon Treaty on 1 December 2009, the EU Charter of Fundamental Rights (the 'Charter' or the 'EUCFR') has finally become a legally binding, core element of the Union's legal order and thus the point at which the Luxembourg judge must start when assessing the compatibility of EU institutions' or Member States' measures with fundamental rights.[2] What impact will this have on the scope of the protection that fundamental rights provide EU citizens, who now have two legally binding instruments both claiming to protect them, and two supranational courts to turn to? How will these 'new' rights impact on the 'old' human rights in Europe?

This chapter will seek to address these questions by evaluating the Strasbourg and Luxembourg legal orders. It will do so by first comparing the material and personal scope of the Charter with those of the European Convention on Human Rights (ECHR).[3] A wider scope of protection may give individuals greater opportunities to rely on fundamental arguments in litigation, and might even provide the Strasbourg Court with a source of inspiration in extending the scope of ECHR rights, but carries with it

[1] A. Rosas, 'Fundamental rights in the Luxembourg and Strasbourg courts' in C. Baudenbacher *et al.* (eds), *The EFTA Court: Ten Years on* (Oxford: Hart Publishing, 2005).

[2] Opinion of AG Bot in Case C–108/10 *Ivana Skattolon* [2011], nyr. See also Joint Communication of Presidents Skouris and Costa on 17 January 2011, available throught the ECtHR website (www.echr.coe.int).

[3] This analysis is complicated by the fact that many of the Charter rights were already protected by the Court of Justice of the European Union (CJEU) as general principles of EU law, the scope of application for which may be different from the Charter rights. This chapter does not address those issues; the focus is primarily on the Charter rights.

dangers, both to the ECHR as a 'constitutional instrument of the European public order'[4] seeking to promote a 'common understanding and observance'[5] of the rights set out in it, and to that harmony between the two legal orders to which CJEU judge Alan Rosas alluded in the epigraph above.

Second, this chapter will look in detail at Article 52(3) of the Charter, which can be described as the 'homogeneity clause', tasked with ensuring that the Charter does not undermine the protection provided by the ECHR and that the two legal orders can co-exist harmoniously. How must this provision be interpreted by the Court of Justice of the European Union (CJEU) if it is to achieve these tasks?

The recent CJEU case *NS*,[6] and an earlier case from the ECtHR, *MSS* v. *Belgium and Greece*,[7] show the two courts vigorously staking their respective pitches as protectors of fundamental rights in the European legal order. Given this, it is crucial that they each have an understanding of the scope of their respective fundamental rights that ensures, if not coherence (as coherence between these two legal orders with fundamentally different 'normative umbrellas'[8] is not achievable), then the harmony that judge Rosas described: a harmony that respects the different normative goals of each legal system and ensures that the fundamental rights set out in both instruments are respected.

1. Material and personal scope of the ECHR *versus* the Charter

> The objective of the Charter is not to create new rights but rather to permit them to apply correctly and properly within the EU.[9]

1.1 Material scope of the Charter versus *the ECHR*

The EU Charter of Fundamental Rights is articulated around six values (each reflected in one of its chapters): Dignity, Freedoms, Equality,

[4] ECtHR (GC), *Loizidou* v. *Turkey*, 18 December 1996, para. 75.

[5] Preamble to the ECHR.

[6] Cases C–411/10 and C–493/10, *NS* v. *Secretary of State for the Home Department* and *ME and others* v. *Refugee Applications Commissioner* [2011] nyr.

[7] ECtHR (GC), *MSS* v. *Belgium and Greece*, judgment of 21 January 2011.

[8] The term 'normative umbrella' refers to the general purposes that are common to all texts within a particular legal system, and that reflect that legal system's accepted principles, fundamental objectives and basic standards (A. Barack, *Purposive Interpretation in Law* (Princeton, NJ: Princeton University Press, 2005), p. 149).

[9] See E. Guild in The House of Lords EU Select Committee Report, 'Fundamental Rights', 2008, 10th Report, House of Lords, para. 5.37.

Solidarity, Citizen's rights and Justice.[10] The text of the Charter follows a wide conception of fundamental rights based on a multitude of legal sources, e.g. the constitutional traditions and international obligations common to the Member States, the ECHR and its case law and the social charters adopted by the Union and by the Council of Europe.[11] This wide conception is perhaps a reflection of the plurality of sources used by the Court of Justice in the elaboration of general principles of EU law. The Charter is far from being a perfect legal instrument and should be seen as the outcome of a politico-judicial compromise. It carries the marks of a harsh and intensive battle during the nine months of negotiations and this has unfortunately resulted in obvious drafting deficiencies, particularly in Title IV (solidarity rights) and the horizontal provisions.

Yet it is a revolutionary text: first in the sense that the twenty-seven Member States, each with its own history and culture, have declared their adhesion to these common fundamental values; second, in the sense that it constitutes a document without equivalent in Europe as it embodies civil and political rights, economic and social rights and rights of a third generation (environment, consumption, right to peace)[12] within one document. This remarkable breadth of substantive reach in the Charter might be due, paradoxically, to the fact that the most reticent observers were convinced that the Charter would not acquire binding effect.[13] Drawing a comparison with the ECHR, it appears clear to us that the Charter contains more substantive rights (such as the social rights) than the ECHR does.[14] Furthermore, some of the rights are not expressly stated by the ECHR, such as freedom of the arts and sciences (Article 13 EUCFR) and the rights of the child (Article 24 EUCFR), even though these rights appear in the case law of the ECHR, respectively in cases on Articles 10 ECHR (freedom of expression) and 8 ECHR (right to respect for family

[10] Cf. Preamble of the EUCFR, recital 7 which recognises rights, freedoms and principles.

[11] *Ibid.*, recital 5. The Charter itself explains that – with due regard for the powers and tasks of the EU and for the principle of subsidiarity – it 'reaffirms' fundamental rights as they result from various sources, including the ECHR, national constitutional traditions and international obligations of Member States, the Social Charters of the EU and the Council of Europe, and the case law of the ECJ and the ECtHR.

[12] See Case C–282/10 *Maribel Dominguez* [2012] nyr. See also Opinion of AG Trstenjak on the same case, delivered on 8 September 2011.

[13] M. Wathelet, 'La Charte des droits fondamentaux: un bon pas dans une course qui reste longue', (2000) 5–6 *Cahiers de droit européen* 585, p. 590.

[14] The Charter contains fifty substantive Articles, while the ECHR contains eighteen substantive provisions (not including the protocols).

life).[15] Some of the Charter's rights also contain a modern drafting style, e.g. Article 7 of the Charter uses the word 'communication' in place of the 'correspondence' used in Article 8 ECHR, and Article 9 of the Charter does not include an explicit reference to 'men and women' when it comes to the right to marry (compare with Article 12 ECHR).

The Charter may best be described as a crystallisation of existing fundamental rights contained in the sources previously mentioned. Its language reflects existing national, EU and international provisions. A little more than half of the Charter's rights codify general principles of Union law that were already recognised as binding by the CJEU. However, some of the Charter's rights are 'new' to the extent that the CJEU has yet to explicitly guarantee them as general principles of law, and the EUCFR contains more fundamental rights than the CJEU has guaranteed through its case law.[16] However, what can be said to be 'new' is not the modern and innovative rights the Charter occasionally refers to (e.g. the right to the protection of personal data, the right to a high level of environmental protection, the right to good administration). Rather, it is the fact that these rights, while arguably not new rights, had not hitherto been regarded as *fundamental* rights in the EU context. To put it differently, while rights such as the right to good administration or the right of access to preventative health care already enjoyed a variable degree of protection under EU law and in most Member States on the basis of national and/or international law obligations, their consecration as *fundamental* rights was still missing.

As pointed out previously, one of the main sources for the EUCFR is the European Convention on Human Rights. Many rights enshrined in the Charter – contained chiefly in Title I (Dignity), Title II (Freedoms) and Title VI (Justice) – in fact correspond with the Convention. According to the explanatory notes of the EUCFR, twelve Charter rights correspond with the ECHR. It is also stated in these explanatory notes – which are not binding under Article 52(7) Charter – that the Charter contains six provisions in which the meaning is the same as the corresponding Articles of the ECHR, but where the scope is wider.[17] But what does this mean? Do

[15] P. Lemmens, 'The relation between the Charter of Fundamental Rights of the European Union and the European Convention on Human Rights – substantive aspects', (2001) 8 *Maastricht Journal of European and Comparative Law* 49, pp. 55–67.

[16] K. Lenaerts and E. de Smijter, 'A Bill of Rights for the European Union', (2001) 38 CML Rev 273.

[17] Art. 9 EUCFR covers the same field as Art. 12 ECHR, but its scope may be extended to other forms of marriage if these are established by national legislation. Art. 12(1) EUCFR corresponds to Art. 11 ECHR, but its scope is extended to the European Union level. Both

rights with a wider scope constitute rights with a higher level of protection as defined under the last sentence of Article 52(3) EUCFR? If this is the case we might wonder why there is no reference in the explanatory notes of Article 52(3) to Article 47(1) EUCFR on effective judicial protection or to Article 49 EUCFR concerning specifically the retroactivity of lighter criminal penalties, what has been called retroactivity *in mitius*. It is argued in this chapter that the definition of corresponding rights provided in the explanatory notes is misleading and should be used extremely carefully.[18] We shall come back to this point in the next section.

The Charter is a more progressive and innovative instrument than the ECHR for protecting fundamental rights in Europe.[19] Many provisions of the Charter do not find an explicit counterpart in the ECHR. Therefore, the Charter might constitute a source of inspiration for the ECtHR if it wishes to extend the level of human rights protection in the Strasbourg regime.[20] In that sense, it is worth noting that the ECtHR's recent references to the Charter are often made in relation to 'progressive' interpretation of Convention rights. In *Hatton I* and *II*,[21] Article 37 EUCFR (right to protection of the environment) was quoted by the ECtHR

Art. 14(1) and (3) EUCFR correspond to Art. 2 of Protocol No. 1 ECHR but their scope is extended to cover access to vocational and continuing training, Art. 47(2) and (3) EUCFR correspond to Art. 6(1) ECHR, but the limit they set on the determination of civil rights and obligations or criminal charges does not apply to Union law and its implementation. Art. 50 EUCFR corresponds to Art. 4 of Protocol No. 7 ECHR, but its scope is extended to the European Union level between the courts of the Member States. Finally, citizens of the European Union may not be considered as aliens in the scope for the application of Union law, because of the prohibition of any discrimination on grounds of nationality. The limitations provided under Art. 16 ECHR as regards the rights of aliens therefore do not apply to them in this context.

18 Cf. W. Weiß, 'Human rights in the EU: rethinking the role of the European Convention on Human Rights after Lisbon', (2011) 7 *European Constitutional Law Review* 64.

19 The well known example here is the influence of Case 13/94 *P* v. *S and Cornwall CC*, [1996] ECR I–2143 on the ECtHR case law on transsexuals (e.g. in ECtHR (GC), *Goodwin* v. *United Kingdom*, 11 July 2002).

20 Indeed, between 2006 and 20012 references to the Charter have noticeably increased. See ECtHR (GC), *Demir and Baykara* v. *Turkey*, 12 November 2008 (referred in the dissenting opinion to Art. 28 EUCFR, the right to negotiate and conclude collective agreements); ECtHR (GC), *Sørensen and Rasmussen* v. *Denmark*, 11 January 2006, para. 37 (Art. 12 EUCFR, freedom of association); ECtHR (GC) *Anheuser-Busch Inc* v. *Portugal*, 11 January 2007, para. 38 (Art. 17 EUCFR, right to property); ECtHR (GC) *Saadi* v. *United Kingdom*, 29 January 2008, para. 39 (Art. 18 EUCFR, right to asylum); and ECtHR (GC) *Zolotukhin* v. *Russia*, 10 February 2009, para. 79 (Art. 50 EUCFR, right not to be tried or punished twice for same offence).

21 ECtHR, *Hatton and others* v. *United Kingdom*, 2 October 2001 (*Hatton I*) and ECtHR (GC), *Hatton and others* v. *United Kingdom*, 8 July 2003 (*Hatton II*).

judges.[22] In *Christine Goodwin*, the Strasbourg Court noted that Article 9 EUCFR departs, no doubt deliberately, from the wording of Article 12 of the Convention in removing the reference to men and women.[23] Similarly, in the joint dissenting opinion in *Künstler*, the judges made reference to the right to dignity, enshrined in Article 1 Charter, and to the *Omega* case.[24] A provision directly related to dignity is not present in the ECHR. In the dissenting opinion to the *Fretté* case, the judges relied on Article 21 EUCFR to argue that a European consensus is now emerging in the area of sexual orientation.[25] The development continued with *Schalk and Kopf*,[26] in which the ECtHR considered that same-sex couples now fall within the definition of 'family life'. As justification for the shift in approach to same-sex couples, the court referred to the rapid evolution in social attitudes towards such couples in many Member States. Reference was also made to an 'emerging European consensus towards legal recognition of same-sex couples'.[27] In *Scoppola*, the ECtHR relied on the *Berlusconi* case of the CJEU and its progressive interpretation of retroactivity *in mitius*,[28] which is also reflected in Article 49 EUCFR.[29] In a similar vein, in *Neulinger and Shuruk* the ECtHR made reference to the progressive Article 24 EUCFR and the concept of 'best interests of the child'.[30] Finally, the Strasbourg court in *Vilho Eskelinen* mentioned the provisions of the Charter on effective judicial protection in order to show that the scope for applicability of judicial control in EU law has widened.[31] Going further, the dissenting judge in

22 In *Hatton II* (*ibid.*), the judges offering the dissenting opinion considered that Art. 37 EUCFR on the right to the protection of the environment constitutes an 'interesting illustration' and that it 'shows clearly that the Member States of the European Union want a high level of protection and better protection, and expect the Union to develop policies aimed at those objectives'.

23 See note 19 above, para. 100.

24 ECtHR, *Vereinigung Bildender Künstler* v. *Austria*, 25 January 2007, joined dissenting opinion, fn 5. C–36/02 *Omega Spielhallen* [2004] ECR I–09609.

25 ECtHR, *Fretté* v. *France*, 26 February 2002, joint dissenting opinion: 'in Chapter III [on equality] of the EU's Charter of Fundamental Rights of 7 December 2000, Article 21 expressly prohibits "any discrimination based on any ground such as sex ... or sexual orientation". It may therefore be reasonably argued that a European consensus is now emerging in this area.'

26 ECtHR, *Schalk and Kopf* v. *Austria*, 24 June 2010.

27 *Ibid.*, para. 105.

28 Joined cases C–387/02, C–391/02 and C–403/02 *Berlusconi and others* [2005] ECR I–03565.

29 ECtHR (GC), *Scoppola* v. *Italy (No. 2)*, 17 September 2009.

30 ECtHR (GC), *Neulinger and Shuruk* v. *Switzerland*, 6 July 2010.

31 ECtHR (GC), *Vilho Eskelinen and others* v. *Finland*, 19 April 2007, para. 60. The ECtHR considered that the Luxembourg Court applies a wider approach in favour of judicial control, as shown by its landmark judgment in Case 222/84 *Johnston* v. *Chief Constable of*

Martinie suggested a revision of the ECHR case law in light of Article 47 EUCFR.[32] In this last case, and also in *Saadi* v. *UK*, the separate opinions considered that EU law should be used as a minimum threshold.[33]

This approach may lead to a problematic situation since the Charter includes not only rights that are specifically designed for the EU law context, e.g. free movement rights (directly Articles 15 and 16 EUCFR or indirectly Article 47 EUCFR) or the principle of *non bis in idem* with a cross-border element (Article 50 EUCFR). It also more generally reflects EU policies such as the internal market or the migration/asylum policies. Ultimately, if the ECtHR is exclusively influenced by EU law it runs the risk of replacing the Strasbourg legal order with EU law rights that are not always designed to reinforce human rights protection but instead pursue a specific goal of EU market integration.[34] So far, however, even though EU law and its Charter have been of extreme relevance in some cases, no case has been detected in which EU law was invoked as the sole evidence of a consensus justifying a departure from previous case law.[35] In that sense, it can be concluded that the risk of seeing EU legal rights pursuing specific EU policies and influencing and modifying the material scope of the ECHR is limited since those rights are not common to all the laws of the states on the Council of Europe; in fact many of those states are still outside the European Union.

1.2 The personal scope of the Charter versus *the ECHR*

Generally speaking, it is often said that the material scope of the Charter is broader than that of the ECHR and that, in contrast, the personal scope of the ECHR is wider than the Charter, since the ECHR is not limited to cases brought under EU law and covers what are called purely internal situations (i.e. situations where EU law is not applicable due to the absence of an extraneous element). Such an assertion appears to be true at first blush, but this is not the full picture. As rightly put by Alonso García, 'the Charter

RUC [1986] ECR 01651. Referring to the operative part of this latter judgment, it noted that if an individual can rely on a material right guaranteed by Community law, his or her status as a holder of public power does not render the requirements of judicial control inapplicable.

32 ECtHR (GC), *Martinie* v. *France*, 12 April 2006.

33 See note 20 above.

34 C. Dautricourt, 'A Strasbourg perspective on the autonomous development of fundamental rights in EU law: trends and implications', Jean Monnet Working Paper 10/10, available at http://centers.law.nyu.edu/jeanmonnet/papers/10/101001.html, at p. 61.

35 *Ibid.*

is part of a context, the Union context which is constructed in conceptual terms as an autonomous legal order with an integrating vocation, that tends to displace, by means of the principle of supremacy, the disparities between the Member States'.[36] In other words, as discussed in the previous section, the Charter's rights rub shoulders with or can even be said, sometimes, to form an integral part of the EU policies fostering European integration. This has important consequences for how fundamental rights are protected. On one hand, the coupling of fundamental rights with the drive for European integration can greatly reinforce the legal impact of those rights at a national level. The existence of strong constitutional principles such as the principle of supremacy, which renders the enforcement of EU law rights mandatory, and the duty of loyal cooperation, which requires Member States to disapply any national measure, including national constitutional provisions, to the extent they conflict with an EU legal right, may give these rights much greater 'traction' at national level than ECHR rights.[37]

On the other hand, this linkage between fundamental rights and integration can lead to situations where the distinctions between a (personal) right and a (collective) policy are dangerously blurred. Two cases illustrated this danger very clearly: *Familiapress* and *Omega*. In *Familiapress*,[38] when considering whether an Austrian measure prohibiting a German

[36] R. Alonso García, 'The general provisions of the Charter of Fundamental Rights of the European Union', (2002) 8 *European Law Journal* 492, at p. 508.

[37] The status of the ECHR within the legal orders of the Contracting Parties varies considerably. Whilst in some countries, such as the Netherlands, the judgments of the ECtHR enjoy primacy over all conflicting laws, in Germany the ECHR has a legal status below that of the German Basic Law, and in the UK the courts are not empowered to disapply Acts of Parliament where they conflict with the ECHR, and are required merely to take into account the judgments of the ECtHR. In Sweden, the Supreme Court has often been reluctant to use the methods of interpretation relied on in the ECHR legal order. Moreover, we can find examples of the Swedish Supreme Court simply refusing to apply ECHR decisions, e.g. in the context of taxation and the principle of *non bis in idem*. This situation would simply be impossible in the EU legal order if a national legislation were found in violation of a Charter's rights. To put it differently, the national court would be under a duty (Art. 4(3) TEU) to disapply the national legislation that conflicts with a Charter's right. In the *Pastor Green* case (NJA 2005, s. 805) the Supreme Court has shown some signs of constitutional pluralism by interpreting the constitutional provisions relating to the freedoms of expression and religion in light of the European human rights regime and thus has departed from the traditional methodology based on preparatory works. See J. Nergelius, '2005 – the year when European law and its supremacy was finally acknowledged by Swedish courts' in P. Cramer and T. Bull, *Swedish Studies in European Law*, vol. 1 (Oxford: Hart Publishing, 2007), p. 145.

[38] C–368/95 *Familiapress* [1997] ECR I–03689.

publisher from distributing its magazines in Austria was justified as necessary to protect press diversity and media pluralism, the CJEU extended the scope of the right of freedom of expression to include protection of the Austrian state's interest in having a diverse and pluralistic media. In *Omega*,[39] the CJEU considered a German measure that prohibited a company from providing laser games to the public in the city of Bonn, on the grounds that the games that took place in Omega's establishment constituted a danger to public order, since the acts of simulated homicide and the trivialisation of violence thereby engendered were contrary to fundamental values prevailing in public opinion. The CJEU held that this measure was justified as protecting the 'right' to human dignity. Whilst the Court of Justice was not entirely clear on where this fundamental right to human dignity derives from, under EU law it is undeniable that the Court considered the measure justified because it protected fundamental rights recognised by EU law;[40] that is to say, that the matter was one which fell within the scope of a fundamental right.

In both these cases, the CJEU extended the scope of fundamental rights to include the protection of what are in fact collective goods (media pluralism and public order respectively). It effectively extended the personal scope of fundamental rights to situations where there was no 'person' as such who could claim to be a bearer of those rights. The *Omega* case illustrates this very clearly – whose rights were the German authorities protecting? Clearly not the rights of the players of the laser game: they would pay money to play;[41] even less the rights of the company that wanted to provide the games. The only persons that could claim 'rights' would be a putative 'moral majority' in the population of Bonn who disapproved of the fact that the games might be played in their city.[42]

39 *Omega Spielhallen*, note 24 above.

40 *Ibid.*, para. 35. It accepted that it was 'a general principle of law', and 'an objective compatible with EU law' (both at para. 34), but the Court made no reference to Art. 1 EUCFR (even though that point was raised by the Advocate-General in his Opinion – at para. 91).

41 *Ibid.* In his Opinion (at para. 94) the Advocate-General refers to a case decided by the Human Rights Committee (HRC) of the UN (Communication No 854/1999: France. 26/7/2002. CCPR/C/75/D/854/1999), which makes an interesting contrast. In that case, concerning a ban on 'entertainment' involving the throwing of dwarves in nightclubs, the person who claimed that his fundamental right was being breached was the dwarf himself, who was prevented from working by the ban. The HRC accepted the French state's references to human dignity, not as a fundamental right, but as a *consideration* when deciding what measures are necessary to protect public order.

42 *Omega Spielhallen*, note 24 above. As the Advocate-General notes in his Opinion (at para. 10), there were protests against the 'Laserdrome' from members of the public from the very start.

However, this type of 'moral right' attaching to the majority is usually seen by the ECtHR not as a fundamental right,[43] but as a public interest that might justify the limitation of a fundamental right.[44] This extension by the CJEU of the personal scope of a fundamental right, conflating the concept of 'right' with that of collective good might be difficult to reconcile with the methodology of the ECtHR.[45]

The essential problem of EU fundamental rights remains in the definition of their scope of personal application after the entry into force of the Lisbon Treaty and of the Charter. It is well known that, in relation to general principles of EU law, the CJEU has consistently held that there are two types of instance in which a matter will fall within the scope for application of fundamental rights:

> (1) *National measures implementing or applying EU law* (the *Wachauf* line of cases):[46] Member States are bound by EU fundamental rights when they adopt measures to implement regulations or transpose directives or more generally, when they apply national rules the subject matter of which is governed by provisions of EU primary and/or secondary legislation and
>
> (2) *National measures derogating from EU law* (the *ERT* line of cases):[47] Member States are also bound by EU fundamental rights when they invoke reasons of public interest under EU law to justify a national measure that limits any Treaty rights and in particular when they adopt measures that obstruct or that are merely liable to hamper the exercise of EU free movement rights.

It is not yet clear whether this understanding of the scope for application of general principles will also be applicable to the Charter, given the wording of Article 51 EUCFR, which states that its provisions are applicable to Member States 'only when they are implementing Union law'. This would seem at first reading to limit the scope for application to the first type of instance above. However, the case law of the CJEU seems to contradict

[43] C. Nowlin, 'The protection of morals under the ECHR', (2002) 27 *Human Rights Quarterly* 264.

[44] See for example ECtHR (GC), *Handyside*, 7 December 1976, para. 47 (restricting right to free speech of book publisher justified on grounds of protecting public morals), or ECtHR (GC), *Dudgeon*, 22 October 1981 (regulating sexual conduct through the criminal law might be justified on grounds of protecting public morals).

[45] This point is also made by M. Avbelj in 'The European Court of Justice and the question of value choices – fundamental human rights as an exception to the freedom of movement of goods', Jean Monnet Paper n. 6/04, available at http://centers.law.nyu.edu/jeanmonnet/archive/papers/04/040601.pdf.

[46] Case 5/88 *Wachauf* [1989] ECR 2609.

[47] Case C–260/89 *Elliniki Radiophonia Tileorassi* [1993] ECR I–2925.

this,[48] and indeed it would seem illogical to have different scopes for application depending on whether the fundamental rights derived from the Charter or had been developed by the CJEU as general principles.

A further uncertainty is whether the Charter will be considered to apply between private parties in the same way as fundamental rights derived from general principles. If the CJEU holds that it does, this will extend the scope for personal application of EU law significantly beyond the doctrine of positive obligations of the states as developed in the ECHR legal order. Therefore, the question we shall now focus on is whether the legally binding status of the Charter may increase the opportunities for individuals to invoke EU fundamental rights in the context of legal proceedings between private parties. Advocate-General Bot, in the conclusive paragraph of his Opinion in *Kücükdeveci*, offered an interesting prediction:

> [G]iven the ever increasing intervention of Community law in relations between private persons, the Court will, in my view, be inevitably confronted with other situations which raise the question of the right to rely, in proceedings between private persons, on directives which contribute to ensuring observance of fundamental rights. Those situations will probably increase in number if the Charter of Fundamental Rights of the European Union becomes legally binding in the future, since among the fundamental rights contained in that charter are a number which are already part of the existing body of Community law in the form of directives.[49]

The Advocate-General, unfortunately, did not go on to explain why one should expect the number of instances of EU fundamental rights being applied in horizontal situations to increase after the Lisbon Treaty. The sole argument proposed would appear to be that a series of Directives have spelled out in greater detail how some of the Charter's rights are to apply to particular situations. One might wonder whether this is not also true of most general principles of EU law. The Charter, however, does increase the visibility of the rights it contains and may therefore lead more applicants and their counsel to seek to rely on those rights or,

48 See in particular *NS*, note 6 above, in which the CJEU considered the 'sovereignty' clause in the Dublin Regulation, which allows a Member State to examine an asylum application itself, in derogation from the principles that otherwise would determine the Member State responsible. The CJEU held that 'a Member State which exercises that discretionary power must be considered as implementing European Union law within the meaning of Article 51(1) of the Charter' [*NS*, note 6 above, para. 68].

49 Opinion of AG Bot in Case C–555/07 *Kücükdeveci* [2010] ECR I–00365, para. 90. For more developments on the concept of direct and indirect horizontal effects of EU fundamental rights, see M. Safjan and P. Miklaszewicz, 'Horizontal effect of the general principles of EU law in the sphere of private law', (2010) 18 *European Review of Private Law* 475.

at the very least, to test their cognizability. Nonetheless, it remains to be seen whether this will occur in the context of proceedings between private persons. In the ECHR legal order, horizontal application of fundamental rights is often limited to the doctrine of positive obligations of the state.[50] In Union law, the spectrum of EU *Drittwirkung* as developed by the CJEU case law is in fact much wider. We find, in that respect, three main lines of case law reflecting horizontal application of fundamental rights:

(a) Case law on positive obligations of the State (*Commission* v. *France* [1996], *Schmidberger* [2003]) [vertical situation with horizontal applications].[51]
(b) Case law on bodies with 'collective/regulative powers' (*Walrave-Laval-Ferlini* and *Wouters*) [sport associations, trade unions].[52]
(c) Case law on 'mandatory nature' (*Defrenne, Angonese*)[53] and/or 'constitutional nature' (*Audiolux, Mangold*).[54]

Whilst the situations in categories (a) and (b) may find their parallel in some cases of the ECtHR, it seems to us that situation (c) has no equivalent within the ECtHR jurisprudence. It should be noted that

50 See L. Garlicki, 'Relations between private actors and the European Convention on Human Rights' in A. Sajo and R. Utiz (eds), *The Constitution in Private Relations: Expanding Constitutionalism* (Utrecht: Eleven International Publishing, 2005), pp. 129–43.

51 Case C–265/95 *Commission* v. *France* [1997] ECR I–6959; Case C–112/00 *Schmidberger* [2003] ECR I–5659.

52 Case C–36/74 *Walrave and Koch* [1974] ECR 1405; Case C–341/05 *Laval* [2007] ECR I–11767; Case C–411/98 *Ferlini* [2000] ECR I–8081; Case C–309/99 *Wouters* [2002] ECR I–1577. This is the so-called 'stretched state action' doctrine. Cases such as *Viking Line* (Case C–438/05 *Viking Line* [2007] ECR I–10779, para. 43), *Laval* (para. 90) and also *Bosman* (Case C–415/93 *Bosman* [1995] ECR I–4921) are here relevant. These cases oppose natural or legal persons (regulatory bodies, trade unions, economic operators) and offer striking examples of free movement claims conflicting with defences grounded in fundamental rights.

53 Case 43/75 *Defrenne I* [1975] ECR–455, para. 39. See also Case C–281/98 *Angonese* [2000] ECR I–4139, para. 36 and the analysis offered by AG Bot in *Kücükdeveci*, note 49 above, para. 85. The so-called horizontal effect of certain EU law provisions, the right to rely on these provisions in the context of legal proceedings between private parties, was made clear in *Defrenne II* (149/77 *Defrenne* [1978] ECR 01365) in which the Court held that the Treaty principle of equal pay for male and female workers for equal work, now laid down in Art. 157 TFEU, applies not only to public authorities, but also to all agreements intended to regulate paid labour collectively, as well as to contracts between individuals.

54 Case C–101/08 *Audiolux* [2009] ECR I–9823; Case C–144/04 *Mangold* [2005] ECR I–09981. The case law on 'mandatory nature' and 'constitutional principles' reflects direct and indirect horizontal effects.

these cases of direct horizontal effect have been limited so far to the right against non-discrimination enshrined in Treaty provisions. This raises the question whether such effect might also apply to other general principles of EU law and in particular the fundamental rights that may simultaneously be found in the Charter.[55] One might suggest that the Court think twice before extending the *Mangold/Kücükdeveci* approach (which leads to horizontal applications of EU law when a directive explicitly enshrines/codifies a EU fundamental right/general principle of EU law)[56] to areas beyond those governed by EU anti-discrimination law where naturally the (general) principle of equal treatment enjoys a special standing.[57] This would suggest, however, that the principle of equal treatment is in a preferred position amongst fundamental rights and this is not a position we would advocate. Similarly, we submit that most if not all provisions of the Charter, while primarily aimed at protecting individuals against public authorities, are capable of application in the context of judicial proceedings between individuals.[58] If anything, the case law of the ECtHR indicates that many of the rights guaranteed by the Convention can affect relations between private individuals.[59]

To put it differently, it is likely that the CJEU will interpret the scope *ratione personae* of the rights contained in the Charter in a way similar to the general principles of EU law. However, the material scope for application of the Charter is broader than the scope of both general principles and ECHR rights. When one adds this to the more highly visible nature of the Charter and the binding character of EU primary legislation, one cannot exclude the possibility that claimants and their

[55] See Case C–73/07 *Satamedia* [2008] ECR I–9831. In this case, the European Commission relied on the general principle protecting the right to privacy in relation to a directive that had not been implemented. See also AG Kokott's Opinion in C–104/09 *Roca-Álvarez* [2010] nyr, para. 55: 'it remains to be seen whether the Court will extend such horizontal direct effect to other general legal principles'.

[56] In these two cases, the fundamental right at stake was the general principle of non-discrimination on grounds of age.

[57] See E. Muir, 'Of ages in – and edges of – EU law', (2011) 48 CMLRev 56.

[58] An alternative approach would be to deny the horizontal application of the Charter's rights, since its Art. 51 provides that they are only addressed to EU institutions and Member States (when they implement EU law) and instead, recognise the horizontal direct effect of the general principles of EU law as in *Kücükdeveci*.

[59] For further discussion of the *Drittwirkung* effect of the provisions of the ECHR, see e.g. P. van Dijk *et al.*, *Theory and Practice of the European Convention on Human Rights*, 3rd edn (The Hague: Intersentia, 2006), p. 15.

counsel might seek to test the applicability of the Charter's rights in 'horizontal' litigation on a more regular basis.[60]

To end, let us come back to where we started this section, in stating that the personal scope of Charter rights is less comprehensive than that of ECHR rights. Even if this statement appears to be true *prima facie*, it should be kept in mind that the Charter's rights might have wider impact than ECHR rights in relation to private parties and in horizontal situations. In particular, the CJEU case law on the direct horizontal application of Treaty provisions and on the indirect horizontal application of EU fundamental rights enshrined in secondary legislation demonstrates the width of EU law in comparison to ECHR law and can also be applicable by analogy to Charter rights. Let us shift now to the analysis of the relationship between the Charter and the Convention.

2. The relationship between the Charter and the ECHR in light of Article 52(3) EUCFR

During the drafting of the Charter, its relationship with the ECHR was a matter for constant consideration.[61] It is apparent that one of the problems that a binding Charter could raise is that of interpretations that diverge from the Convention. It may be argued, in that sense, that the Charter could increase the risk of divergence, since its text does not correspond exactly to the text of the ECHR. Lenaerts and de Smijter contended, however, that '[w]here the text of the Charter departs from that of the ECHR, it can never be at the expense of the level of protection offered by the ECHR'.[62] Furthermore, if the Convention is amended in the future, these amendments will automatically become the minimum standard for the protection of fundamental rights within the European Union.[63] The risk of diverging *interpretation* is in reality rather low, since the ECtHR jurisdiction is 'subsidiary' to the preliminary ruling procedure under

60 AG Trstenjak argued for the lack of horizontal effect of the Charter's rights. As argued in this chapter, we disagree with that stance (see Opinion of AG Trstenjak in *Dominguez*, note 12 above).

61 See M. Lindfelt, *Fundamental Rights in the European Union: Towards Higher Law of the Land? A Study of the Status of Fundamental Rights in a Broader Constitutional Setting* (Turku, Finland: Åbo Akademi University Press, 2007), at p. 144.

62 Lenaerts and de Smijter, 'A Bill of Rights', note 16 above, p. 297.

63 T. Lock, 'The ECJ and the ECtHR: the future relationship between the two European courts', (2009) 8 *The Law and Practice of International Courts and Tribunals* 382.

Article 267 TFEU.[64] It will become even lower with the accession to the European Convention on Human Rights.[65]

The horizontal provisions of the EU Charter of Fundamental Rights are particularly interesting when it comes to regulating the relationship between the Charter and Convention rights and offering a framework for preventing conflicts between the CJEU and the ECtHR. In that sense, Articles 52(3) and 53 EUCFR are of special significance since essentially they seek to guarantee a harmonious relationship between the Charter and the Strasbourg regime. These provisions have the ambition of preventing conflict of interpretation between the various jurisdictions that might arise from the plurality of the legal sources. Article 52(3) EUCFR aims to ensure equivalent protection of rights in Strasbourg and Luxembourg. Article 53 EUCFR establishes a 'non-regression' clause over the rights enshrined in the Charter, the ECHR and national constitutions.[66]

Article 52(3) has the purpose of ensuring consistency between the Charter and the ECHR by establishing the rule that, insofar as the rights in the Charter correspond to rights guaranteed by the ECHR, the meaning and scope of those rights, including authorised limitations, are the same as those laid down by the ECHR. It goes on to add that this will not prevent Union law providing more extensive protection.[67] In *Solvay* Advocate-General Kokott rightly considered that the first sentence of

[64] By 'subsidiary' character we mean that the preliminary ruling procedure is integrated within 'exhaustion of remedies' under Art. 35 ECHR. Therefore, in this context, the ECtHR may have the last word on the interpretation of the ECHR rights.

[65] A risk of divergence will always exist even after accession since the Convention sets minimum standards. The argument often used, that accession to the ECHR will bring coherence to fundamental rights, is thus doubted.

[66] According to Art. 53 EUCFR,

> [n]othing in this Charter shall be interpreted as restricting or adversely affecting human rights and fundamental freedoms as recognised, in their respective fields of application, by Union law and international law and by international agreements to which the Union or all the Member States are party, including the European Convention for the Protection of Human Rights and Fundamental Freedoms, and by the Member States' constitutions.

This provision constitutes a non-regression clause and is intended to maintain the level of protection currently afforded within their respective scope by Union law, national constitutions and international law (particularly the ECHR). Its purpose, in the end, is to avoid conflicts of interpretation and of jurisdiction between (on one hand) the Court of Justice and (on the other) the ECtHR and national courts.

[67] According to Art. 52(3) EUCFR, '[i]nsofar as this Charter contains rights which correspond to rights guaranteed by the Convention for the Protection of Human Rights and Fundamental Freedoms, the meaning and scope of those rights shall be the same as those

Article 52(3) contains a 'homogeneity clause'.[68] As it stems from the explanatory notes to the Charter, the meaning and the scope of the rights guaranteed are determined not only by the text of those instruments, but also by the case law of the European Court of Human Rights and by the Court of Justice of the European Union. This paragraph is essential to make sure that the Charter's rights incorporate as a minimum the standards of the Convention.

As Advocate-General Trstenjak noted in *NS*,[69] under Article 52(3) EUCFR the CJEU must ensure that the protection provided by the Charter rights is no less than the protection granted by the corresponding ECHR rights.[70] In other words, by Article 52(3) the EU has committed itself to 'secure to everyone within [its] jurisdiction the rights and freedoms defined in . . . the Convention'.[71] To be sure, that commitment is only made in respect of matters that fall within the competence of EU law, and only in respect of those ECHR rights that find correspondents in the Charter. The key point to note, however, is that the EU has committed itself to respect ECHR rights, that is to say, the rights *defined* in the ECHR. This commitment entails a legal duty, derived from EU primary law, on the part of all EU institutions (including the CJEU), and of the Member States when acting within the scope of EU law,[72] to respect the relevant ECHR right. This legal duty to respect the Convention derives from the Charter, and is not contingent on any accession by the EU to the ECHR or on any power of the Council of Europe or the ECtHR to sanction the EU for breaches of the ECHR.

Even though, during the drafting of the Charter, there were many attempts to include an explicit reference to ECtHR case law, Article 52(3) does not make any explicit reference to it. Is the CJEU, now that the Charter is in force, bound by the jurisprudence of the Strasbourg Court? One could argue this, since the rights contained in the Convention and interpreted in the case law of the Strasbourg Court form an integral part of the meaning, interpretation and scope of the rights guaranteed within

laid down by the said Convention. This provision shall not prevent Union law providing more extensive protection.'

68 AG Kokott in Case C–110/10 P *Solvay* [2011] nyr, para. 95.

69 AG Opinion in *NS*, note 6 above. 70 *Ibid.*, at para. 145.

71 Which is the duty set out in Art. 1 ECHR.

72 See X. Groussot, L. Pech and G. Petursson, 'The scope of application of fundamental rights on Member States', (2011) Eric Stein Working Paper 1/2011, available at www.ericsteinpapers.eu/info/papers/2011-01.

the EU legal order.[73] In contrast, Article 52(7) EUCFR merely states that its explanatory notes 'shall be given due regard'. In the explanatory notes, it is established that the reference to the ECHR in Article 52(3) covers both the ECHR and its additional Protocols and that 'the meaning and the scope of the guaranteed rights are determined not only by the text of those instruments, but also by the case law of the European Court of Human Rights and by the Court of Justice of the European Union'.[74] But since the interpreter of the Charter only has to give due regard to the case law of the ECtHR, there is nothing in these explanatory notes that imposes an explicit obligation to respect that jurisprudence. This perhaps stems from the fact that the Convention sets a minimum standard of protection, as emphasised by Article 52(3) EUCFR. Also, in view of the recent case law of the CJEU on fundamental rights – based on the doctrine of general principles – it is possible to consider that the substantive content of the Convention has been incorporated into EU law.[75] If this is the scenario, one should not worry about the lack of unequivocal reference.[76]

It might even be said that there has never been an instance in which the CJEU openly challenged the ECtHR's interpretation of the Convention. This is not so surprising since the case law of the CJEU often takes into consideration the case law of the ECtHR on the relevant provisions of the ECHR in interpreting the provisions of the Charter of Fundamental Rights.[77] And in that sense, one can state that 'the ECJ has not only helped to maintain a high standard of human rights protection in Europe but also contributed to the development of these human rights. It is to

[73] K. Lenaerts and E. de Smijter, 'The Charter and the role of the European courts', (2001) *Maastricht Journal of European and Comparative Law* 90.

[74] 'Explanations relating to the Charter of Fundamental Rights' (OJ 2007/C 303/33).

[75] J.P. Jacqué, 'The accession of the European Union to the European Convention on Human Rights and Fundamental Freedoms', (2011) 48 CMLRev 995, at p. 1000.

[76] Lock, 'The ECJ and the ECtHR', note 63 above, at p. 387. The author argues against the binding effect of ECtHR case law. According to him, during the drafting of the Charter there were many attempts to include an explicit reference to ECtHR case law in the Charter's text. Nevertheless it was impossible to agree on such reference. Neither the wording of the provision nor the history of the drafting support the view that the CJEU is to be bound by the case law of the Strasbourg Court.
Ibid., p. 387.

[77] See AG Trstenjak's opinion in *NS*, note 6 above, at para. 127. See also Case C–400/10 PPU *McB* [2010] ECR I–08965, para. 53 in which the Court expressly found, with regard to Art. 7 EUCFR, that this provision must be given the same meaning and the same scope as Art. 8(1) ECHR, *as interpreted by the case law of the European Court of Human Rights.* NB: PPU refers to the Urgent Preliminary Ruling procedure under Art. 107 of the Rules of the Court.

be expected that [after accession] the two Courts will keep an eye on the development of the other's case law.'[78] It can even be argued – in light of Article 52(3) EUCFR – that since the Treaty of Lisbon came into force, the EU has unilaterally bound itself to the jurisdiction of the ECtHR.[79]

As put by Advocate General Trstenjak in *NS*:

> [b]ecause the protection granted by the ECHR is constantly developing in the light of its interpretation by the European Court of Human Rights, the reference to the ECHR contained in Article 52(3) of the Charter of Fundamental Rights is to be construed as an essentially dynamic reference which, in principle, covers the case-law of the European Court of Human Rights.

However, in the same case the Advocate-General made a remark that is important to address:

> It should be borne in mind in this connection that the judgments of the European Court of Human Rights essentially always constitute case-specific judicial decisions and not the rules of the ECHR themselves, and it would therefore be wrong to regard the case-law of the European Court of Human Rights as a source of interpretation with full validity in connection with the application of the Charter. This finding, admittedly, may not hide the fact that particular significance and high importance are to be attached to the case-law of the European Court of Human Rights in connection with the interpretation of the Charter of Fundamental Rights, with the result that it must be taken into consideration in interpreting the Charter.[80]

This passage quoted above may be interpreted as depicting the judgments of the ECtHR as *merely* case-specific judicial decisions that do not provide rules for general application, and that as such cannot determine the scope and application of the corresponding rights. We consider that, if that was the meaning intended by the Advocate-General, then it does not reflect the true nature of the judgments of the ECtHR. Through the application of the Convention to the specific cases at hand, the ECtHR does interpret the meaning and scope of the Convention rights, and of

[78] T. Lock, 'EU accession to the ECHR: consequences for the European Court of Justice', EUSA Conference, Boston MA, paper for conference, 3 March 2011.

[79] See C. Timmermans, 'Relationships between the Strasbourg Court and the ECJ', Intervention Round Table CCBE, Luxembourg, 20 May 2011, at p. 3, quoting C–92 and 93/09 *Volker and Schecke* [2010] ECR I–11063 and Case C–279/09 *DEB* [2010] ECR I–13849. Quotation is from AG Trstenjak's opinion in *NS*, note 6 above.

[80] *Ibid.*, at paras 145 (first quotation) and 146 (second quotation).

the concepts contained within those rights, and this interpretation will be autonomous.[81]

As Letsas points out,[82] in autonomous concept cases the problem arises at a conceptual sublevel, where the state has excluded some instances from the 'extension' of the right.[83] For example, in one case the state considered that 'public law, para-administrative bodies' do not fall within the extension of the right of association under Article 11 ECHR.[84] So the state excluded this type of body from the extension of the right, and this exclusion happened before the application of the concept to specific cases. The task of the ECtHR was then to determine whether the state had been correct in so delineating the extension of the concept 'association'. In effect this was a determination of what it is that the ECHR entitles people to *as a matter of law*, and the ECtHR alone is qualified to undertake such a determination.[85] As Callewaert notes:

> The interpretation of the Convention, and the definition of its requirements [is] a domain reserved for the ECtHR . . . : by definition any interpretation of the Convention produces effects *ratione loci et temporis* on a Convention wide scale. Consequently, an authentic interpretation thereof . . . can only come from the ECtHR.[86]

So, in giving the Charter binding force as EU primary law, the EU has committed itself to protecting the rights guaranteed by the ECHR, where they find a correspondent in the Charter and, we argue, this means protecting the rights as defined by the ECtHR.

2.1 The problem of 'more extensive protection'

As seen above, Article 52(3) requires the EU institutions and Member States implementing EU law to secure the rights in the Convention that

[81] See for instance ECtHR (GC) 29 April 1999, *Chassagnou and others* v. *France* (1999) 29 EHRR 615, at para. 100, in which the ECtHR held that the term 'association' in Art. 11 has an autonomous meaning which does not depend on domestic classification.

[82] G. Letsas, *A Theory of Interpretation of the European Convention on Human Rights* (Oxford University Press, 2007), p. 44.

[83] *Ibid.* Letsas uses the term 'extension' following the writings of Fredde, where extension (in contrast to intension) is the object, person or situation in the world to which the concept applies.

[84] *Chassagnou*, note 81 above, para. 100.

[85] See Art. 32 ECHR.

[86] J. Callewaert, 'Is there a margin of appreciation of Articles 2, 3 and 4 of the Convention?', (1998) 19 *Human Rights Law Journal* 8.

correspond to rights in the Charter. However, Article 52(3) also permits Union law to provide more extensive protection. How can these provisions be reconciled? How must the scope of these corresponding rights be understood in order to enable both requirements to be met?

To give an example of the difficulties this can give rise to, the legal explanations in the Charter merely assert that the first paragraph of Article 47 EUCFR is based on Article 13 ECHR, while the second paragraph corresponds to Article 6(1) ECHR.[87] It is also stated in the legal explanations that in Union law only Article 47(1) affords a protection that is more extensive since it guarantees the right to an effective remedy before a court. By contrast, paragraphs (2) and (3) of Article 47 are said to be 'corresponding rights with wider scope' in the explanatory notes related to Article 52 EUCFR. However, it is arguable from the CJEU's case law that the protection under paragraphs (2) and (3) is also more extensive (and thus not just paragraph (1)). What, then, is the dividing line between the 'corresponding rights with wider scope' and the rights where the 'protection is more extensive'? The *DEB* case offers an interesting illustration since Article 47(3) was interpreted by the Court as clearly applying to legal persons.[88] In *DEB*, the CJEU considered that, though the right of legal persons to receive legal aid is not deeply rooted in the ECHR, it is apparent from the examination of the case law of the ECtHR that the grant of legal aid to legal persons is not in principle impossible.[89] Importantly, for the CJEU Article 47(3) must be interpreted in its context, in the light of other provisions of EU law, the law of the Member States and the case law of the ECtHR.[90] In the light of *DEB*, Article 47(3) EUCFR can be viewed as a right 'where the protection is more extensive' whereas it is not explicitly categorised as such in the legal explanations that the Charter supplies for this specific Article.

The conclusion to which we are inescapably drawn is that the Explanatory Notes do not help to draw a clear-cut distinction between corresponding rights and rights affording more extensive protection.[91] It appears from Article 47 EUCFR that the corresponding rights having a wider

87 See Case C–69/10 *Samba Diouf* [2011] nyr, paras 37–8. This confirms the Opinion of AG Cruz Villalón in the same case.

88 *DEB*, note 79 above, para. 30.

89 *Ibid.*, para. 52. It must be assessed in the light of the applicable rules and the situation of the company concerned.

90 *Ibid.*, para. 37.

91 Cf. Weiß, 'Human rights in the EU', note 18 above.

scope can also be viewed as rights affording a wider protection. This position is also verified by Article 50 EUCFR. This provision, which enshrines the *non bis in idem* principle, corresponds to Article 4 of Protocol No. 7 to the ECHR, but its scope is wider since it also applies to cross-border situations involving different courts of the Member States.[92] In other words, in certain circumstances (when there is a cross-border element) it may be viewed as a non-corresponding right. The practical consequence of this is that there is no obligation under Article 52(3) EUCFR for the CJEU to respect ECtHR case law.[93]

In addition, Article 49 EUCFR, which enshrines the principle of retroactivity *in mitius*, is not explicitly viewed, in the Explanatory Notes, as a right affording more extensive protection than Article 7 ECHR or even a corresponding right having wider scope. Furthermore, looking at Title II of the Charter and more particularly at Article 7 EUCFR, it is stated in the Explanatory Notes that this provision corresponds to Article 8 ECHR. However, it is well known that CJEU cases like *Carpenter* and *Chakroun*, concerning the rights of third-country nationals (TCN) in the context of both free movement and migration policies, afford more extensive protection to TCNs, since the margin of discretion afforded to the state is narrower than in the ECtHR case law.[94] Once again, the Explanatory

[92] Art. 4 of Protocol 7 ECHR applies only in internal situations.

[93] If this is true, it means that the CJEU was right in the recent *Toshiba Corporation* case from 14 February 2012 (Case C–17/10 *Toshiba Corporation and others* [2012] nyr). In this case, the Court refused to follow the (single) criterion established by the ECtHR in *Zolotukhin*, note 20 above, and instead relied on its own (three-pronged) *Aalborg* criteria to assess the *'idem'* (Joined Cases 204/00 P *et al.*, *Aalborg* [2004] ECR I–00123, para. 338). Cf. Opinion of AG Kokott in *Toshiba Corporation and Others*, paras 119–20. She considered that the homegenity clause applied. For the purposes of identifying the criteria relevant for defining *idem*, it must be borne in mind that the *ne bis in idem* principle is based largely on a fundamental right enshrined in the ECHR, more specifically Art. 4(1) Prot. 7 ECHR, although that protocol has not yet been ratified by all the EU Member States. That close proximity to the ECHR is indicated not only by the Explanations on Art. 50 of the Charter of Fundamental Rights, which must be duly taken into account by the courts of the European Union and of the Member States, but also by the previous case law of the Court of Justice concerning the general EU legal principle *ne bis in idem*... The requirement for homogeneity is therefore applicable. It follows from that requirement that rights contained in the Charter that correspond to rights guaranteed by the ECHR are to have the same meaning and scope as those laid down by the ECHR. In other words, Art. 4(1) Prot. 7 ECHR, as interpreted by the ECtHR, describes the minimum standard that must be guaranteed in the interpretation and application of the *ne bis in idem* principle in EU law.

[94] Case C–60/00 *Carpenter* [2002] ECR I–6279, para. 41, Case C–578/08 *Chakroun* [2010] nyr, para. 44.

Notes do not offer a perfect tool to assess the notion of corresponding rights. This is regrettable, since the concept of corresponding rights has an important legal consequence, i.e. the obligation to respect ECtHR case law.

2.2 The primary duty under Article 52(3)

Another point of crucial importance is that the discretion to provide more extensive protection does not affect the primary duty to secure the corresponding right.[95] So any measure that fails to respect the corresponding right, within the meaning and scope given to that right by the ECtHR, will breach the Charter, regardless of whether it also provides more extensive protection.

A recent CJEU case illustrates the importance of vigilance if this duty to secure the corresponding rights is to be honoured. *Roj TV* concerned a TV company established in Denmark broadcasting into Germany.[96] Germany considered that the broadcasts breached principles of international understanding since, in their view, the broadcasts called for the resolution of differences between Kurds and Turks by violence. Germany therefore prohibited Roj TV from carrying out its activities in Germany. After the broadcaster challenged that decision, the German court referred to the CJEU a question on whether that prohibition had been compatible with the Television Without Frontiers Directive.[97] The CJEU ruled that, whilst the Directive prohibited Germany from blocking retransmission of Roj TV's broadcasts into its territory, it did not preclude Germany from taking other measures against the broadcaster, such as prohibiting the production of broadcasts in Germany, the public screenings of Roj TV broadcasts, and sympathy actions connected to the broadcasts.

The surprising point about the judgment is that no consideration is given to any potential restriction on freedom of expression that such measures might entail. This right is protected by Article 11 EUCFR, which corresponds exactly to Article 10 ECHR. As Advocate-General Bot pointed out in his Opinion, the fundamental right to freedom of expression laid down in Article 11 EUCFR is the principle behind the

[95] See AG Trsentjak in *NS*, note 6 above.

[96] Cases C–244/10 and C–245/10 *Mesopotamia Broadcast and Roj TV* [2011] nyr.

[97] Council Directive 89/552/EEC of 3 October 1989 on the coordination of certain provisions laid down by law, regulation or administrative action in Member States concerning the pursuit of television broadcasting activities.

Directive.[98] Therefore any limitations on this principle must be interpreted restrictively. The measures taken by the German authorities clearly had the potential to place limitations on Roj TV's right of free expression: prohibiting public showings of the transmissions would clearly have an impact on the reach of the broadcasts. Further, prohibiting programmes from being produced in Germany might have an impact on the issues that could be covered, and how they could be covered: it might limit the range of people that could be interviewed and the footage that could be obtained.

As the Court made clear in *Karner*, where a national measure falls within the field of application of Union law the Court, in a reference for a preliminary ruling, must give the national court all the guidance as to interpretation necessary to enable it to assess the compatibility of that legislation with the fundamental rights the observance of which the Court ensures.[99] But in *Roj TV* the guidance given by the CJEU was only to check that there was no restriction on freedom to provide services. Once that was done, EU law would have nothing more to say about the lawfulness of any further measures, regardless of the impact that they might have on fundamental rights. It is suggested that this approach would not enable the CJEU to discharge its primary duty under Article 52(3) of ensuring that corresponding rights are secured.

2.3 More extensive protection

But once that duty is secured, is the Court of Justice then free to interpret the scope of a corresponding right in a way that provides more extensive protection? It is argued that, if the Union wishes to do so, then that more extensive protection must come from Union law, as the wording of the last paragraph of Article 52(3) EUCFR requires. This point is made clear if Article 52(3) is read in conjunction with Article 53 ECHR. The ECHR article states that:

> [n]othing in this Convention shall be construed as limiting or derogating from any of the human rights and fundamental freedoms *which may be ensured under the laws* of any High Contracting Party or *under any other agreement* to which it is a party.[100]

[98] AG Bot in *Mesopotamia Broadcast and ROJ TV*, note 96 above, para. 51.

[99] C–71/02 *Karner* [2004] ECR I–03025, at para. 49.

[100] Our emphasis.

So, according to the ECHR, the Union is fully entitled to provide more extensive protection for a right under its own laws.[101] To do this will not breach the ECHR. But what the Union cannot do is to claim that such a right is protected under the Convention, because (as we have seen) only the ECtHR has the competence to interpret the scope and application of the Convention. As the rights in the Charter must have the same scope and meaning as the corresponding Convention rights, the necessary implication must be that the Union is precluded from claiming that this more extensive protection derives from the corresponding right.

This point may be usefully illustrated by an example. The right to respect for private and family life, home and communications under Article 7 EUCFR corresponds to the right to respect for private and family life, home and correspondence in Article 8 ECHR. In some circumstances the processing of information about a person can fall within the scope of this right. However, in addition to this general right to privacy, the Charter also provides a specific right to protection of personal data, under Article 8. This right has no corresponding right in the ECHR, and is therefore 'purely' a right under EU law. So, applying the analysis of Article 52(3) to these two Charter rights, it could be said that the EU must ensure that Article 7 EUCFR secures the right as defined in Article 8 ECHR. However, it may provide more extensive protection to personal data under its own law, applying Article 8 EUCFR.

This is not always the approach that the Court has taken. Whilst in one recent case the CJEU expressly acknowledged that EU law grants an individual the right to protection of personal data in circumstances that fall outside the scope of Article 8 ECHR,[102] in other cases the CJEU has adopted an expansive interpretation of the case law of the ECtHR, providing greater protection than does the ECtHR. This is particularly clear in cases involving the processing of information about legal persons. As is well known, the Convention protects the rights of both legal and natural persons, in some circumstances. However, the ECtHR has not yet held that the right to respect for private life under Article 8 extends to legal persons, nor that the collection or use of information about a legal person engages the Article 8 rights of that legal person. On the other hand

101 And in fact, under Art. 53 EUCFR, the Union makes the same commitment that nothing in the Charter should be interpreted as restricting or adversely affecting human rights recognised by (among others) the ECHR, or by the Member States' constitutions.

102 Case C–28/08 P *Bavarian Lager* [2010] ECR I–06055.

the CJEU has interpreted the right to privacy in a way that goes much further.

Varec is a good example of this.[103] The case concerned a request by one company (Varec) to be given details of a tender application submitted by another company (Diehl) in response to a public tendering procedure announced by the Belgian state. The Court held that the disclosure of the document would be an interference with Diehl's right to respect for private life under Article 8.[104] The Court referred to the ECtHR cases of *Peck* and *Colas Est* in support of their findings that Article 8 was engaged,[105] and stated that 'it follows from the case law [of the ECtHR that] the notion of "private life" cannot be taken to mean that the . . . commercial activities of . . . legal persons are excluded'. However, *Colas Est* was not about the notion of 'private life' but was in fact about the right to respect for the home, or domicile, of a company.[106] The ECtHR is generally careful to distinguish between the different rights protected by Article 8, and the justification for protecting the home can be seen to rest on different grounds than the concept of private life.[107]

The CJEU's reference to *Peck* is also curious. In this case closed-circuit television images of Mr Peck carrying a knife in a public street were shown on national television, in a way that allowed him to be recognised by the audience. This was found to be an interference with his right to respect for private life. Mr Peck was suffering from mental illness and was carrying the knife in order to cut his own wrists (he did cut his wrists but paramedics reached him in time). Whilst he was in a public street, he was not there to take part in any public event and he was not a public figure, nor had he been charged with any offence. He was in a very distressed and vulnerable state and the broadcast was deeply embarrassing for him. It is difficult to see the parallels between (on one hand) broadcasting on national television footage of a mentally ill man, in a very vulnerable state, minutes before attempting suicide, and (on the other) requiring that a

[103] Case C–450/06 *Varec SA* v. *Belgian State* [2008] ECR I–00581. [104] *Ibid.*, para. 48.

[105] ECtHR, *Peck*, 28 January 2003. ECtHR, *Colas Est*, 16 April 2002.

[106] *Colas Est*, *ibid.*, at para. 42.

[107] It can be argued that the right to respect for the home can be considered related philosophically to the right to property. One's home, as well as being an important component of one's private life, is also often one's property. So a search by the state authorities of one's home can be seen to impact on the right to the peaceful enjoyment of one's property. Whilst it is not a deprivation or control of use, and so will not engage Art. 1 Prot. 1, it is a clear intrusion. For those reasons it is easy to extend the protection of the company's right to property that the Convention affords, to protect their 'homes' from intrusion.

company that submitted a tender in a public tendering process disclose that tender to a rival company.

This case illustrates the very expansive approach that the CJEU can take when applying ECtHR case law in corresponding rights cases.[108] It is argued that it would be preferable and more in line with the requirements of Article 52(3) to ensure that Charter rights are interpreted with the same scope and meaning as the corresponding Convention rights, and that whenever more extensive protection is afforded, this is explicitly acknowledged by the CJEU.

3. Conclusion

It transpires from this analysis that the 'new' rights may have an impact on the scope of application of 'old' human rights in Europe. As described above, the material scope of application of the Charter is broader than that of the ECHR rights. The 'new' rights may therefore influence the development of 'old' rights, as a source of inspiration for the Strasbourg court. Also, the Charter rights have wider impact than ECHR rights on private parties, 'horizontal' situations, and in relation to the enforcement of rights through the prism of EU constitutional principles. Since the Lisbon Treaty came into force, the relationship between the Strasbourg and Luxembourg legal orders is governed by Article 52(3) EUCFR. It is argued that Article 52(3) EUCFR has unilaterally bound the EU to the jurisdiction of the ECtHR when the rights correspond. This legal duty to respect the Convention derives from the Charter, and is not contingent on any accession by the EU to the ECHR.

Problematically, the definition of corresponding rights provided by the Explanatory Notes in the Charter is misleading and should be used with extreme care. Furthermore, the CJEU may sometimes take a very expansive approach when applying ECtHR case law in corresponding rights cases. It would be preferable and more in line with the requirements of Article 52(3) to ensure that Charter rights are interpreted with the same scope and meaning as the corresponding Convention rights. Article 52(3) effectively extends the scope for application of Convention rights into all areas of EU law, but with the proviso that it imposes duties on the CJEU that must be taken seriously. These duties are, first, the duty to ensure the protection of Convention rights as minimum standards in all areas of EU law, and second, the duty to ensure that different normative

[108] This approach was also taken in *Volker*, note 79 above, see in particular para. 52.

considerations are not permitted to shape the CJEU's understanding of the meaning and scope of the rights. EU legal rights are not always designed to reinforce human rights protection, but instead pursue a specific goal of EU market integration. The Strasbourg court and the Luxembourg court should be completely aware of the different normative goals of the two legal systems in order to ensure that the fundamental rights set out in both instruments are respected.

12

European human rights as universal rights

In defence of a holistic understanding of human rights

MARTIN SCHEININ

1. Introduction

The European Convention on Human Rights is but one of many human rights treaties binding upon European states. In particular at the level of the United Nations, numerous – general and specific – human rights treaties have been adopted, to which most Council of Europe member states adhere. This chapter examines how far the scopes of human rights at the UN and the Council of Europe levels are coherent. It promotes an 'interdependence approach' based on the idea of universal and indivisible human rights. This does not mean that the scope of every human rights provision should be interpreted in the widest possible way but that every human rights provision should be interpreted as being compatible with all other human rights, including through the principle of avoiding any 'cracks' between human rights, through which important issues could fall. In addition, the chapter proposes an integrated approach to human rights obligations, which would in the author's view require the creation of a World Court of Human Rights, the jurisdiction of which would not be limited to states only, but would also allow for the human rights accountability of other actors besides states as duty-bearers.

The determination of the scope of an article in a human rights treaty is an issue that pertains to the interpretation of the treaty in question. It is asserted that the determination of the scope of a treaty provision is neither something predefined, before even addressing the case at hand, nor an operation that could be isolated into a specific step in the course of the overall consideration of a case. True, comparing the human rights claim made by the applicant with reference to an allegedly violated provision of the ECHR to the actual scope of the invoked provision, as understood by the Court, is primarily an admissibility issue. That said, addressing the issue of scope will engage a number of admissibility questions, some of which require a feedback loop from the body of the Court's jurisprudence on the merits. Hence, a single decision that a particular claim falls within or outside the scope of an ECHR provision requires interaction with the institutionalised interpretative practice of the ECHR as a whole. This is one of the two positions this chapter wishes to defend.

The other position to be presented and defended is one of interdependence between the ECHR as a single human rights treaty and the broader phenomenon of human rights law. Ultimately, human rights are universally applicable, fundamental rights of the individual and therefore the application and interpretation of any regional human rights treaty will need to strive for a universalist view and allow itself to be informed by treaties and interpretative practices on the global (United Nations) level as well as within other regional human rights systems. The discussion below will first articulate the latter position and then move to the former one. This chapter will conclude with two remarks on the value a world court can have if a holistic perspective on human rights is taken.

2. ECHR and universal human rights

In an earlier article, the author of this chapter proposed a differentiation between a school of distinction and a school of interdependence as two ways to read a treaty.[1] Adherents of the school of distinction would emphasise reasoning *a contrario* and argue that if something falls within the scope of treaty provision (or human right) A, it cannot also sit within the scope of provision (or right) B. Under this approach, the respective scopes of various human rights are exclusive, so that potential cases of overlap are to be resolved by excluding from the scope of one right anything that might fall within the scope of another. If this sometimes results in excluding an issue from the scope of both potentially applicable human rights provisions, that just has to be accepted. As examples of the school of distinction in practice, reference can be made to the Human Rights Committee case *JB et al.* v. *Canada*,[2] to its General Comment

[1] M. Scheinin, 'The right to self-determination under the Covenant on Civil and Political Rights' in P. Aikio and M. Scheinin (eds), *Operationalizing the Right of Indigenous Peoples to Self-Determination* (Turku, Finland: Åbo Akademi University Institute for Human Rights, 2000), pp. 179–99.

[2] Because the right to strike was explicitly mentioned in Art. 8 of the Covenant on Economic, Social and Cultural Rights (ICESCR), the committee concluded that 'the right to strike cannot be considered as an implicit component of the right to form and join trade unions', a right explicitly mentioned in Art. 22 of the International Covenant on Civil and

No. 23 on minority rights,[3] and to a dissenting opinion in the case of *Hopu and Bessert* v. *France*.[4]

In contrast, the school of interdependence seeks to interpret and apply each treaty provision (or human right) in its context, as being informed and enriched by other provisions in the same treaty or within the broader family of all human rights. Examples include the majority opinion in *Hopu and Bessert*, as well as subsequent case law acknowledging the interpretative effect of Article 1 ICCPR – the right of peoples to self-determination which, unlike other rights in the ICCPR, is not acknowledged as being on its own subject to the procedure of individual complaint – upon other provisions, such as Article 27 on minority rights and Article 25 on rights of participation.[5] To operationalise the (collective) right of a people to self-determination, the acknowledgement of interdependence between various treaty provisions is a crucial step. This was the basic point made in that earlier article, but of course the issue has much broader implications for human rights law, including in the determination of the scope of specific treaty provisions.

The school of interdependence finds support in various intergovernmental declarations and documents adopted at the United Nations level, emphasising the universal, interdependent and inter-related nature of all human rights.[6] In Europe, the adoption and subsequent incorporation in the framework of the EU's constituting treaties of the Charter on Fundamental Rights were important milestones in the recognition of

Political Rights (ICCPR) as a dimension of freedom of association. *JB et al.* v. *Canada*, Communication 118/1982, para. 6.4.

3 This general comment on ICCPR Art. 27 appears to seek justification for minority rights through: (over)emphasising their distinctiveness as compared to universally applicable human rights. See, in particular, paras 1, 3.1 and 5.3 of the General Comment, available at www2.ohchr.org/english/bodies/hrc/comments.htm.

4 Owing to a declaration by France (amounting to a reservation), ICCPR Art. 27 was not applicable in a case that concerned the construction of a hotel complex on traditional burial grounds and at a fishing lagoon still used for the subistence of indigenous Polynesians in Tahiti. The Committee's majority, however, found a violation of other ICCPR provisions, namely Arts 17 and 23, as there had been an arbitrary interference with the complainants' right to family and privacy due to the importance of the burial grounds in question for their 'history, culture and life' (para. 10.3). A minority of four members dissented, arguing that the values cited by the majority 'are protected under Article 27 of the Covenant and not the provisions relied on by the Committee', *Hopu and Bessert* v. *France*, Communication 549/1993.

5 *Mahuika et al.* v. *New Zealand*, Communication 547/1993 (Art. 27 informed by Art. 1) and *Gillot et al.* v. *France*, Communication 932/2000 (Art. 25 informed by Art. 1).

6 See, in particular, paras 5 and 8 in Part I of the 1993 Vienna Declaration and Programme of Action, UN doc. A/CONF.157/23.

interdependence between all fundamental rights. In its Article 52, the EU Charter, which carries the title 'Scope and interpretation of rights and principles', on one hand supports interdependence, for instance in paragraph 3 (seeking to integrate its own interpretation with that of the ECHR) and paragraph 4 (providing for harmonising interpretation with national constitutions), but on the other hand suggests a problematic distinction between 'rights' and 'principles' in its title and in paragraph 5.

Within the Council of Europe system, the ECHR clearly has a special status as compared to other conventions in the field of human rights, so that the school of distinction may still be alive and well, manifesting itself in efforts to restrict the scope of a particular ECHR provision under the argument that the proposed dimension of the human right in question would find its protection under another treaty and hence, *a contrario*, not under the ECHR.[7] That said, the alternation and dialogue between the schools of distinction and interdependence are visible also in the operation of the Court.

In line with the lessons of the school of interdependence, the indivisible and holistic nature of human rights is illustrated by Figure 1 through the example of ECHR Article 8. Even though that provision lists a number of subject-matter areas protected under one single provision – namely private life, family life, honour and reputation – it is still more narrow in language than subsequent formulations of the same human right, here to be referred to through the shorthand expression 'privacy'. The right to privacy has given rise to the gradual emergence of the right to the protection of personal data as a semi-autonomous human right, so that the European Union Charter on Fundamental Rights now recognises it as a separate fundamental right in Article 8, while the privacy provision in Article 7 of the Charter lists exactly the same subject-matter areas as Article 8 ECHR. Data protection was also addressed as falling within the scope of Article 17 ICCPR in General Comment 16 by the Human Rights Committee. The provision in question is closely related to Article 8 ECHR as it lists the same protected subject matters, using the term 'privacy' instead of 'private life' and adding 'correspondence' to the list. More importantly, the ICCPR includes a separate provision on the protection

[7] In *Chapman* v. *United Kingdom* (Application 27238/95), the Court dismissed the claim of a violation of ECHR Art. 8 through a traveller/Gypsy family being denied from settling down in their caravan, with reference to the existence of a separate European Framework Convention for the Protection of National Minorities as support for a deferential standard in reading into ECHR Art. 8 any minority rights dimension. See paras 93–4.

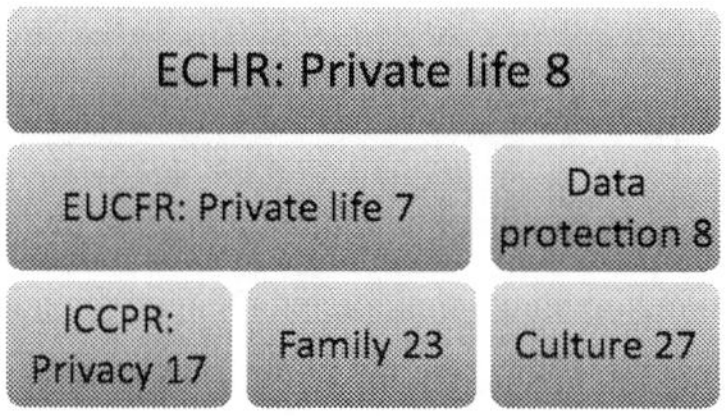

Figure 1 The indivisibility and holistic nature of human rights: scope

of the family, in Article 23, even though the basic notion of the family is already included in Article 17. Further, the ICCPR has a separate provision, in Article 27, on the rights of members of minorities, including their right to enjoy their own 'culture' in community with other members of the group. This community dimension of the right to private life has been recognised and developed in the jurisprudence of the Court and its predecessor the European Commission of Human Rights under Article 8 ECHR.[8] Under Article 8 ECHR it has been explicitly acknowledged that such a community dimension of the right to private life may have particular application in the case of persons belonging to minorities and leading a distinctive way of life – their culture.

Drawing upon these considerations, Figure 1 illustrates that at least as a point of departure for a concrete assessment in a case, the scope of Article 8 ECHR should be assumed to include the right to the protection of personal data (Article 8 EU Charter), as well as those dimensions of Articles 23 and 27 ICCPR that are not textually represented in the wording of Article 8 ECHR but have a strong substantive connection to the protection afforded by it. Instead of making conclusions *a contrario* from the fact that the text of Article 8 ECHR does not provide for data protection or minority rights, an interdependence-based model of interpretation seeks to respect the indivisible and holistic nature of all human rights and to assume an expansive scope for the provision in case of doubt.

[8] As an early case, see ECommHR, *G and E* v. *Norway*, Applications No. 9278/81 and 9415/81, European Commission of Human Rights, *Decisions and Reports*, vol. 35 (1984), pp. 30–45. As a much more recent case, reference is made to ECtHR, *Noack* v. *Germany*, 25 May 2005 (Application 46346/99), which concerned the dislocation of a Sorbian minority village because of a mining project. Here, the Court stated 'for the purposes of Article 8 of the Convention, a minority's way of life is, in principle, entitled to the protection guaranteed for an individual's private life, family life and home'. Notably, both of these cases are inadmissibility decisions and therefore the actual consequences of these statements was not tested.

Not all of the scope covered jointly by Articles 27 or 23 ICCPR will be likely to fall under Article 8 ECHR. Rather, it would be the dimensions of 'privacy and family' and 'culture', respectively, in those provisions that in the ECHR system seek their home under Article 8. For instance the right to marry, protected by Article 23 ICCPR, is to be found explicitly elsewhere in the ECHR, namely in Article 12. When, in addition to minority culture, Article 27 ICCPR protects minority language and minority religion, in the ECHR system those aspects of minority rights may ultimately find their protection under, respectively, Articles 10 and 9, rather than under Article 8. That said, as Article 8 has proven to be perhaps the most dynamic provision of the ECHR, often providing a platform for the recognition of 'new' claims as triggering human rights protection, such as in issues related to sexuality, euthanasia and migration, it is tempting to predict that in the future its scope will continue to be subject to expansion through interpretation.[9]

In relation to issues covered by the ICCPR but not in the text of the ECHR, one intriguing question is whether Article 24 ICCPR and its close relationship with preceding Article 23 on the family could encourage the Court towards reading into Article 8 ECHR the rights of the child,[10] including through developing the idea of the autonomy of the person being an important dimension of the right to one's private life. Quite rightly, the ECHR has been criticised for being a very old-fashioned human rights treaty in that it does not give much room to the rights of the child. Sadly, on both occasions on which the ECHR or its Protocols explicitly or implicitly make reference to children, focus is on the rights of the parents.[11] If Article 8 ECHR were to become the platform for child rights claims, then Figure 1 should be modified to include Article 24 ICCPR as well, in addition to Articles 17, 23 and 27.

Article 8 ECHR may be a particularly well suited case for the interdependence-based assessment of scope, owing to the dynamic and multifaceted nature of this provision. That said, there are certainly other areas in which ECHR provisions, when read against the broader background of the universal catalogue of human rights, will need to be informed by other human rights, in addition to the one that is already

[9] On this, see the chapter in this volume written by Maris Burbergs.

[10] Article 24 ICCPR includes a general clause on the rights of the child to 'such measures of protection as are required by his status as a minor, on the part of his family, society and the State', as well as special clauses on a child's right to registration, name and nationality.

[11] See ECHR Protocol 1, Art. 2, and Protocol 7, Art. 5.

covered in the text of the provision (obviously). Trade union rights under the freedom of association (Article 11), as well as social rights under the right to a fair trial (Article 6) and under the freedom of movement (Protocol 4, Article 2) are some further illustrations.[12]

3. Phases of scope determination

I am now moving to the question how the determination of whether a particular human rights claim falls within or outside the scope of a specific ECHR provision represents a contextual comparison between the case at hand and institutionalised practices of interpretation, e.g. earlier case law by the Court. The Court's determination of issues of scope cannot be isolated into one single step in the overall consideration of a case. Rather, questions of scope will be asked at various stages of the proceedings. Human rights claims made by applicants to the Court are often broader than what the Court's established understanding, represented by its case law, would suggest. While the scope determination made by the Court will result in excluding some claims from ECHR protection, the scope of each substantive provision is not static, since new human rights claims will always require fresh consideration of the scope of the human right invoked. Therefore, the question whether a case falls within the scope of an ECHR provision cannot be isolated into one single admissibility issue but may occur also at the stage of the merits, through substantive reinterpretation of ECHR provisions.

Figure 2 seeks to illustrate the various phases in which scope is determined by the Court. For each human rights claim presented by way of an application to the Court, there are three possible outcomes: inadmissibility (represented in the figure by a waste-paper basket), and two alternative conclusions on the merits, namely that a violation of the ECHR occurred or that no violation occurred. Seemingly the most important phase, in which the Court addresses whether a particular complaint falls within the scope of an ECHR provision, is represented in the figure by the notion of 'general incompatibility'. Among the inadmissibility grounds prescribed in Article 35 ECHR, paragraph (3)(a) lists the situation in which the complaint is 'incompatible with the provisions of the Convention or the Protocols thereto'. If scope determination were to be reduced to one single phase in the consideration of a case, this would be it.

[12] For the 'socialising' effect of Art. 14 ECHR, see the chapter by Oddný Arnardóttir in this volume.

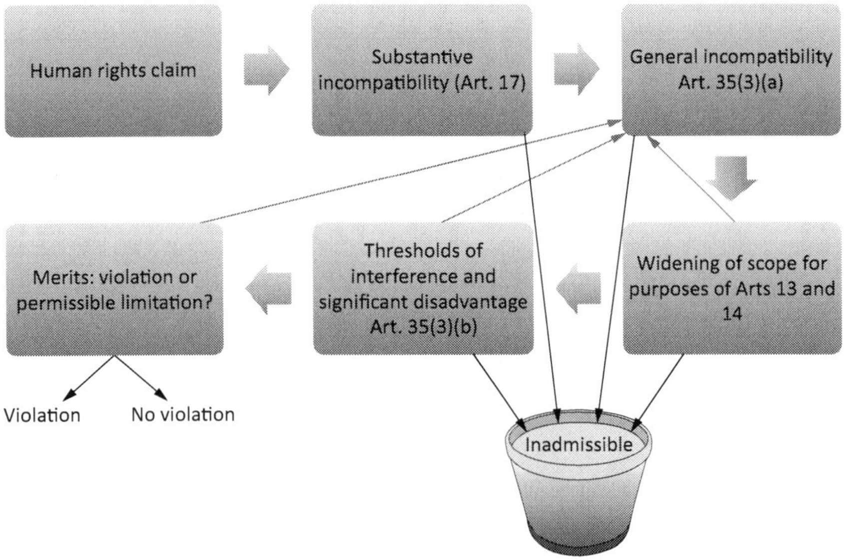

Figure 2 Issues and phases of scope determination

The view defended in this part of the current chapter, however, is that the issue of scope cannot be isolated into one single phase in the overall process of dealing with a case. Already prior to addressing the question of general incompatibility, the Court may be confronted with the issue whether the claim presented to it is at all worthy of human rights protection. In the figure this is referred to as 'substantive incompatibility' as prescribed in Article 17 ECHR. This provision has the word 'abuse' in its title and excludes from protection all claims that aim at the 'destruction' of human rights.[13] Rightly, the Court has been cautious in applying the provision as an independent ground for inadmissibility.[14] To understand the process of determining scope, however, it is useful to keep in mind that methodologically it also includes this phase of assessing substantive incompatibility.

[13] See the chapter by Antoine Buyse in this volume.

[14] See, for instance, the unanimous Grand Chamber judgment in the case of ECtHR (GC) 8 December 1999, *Freedom and Democracy Party (ÖZDEP)* v. *Turkey* (Application 23885/94) (para. 47) in which the Court dismissed the application of ECHR Art. 17 (this had been referred to by the Turkish Constitutional Court) and found a violation of ECHR Art. 11 (para. 48).

Reference to these two admissibility issues does not exhaust the discussion on the scope of the ECHR and on whether a complaint falls within it. Figure 2 includes two further boxes that both provide for the possibility of declaring a case inadmissible for reasons related to the scope of ECHR provisions. Hence, there are four parallel routes through which a case may end up in the waste-paper basket of inadmissibility. One of them, however, referring to Articles 13 and 14 ECHR, provides for a *widening* of the range of admissible complaints. In order to be declared admissible in relation to Article 13 or 14, in conjunction with another substantive human rights provision, it is not required that a case should fall straightforwardly within the scope of that other provision. Rather, it is sufficient that the complainant has raised an arguable claim that the other provision has been violated; then a claim concerning discrimination (Article 14) or absence of effective remedies (Article 13) brings the case within the ECHR.

Article 35 ECHR, paragraph (3)(b), introduced through Protocol 14, operates in the opposite direction. Even when a complaint has passed muster under subparagraph (a) of the provision as not being incompatible with the ECHR and hence *prima facie* falling within the scope of a substantive provision, it can be declared inadmissible if the complainant has not suffered a 'significant disadvantage'. This provision introduces a seriousness threshold for human rights violations, as a condition for their being acknowledged as falling within the scope of the Court's jurisdiction under a substantive provision. Even though the provision is somewhat discretionary in its borderlines, Article 35, paragraph (4), makes it clear that the provision is to be seen as a mandatory condition for admissibility and hence as reflecting a genuine question of scope determination.

In Figure 2, the admissibility condition just referred to as a seriousness threshold is illustrated together with another threshold, namely whether there was an *interference* with the human right claimed. Even though that question is routinely addressed by the Court at the merits stage, it is grouped together with admissibility issues here because of its importance for the application of the main phase of scope determination, namely that of general incompatibility. Factors that in the view of lay people affect their enjoyment of human rights, and that therefore trigger their decision to file a complaint before the Court, are treated by professionals as falling outside the scope of the invoked right if the Court in its case law has decided that the measures in question do not amount to an interference with any of the ECHR rights. Such decisions will inform subsequent practice by the Court, so that new applications related to the same issue are declared inadmissible at the outset for being incompatible with the ECHR.

This is the first of three feedback loops illustrated in Figure 2. What is not an interference with any ECHR right cannot be subject to a successful subsequent complaint, since the corresponding claim is seen as incompatible with the ECHR. Similarly, the threshold of significant disadvantage and the determination of what constitutes an arguable claim for purposes of Articles 13 or 14 will inform the Court, in future cases, what kind of complaints are to be declared incompatible with the ECHR.

Finally, there is also a feedback loop from the last box in Figure 2. A case that has passed all admissibility conditions and the preliminary merits issue (whether there was an interference with an ECHR right), will be addressed from the perspective of whether the recognised interference was permissible under the ECHR, for instance under the explicit restriction clauses in Articles 8–11, or whether all things considered the interference was impermissible. In the former case the Court makes a finding of no violation, while in the latter it establishes that a violation of the ECHR had taken place. Additionally, these decisions made at the merits stage by the Court through interpretation of the substantive human rights provisions will affect the issues affecting determination of scope in any future cases.

4. Two short remarks about the World Court of Human Rights

So far, this chapter has made two arguments about the scope of ECHR rights: one is about the need to read ECHR rights in the light of universal human rights, and the other is about the different stages in the European Court's reasoning at which determinations of scope can take place, as well as about the feedback loops from the Court's earlier case law. To conclude, I want to make a few remarks that build upon the holistic view of human rights put forward in the first argument, while adding to the holistic approach *ratione materiae*.

Some years ago I was involved in the drafting of a Statute for a future World Court of Human Rights. The proposal, submitted to the Swiss Initiative to commemorate the sixtieth anniversary of the Universal Declaration of Human Rights,[15] represents both a serious idea for reforming the international adjudication and enforcement of human rights whenever

[15] See www.udhr60.ch.

there is political momentum for change, and a reflection over developments in human rights law to that point, over the more than sixty years since the adoption of the UDHR.

There are two reasons for referring to the World Court project in the context of this chapter. First, one dimension of the proposal is in taking seriously the evolution of human rights law beyond the traditional and narrow idea of human rights as strictly vertical norms between the individual and the territorial state. When human rights are looked into as individual entitlements, their scope should not be restricted to those dimensions of the right that are applicable in relation to one single duty-bearer, the state of which the individual is a citizen or resident. With some discomfort, courts and expert bodies that monitor state compliance with their human rights obligations have sought to apply standards such as due diligence in order to attribute to the state conduct that in fact was undertaken by some other actor, such as a private corporation or an international organisation. Since all monitoring mechanisms under traditional human rights treaties, including procedures for individual complaints, are geared towards the States Parties, there is no-one to hold to account other than the state. The innovation in the World Court project is to see this as a procedural defect of existing human rights treaties, rather than as an essential feature of human rights norms themselves, which would be understood to constrain their scope to the relationship between the individual and the state that has jurisdiction over him or her.

The World Court Statute would extend the binding jurisdiction of the proposed Court not only to states that ratify the Statute but also to 'entities' that accept the Court's jurisdiction,[16] through an act analogous to ratification by a state.[17] Through this provision the World Court would represent a major leap towards a uniform paradigm of human rights obligations, applicable in equal terms to states and to other powerful organisations when they engage in activities that result in violating the human rights of individuals. The scope of substantive human rights norms need not

[16] J. Kozma, M. Nowak and M. Scheinin, *A World Court of Human Rights – Consolidated Statute and Commentary, Studienreihe des Ludwig Boltzmann Instituts für Menschenrechte 22* (Vienna: Neuer Wissenschaftlicher Verlag, 2010). The draft Statute is also available at www.eui.eu/Documents/DepartmentsCentres/Law/Professors/Scheinin/ConsolidatedWorldCourtStatute.pdf.

[17] *Ibid.*, Art. 51 (p. 27). See, also, Art. 4, para. 1 (p. 11), where the term 'entity' is defined as follows: 'any inter-governmental organization or non-State actor, including any business corporation, which has recognized the jurisdiction of the Court in accordance with Article 51', Art. 6, para. 1 on attribution and Art. 7 on individual complaints (both on p. 12).

be limited to those dimensions that pertain to the vertical relationship between the individual and the jurisdictional state but can be extended adequately to cover other relationships as well, when the procedural defect inherent in present-day human rights treaties is remedied.

Second, the World Court project corresponds to the holistic and interdependence-based approach to human rights as universal and mutually reinforcing, so that each treaty provision will need to be read in the light of the other provisions in the same treaty and in other human rights treaties. Article 6, paragraph 2, of the draft World Court Statute is entitled 'General Principles' and reads as follows:

> In exercising its jurisdiction, the Court shall be guided by the principles of universality, interdependence and indivisibility of all human rights, by general international law, general principles of law and by the jurisprudence of other international and regional courts.[18]

In the context of the World Court Statute, this provision is intended as a partial remedy to the problem of 'variable geometry' that results from different states and entities being allowed to recognise the jurisdiction of the Court in respect of some but not all human rights treaties or their provisions. Through elevating universality, interdependence and indivisibility into a principle of law, the proposed provision would secure a harmonising interpretation of any human right. At the same time, the provision reflects a broader trend in human rights law towards the recognition of such a principle as already within the framework of existing law.

[18] *Ibid.*, Art. 6, para. 2 (p. 12).

PART 4

A closer look at specific rights

13

The 'absolute' prohibition of torture and inhuman or degrading treatment in Article 3 ECHR

Truly a question of scope only?

STIJN SMET

1. Introduction

In its principled rhetoric, the European Court of Human Rights (ECtHR; the Court) consistently refers to the prohibition of torture and inhuman or degrading treatment in Article 3 of the European Convention on Human Rights (ECHR; the Convention) as absolute. The Court has declared that '[e]ven in the most difficult of circumstances, such as the fight against terrorism or crime, the Convention prohibits in absolute terms torture or inhuman or degrading treatment or punishment'[1] and that '[t]he philosophical basis underpinning the absolute nature of the right under Article 3 does not allow for any exceptions or justifying factors or balancing of interests'.[2]

Taken at face value, these statements lead to a straightforward, principled conclusion: because Article 3 is absolute, its application is purely a matter of scope.[3] Unlike most Convention articles,[4] Article 3 does not fit a two-stage model of human rights adjudication, in which the Court first establishes whether the right has been interfered with, then determines whether such interference could be justified as necessary in a democratic society to achieve a legitimate aim.[5] Instead, its application only requires

[1] ECtHR (GC), *Ramirez Sanchez* v. *France*, 4 June 2006, para. 115.

[2] ECtHR (GC), *Gäfgen* v. *Germany*, 1 June 2010, para. 107.

[3] H. Battjes, 'In search of a fair balance: the absolute character of the prohibition of *refoulement* under Article 3 ECHR re-assessed', (2009) 22 *Leiden Journal of International Law* pp. 587–8; A. Barak, *Proportionality: Constitutional Rights and their Limitations* (Cambridge University Press, 2012), p. 27.

[4] Arts 8–11 ECHR are the prime examples.

[5] On the two-stage model of human rights adjudication, see G. van der Schyff, *Limitation of Rights: A Study of the European Convention and the South African Bill of Rights* (Nijmegen: Wolf Legal Publishers, 2005); Barak, *Proportionality*, note 3 above, at pp. 19–20.

that a certain threshold has been reached: 'ill-treatment must attain a minimum level of severity if it is to fall within the scope of Article 3'.[6] When treatment falls within the scope of Article 3, it is absolutely prohibited: under no circumstances can it be justified.[7] In its principled rhetoric, the Court thus excludes any and all considerations of proportionality or balancing from holding relevance over the application of Article 3.[8] As such, the prohibition of torture and inhuman or degrading treatment offers formidable protection; at least in theory.

At least in theory, because, as Hemme Battjes has argued, the Court's case law does not live up to this picture of an 'absolute' Article 3.[9] Instead, Battjes concludes from his analysis of the Court's judgments on *refoulement* that 'the absolute character of the prohibition [of Article 3] does not preclude each and every form of balancing of interests'.[10] He consequently proposes an alternative reading of the Court's language on 'the absolute nature' of Article 3. He argues that the Court uses 'the label "absolute" ... for rhetorical effect',[11] as 'an argument, if not the decisive argument' that 'adds weight to the interest of the individual concerned'.[12] If this interpretation of the case law were correct, not much would be left of the firewall erected by the 'absolute nature' of Article 3. It would be liable to come crashing down in the face of proportionality considerations.

In this chapter, I will approach the issue rather differently from Battjes. Instead of proposing alternative readings of the Court's principled stance on the 'absolute nature of Article 3', I will take that principle as my starting

[6] ECtHR (Plenary), *Ireland* v. *United Kingdom*, 18 January 1978, para. 162.

[7] N. Mavronicola, 'What is an "absolute right"? Deciphering absoluteness in the context of Article 3 of the European Convention on Human Rights', *Human Rights Law Review*, advance access published 30 November 2012, doi:10.1093/hrlr/ngs020, p. 16; M.K. Addo and N. Grief, 'Does Article 3 of the European Convention on Human Rights enshrine absolute rights?', (1998) 9 *European Journal of International Law* 522.

[8] Mavronicola, 'What is an "absolute right"?', note 7 above, at pp. 14–15; S. Palmer, 'A wrong turning: Article 3 ECHR and proportionality', (2006) 65 *Cambridge Law Journal* 448; Battjes, 'In search of a fair balance', note 3 above, at p. 584.

[9] Battjes, *ibid.*

[10] *Ibid.*, at pp. 617–18. Battjes maintains that the Court's principle in *Soering*, to the effect that the qualification of treatment as inhuman or degrading involves an assessment in light of the 'search for a fair balance', which is 'inherent in the whole of the Convention', is still standing case law. See ECtHR (Plenary), *Soering* v. *United Kingdom*, 7 July 1989, para. 89. However, it seems to me that, in *Chahal*, the Court later clarified (or overruled) the principle it initially stated in *Soering*: 'it should not be inferred from the Court's remarks ... in paragraph 89 of ... [*Soering*] ... that there is any room for balancing the risk of ill-treatment against the reasons for expulsion in determining whether a State's responsibility under Article 3 is engaged'. See ECtHR (GC), *Chahal* v. *United Kingdom*, 15 November 1996, para. 81.

[11] Battjes, 'In search of a fair balance', note 3 above, at p. 584.

[12] *Ibid.*, at p. 618.

point and examine what it would take for the Court to hold fast to it in all instances. To that end, I will first paint a picture of a truly absolute prohibition of torture and inhuman or degrading treatment, illustrating how Article 3 should function for its application to really be purely a matter of scope. I will then show, in line with Battjes's findings, that currently the Court's case law does not live up to the promise of such an absolute right. However, unlike Battjes, I will not draw the conclusion that, upon closer examination, Article 3 is not really absolute. Instead, I will analyse whether – and if so, how – the Court can amend its reasoning in the problematic cases, i.e. those in which it introduces elements of proportionality and balancing, in order to bring it in line with its own principled stance on the 'absolute nature of the right under Article 3'. In doing so, I aim to contribute to the topic of the current volume by demonstrating what it would take for application of Article 3 to be truly a matter of scope only.

2. How Article 3 should function for it to be truly absolute

Before I spell out my understanding of a truly absolute Article 3, one preliminary clarification should be made. Given the importance of the notion of proportionality to the current contribution, I should explain what I mean when I use this term. To fully grasp the arguments set out in this chapter, it is vital to avoid potential confusion between two ways in which the word 'proportionality' can be used. Proportionality can firstly refer to the proportionality test, i.e. the test the Court employs to determine whether an interference with a qualified Convention right can be justified as necessary in a democratic society in pursuit of a legitimate aim. When I argue, throughout this chapter, that Article 3 can only be truly absolute if all considerations of proportionality are eliminated from the Court's reasoning under Article 3, I refer to proportionality in this first sense.

But the same concept can also be used to express a different, relational notion. In this second sense proportionality expresses, for example, the relationship between the force used by a police officer and the force used by a suspect who resists arrest. As will be explained immediately below, use of the term 'proportionate' in this scenario has nothing to do with the first use of the term 'proportionality'. Instead, 'disproportionate' violence in this second sense equates to 'excessive' violence, a term that is perhaps to be preferred in order to avoid confusion.

With that clarification out of the way, let us move on to consider a picture of a truly absolute Article 3.

According to the Court,[13] application of Article 3 is purely a matter of scope: 'ill-treatment must attain a minimum level of severity' to come within the article's scope,[14] but as soon as that threshold is crossed, there can be no question of balancing or justification.[15] However, this does not mean that the threshold is identical in all cases. Instead (the Court has held) the threshold varies, depending on the concrete circumstances of the case: '[t]he assessment of this minimum is, in the nature of things, relative; it depends on all the circumstances of the case, such as the nature and context of the treatment, the manner and method of its execution, its duration, its physical or mental effects and, in some instances, the sex, age and state of health of the victim'.[16] Giving content to the relative threshold is thus a matter of contextualisation.[17] But for Article 3 to maintain its absolute nature, considerations of proportionality and balancing against a public interest or the rights of others cannot be brought into the threshold question.[18]

How Article 3 can nevertheless function as an absolute prohibition, in some circumstances allowing treatment that it prohibits in others, will be illustrated through a set of scenarios on the use of force.

In Scenario 1, a police officer, Zoë, is observing a peaceful demonstration. Suddenly, she decides – for whatever 'reason' – to arrest a peaceful protester, chosen at random. She punches the protester twice, shoves him to the ground, handcuffs him and leads him away to a police car. Because the context in which Zoë acts is not one in which the use of force can be considered necessary, the Court will employ a low threshold for application of Article 3. Both the arbitrary violence committed by Zoë and the degrading use of handcuffs on a random, innocent, person pass the threshold for application of Article 3 and will thus constitute a violation of that article.[19]

[13] The positive obligation to protect individuals from ill-treatment by other individuals adds a layer of complexity to the application of Art. 3, which will be dealt with extensively below.

[14] ECtHR (GC), *Kudła* v. *Poland*, 26 October 2000, para. 91.

[15] *Gäfgen*, note 2 above at para. 107. Cf., with regard to cruel, inhuman and degrading treatment, M. Nowak, 'Challenges to the absolute nature of the prohibition of torture and ill-treatment', (2005) 23 *Netherlands Quarterly of Human Rights*, pp. 676–8.

[16] *Kudła*, note 14 above at para. 91.

[17] Addo and Grief, 'Does Article 3 enshrine absolute rights?', note 7 above, at p. 522; Palmer, 'A wrong turning', note 8 above, at p. 439.

[18] Mavronicola, 'What is an "absolute right"?', note 7 above, at p. 25.

[19] For cases from the Court's case law comparable to Scenario 1, see ECtHR, *Güler and Öngel* v. *Turkey*, 4 October 2011, paras 209 and 231; ECtHR, *Muradova* v. *Azerbaijan*, 2 April 2009, paras 133–4; ECtHR, *Saya and others* v. *Turkey*, 7 October 2008, paras 20–23.

In Scenario 2, Zoë is called to the scene of a violent burglary. When she arrives, she spots the suspect and shouts 'stop, police!', but the suspect flees. When Zoë catches up to him, he violently resists arrest. She then proceeds as in Scenario 1: she punches the suspect twice, shoves him to the ground, handcuffs him and leads him to her police car. The context of Scenario 2 is clearly different from that in Scenario 1. Zoë is now confronted with a violent suspect, not a peaceful demonstrator. Because the behaviour of the suspect makes the use of force necessary, the threshold for application of Article 3 will be higher. As the Court has held, 'Article 3 does not prohibit the use of force for effecting an arrest. However, such force may be used only if indispensable and must not be excessive.'[20] Since the force used by Zoë in Scenario 2 is not excessive, it does not cross the threshold for application of Article 3.[21]

In Scenario 3, Zoë is again called to attend a violent burglary; only, this time, the suspect immediately surrenders, dropping to his knees and putting his hands on his head. To achieve the public interest aims of prevention of crime and protection of public order, arresting and detaining the suspect is justified. This may include handcuffing him and certainly includes leading him to a police car. But because Scenario 3 involves a suspect who does not resist arrest, the threshold for application of Article 3 will be lower than in Scenario 2. If Zoë were nevertheless to use the same amount of force as in Scenario 2, she will violate Article 3, given that the suspect in this scenario has not made such use of force necessary by his own conduct.[22]

When comparing Scenarios 2 and 3, it becomes clear that what goes on in Scenario 2 does *not* involve application of the proportionality test, but is instead a matter of context.[23] In both Scenarios 2 and 3, Zoë's use of force is not assessed in terms of proportionality to some public interest aim – e.g. the prevention of crime and the protection of public order – to determine whether Article 3 has been violated. Only the suspect's arrest and detention stand in such a relation of proportionality with the cited

[20] ECtHR, *Kuzmenko* v. *Russia*, 21 October 2010, para. 41; ECtHR, *Ivan Vasilev* v. *Bulgaria*, 12 April 2007, para. 63.

[21] For cases from the Court's case law comparable to Scenario 2, see ECtHR, *Stojnsek* v. *Slovakia*, 23 June 2009, paras 92–3 and 96; and, *mutatis mutandis*, ECtHR, *Julin* v. *Estonia*, 29 May 2012, paras 121 and 133.

[22] For cases from the Court's case law comparable to Scenario 3, see ECtHR, *Erdoğan Yağız* v. *Turkey*, 6 March 2007, paras 42 and 45–8; ECtHR, *Rehbock* v. *Slovenia*, 28 November 2000, paras 72 and 76; ECtHR, *Grigoryev* v. *Russia*, 23 October 2012, paras 82–4.

[23] See also N. Mavronicola, '*Güler and Öngel* v. *Turkey*: Article 3 of the European Convention on Human Rights and Strasbourg's discourse on the justified use of force', *76 Modern Law Review* (2013), pp. 375–6 and 378.

public interest aims: because he is clearly suspected of a violent crime in both scenarios, Zoë can justifiably arrest and detain him. Her use of force, by contrast, stands only in relation to what is required to achieve the arrest. Because the context in which she acts in Scenario 2 is one in which the suspect resists arrest, the use of force becomes necessary. However, use of the same amount of force is not justified in Scenario 3. This is so because the context in which Zoë acts is different in the third scenario (arresting a violent suspect *versus* arresting a non-violent suspect). That Scenario 2 (violent suspect) does not involve application of the proportionality test is further demonstrated by the fact that Article 3 *will* be violated in that scenario if Zoë uses excessive force or if she punches the suspect after he has been restrained by handcuffs.[24]

To recapitulate, the three scenarios illustrate how the prohibition of torture and inhuman or degrading treatment should function for it to live up to its own standard of an absolute prohibition, application of which is a matter of scope only. But the Court does not always comply with the principle in this manner. As I will show in the following sections, the Court employs considerations of proportionality (in the first sense explained above) and balancing in certain types of Article 3 case, thereby contradicting the article's absolute nature. In each section, I will assess whether – and if so, how – the resulting cracks in the armour of Article 3 could be mended.

3. The negative dimension of Article 3: the role of illegitimate purposes and legitimate objectives

According to the Court, the purpose for which ill-treatment is inflicted is a relevant, though not necessarily decisive, consideration in the application of Article 3. Whether treatment is categorised as torture is determined by its purpose: '[i]n addition to the severity of the treatment, there is a purposive element [to torture], as recognised in the United Nations Convention . . . which defines torture in terms of the intentional infliction of severe pain or suffering with the aim, *inter alia*, of obtaining information, inflicting punishment or intimidating'.[25] But the purpose is not a decisive factor in determining whether the ill-treatment is categorised as

24 See, for example, *Kuzmenko*, note 20 above, at paras 42–3; ECtHR, *Sylenok and Tekhnoservis-Plus* v. *Ukraine*, 9 December 2010, paras 69–70.

25 ECtHR (GC), *Ilhan* v. *Turkey*, 27 June 2000, para. 85. Mavronicola, 'What is an "absolute right"?', note 7 above, at pp. 32–3.

degrading: '[a]lthough the purpose of such treatment is a factor to be taken into account, in particular whether it was intended to humiliate or debase the victim, the absence of any such purpose does not inevitably lead to a finding that there has been no violation of Article 3'.[26]

The purpose for which ill-treatment is inflicted is likewise relevant to, but not determinative of, the absolute nature of Article 3. Analysis of the Court's case law shows that a distinction should be drawn between treatment inflicted for illegitimate purposes and treatment inflicted in pursuit of legitimate objectives.

The Court has been perfectly consistent in applying its principled rhetoric on the absolute nature of Article 3 whenever ill-treatment was inflicted for illegitimate purposes.[27] Considerations of proportionality and balancing do not feature in cases that involve authorities using ill-treatment to extract a confession or for punitive reasons;[28] using excessive force to subdue a suspect or detainee;[29] force-feeding a detainee to break his or her will;[30] publicly leading around in handcuffs a person who clearly does not intend to flee, nor presents a threat to others;[31] at trial, putting harmless suspects in a metal cage as a matter of routine;[32] or inflicting degrading treatment motivated by ethnic discrimination.[33]

Matters are different, however, when seemingly legitimate objectives underlie the inflicted treatment. Balancing and proportionality do not necessarily enter the Court's reasoning at that point. As explained above, the proportionality test, for instance, is not relevant to the use of non-excessive force to arrest a violent suspect or to subdue a violent detainee.[34] But considerations of proportionality do find their way into the Court's reasoning in specific types of Article 3 case, particularly when security

[26] ECtHR, *Csüllög* v. *Hungary*, 7 June 2011, para. 28. See also ECtHR (GC), *Stanev* v. *Bulgaria*, 17 January 2012, para. 211.

[27] On the relevance of the purpose of the treatment, see also Mavronicola, '*Güler and Öngel*', note 23 above, at pp. 9–10.

[28] ECtHR (GC), *Salman* v. *Turkey*, 27 June 2000, paras 113 and 115; ECtHR (GC), *Ilascu and others* v. *Moldova*, 8 July 2004, paras 268–70, 443 and 447; ECtHR, *Davydov and others* v. *Ukraine*, 1 July 2010, paras 266–7 and 271.

[29] ECtHR, *Vladimir Romanov* v. *Russia*, 24 July 2008, paras 67–8 and 70.

[30] ECtHR, *Ciorap* v. *Moldova*, 19 June 2007, para. 89. See also ECtHR, *Nevmerzhitsky* v. *Ukraine*, 5 April 2005, paras 96–8.

[31] *Yağız*, note 22 above, at paras 45–8.

[32] ECtHR, *Ashot Harutyunyan* v. *Armenia*, 15 June 2010, paras 126–9; ECtHR, *Ramishvili and Kokhreidze* v. *Georgia*, 27 January 2009, paras 99–102.

[33] ECtHR (GC), *Cyprus* v. *Turkey*, 10 May 2001, paras 307 and 309–10.

[34] On this latter case, see ECtHR, *Sharomov* v. *Russia*, 15 January 2009, paras 27, 29 and 30; *Julin*, note 21 above, at paras 121 and 133.

reasons are invoked, for instance to justify solitary confinement.[35] Similarly, although the Court has refused to balance the Article 3 rights of one person against the qualified rights of others, including their right to life,[36] it does make room for such balancing when the case concerns 'conflicting rights' of the same person, such as when a detainee is force-fed out of medical necessity.[37]

3.1 Contradictions in cases concerning solitary confinement and force-feeding

In cases concerning the use of security measures in prison, such as solitary confinement or punishment cells, the Court has explicitly used language identical to the proportionality language it uses when applying relative Convention rights.[38] It has thus held that '[a] measure of disciplinary confinement may not in itself be in breach of [the] requirements [of Article 3]. It is rather the *proportionality* of its imposition and the conditions of the confinement which may be questionable under the above provision.'[39] The Court has also ruled that 'the measures taken must . . . be necessary to attain the legitimate aim pursued'[40] and that it is up to the Court 'to determine whether [solitary confinement for a lengthy period] was justified [and] whether the measures taken were necessary and proportionate'.[41]

Similar considerations apply to cases involving force-feeding of detainees: 'a measure which is of therapeutic necessity . . . cannot in principle be regarded as inhuman and degrading . . . The same can be said about force-feeding that is aimed at saving the life of a particular detainee

35 See section 3.1 of this chapter, 'Contradictions arising in cases on solitary confinement and force-feeding'.

36 *Gäfgen*, note 2 above. See further Mavronicola, 'What is an "absolute right"?', note 7 above, at p. 13.

37 *Ciorap*, note 30 above, at paras 76–7.

38 Similar conclusions might apply, but not always as obviously, to the use of handcuffs and other restraints for security reasons (see ECtHR, *Hénaf* v. *France*, 27 November 2003, paras 48 and 56; *Julin*, note 21 above, at para. 127, compare paras 129–30; ECtHR (GC), *Öcalan* v. *Turkey*, 12 May 2005, paras 184–5; ECtHR, *Bureš* v. *The Czech Republic*, 18 October 2012, paras 90–91, 96 and 100) and to the use of a metal cage to hold dangerous applicants at trial (see *Ramishvili and Kokhreidze*, note 32 above, paras 99–102, *a contrario*; see also ECtHR, *Fyodorov and Fyodorova* v. *Ukraine*, 7 July 2011, para. 60).

39 *Ramishvili and Kokhreidze*, note 32 above, para. 82 (emphasis added).

40 *Ramirez Sanchez*, note 1 above, at para. 119. See also ECtHR, *Khider* v. *France*, 9 July 2009, para. 102; ECtHR, *Alboreo* v. *France*, 20 October 2011, para. 109.

41 *Ramirez Sanchez*, note 1 above, at para. 136.

who consciously refuses to take food.'[42] The underlying *rationale* of this principle, in the opinion of the Court, is that hunger strikes in prison involve a conflict of Convention rights: '[w]hen . . . a detained person maintains a hunger-strike this may inevitably lead to a conflict between an individual's right to physical integrity and the High Contracting Party's positive obligation under Article 2 of the Convention – a conflict which is not solved by the Convention itself'.[43] Provided that force-feeding is medically necessary and does not involve the use of excessive force,[44] the Court resolves this conflict to the benefit of Article 2 through a balancing act.

The above picture is at odds with the Court's principled rhetoric on an absolute prohibition of torture and inhuman or degrading treatment,[45] which 'does not allow for any exceptions or justifying factors or balancing of interests'.[46] Incorporating considerations of proportionality and balancing into the threshold question under Article 3, as the Court does in cases on solitary confinement and force-feeding, does not contradict that conclusion.[47] There is little difference between (i) applying proportionality during the second stage of a two-stage model of rights adjudication to determine that a certain measure is justified and (ii) relying on considerations of proportionality to determine that a certain measure does not fall within the scope of Article 3 after all. In both situations, the Court effectively rules that public interests or other (Convention) rights 'outweigh' the interest of the applicant. However, the aim of declaring a right to be absolute is precisely to shield it from such balancing, no matter at what stage it takes place. To be truly absolute, Article 3 should resist the use of proportionality and balancing considerations in the determination of the threshold question.[48]

3.2 Addressing the contradiction: possible ways forward

The Court could walk a number of paths to rectify the contradiction between declaring, as a matter of principle, that Article 3 is absolute and

42 *Ciorap*, note 30 above, at para. 77. On the application of Art. 3 in cases of medical necessity, see also Battjes, 'In search of a fair balance', note 3 above, at pp. 613–15.

43 *Ciorap*, note 30 above, at para. 76.

44 *Ibid.*, at para. 77.

45 See also Mavronicola, '*Güler and Öngel*', note 23 above, at pp. 4–5. Cf., Palmer, 'A wrong turning', note 8 above, at p. 439.

46 *Gäfgen*, note 2 above at para. 107.

47 Nowak, 'Challenges to the absolute nature', note 15 above, at p. 677.

48 See also *ibid.* (Nowak does not, however, object to the prohibition of cruel, inhuman or degrading treatment being subjected to a proportionality test.)

using considerations of proportionality and balancing to determine the threshold question in certain concrete cases.

The first path would entail admitting that certain types of ill-treatment must be tested for proportionality. The Court could follow Manfred Nowak, for instance, in holding that the proportionality test applies to cases involving inhuman and degrading treatment, while maintaining the absolute prohibition for torture.[49] However, this would require it to abandon its established principle – Article 3 is absolute – in order to address inconsistencies in applying the article to specific cases. Given that such inconsistencies only arise in a limited number of situations, and in light of the Court's clear rhetorical position on the absolute character of Article 3, a more fruitful option is to look for ways to remove the contradiction without sacrificing the absolute nature of Article 3.

A second way forward could see the Court radically changing its stance on solitary confinement and force-feeding by ruling that they always violate Article 3 – no matter what circumstances obtain. However, it is highly unlikely that the Court would follow this line of thought, given that it has traditionally granted Member States leeway in determining the type of detention measures they consider appropriate.[50] Moreover, pursuing this route would create room for new contradictions within the Court's case law, for instance where prisoners are shackled for security reasons.[51] Such practices would still be allowed while solitary confinement would not, although reasons of public interest motivate both measures. Similar considerations would apply to force-feeding and the positive obligation of Member States to preserve the life of prisoners who attempt to commit suicide.[52] If force-feeding were to be absolutely prohibited, states would be forced to let detainees die on hunger strikes, while being obliged to save them when they attempt to commit suicide.

Rather than expecting the Court to radically change its normative stance on the absolute nature of Article 3 or the permissibility of solitary confinement and force-feeding, attempts should be made to *reconcile* the principle of the absolute nature of Article 3 with its application to concrete cases. Such reconciliation can only be achieved by removing all considerations of proportionality and balancing from the Court's reasoning in

49 *Ibid.*, at p. 678. See also Battjes, 'In search of a fair balance', note 3 above, at pp. 595–7.

50 *Ramirez Sanchez*, note 1 above, at para. 119; ECtHR, *Van der Ven* v. *The Netherlands*, 4 February 2003, para. 50.

51 See the cases mentioned in note 38 above.

52 See for instance ECtHR, *Keenan* v. *United Kingdom*, 3 April 2001; ECtHR, *Shumkova* v. *Russia*, 14 February 2012.

the cases that have been identified as problematic. This aim could, *prima facie*, be achieved in two ways.

A first attempt at reconciliation, made by Natasa Mavronicola, involves specification. Mavronicola argues that defining the prohibition in Article 3 more narrowly would protect its absolute character against erosion by considerations of proportionality. To that end, she claims that Article 3 does not protect against all infringements of physical and psychological integrity, but only against those that affront dignity and agency.[53] She thus argues that the threshold of Article 3 is not crossed when 'force used against an individual . . . is immediately necessitated by the individual's actions . . . because the dignity of the individual is respected'.[54]

Mavronicola suggests that her principle can also be applied to the cases that have been identified as problematic in this chapter. In respect of cases involving security measures, she argues that 'there is no affront to dignity or agency in shackling a potentially violent and dangerous individual for the purpose of preventing harm to himself or others'.[55] With regard to cases involving medical necessity, she claims that '[i]t could be argued that force used . . . to secure the health of someone . . . is not wielded with the primary purpose of inflicting suffering . . . but seeks to secure the dignity and agency of the individual through securing their health'.[56] Thus, both types of measures are excluded from the scope of Article 3, because they do not meet Mavronicola's redefined threshold for its application.

However, Mavronicola's suggestion does not *really* exclude considerations of proportionality and balancing from entering the threshold question under Article 3. It just renders them less immediately visible. There is ultimately little difference between what the Court does in cases concerning solitary confinement and force-feeding and Mavronicola's alternative reasoning. While the Court explicitly makes considerations of proportionality and balancing relevant to the threshold question of Article 3, thereby contradicting the article's absolute nature, Mavronicola risks doing the same, only less explicitly. The reason for this is that the specification that Article 3 only protects against treatment that affronts agency and dignity appears to be underscored by a 'balancist' position, namely that agency and dignity will not be affronted when a measure is motivated by security reasons or medical necessity. Thus, public interest aims and conflicting rights are brought, once again, into the threshold question of Article 3, only indirectly.

[53] Mavronicola, '*Güler and Öngel*', note 23 above. [54] *Ibid.*, at p. 8.
[55] *Ibid.*, at p. 9. [56] *Ibid.*, at pp. 10–11.

Nevertheless, Mavronicola appears to be on to something. Inspired by her starting-point, I will suggest another path towards reconciling the principled absolute nature of Article 3 with its concrete application in cases involving solitary confinement and force-feeding. The path I have in mind also calls for renewed attention by the Court to the object and purpose of Article 3, to prohibit particularly serious infringements of physical and psychological integrity, namely those that *exceed* a certain threshold, as defined in the Court's case law. However, it seems to me that this does not require a redefinition of the prohibition, for instance by referencing dignity and agency. Instead, it suffices for the Court to consistently rely on the factors that determine when the threshold for application of Article 3 is reached, as both the starting- *and* the ending-point of its reasoning.

Rather than ruling, as it does now, that solitary confinement does not violate Article 3 when it is imposed for security reasons and is proportionate to that legitimate aim, the Court should amend its starting position. In keeping with the object and purpose of Article 3, the Court could for instance extend the principle that there is an unavoidable level of suffering inherent in detention to encompass measures of solitary confinement.[57] Accordingly, such measures would not come within the scope of Article 3, *unless* certain elements – defined in the Court's case law – 'lift' them above the required minimum level of severity. Thus, solitary confinement would still violate Article 3 when its nature is excessive (i.e. complete sensory isolation and total social isolation);[58] when the manner and method of its execution are degrading or inhuman (e.g. when solitary confinement takes place in poor hygienic conditions);[59] when its duration is not limited in time;[60] when it is imposed for illegitimate purposes (e.g. to humiliate inmates or break their will); or when its physical or mental effects lead to substantial deterioration of the inmate's health.[61]

However, so long as none of those elements are present, solitary confinement would be excluded from the scope of Article 3, without there being a need to refer to any legitimate aims to justify such exclusion. By focusing exclusively on the factors that determine the threshold question under Article 3, the Court would thus eliminate proportionality language

57 *Van der Ven*, note 50 above, at para. 50.

58 *Öcalan*, note 38 above, at para. 191.

59 *Ilascu*, note 28 above, at paras 438 and 444; *Ramishvili and Kokhreidze*, note 32 above, at para. 88.

60 ECtHR, *Babar Ahmad and others* v. *United Kingdom*, 10 April 2012, para. 210.

61 *Khider*, note 40 above, at para. 122.

from its judgments in solitary confinement cases, thereby living up to the promise of an absolute right in those cases. By removing all elements of proportionality from the Court's reasoning, the approach I suggest might even lead to increased protection against excessive measures of solitary confinement. Even where a security risk exists, it can never *justify* treatment that exceeds the threshold for application of Article 3. Therefore, as soon as one of the elements described above is present, Article 3 applies and is violated, without security considerations being able to 'trump' that conclusion.

Similar reasoning could be applied to force-feeding. The Court could rule that, when administered with the use of the proper techniques, for instance, force-feeding does not reach the threshold for application of Article 3. Force-feeding would instead be included under the scope of Article 8 ECHR, as an infringement of the prisoner's physical integrity and her right to decisional privacy. Given that those rights are qualified by Article 8(2), they would be open to balancing against the state's positive obligation under Article 2 to protect the detainee's life. In keeping with its object and purpose, the absolute Article 3 would only come into play when *additional* elements are present, for instance when force-feeding is imposed for illegitimate purposes (e.g. to break an inmate's will)[62] or when it is applied with excessive force.[63] Once again, these suggestions would not alter the substantive outcome of the Court's judgments on force-feeding. But following them *would* remove any considerations of balancing from holding relevance under the Court's Article 3 reasoning, and thus reconcile the principled absolute nature of Article 3 with its application in force-feeding cases.

By focusing on issues of definition and scope, the Court would avoid turning Article 3 into a qualified right, application of which (explicitly or implicitly) follows a two-stage model. Instead, the Court would return to the roots of Article 3 as a one-stage, absolute right, application of which is purely a matter of scope.

4. The positive dimension of Article 3: is absolute protection possible?

As is well known, the prohibition of torture and inhuman or degrading treatment does more than offer protection against negative interferences

[62] *Nevmerzhitsky*, note 30 above, paras 96–8; *Ciorap*, note 30 above, at para. 83.
[63] *Ciorap*, note 30 above, at para. 85.

by state agents. It also imposes a number of positive obligations on Member States, both substantive and procedural. In what follows, I will largely leave procedural obligations aside and will focus instead on the relationship between the absolute nature of Article 3 and substantive positive obligations. The chief question to be addressed is: can an obligation to protect against torture and inhuman or degrading treatment be absolute? The question is once again relevant to the subject matter of this volume, for if the obligation to protect is open to balancing, application of Article 3 – this time in its positive dimension – cannot be only a matter of scope.

4.1 Protection in mixed cases

Certain Article 3 cases in which the obligation to protect plays a crucial role are, in fact, cases of a mixed nature.[64] Expulsion, extradition and deportation cases, for instance, arguably entail both a negative and a positive element.[65] When a person claims that her expulsion by a Member State would expose her to treatment contrary to Article 3 in the receiving state, what she effectively argues is that the Member State is under a negative obligation to not put her on a plane and expel her, which is an obligation to refrain from acting. However, the Member State can only be under such a negative obligation *because* it is under a positive obligation to protect persons under its power against treatment contrary to Article 3, even when administered by third parties in a third state. The Court appears to have recognised this mixed nature in *Saadi* v. *Italy*:

> Since *protection* against the treatment prohibited by Article 3 is absolute, that provision imposes an *obligation not to* extradite or expel any person who, in the receiving country, would run the real risk of being subjected to such treatment.[66]

The quotation also demonstrates that the Court considers the positive obligation to be absolute: 'protection against the treatment prohibited by

[64] In this section I leave aside procedural obligations, which are also positive obligations, and focus on substantive positive obligations instead. Needless to say, cases that involve a negative obligation and a procedural obligation (for instance, cases in which a person was tortured or killed by state agents but the authorities did not conduct an (effective) investigation) are also mixed cases. See also Chapter 7 by Brems in this volume.

[65] Cf. Battjes, 'In search of a fair balance', note 3 above, at pp. 600–3 (who refers to the 'liability for taking action' – the act of *refoulement* – as a 'negative obligation', but ultimately concludes that expulsion cases are best understood as involving positive obligations).

[66] ECtHR (GC), *Saadi* v. *Italy*, 28 February 2008, para. 138 (emphasis added).

Article 3 is absolute'.[67] As a result, 'it is not possible to weigh the risk of ill-treatment against the reasons put forward for the expulsion in order to determine whether the responsibility of a State is engaged under Article 3, even where such treatment is inflicted by another State.'[68] Once the person to be expelled faces a real risk of being subjected to treatment contrary to Article 3 in the receiving state, there can be no question of balancing her Article 3 rights against any public interest, nor against the Convention rights of others, in the Member State.[69]

The Court has consistently applied the above principle whenever the treatment would be inflicted by human actors in the receiving state – i.e. state agents or private actors – against whom the receiving state could not offer protection.[70] It has also adhered to the principle whenever the person to be expelled would find herself the victim of inhuman and degrading living conditions that are directly attributable to actions or omissions by the receiving state.[71]

However, a contradiction arises between the principle – protection against treatment contrary to Article 3 is absolute – and its application in cases in which the person to be deported would face pain and suffering attributable to 'natural causes'. Thus, the Court has repeatedly ruled that the deportation of an applicant who suffers from AIDS would not violate Article 3, despite the fact that she would inevitably suffer a deterioration in her health and her life expectancy would reduce in the receiving state.[72]

In *N* v. *the United Kingdom*, the Court held that even the fact that 'the applicant's circumstances, including his life expectancy, would be significantly reduced if he were to be removed from the Contracting State is not sufficient in itself to give rise to breach of Article 3'.[73] In defending that position, the Court referenced the 'search for a fair balance between the demands of the general interest of the community and the requirements of the protection of the individual's fundamental rights' that is 'inherent in the whole of the Convention'.[74] This 'search for a fair balance' led the Court to rule that it should not 'place an obligation

[67] See also *Chahal*, note 10 above, para. 80.

[68] *Saadi*, note 66 above, at para. 138.

[69] *Ibid.*, at paras 139–40.

[70] See *ibid.*; *Chahal*, note 10 above; ECtHR (GC), *Hirsi Jamaa and others* v. *Italy*, 23 February 2012; ECtHR, *Sufi and Elmi* v. *United Kingdom*, 28 June 2011.

[71] See ECtHR (GC), *MSS* v. *Belgium and Greece*, 21 January 2011, paras 365–8; *Sufi and Elmi*, note 70 above, at paras 282–3 and 291–2.

[72] For an overview of the relevant case law, see ECtHR (GC), *N* v. *United Kingdom*, 27 May 2008, paras 35–41.

[73] *Ibid.*, at para. 42.

[74] *Ibid.*, at para. 44.

on the Contracting State to alleviate [disparities in health care standards between states] through the provision of free and unlimited health care to all aliens without a right to stay within its jurisdiction' by prohibiting the applicant's expulsion.[75] Doing this 'would place too great a burden on the Contracting States'.[76] Both references – to a 'fair balance' and to a 'too great burden [imposed] on the Contracting States' – cannot co-exist with 'the absolute nature' of the prohibition of torture and inhuman or degrading treatment.[77]

At least two approaches appear to be available to redress the contradiction.[78]

The first, 'agent-relative', approach would entail approaching the question of the applicability – and violation – of Article 3 from the perspective of the applicant only. It would require the Court to rule that, if the applicant would become the victim of serious pain and suffering in the receiving state, her expulsion would violate Article 3, regardless of the origin of her pain and suffering. The 'agent-relative' approach would thus guarantee consistency between the principle and its application by bringing serious pain and suffering within the scope of Article 3, no matter the cause of said pain, and by barring any potential countervailing reasons – including the burden placed on the sending state – from 'trumping' that conclusion.

The second, 'state-relative', approach would entail approaching the applicability of Article 3 from the perspective of the state by asking whether the state (sending or receiving) can be held directly responsible – through act or omission – for the pain and suffering the applicant would face. Given that states cannot be held directly responsible for the pain and suffering caused by natural illnesses, applicants with AIDS could be expelled under an exclusively 'state-relative' approach, even when they would suffer a deterioration of their health and their life expectancy would reduce in the receiving state. Thus, the 'state-relative' approach would also guarantee consistency between the principle and its application, but at the expense of categorically excluding the pain and suffering of the applicant from the scope of Article 3.

In its case law, the Court – presumably for pragmatic reasons – has borrowed a bit from both perspectives. In the process, it has ended up sacrificing the absolute nature of Article 3. It has drawn on the

[75] *Ibid.* [76] *Ibid.*

[77] See the joint dissenting opinion of Judges Tulkens, Bonello and Spielmann in *ibid.*, at paras 7–8; Battjes, 'In search of a fair balance', note 3 above, at p. 598.

[78] For an alternative approach, suggesting three possible ways to (re)interpret the prohibition of *refoulement* under Art. 3, see Battjes, 'In search of a fair balance', note 3 above, at pp. 598–9 and 611.

state-relative approach to rule that 'AIDS cases' do not principally raise an issue under Article 3, 'given that in such cases the alleged future harm would emanate not from the intentional acts or omissions of public authorities or non-State bodies, but instead from a naturally occurring illness and the lack of sufficient resources to deal with it in the receiving country'.[79] However, the Court has also allowed for such cases to 'very exceptional[ly]' come within the scope of Article 3 when certain agent-relative circumstances are present that render 'the humanitarian grounds against the removal... compelling' (e.g. when an applicant is close to death and will not find family able to provide material and social support in the receiving state).[80]

The outcomes to which the Court's intermediate position leads could theoretically be reconciled with the absolute nature of Article 3, but only if the reasoning would follow suit, i.e. if the Court could provide balancing-free reasons why Article 3 would only be engaged when certain very exceptional, agent-relative, circumstances were present. Such reasons could be related, for instance, to the *extent* to which the applicant's pain and suffering would increase if she were expelled to the receiving state. Given that the applicant will face a certain amount of pain and suffering from her illness no matter which country she lives in, the relevant question should be whether the difference between the pain and suffering she faces in the sending state and what she would face in the receiving state is sufficient to bring Article 3 into play. Agent-relative circumstances, such as the stage of the disease and the presence of family members, should play a central role in determining the answer to that question. But because the Court currently relies on balancing, state-relative, considerations in establishing the relevant principles, its standing case law cannot convincingly be squared with the absolute nature of Article 3. Until the Court amends its reasoning, the 'AIDS cases' thus fall to be characterised as one of the cracks in the absolute prohibition of Article 3.

4.2 Strictly positive obligations to protect and to fulfil

A final category of substantive obligations under Article 3 that requires analysis contains strictly positive obligations, namely those to protect and to fulfil.[81]

[79] *N*, note 72 above, at para. 43. Confirmed in *Sufi and Elmi*, note 70 above, at paras 282–3 and in *Babar Ahmad*, note 60 above, at para. 177.

[80] ECtHR, *D* v. *United Kingdom*, 2 May 1997, paras 51–3; *N*, note 72 above, at para. 42.

[81] See Lavrysen's chapter in this volume.

The Court generally lives up to its principled rhetoric on the absolute character of Article 3 in adjudicating cases involving positive obligations to fulfil. No hints of proportionality or balancing can be found in the Court's case law on conditions of detention;[82] on the treatment of asylum seekers during their deportation;[83] on the poor living conditions of asylum seekers in certain Member States;[84] and on the treatment of close family members of missing or deported persons.[85]

Matters get more complex when cases involve the state's positive obligation to protect individuals against ill-treatment by other private actors. When such treatment exceeds the threshold for application of Article 3, the state is under a positive obligation to protect said individuals.[86] In certain cases, namely those related to corporal punishment of children by private actors, considerations of proportionality and balancing do not enter the Court's reasoning.[87] But in other cases, things are not as straightforward. Particularly noteworthy are cases concerning sexual and physical abuse within the family.[88] As soon as domestic authorities are aware (or ought to be aware) that a person is the victim of such abuse, the state is under an obligation to put an end to it.[89] But in establishing the existence of such a positive obligation, the Court has immediately limited its scope by indicating that the state should take 'reasonable steps' to protect the victim.[90]

The reference to 'reasonable steps' can be interpreted in two ways. A first interpretation would read it as *ipso facto* negating the absolute character of the positive obligation. However, along with Stephanie Palmer, I submit that such an interpretation would be erroneous.[91] It confuses the

[82] ECtHR (GC), *Enea* v. *Italy*, 17 September 2009, para. 57; ECtHR (GC), *Idalov* v. *Russia*, 22 May 2012, paras 97 and 101; *Stanev*, note 26 above, paras 207 and 210; *MSS*, note 71 above, at paras 223, 230 and 233; ECtHR, *Mubilanzila Mayeka* v. *Belgium*, 12 October 2006, paras 50, 54–5 and 58.

[83] *Mubilanzila Mayeka*, note 82 above, at paras 66–9.

[84] *MSS*, note 71 above, at para. 263.

[85] *Cyprus*, note 33 above, at paras 156–7; *Mubilanzila Mayeka*, note 82 above, at para. 70.

[86] ECtHR, *Opuz* v. *Turkey*, 9 June 2009, para. 159; ECtHR (GC), *Z and others* v. *United Kingdom*, 10 May 2001, para. 73.

[87] ECtHR, *A* v. *United Kingdom*, 17 December 2002, paras 21–4; ECtHR, *Costello-Roberts* v. *United Kingdom*, 25 March 1993, paras 31–2.

[88] For an example of a case in which the violence was not intrafamilial, see ECtHR, *97 members of the Gldani Congregation of Jehovah's Witnesses and 4 others* v. *Georgia*, 3 May 2007, particularly paras 111 and 124.

[89] ECtHR, *E and others* v. *United Kingdom*, 26 November 2002, para. 92.

[90] *Opuz*, note 86 above, at para. 162; *E*, note 89 above, at para. 92.

[91] Palmer, 'A wrong turning', note 8 above, at pp. 446, 448 and 450. See also Mavronicola, 'What is an "absolute right"?', note 7 above, at pp. 12 and 15–16.

question of the scope of the positive obligation with the question whether any considerations of public interest or the rights of others might *outweigh* that positive obligation.[92] In the Court's case law, it transpires that domestic authorities are granted some leeway in fulfilling their positive obligation to protect in abuse cases.[93] Thus, they may require some time to act, for example to prepare a successful rescue operation, without failing to adhere to their positive obligation.[94] But this does not alter the fact that they are under a positive obligation to protect the victim. If they fail to act at all or do not do all that lies within their power, they will have violated that positive obligation.[95] Interpreting the reference to 'reasonable steps' as limiting the scope of the positive obligation to what lies in the authorities' power does not necessarily contradict the notion of an absolute positive obligation,[96] provided that no considerations of proportionality or balancing are brought into the Court's reasoning to justify the state's failure to meet its positive obligation.[97] Thus, the question is not whether the reference to 'reasonable steps' *ipso facto* negates the absolute nature of Article 3, but whether it opens the positive obligation up to balancing against the public interest or the Convention rights of others.

To answer this question, it is crucial to distinguish two types of positive obligation. First, the state may be held under a general, abstract obligation to *prevent* ill-treatment contrary to Article 3 by private actors (e.g. domestic violence, rape, severe negligence of children). Second, the state may be held under a concrete obligation to *protect* identified individuals from a specific instance of ill-treatment of which the state is or ought to be aware. Both are positive obligations, but naturally, the former – the abstract obligation to prevent – cannot be regarded as absolute, given the 'difficulties involved in policing modern societies, the unpredictability of human conduct and the operational choices which must be made in terms of priorities and resources',[98] as well as the need to consider the

[92] See Lavrysen's chapter in this volume.

[93] *Opuz*, note 86 above, at para. 165. See also Mavronicola, 'What is an "absolute right"?', note 7 above, at pp. 12 and 15–16.

[94] ECtHR, *M and others* v. *Italy and Bulgaria*, 31 July 2012, paras 102–3.

[95] *Opuz*, note 86 above, at paras 165 and 166–70.

[96] This interpretation is supported by the language used in *E*, note 89 above, at para. 92: 'whether [the local authority] took the steps reasonably available to them to protect [the applicants] from that abuse'.

[97] Mavronicola, 'What is an "absolute right"?', note 7 above, at p. 16.

[98] ECtHR (GC), *Osman* v. *United Kingdom*, 28 October 1998, para. 116. The Court ruled in this manner under Art. 2, but similar considerations clearly apply to the abstract obligation to prevent ill-treatment by private actors under Art. 3.

countervailing rights of other individuals to private life and liberty of person. The concrete positive obligation to protect, conversely, *can* function as absolute; and it in fact does so under the Court's case law, as indicated above. Domestic authorities may be granted some leeway in fulfilling their positive obligation to protect in concrete cases, but they cannot justify a failure to act by invoking overriding interests or rights as justification. To put it sharply, budgetary restrictions, physical impossibility and the countervailing rights of others may put limits on the state's ability to prevent each and every instance of rape or physical abuse from occurring, but they cannot justify a failure to act in actual cases of rape or abuse.[99]

There is one case, however, in which the Court appears to reason against the above interpretation of concrete positive obligations to protect. In *Z and others* v. *the United Kingdom*, the Court acknowledged 'the difficult and sensitive decisions facing social services and the important *countervailing* principle of respecting and preserving family life'.[100] The reference to the 'countervailing principle of respecting and preserving family life' might entice us to conclude that balancing is possible in concrete positive cases under Article 3 after all. I would argue that such an interpretation of *Z* would be mistaken. It seems to me that, rather than being read as allowing for balancing, the statement should be understood as a recognition that the search for a solution within the family may be worth striving for, but under the condition – not to be surrendered, because absolute – that the abuse is put to an end. This reading of *Z* is further strengthened by the fact that the quoted principle is immediately followed by firm confirmation by the Court that 'the present case . . . leaves no doubt as to the failure of the system to protect these applicant children from serious, long-term neglect and abuse'.[101] This conclusion is in line with what has been suggested above: domestic authorities may have some leeway in deciding *how* to fulfil their positive obligations, but they cannot rely on countervailing reasons of public interest, nor on the Convention rights of others, to justify a failure to protect victims of abuse. In that

[99] Cf. ECtHR, *Đorđević* v. *Croatia*, 24 July 2012, paras 138–40, in which the Court – exceptionally and erroneously – held, under the heading 'general principles', that the principles it developed in *Osman* also apply to concrete cases of ill-treatment by private actors under Art. 3. However, the Court did not apply any of those principles to the case at hand. Instead, it found that the authorities did not do enough to put a halt to the ill-treatment, without referencing any need to balance the applicant's Art. 3 rights against the Convention rights of the perpetrators. See *ibid.*, paras 146–50.

[100] *Z*, note 86 above, at para. 74 (emphasis added).

[101] *Ibid.*, at para. 74.

sense, the Court's case law on the positive obligation to protect victims of domestic abuse can be interpreted as being in line with the proclaimed 'absolute nature' of Article 3.

5. Conclusion

In this chapter I have demonstrated that the ECtHR relies on considerations of proportionality and balancing in adjudicating certain types of Article 3 case. The Court thereby undermines its own principled rhetoric on the absolute nature of the prohibition of torture and inhuman or degrading treatment. In some cases (positive obligation to protect victims of domestic abuse) the ensuing contradiction is one in appearance only: it can be 'rationalised' through an 'absolute-friendly' interpretation of the Court's judgments.

In other cases, however, the contradiction is genuine. Mending the resulting cracks in the absolute armour of Article 3 will sometimes require the Court to walk a path of reconciliation between the principle and its application to actual cases (negative cases on solitary confinement and force-feeding). The Court might achieve such reconciliation by paying increased attention to the object and purpose of Article 3 and by exclusively relying on the elements that it has identified as being principally relevant to the application of the article's threshold.

At other times (mixed cases involving deportation of a person suffering from AIDS), staying faithful to the principled, absolute nature of Article 3 will require the Court to make a clear normative choice, i.e. to abandon a predominantly 'state-relative' approach in favour of an exclusively 'agent-relative' one. Only then will application of Article 3 truly be purely a question of scope.

14

The right to a fair trial and its multiple manifestations

Article 6(1) ECHR

PAUL LEMMENS

1. Introduction

In this chapter the case law of the European Court of Human Rights will be examined insofar as it contains interpretations relating to the scope of application of Article 6(1) ECHR as well as to the substance of some of the rights guaranteed by that provision. The focus will be on a number of issues for which the text of the ECHR in itself is not sufficiently clear, and where an effort at interpretation by the Court has been – and sometimes still is – necessary. The analysis will follow the structure of Article 6(1), element by element.

In the concluding remarks an attempt will be made to find the logic behind the Court's interpretations, which are sometimes extensive and sometimes restrictive.

2. Interpretation of the various elements of Article 6(1) ECHR

2.1 Scope of application

According to Article 6(1) ECHR, its provisions apply to 'the determination of (a person's) civil rights and obligations or of any criminal charge against him'. From the very beginning, the Court has considered this enumeration as referring to only some of all possible cases that can be brought before a court: 'there are some cases . . . which are not comprised within either of these categories and which thus fall outside the ambit of Article 6(1)'.[1] Such a view makes it necessary to verify in each case whether the case

[1] ECtHR, *Le Compte, Van Leuven and De Meyere* v. *Belgium*, 23 June 1981, para. 41; ECtHR, *Albert and Le Compte* v. *Belgium*, 10 February 1983, para. 25.

falls within the scope of Article 6(1). This has resulted in an abundant case law.

2.1.1 Applicability under the civil head

According to the most recent case law of the Court,

> Article 6(1) applies to disputes (*contestations*) concerning civil 'rights' which can be said, at least on arguable grounds, to be recognised under domestic law, whether or not they are also protected by the Convention . . . The dispute may relate not only to the actual existence of a right but also to its scope and the manner of its exercise; and, finally, the result of the proceedings must be directly decisive for the right in question . . . [2]

Within this formula one can discern two conditions: first, there must be a dispute over rights (or obligations), and second, these rights (or obligations) must be of a civil nature.

The term 'dispute' is interpreted by the Court in a wide sense. The Court holds that 'the spirit of the Convention requires that this word should not be construed too technically and that it should be given a substantive rather than a formal meaning'.[3] Nevertheless, not all disagreements attract the application of Article 6(1). A dispute must be justiciable, in the sense that it must lend itself to a judicial decision 'in the exercise of the normal judicial function'.[4]

In order for a 'right' to attract the application of Article 6(1), it must be a right, as indicated above, that 'can be said, at least on arguable grounds, to be recognised under domestic law'. This does not mean that the right should actually exist in domestic law. It is precisely the task of the courts, before which the existence of the right in question may be the actual object of the dispute, to decide that issue. The fact that the domestic courts eventually might hold that the claimant does not have a legally enforceable claim does not necessarily make the claim retroactively unarguable.[5] The limits of the notion are not yet fully explored. The Court has left open, for instance, the question whether the autonomous concept of a 'right' applies not only to subjective rights, but also to legitimate

[2] ECtHR (GC), *Sabeh El Leil* v. *France*, 29 June 2011, para. 40. In the same sense, ECtHR (GC), *Boulois* v. *Luxembourg*, 3 April 2012, para. 90.

[3] ECtHR (GC), *Gorou* v. *Greece (no. 2)*, 20 March 2009, para. 29.

[4] ECtHR, *van Marle* v. *The Netherlands*, 26 June 1986, paras 35 and 36; ECtHR (GC), *Athanassoglou* v. *Switzerland*, 6 April 2000, para. 45.

[5] ECtHR(GC), *Z and others* v. *United Kingdom*, 10 May 2001, para. 89; ECtHR (GC), *Marković* v. *Italy*, 14 December 2006, para. 101.

interests,[6] although it has indicated 'that the mere fact that the wording of a legal provision affords an element of discretion does not in itself rule out the existence of a right'.[7]

Finally, the link between the dispute and the rights invoked must be sufficiently direct. This excludes from the scope of application of Article 6(1) disputes raised e.g. by associations for the defence of the environment, relating to general interests, where there is only an indirect link with individual rights.[8] The requirement of a direct link also excludes from the scope of application of Article 6(1) proceedings in which rights or obligations are not 'determined'. However, adopting a realistic view of the actual way in which disputes are often solved, the Court accepts that Article 6(1) applies to injunction proceedings in which, albeit for a limited period, rights are determined.[9]

As regards the 'civil' character of the rights at issue, the Court does not proceed on the basis of an abstract definition of the term 'civil'.[10] Rather, it works on a case-by-case basis. For many years, especially in the 1980s, the Court regularly handed down judgments in which it gradually expanded the scope of application of Article 6(1). In its *Ferrazzini* judgment (2001), the Court summarised the development of its case law as follows:[11]

> Relations between the individual and the State have clearly evolved in many spheres during the fifty years which have elapsed since the Convention was adopted, with State regulation increasingly intervening in private-law relations. This has led the Court to find that procedures classified under national law as being part of 'public law' could come within the purview of Article 6 under its 'civil' head if the outcome was decisive for private rights and obligations, in regard to such matters as, to give some examples, the sale of land, the running of a private clinic, property interests, the granting of administrative authorisations relating to the conditions of professional

6 ECtHR (GC), *Mennitto* v. *Italy*, 5 October 2000, para. 27.

7 See the case law quoted in *Boulois*, note 2 above, at para. 93. In the *Boulois* case, however, which concerned a dispute over the refusal of the applicant's request for prison leave, the Court found that there was no 'right' to prison leave recognised in the domestic legal system, but merely a 'privilege'. Art. 6(1) ECHR therefore did not apply to the dispute (paras 96–101 and 104).

8 ECtHR, *Balmer-Schafroth* v. *Switzerland*, 26 August 1997, para. 40; *Athanassoglou*, note 4 above, at para. 55. But see ECtHR, *L'Erablière asbl* v. *Belgium*, 24 February 2009, paras 28–30.

9 ECtHR (GC), *Micallef* v. *Malta*, 15 October 2009, para. 85.

10 See, e.g., ECtHR, *H* v. *Belgium*, 30 November 1987, para. 45.

11 ECtHR (GC), *Ferrazzini* v. *Italy*, 12 July 2001, para. 27.

> practice or of a licence to serve alcoholic beverages....[12] Moreover, the State's increasing intervention in the individual's day-to-day life, in terms of welfare protection for example, has required the Court to evaluate features of public law and private law before concluding that the asserted right could be classified as 'civil'.[13]

This does not mean that all 'public law' rights are to be considered 'civil rights'. Rights and obligations belonging to matters that 'form part of the hard core of public-authority prerogatives, with the public nature of the relationship between the [citizen] and the community [being] predominant', fall outside the scope of 'civil' rights and obligations.[14] This applies in the first place to purely political rights, such as the right to stand for elections,[15] or rights deriving from a political mandate,[16] and to obligations of a political nature.[17] This applies also to rights and obligations in the tax field.[18] Finally, disputes relating to the entry, the stay or the deportation of aliens do not fall within the scope of Article 6(1).[19]

For a long time, disputes relating to the recruitment, the career or the termination of service of civil servants belonged also, at least in principle, to the category of disputes that fell outside the scope of 'civil' rights and obligations. On this point, however, the Court's case law has undergone some remarkable changes. First, in the *Pellegrin* case (1999), the Court held that in principle disputes between administrative authorities and their employees fall within the scope of Article 6(1), leaving outside the scope of that article only disputes 'raised by public servants whose duties typify the specific activities of the public service in so far as the latter is acting as the depositary of public authority responsible for protecting

[12] Reference by the Court to ECtHR, *Ringeisen* v. *Austria*, 16 July 1971, para. 94; ECtHR, *König* v. *Germany*, 28 June 1978, paras 94–5; ECtHR, *Sporrong and Lönnroth* v. *Sweden*, 23 September 1982, para. 79; ECtHR, *Benthem* v. *The Netherlands*, 23 October 1985, para. 36; ECtHR, *Tre Traktörer AB* v. *Sweden*, 7 July 1989, para. 43; ECtHR, *Allan Jacobsson* v. *Sweden (no. 1)*, 25 October 1989, para. 73.

[13] *Ferrazzini*, note 11 above. Reference by the Court to ECtHR, *Feldbrugge* v. *The Netherlands*, 29 May 1986, para. 40, and *Deumeland* v. *Germany*, 29 May 1986, para. 74; ECtHR, *Salesi* v. *Italy*, 26 February 1993, para. 19; ECtHR, *Schouten and Meldrum* v. *The Netherlands*, 9 December 1994, para. 60.

[14] *Ferrazzini*, note 11 above, at para. 29.

[15] ECtHR, *Pierre-Bloch* v. *France*, 21 October 1997, para. 50

[16] ECtHR, *Papon* v. *France*, decision 11 October 2005, para. 1.

[17] ECtHR (GC), *Paksas* v. *Lithuania*, 6 January 2011, para. 66.

[18] *Ferrazzini*, note 11 above, at para. 29.

[19] ECtHR (GC), *Maaouia* v. *France*, 5 October 2000, paras 37–8; ECtHR (GC), *Mamatkulov and Askarov* v. *Turkey*, 4 February 2005, para. 82.

the general interests of the State or other public authorities'.[20] Then, in *Vilho Eskelinen* (2007), the Court found that its case law needed further development. Since 'in very many Contracting States access to a court is accorded to civil servants',[21] it held that where national law allows a dispute with a civil servant to be brought before a court, the rights at issue are deemed to be 'civil'; where according to domestic law there is no right of access to a court, it remains to be seen whether the exclusion can be justified on objective grounds in the state's interest.[22]

The new approach in fact reduces the importance of the nature of the right as the factor to determine whether the right is a 'civil' one or not. While in its earlier case law the Court held that '(the character) of the authority which is invested with jurisdiction in the matter (is) of little consequence',[23] the existence of an adjudicating body and the judicial character thereof are now decisive. One could say that under the new approach a right that is justiciable at domestic law is a 'civil' right.

In *Vilho Eskelinen*, the Court made it clear, however, without giving any reasons for so holding, that the situation envisaged by the new approach

> is distinct from other cases, which due to the claims being made are regarded as falling outside the civil and criminal heads of Article 6(1) of the Convention (see, *inter alia*, for the assessment of tax, *Ferrazzini v. Italy*...; for matters of asylum, nationality and residence in a country, *Maaouia v. France*...; and for the adjudication of election disputes in respect of members of parliament, *Pierre-Bloch (v. France)*). The reasoning in this case is therefore limited to the situation of civil servants.[24]

Thus other areas of public law, in particular those that are explicitly mentioned, are not to be dealt with under the new approach.

Intrinsically, however, the new approach lends itself perfectly to application outside the area of disputes involving civil servants and their employers. Indeed, in a case concerning the right of access to primary education, the Court held that 'where a State confers rights which can be enforced by means of a judicial remedy, these can, in principle, be regarded as civil rights within the meaning of Article 6(1)'.[25] It is true that

[20] ECtHR (GC), *Pellegrin* v. *France*, 8 December 1999, para. 66. In the same sense, e.g., ECtHR (GC), *Frydlender* v. *France*, 27 June 2000, para. 33; ECtHR (GC), *Martinie* v. *France*, 12 April 2006, paras 27–8.

[21] ECtHR (GC), *Vilho Eskelinen and others* v. *Finland*, 19 April 2007, para. 57.

[22] *Ibid.*, at paras 61 and 62. In the same sense, e.g., ECtHR (GC), *Cudak* v. *Lithuania*, 23 March 2010, para. 42; *El Leil*, note 2 above, at para. 38.

[23] *Ringeisen*, note 12 above, at para. 94.

[24] *Eskelinen*, note 21 above, at para. 61.

[25] ECtHR (GC), *Oršuš* v. *Croatia*, 16 March 2010, para. 105.

in that case there was no reference to *Vilho Eskelinen*, and there are no indications that the Court is prepared to withdraw the reservation quoted above. But it seems that the issue is one upon which the last word has not yet been spoken.

2.1.2 Applicability under the criminal head

Under its criminal head, Article 6(1) applies to the determination of 'criminal' charges. In this respect, the Court's case law focuses on the interpretation to be given to the terms 'criminal' and 'determination'.[26]

In order to assess whether a charge is 'criminal' within the meaning of Article 6(1), the Court uses three criteria, formulated for the first time in the *Engel* case (1976):

> [I]t is first necessary to know whether the provision(s) defining the offence charged belong, according to the legal system of the respondent State, to criminal law, disciplinary law or both concurrently. This however provides no more than a starting point. The indications so afforded have only a formal and relative value and must be examined in the light of the common denominator of the respective legislation of the various Contracting States.
>
> The very nature of the offence is a factor of greater import...
>
> However, supervision by the Court does not stop there. Such supervision would generally prove to be illusory if it did not also take into consideration the degree of severity of the penalty that the person concerned risks incurring.[27]

These criteria have not undergone any changes. Over the years, the Court has made it clear that the second and third criteria are alternative and not necessarily cumulative.[28]

In the words of the Court itself,[29] the effect of the 'autonomous' interpretation of the term 'criminal' has been 'a gradual broadening of the criminal head to cases not strictly belonging to the traditional categories of the criminal law, for example administrative penalties...,[30] prison

[26] The term 'charge' is also the object of interpretation by the Court, but this case law will not be examined here.

[27] ECtHR, *Engel* v. *The Netherlands*, 8 June 1976, para. 82. The quotation is from ECtHR (GC), *Ezeh and Connors* v. *United Kingdom*, 9 October 2003, para. 82; ECtHR (GC), *Jussila* v. *Finland*, 23 November 2006, para. 30.

[28] See, e.g., *Ezeh and Connors*, *ibid.*, at para. 86; *Jussila*, *ibid.*, at para. 31.

[29] *Jussila*, note 27 above, at para. 43.

[30] Reference by the Court to ECtHR, *Öztürk* v. *Germany*, 21 February 1984.

disciplinary proceedings . . . ,[31] customs law . . . ,[32] competition law . . . ,[33] and penalties imposed by a court with jurisdiction in financial matters . . . '.[34] Even tax penalties can come within the scope of application of Article 6(1), on the basis of the *Engel* criteria, notwithstanding 'the importance of tax to the effective functioning of the State'.[35]

Not all decisions taken in a criminal context qualify as criminal sanctions. Precautionary or preventive measures, often imposed for reasons of public security, are not considered criminal penalties, not even if they are imposed in the context of criminal proceedings. Article 6(1) therefore does not apply to, e.g., the immediate withdrawal of a driving licence from a potentially dangerous driver,[36] or an exclusion order issued against a convicted alien.[37]

As regards the requirement that, for Article 6(1) to apply, there should be a 'determination' of a criminal charge, the Court has adopted a wide interpretation, which explicitly extends beyond the literal meaning of the text of Article 6(1). Indeed, the Court holds that Article 6(1) may be relevant for stages in the criminal procedure before the opening of the trial at which the charge will be 'determined'. For obvious reasons, this is the case with the reasonable-time requirement: the reasonable time 'begins to run as soon as a person is "charged"; this may occur on a date prior to the case coming before the trial court . . . , such as the date of arrest, the date when the person concerned was officially notified that he would be prosecuted or the date when preliminary investigations were opened'.[38] But the Court goes further, and holds that some of the guarantees that are typical for the trial stage may already play a role at earlier stages: 'Article 6 – especially paragraph 3 – may be relevant before a case is sent for trial if and so far as the fairness of the trial is likely to be seriously prejudiced by an initial failure to comply with its provisions'.[39] The Court is aware of the boldness of this holding: it immediately softens its effect by admitting not only that the manner in which Article 6(3) is to be applied in the

[31] Reference by the Court to ECtHR, *Campbell and Fell* v. *United Kingdom*, 28 June 1984.

[32] Reference by the Court to ECtHR, *Salabiaku* v. *France*, 7 October 1988.

[33] Reference by the Court to ECtHR, *Société Stenuit* v. *France*, 27 February 1992.

[34] Reference by the Court to ECtHR, *Guisset* v. *France*, 26 September 2000.

[35] *Jussila*, note 27 above, at para. 36.

[36] ECtHR (GC), *Escoubet* v. *Belgium*, 28 October 1999, paras 33–9.

[37] *Maaouia*, note 19 above, at para. 39.

[38] ECtHR, *Eckle* v. *Germany*, 15 July 1982, para. 73.

[39] ECtHR, *John Murray* v. *United Kingdom*, 8 February 1996, para. 62; ECtHR (GC), *Salduz* v. *Turkey*, 27 November 2008, para. 50. See also in the same sense ECtHR, *Imbrioscia* v. *Switzerland*, 24 November 1993, para. 36.

initial stages of the criminal proceedings 'depends on the special features of the proceedings involved and on the circumstance of the case',[40] but also that the rights guaranteed by Article 6(3), insofar as they are applied in the initial stages, 'may be subject to restrictions for good cause'.[41]

2.2 Right to a court

Probably the most spectacular example of a wide interpretation of Article 6 is offered by the *Golder* case (1975). In that case the Court read into Article 6(1) a right to a court, of which the right of access to a court is an essential aspect.

The Court reached its conclusion on the basis of extensive reasoning, in which it relied on the rules of interpretation contained in Articles 31 to 33 of the Vienna Convention of 23 May 1969 on the Law of Treaties. It relied in particular on the 'general rule' under Article 31: it took into account the text of Article 6(1) (which is not necessarily limited to pending proceedings, but can also be understood as implying a right to institute proceedings), the preamble to the ECHR (which refers to the rule of law), the object and purpose of the ECHR (intended to protect human rights), and two relevant general principles of law, namely that which requires a civil claim to be capable of being submitted to a judge and that which forbids the denial of justice. The Court concluded that the right of access is an inherent element of the right stated in Article 6(1).[42] And, clearly anticipating the dissenting opinion of Judge Fitzmaurice,[43] it added that 'this is not an extensive interpretation forcing new obligations on the Contracting States: it is based on the very terms of the first sentence of Article 6(1) read in its context and having regard to the object and purpose of the Convention, a lawmaking treaty . . . , and to general principles of

40 *Imbrioscia*, *ibid.*, at para. 38; *Murray*, *ibid.*, at para. 62.

41 *Murray*, *ibid.*, at para. 62. See also *Salduz*, note 39 above, at para. 52.

42 ECtHR, *Golder* v. *United Kingdom*, 21 February 1975, paras 30–35.

43 Sir Gerald Fitzmaurice, dissenting opinion, *Publ. Court*, Series A, vol. 18, p. 53, para. 39:

> These various factors could justify even a somewhat restrictive interpretation of the Convention but, without going as far as that, they must be said, unquestionably, not only to justify, but positively to demand, a cautious and conservative interpretation, particularly as regards any provisions the meaning of which may be uncertain, and where extensive constructions might have the effect of imposing upon the contracting States obligations they had not really meant to assume, or would not have understood themselves to be assuming. . . . Any serious doubt must therefore be resolved in favour of, rather than against, the government concerned.

law'.[44] Having reached a conclusion on the basis of the 'general rule', the Court noted that there was no need to resort to any 'supplementary means of interpretation', as envisaged by Article 32 of the Vienna Convention,[45] thereby avoiding the question whether its conclusion corresponded to the intention of the drafters of the ECHR.[46]

The impact of this interpretation has been enormous, especially on the field of public law. It might not have been clear from the outset, but it soon became clear that the Court had in fact opened the door to a right to judicial review of administrative acts, at least in so far as such acts affect 'civil' rights. That conclusion was explicitly drawn some years later:

> Article 6(1) is not applicable solely to proceedings which are already in progress: it may also be relied on by anyone who considers that an interference with the exercise of one of his (civil) rights is unlawful and complains that he has not had the possibility of submitting that claim to a tribunal meeting the requirements of Article 6(1) . . . It is of little consequence that the *contestation* (dispute) concerned an administrative measure taken by the competent body in the exercise of public authority . . .[47]

It should be noted that the right to judicial review of administrative acts is important in more than just cases coming under the 'civil' head of Article 6(1): that right is relevant in the 'criminal' context as well. Bearing in mind that under the Court's case law administrative, tax or disciplinary sanctions can qualify as 'criminal' sanctions (see section 2.1.2 above), the right of access to a court implies a right to challenge before a court a decision imposing such a sanction.[48]

In *Golder*, the Court tempered its holding (that a right of access to a court is guaranteed by Article 6(1) ECHR) by accepting at the same time that this right is not absolute and that, since the right is not defined as such in the Convention, 'there is room . . . for limitations permitted by implication'.[49] An implied right entails implied limitations.

There are many examples of limitations. Legitimate restrictions may follow from various conditions for the admissibility of a suit or an appeal, such as statutory limitation periods, security for costs orders, or regulations concerning minors and persons of unsound mind.[50] Another

44 *Golder*, note 42 above, at para. 36. 45 *Ibid.*

46 Which it probably did not, as was argued before the Court by the UK Government.

47 *Sporrong and Lönnroth*, note 12 above, at para. 80.

48 *Öztürk*, note 30 above, at para. 56. 49 *Golder*, note 42 above, at para. 38.

50 *Marković*, note 5 above, at para. 99, referring to *Golder*, note 42 above, at para. 39, ECtHR, *Tolstoy Miloslavsky* v. *United Kingdom*, 13 July 1995, paras 62–7, and ECtHR, *Stubbings* v. *United Kingdom*, 22 October 1996.

example of a legitimate restriction is given by the immunity of jurisdiction of foreign states or international organisations.[51] However, there are limits to the limitations as well: 'the limitations applied must not restrict the access left to the individual in such a way or to such an extent that the very essence of the right is impaired. Furthermore, a limitation will not be compatible with Article 6(1) if it does not pursue a legitimate aim and if there is not a reasonable relationship of proportionality between the means employed and the aim sought to be achieved.'[52] Implied limitations entail implied limits.

As indicated above, the right of access is (only) one aspect of the right to a court.

Another important aspect is the right to a judicial determination of the dispute.[53] This right implies the possibility of obtaining a 'decision' by the competent court.[54] Especially in public law cases, the question arises whether Article 6(1) requires the courts to have a minimum scope of judicial review. This is, however, an issue that will not be further examined in this chapter.[55]

The Court has further held that the right of access to a court 'would be illusory if a Contracting State's domestic legal system allowed a final, binding judicial decision to remain inoperative to the detriment of one party. It would be inconceivable that Article 6(1) should describe in detail procedural guarantees afforded to litigants – proceedings that are fair, public and expeditious – without protecting the implementation of judicial decisions . . . Execution of a judgment given by any court must therefore be regarded as an integral part of the "trial" for the purposes of Article 6.'[56]

[51] Foreign states: ECtHR (GC), *McElhinney* v. *Ireland*, 21 November 2001, *Al-Adsani* v. *United Kingdom*, 21 November 2001, and *Fogarty* v. *United Kingdom*, 21 November 2001; *Cudak*, note 22 above; *El Leil*, note 2 above. International organisations: ECtHR (GC), *Waite and Kennedy* v. *Germany*, 18 February 1999.

[52] See, for a recent authority, ECtHR (GC), *Stanev* v. *Bulgaria*, 17 January 2012, para. 230.

[53] *Le Compte et al.*, note 1 above, at para. 51 b; *Albert and Le Compte*, note 1 above, at para. 29.

[54] *Benthem*, note 12 above, at para. 40.

[55] For examples, see, in 'civil' cases, ECtHR, *Bryan* v. *United Kingdom*, 22 November 1995, paras 39–47, and ECtHR (GC), *Kingsley* v. *United Kingdom*, 28 May 2002, paras 32–4, and in 'criminal' cases, ECtHR, *Janosevic* v. *Sweden*, 23 July 2002, paras 81–2; ECtHR, *Segame SA* v. *France*, 7 June 2012, paras 54–60.

[56] ECtHR, *Hornsby* v. *Greece*, 19 March 1997, para. 40; ECtHR (GC), *Immobiliare Saffi* v. *Italy*, 28 July 1999, para. 63.

This also applies to judgments in criminal cases, in particular decisions to acquit the defendant.[57] The right to a fair trial thus extends to post-trial situations; again, an extension that does not immediately follow from a literal reading of Article 6(1).

A precondition for the effective enjoyment of the right to the execution of a judgment is that the judgment, once final, cannot be called into question, other than in exceptional circumstances. The Court thus reads into Article 6(1) a guarantee of the inalterability of final judgments. It bases this guarantee on the principle of legal certainty, considered as one of the fundamental aspects of the rule of law.[58]

2.3 Some structural and procedural guarantees

Article 6(1) and (3) ECHR provide a number of structural and procedural guarantees. These provisions are drafted in very general terms, leaving considerable room for interpretation.

In what follows, a number of these guarantees will be looked at, in the light of the case law of the Court. The focus will be on interpretations upholding guarantees not specifically mentioned, or derogating from a literal reading of Article 6.

2.3.1 Independence

Article 6(1) ECHR provides that everyone has the right to a hearing before an 'independent' tribunal. According to the Court, 'in order to establish whether a tribunal can be considered "independent" within the meaning of Article 6(1), regard must be had, *inter alia*, to the manner of appointment of its members and their term of office, to the existence of guarantees against outside pressures and to the question whether the body presents an appearance of independence'.[59]

While in the first place the guarantee of independence is a guarantee for the parties in judicial proceedings, the Court has developed it into a guarantee for the individual members of the judiciary as well. In the recent *Volkov* case, for instance, the Court found that the procedure leading to the dismissal of the applicant, a Supreme Court judge, did not comply with the principle of the independence of the courts, considered together

57 ECtHR (GC), *Assanidze* v. *Georgia*, 8 April 2004, para. 182.

58 ECtHR (GC), *Brumărescu* v. *Romania*, 28 October 1999, para. 61.

59 ECtHR, *Langborger* v. *Sweden*, 22 June 1989, para. 32; *Bryan*, note 55 above, at para. 37; ECtHR, *Findlay* v. *United Kingdom*, 25 February 1997, para. 73.

with the principle of their impartiality.[60] It thus underlined that judges need to be protected from undue influence by other state bodies and politicians, so as to allow the judiciary to carry out its activities in all independence.

2.3.2 Impartiality

Article 6(1) ECHR further provides that a tribunal must be 'impartial'. From its first judgments on the matter, the Court has distinguished 'between a subjective approach, that is endeavouring to ascertain the personal conviction of a given judge in a given case, and an objective approach, that is determining whether he offered guarantees sufficient to exclude any legitimate doubt in this respect'.[61]

For the purpose of this study, it is interesting to note that many years later the Court explained why it did not limit itself to the (obvious) subjective approach, and had recourse to an objective approach as well:

> In applying the subjective test, the Court has consistently held that the personal impartiality of a judge must be presumed until there is proof to the contrary... Although in some cases it may be difficult to procure evidence with which to rebut the presumption, it must be remembered that the requirement of objective impartiality provides a further important guarantee... In other words, the Court has recognised the difficulty of establishing a breach of Article 6 on account of subjective partiality and for this reason has in the vast majority of cases raising impartiality issues focused on the objective test.[62]

This candid explanation makes clear that, by adopting an objective approach in addition to a subjective approach, the Court has intentionally given a wide interpretation to the guarantee of impartiality.

2.3.3 Oral and public hearing and public judgment

Article 6(1) provides that everyone is entitled to a fair and 'public hearing', and that 'judgment shall be pronounced publicly'. At the same time, it allows for the exclusion of the press and the public from all or part of the trial in a number of circumstances. Both guarantees, that of the public hearing and that of the public judgment, have been the object of interpretations that go against a literal reading of the text.

60 ECtHR, *Oleksandr Volkov* v. *Ukraine*, 9 January 2013, paras 109–22.

61 ECtHR, *Piersack* v. *Belgium*, 1 October 1982, para. 30. See also ECtHR, *De Cubber* v. *Belgium*, 26 October 1984, para. 24; ECtHR, *Hauschildt* v. *Denmark*, 24 May 1989, para. 46.

62 ECtHR (GC), *Kyprianou* v. *Cyprus*, 15 December 2005, para. 119.

As regards the requirement for an oral hearing, which moreover shall be public, the Court makes a distinction between proceedings at first instance and proceedings at second or third instance. In the case of proceedings at first instance (and assuming that there is no oral and public hearing at a later stage of the proceedings), the principle, as indicated in Article 6(1) ECHR, is an entitlement to a 'public hearing'. However, apart from the circumstances mentioned in Article 6(1) that explicitly allow the court to order a closed session, the Court also accepts that there may be 'exceptional circumstances that justify dispensing with such a hearing'.[63] The 'exceptional' character of the circumstances is related to the nature of the issues to be decided by the competent courts, not to the frequency of such situations.[64] A law may therefore allow the courts to decide a given type of case merely on the basis of written submissions if the matter is highly technical (such as in social security cases[65]) and where a personal appearance would not serve any meaningful purpose.[66] However, in principle it would be incompatible with Article 6(1) for a litigant in such cases not to have the opportunity to at least request an oral hearing on the ground that his or her case presents special features, even when the court could refuse such a request on account of the circumstances of the case.[67] For the court, the 'overarching principle of fairness' should be 'the key consideration'.[68]

In the case of proceedings at second or third instance, the Court is even more lenient. Provided that there has been a public hearing at first instance, the absence of public hearings at second or third instance may be justified by the 'special features' of the proceedings at issue. 'Thus, proceedings for leave to appeal or proceedings involving only questions of law, as opposed to questions of fact, may comply with the requirements of Article 6 even where the appellant was not given an opportunity of being heard in person by the appeal or cassation court.'[69] When it comes

63 ECtHR (GC), *Göç* v. *Turkey*, 11 July 2002, para. 47.

64 ECtHR, *Miller* v. *Sweden*, 8 February 2005, para. 29; *Jussila*, note 27 above, at para. 42.

65 See, e.g., ECtHR, *Schuler-Zgraggen* v. *Switzerland*, 24 June 1993, para. 58.

66 According to the Court, the possibility cannot be excluded that even in the 'criminal' sphere the nature of the issues may be such that an oral hearing is not required. This is especially so with cases 'not strictly belonging to the traditional categories of the criminal law' (*Jussila*, note 27 above, at para. 43).

67 *Martinie*, note 20 above, at para. 42. The exclusion of an opportunity to request a public hearing could only be justified 'in wholly exceptional circumstances' (*ibid.*).

68 *Jussila*, note 27 above, at para. 42. In the same sense, *Eskelinen*, note 21 above, at para. 74.

69 ECtHR (GC), *Meftah* v. *France*, 26 July 2002, para. 41, with further references. Compare, with respect to proceedings before a supreme court where fresh evidence can be examined, e.g., ECtHR, *Serrano Contreras* v. *Spain*, 20 March 2012.

to proceedings in cassation, the Court noted that any argument in such proceedings would be particularly technical and concern only points of law; in such circumstances, 'it would be unduly formalistic to interpret the procedural requirements as meaning that the applicants should have been permitted to make oral representations at the hearing before the Court of Cassation'.[70]

It thus appears that, as well as the explicit exceptions to the right to a public hearing, this right is also subject to implied limitations.

As regards the requirement for public pronouncement of the judgment, the Court adopts a reading that departs from the terms of Article 6(1). While the terms might suggest that a 'reading out aloud of the judgment' is required,[71] the Court takes into account the fact that 'many member States of the Council of Europe have a long-standing tradition of recourse to other means, besides reading out aloud, for making public the decisions of all or some of their courts, and especially of their courts of cassation, for example deposit in a registry accessible to the public'.[72] The Court therefore 'does not feel bound to adopt a literal interpretation', and rather considers 'that in each case the form of publicity to be given to the "judgment" under the domestic law of the respondent State must be assessed in the light of the special features of the proceedings in question and by reference to the object and purpose of Article 6(1)'.[73]

It is interesting to note that the 'object and purpose' of Article 6(1) serve as a justification for setting aside an explicit requirement.

2.3.4 Fairness of the proceedings

The requirement of a fair trial, as guaranteed by Article 6(1) and (in criminal cases) paragraphs (2) and (3), presents a myriad of aspects. Quite naturally, the Court has developed an impressive case law. However, it is only exceptionally that the Court 'interprets' the fair trial provision, in the sense of making a general statement about its scope. In what follows, attention will be paid, first, to a few general guarantees that are implied by the right to a fair trial, and second, to the relationship between the general right to a fair trial and the specific aspects of that right mentioned in Article 6(3).

70 *Meftah, ibid.*, at para. 44.

71 ECtHR, *Pretto* v. *Italy*, 8 December 1983, para. 25; ECtHR, *Axen* v. *Germany*, 8 December 1983, para. 30; ECtHR, *Sutter* v. *Switzerland*, 22 February 1984, para. 30.

72 *Pretto, ibid.*, at para. 26; *Axen, ibid.*, at para. 31; *Sutter, ibid.*, at para. 31.

73 *Pretto, ibid.*, at para. 26; *Axen, ibid.*, at para. 31; *Sutter, ibid.*, at para. 31.

Some guarantees implied by the right to a fair trial A first important element of the right to a fair trial is the right to participate effectively in the proceedings.

This right is particularly important in criminal cases. The Court has given the right a very concrete meaning by pointing to a number of specific requirements:

> 'Effective participation' in this context presupposes that the accused has a broad understanding of the nature of the trial process and of what is at stake for him or her, including the significance of any penalty which may be imposed... It also requires that he or she, if necessary with the assistance of, for example, an interpreter, lawyer, social worker or friend, should be able to understand the general thrust of what is said in court. The defendant should be able to follow what is said by the prosecution witnesses and, if represented, to explain to defence counsel his or her version of events, point out any statements with which he or she disagrees and make the trial court aware of any facts which should be put forward for the defence... [74]

The interpretation thus given illustrates that the Convention is intended to guarantee 'not rights that are theoretical or illusory but rights that are practical and effective', and that 'this is particularly so of the rights of the defence'.[75]

Another important element of the right to a fair trial is the right to an adversarial procedure. That right implies that in principle each of the parties has the opportunity to have knowledge of and comment on all evidence adduced or observations filed, even by a third party or an independent actor in the proceedings, with a view to influencing the court's decision.[76]

A specific problem arises with respect to evidence in the possession of the prosecution authorities. The Court considers that, apart from respect for the right to an adversarial procedure, Article 6(1) ECHR also requires 'that the prosecution authorities disclose to the defence all material evidence for or against the accused'.[77] However, the entitlement to disclosure of relevant evidence is not an absolute right. Without speaking

[74] ECtHR, *Güveç* v. *Turkey*, 20 January 2009, para. 124.

[75] See the general statement in ECtHR, *Artico* v. *Italy*, 13 May 1980, para. 33.

[76] See ECtHR (GC), *Kress* v. *France*, 7 June 2001, para. 74. In that judgment, the Court drew a distinction between the general right to an adversarial procedure and the more specific right to equality of arms (which concerns the relationship between opposing parties): see paras 72–3.

[77] ECtHR, *Edwards* v. *United Kingdom*, 16 December 1992, para. 36. In later cases the Court specified that the prosecution authorities have to disclose the material evidence 'in their possession': ECtHR (GC), *Rowe and Davis* v. *United Kingdom*, 16 February 2000, para.

of implied limitations, the Court accepts that 'in any criminal proceedings there may be competing interests, such as national security or the need to protect witnesses at risk of reprisals or keep secret police methods of investigation of crime, which must be weighed against the rights of the accused'.[78] Whether or not withholding certain evidence can still be deemed compatible with the right to a fair trial will depend on how strong the justification is and whether the limitations to the rights of the defence are sufficiently counterbalanced by the procedures followed. On this issue the Court adopts a realistic approach, showing its willingness to take into account the practical needs of police and judicial investigations.

Another issue that has given rise to very specific case law is that of the use of unlawfully obtained evidence. The Court is not inclined to consider that the use of unlawfully obtained evidence in itself makes the trial unfair. The reason is that it considers that Article 6 ECHR does not lay down any rules on the admissibility of evidence as such, leaving it to national law to regulate the matter. The Court therefore puts the issue in a wider perspective, and examines whether the trial as a whole was fair.[79] In this respect a relevant question is whether the party against whom the evidence is used could properly exercise its rights of defence, i.e. challenge the authenticity and the probative value of the evidence adduced.[80]

There is an important exception to the (only) relative importance given to illegality of evidence. Where evidence has been obtained by an act qualified as torture, which is prohibited in absolute terms by Article 3 ECHR, it can never be relied on as proof of the defendant's guilt. Should this nevertheless have happened, normally the trial is automatically rendered unfair.[81] It seems that the same is true where evidence was obtained by an act qualified as inhuman or degrading treatment, but falling short of torture.[82]

However, the trial is not rendered unfair if the inhuman or degrading treatment, or even the act of torture, had no bearing on the outcome of the proceedings; that is, if it had no impact on the defendant's conviction or sentence.[83]

60, and *Fitt* v. *United Kingdom*, 16 February 2000, para. 44; ECtHR (GC), *Edwards and Lewis* v. *United Kingdom*, 27 October 2004, para. 46.

78 *Rowe and Davis*, *ibid.*, para. 61, and *Fitt*, *ibid.*, para. 45; *Edwards and Lewis*, *ibid.*, para. 46.

79 ECtHR, *Allan* v. *United Kingdom*, 5 November 2002, para. 42.

80 ECtHR, *Schenk* v. *Switzerland*, 12 July 1988, paras 46–7; ECtHR (GC), *Jalloh* v. *Germany*, 11 July 2006, paras 95–6; ECtHR (GC), *Gäfgen* v. *Germany*, 1 June 2010, paras 163–4.

81 *Jalloh*, *ibid.*, at para. 107; *Gäfgen*, *ibid.*, at para. 167.

82 *Gäfgen*, *ibid.*, at paras 176–7.

83 *Ibid.*, at para. 178.

Another set of guarantees, identified as separate rights under the umbrella of the right to a fair trial, is constituted by the right to silence and the privilege against self-incrimination. According to the Court, these are 'generally recognised international standards, which lie at the heart of the notion of fair procedures under Article 6. Their rationale lies, *inter alia*, in the protection of the accused against improper compulsion by the authorities, thereby contributing to the avoidance of miscarriages of justice and to the fulfilment of the aims of Article 6'.[84]

It seems that the case law on the contents of these rights shows some hesitation on the part of the Court. On several occasions, it has affirmed that the right not to incriminate oneself is primarily concerned with respecting the intention of an accused person to remain silent.[85] Referring to the common understanding of that right in the legal systems of the Contracting States, the Court further holds that generally the right 'does not extend to the use in criminal proceedings of material which may be obtained from the accused through the use of compulsory powers, but which has an existence independent of the will of the suspect such as, *inter alia*, documents acquired pursuant to a warrant, breath, blood, urine, hair or voice samples and bodily tissue for the purpose of DNA testing'.[86] The Court admits, however, that 'on occasion' it has given the principle of self-incrimination 'a broader meaning so as to encompass cases in which coercion to hand over real evidence to the authorities was in issue'.[87] A cautious conclusion could therefore be that the answer to the question whether or not the principle of self-incrimination applies in a given case depends on the circumstances, including the degree of coercion used.

A last guarantee to be mentioned is that of the obligation for courts to give reasons for their decisions. It is an obligation that must be understood and applied in a reasonable way: 'it cannot be understood as requiring a detailed answer to every argument'. Nor is the adequacy of the answer a condition for its sufficiency, from the point of view of Article 6(1) ECHR.[88]

84 *John Murray*, note 39 above, at para. 45; ECtHR (GC), *Saunders* v. *United Kingdom*, 17 December 1996, para. 68; *Jalloh*, note 80 above, at para. 100; *Gäfgen*, note 80 above, at para. 168.

85 See, e.g., *Saunders*, *ibid.*, at para. 69; *Jalloh*, *ibid.*, at para. 102.

86 *Jalloh*, *ibid.*, at para. 102, with further references. See also at para. 110.

87 *Ibid.*, at para. 111, referring to, *inter alia*, ECtHR, *Funke* v. *France*, 25 February 1993.

88 ECtHR, *van de Hurk* v. *The Netherlands*, 19 April 1994, para. 61. See also *Gorou (no. 2)*, note 3 above, at para. 37, with respect to the varying extent of this duty, in the light not only of the diversity of the submissions by the parties, but also of the differences existing in the Contracting States with regard to the applicable legal and practical framework.

Recently, the Court held that the obligation to give reasons does not apply as such to decisions handed down by a lay jury. Nevertheless, the fairness of the trial implies that the accused and even the public must be able to understand the verdict. For the Court, this is 'a vital safeguard against arbitrariness'. While in proceedings before professional judges the obligation to explain why an accused is convicted is normally fulfilled by giving reasons in the judicial decision itself, there may be other ways to fulfil that obligation in proceedings before a jury, e.g. through directions or guidance provided by the presiding judge to the jurors or through precise, unequivocal questions put to the jury by the judge.[89] This is an example of the result being more important than the means adopted to achieve it.

Relationship between the general right to a fair trial (Article 6(1)) and the specific aspects of that right (Article 6(3)) The rights mentioned above are all features of the right to a fair trial. The same is true of the more specific guarantees in criminal cases, mentioned in Article 6(3) ECHR.

With respect to the latter rights the question arises what the relationship is between the general right to a fair trial and the specific aspects of that right. Should the specific rights be respected as such, or do they merely serve to give content, together with other elements, to the right to a fair trial?

In its earlier cases, the Court held that paragraph (3) of Article 6 ECHR contains an enumeration of specific applications of the 'general principle' stated in paragraph (1), and that 'when compliance with paragraph 3 is being reviewed, its basic purpose must not be forgotten nor must it be severed from its roots'.[90] This seemed to indicate that the various guarantees in Article 6(3) have only a relative meaning, and must be assessed in light of the general right to a fair trial.

However, it does not seem that the Court has consistently followed such an approach. An example of a case in which a guarantee of Article 6(3) was rather detached from the general right to a fair trial, is the *Salduz* case (2008). That case concerned the right to assistance by a lawyer, a right guaranteed by Article 6(3)(c) ECHR. The Court held that this right could play a role even in the pre-trial stages of the criminal proceedings, including during police interrogations.[91] It then went on to hold that Article 6(1):

[89] ECtHR (GC), *Taxquet* v. *Belgium*, 16 November 2010, paras 90–92.

[90] *Artico*, note 75 above, at para. 32.

[91] *Salduz*, note 39 above, at para. 52.

> requires that, as a rule, access to a lawyer should be provided as from the first interrogation of a suspect by the police, unless it is demonstrated in the light of the particular circumstances of each case that there are compelling reasons to restrict this right. Even where compelling reasons may exceptionally justify denial of access to a lawyer, such restriction – whatever its justification – must not unduly prejudice the rights of the accused under Article 6.[92]

It seems that by requiring 'as a rule' that the specific guarantee of Article 6(3)(c) should be afforded, the Court interprets that specific aspect of the right to a fair trial as a right on its own. In such an interpretation the means acquire more importance than the overall result to be reached.

In the more recent case *Al-Khawaja and Tahery* (2011), the Court seems to have reverted to the initial relationship between the general right to a fair trial and the specific aspects of that right. It considers that

> the guarantees in paragraph 3(d) of Article 6 are specific aspects of the right to a fair hearing set forth in paragraph 1 of this provision, which must be taken into account in any assessment of the fairness of the proceedings. In addition, the Court's primary concern under Article 6(1) is to evaluate the overall fairness of the criminal proceedings.[93]

Further, in the judgment it emphasises that the impact of any shortfall from a specific guarantee of Article 6(3) should be assessed against the overall fairness of the trial,[94] and that Article 6(3) should be interpreted in the context of an overall examination of the fairness of the proceedings.[95] This leads to the conclusion that what the Court calls the 'sole or decisive rule', which is an element of the legal framework of the right to examine or have examined witnesses (Article 6(3)(d)),[96] should not be applied in an inflexible manner. Rather, it should be applied in the context of an assessment of the 'overall fairness of the proceedings', which involves

92 *Ibid.*, at para. 55.

93 ECtHR (GC), *Al-Khawaja and Tahery* v. *United Kingdom*, 15 December 2011, para. 118, referring to *Taxquet*, note 89 above, at para. 84.

94 *Al-Khawaja and Tahery*, *ibid.*, para. 143.

95 *Ibid.*, para. 143, referring to *Salduz*, note 39 above, at para. 50 (which does not exactly state the same thing).

96 The 'sole or decisive rule' means that 'when a conviction is based solely or to a decisive degree on depositions that have been made by a person whom the accused has had no opportunity to examine or to have examined, whether during the investigation or at the trial, the rights of the defence may be restricted to an extent that is incompatible with the guarantees provided by Article 6' (*Al-Khawaja and Tahery*, note 93 above, para. 119). The question to be examined in *Al-Khawaja and Tahery* was whether the 'sole or decisive rule' was to be considered as an absolute rule breach of which automatically leads to a finding that the proceedings had not been fair in violation of Art. 6(1) ECHR (*ibid.*).

'(weighing) in the balance the competing interests of the defence, the victim and witnesses, and the public interest in the effective administration of justice'.[97]

The new approach – or better, the return to the original approach – somewhat lowers the level of protection afforded to the accused. As such, it seems to respond to the criticism levelled against e.g., the *Salduz* judgment, for having imposed strict requirements that might not be necessary in all legal systems, when attention is paid to the overall fairness of the relevant proceedings.

3. Concluding remarks

What are the conclusions that can be drawn from this overview of some relevant aspects of the Court's case law on Article 6(1) ECHR?

It seems fair to say that the Court has consistently widened the scope of application of Article 6(1) ECHR. There are, however, limits to the scope of application, and the Court does not seem inclined to extend these limits further. The result is a complex system that gives the impression of not yet being fully developed.

The Court's reading of a right to a court into Article 6(1) ECHR constitutes one of its most important jurisprudential constructions. This has had the effect of submitting large segments of administrative action to the requirement for judicial review.

As for the structural and procedural guarantees, a recent development in the case law is the Court's return to the view that what matters is the overall fairness of proceedings. Specific aspects of the right to a fair trial are important indicators, but a failure to guarantee them in full does not necessarily lead to the conclusion that the parties were denied a fair trial. The Court seems to have become more 'result'-oriented, which allows it to leave more room for domestic policy considerations when it comes to creating the framework for judicial proceedings. This development seems to fit with an increased emphasis on the 'subsidiary' character of the Convention protection system.[98]

Is there a logic behind the various interpretations of the provisions of Article 6(1) ECHR? The answer can only be a cautious one. Like any other court the European Court's mission is to solve disputes. This involves

[97] *Ibid.*, para. 146. See also para. 118.

[98] See e.g., the Brighton Declaration, adopted by a High Level Conference on the Future of the European Court of Human Rights (19–20 April 2012), points 3, 11, 12 and 29 and the new recital to the ECHR's Preamble, inserted by Protocol 15, signed on 24 June 2013.

taking decisions on a case-by-case basis. While the Court is also called to give authoritative interpretations of the Convention, its case law is not necessarily driven by an overriding concern to follow a strictly logical path. Depending on the circumstances, a given principle of interpretation may receive lesser or greater weight.

Having said that, there are at least two elements that regularly recur when the Court adopts a wide interpretation of Article 6(1) ECHR. A first one is the importance of the rule of law, which has been particularly important for the recognition of the right to a court. This should not come as a surprise: the rule of law is practically inconceivable without the possibility to bring claims before courts. Another element is the need to avoid the guarantees of Article 6(1) becoming merely theoretical or illusory and to ensure that they are practical and effective. This element has been important as regards the right to obtain the execution of an enforceable judgment and the right to effective participation in proceedings.

When the Court tends to a more restrictive interpretation of Article 6(1) ECHR, other considerations come into play. Two should be mentioned in particular. First, the Court tries to avoid reading Article 6(1) in such a way that the result would be wholly unrealistic. This has been the case, e.g., with the right to public pronouncement of judgments and with the obligation on prosecuting authorities to disclose all relevant material in their possession. Second, and especially in recent years, the Court seems to attach more importance to the overall fairness of proceedings than to respect for each of the specific guarantees, considered separately. This has led it to accept, under certain conditions, the use of unlawfully obtained evidence, the absence of formal reasons for a judicial decision, and restrictions of the right to examine witnesses or have them examined.

Thus it seems that the Court is looking for an interpretation of Article 6(1) that offers effective protection to individuals without unduly restricting legislatures in the way they deal with affairs of justice or courts in the way they adjudicate cases. Whether the Court always manages to strike the right balance is of course a matter on which views may differ.

15

How the right to respect for private and family life, home and correspondence became the nursery in which new rights are born

Article 8 ECHR

MARIS BURBERGS

1. Introduction

The first paragraph of Article 8 ECHR reads '[e]veryone has the right to respect for his private and family life, his home and his correspondence'.

Looking at that text helps us realise the amount of work that the former European Commission of Human Rights (the Commission, ECommHR) and the European Court of Human Rights (the Court; ECtHR) (together – Strasbourg organs) have done to give shape to this article. Back in the 1950s the four notions – private life, family life, home and correspondence – were just the bare notions we can see above. This is the material the Commission looked at when it started its work. And now, for those who know the Strasbourg case law, a myriad of sub-rights and interests associated with each notion start running through the mind. Indeed, Article 8 has become a particularly content-rich Convention article. It has accumulated developments in communication technologies under the notion of 'correspondence'. A variety of living premises with which a person has sustained substantial and permanent links have found protection under the concept 'home' in Article 8. It covers *de facto* family life – a notion that has been applied to a variety of relationship arrangements. The article encompasses multiple sub-rights and interests under 'private life', the majority of which have been categorised under spheres of

The research for this chapter was conducted within the framework of the ERC Starting Grant project 'Strengthening the European Court of Human Rights: More Accountability Through Better Legal Reasoning'.

physical and moral integrity, the collection and use of data, establishing relationships with others, identity, and personal autonomy.[1]

What else, besides the text of the Article, was 'on the table' when cases involving alleged Article 8 violations started to reach the Strasbourg organs? There were also the history of the drafting of the Convention and the history of Europe, of a continent that was recovering from the Second World War. Gradually, cases were decided that gave shape to Convention rights and that constituted materials that could be used for further developments.

In the first part of this chapter I will explore, first, the transforming processes that the Convention went through in realising its envisaged purpose for Europe and how that affected the scope of Article 8, and, second, how the general methods for interpreting the Convention shaped Article 8 and vice versa. In the second part I will look deeper inside Article 8 and explore the use of previous case law to develop the scope of the Article further. Several authors have commented on the role of the interpretation doctrines in the development of the Convention;[2] and the use of argumentative techniques in the Court's case law has been the subject of an academic inquiry.[3] These publications show the great impact that the doctrines of interpretation and argumentative techniques employed by the Strasbourg organs have had on the scope of Convention rights. Thus, in this chapter I will look into both of them when looking for explanations of how Article 8 was shaped.

2. The Convention's evolution and Article 8

2.1 Pact against totalitarianism or European bill of rights?

For the aim of this volume – to discuss the scope of Convention rights – an understanding of the general purpose of the Convention is important,

1 See P. van Dijk, F. van Hoof, A. van Rijn and L. Zwaak (eds), *Theory and Practice of the European Convention on Human Rights*, 4th edn (The Hague: Intersentia, 2006), pp. 666–90; D.J. Harris, M. O'Boyle, E.P. Bates and C.M. Buckley, *Harris, O'Boyle and Warbrick, Law of the European Convention on Human Rights*, 2nd edn (Oxford University Press, 2009), pp. 364–76; I. Roagna, *Protecting the Respect for Private and Family Life under the European Convention on Human Rights*, Human Rights Handbooks, No. 11 (Strasbourg: Council of Europe, 2012), pp. 12–24, available at: www.coe.int/t/dghl/cooperation/capacitybuilding/Source/documentation/hb11_privatelife_en.pdf (accessed on 5 March 2013).

2 See A. Mowbray, 'The creativity of the European Court of Human Rights', 2005 5(1) *Human Rights Law Review* 57; G. Letsas, *A Theory of Interpretation of the European Convention on Human Rights* (Oxford University Press, 2007).

3 See J.H. Gerards, 'The prism of fundamental rights', 2012 8(2) *European Constitutional Law Review* 173, and the sources cited therein.

as it has an impact on the interpretation of each of the Convention rights. To this end Bates, who has made a historical study of the developments of the Convention, points out that 'the primary aim of those who drafted the Convention in 1950 was to create a type of collective pact against totalitarianism'.[4] Drafted in the aftermath of the Second World War, the Convention was envisaged as 'an alarm that would bring . . . large-scale violations of human rights to the attention of other Western European States in time for action to be taken to suppress them'.[5] Another view on the overall mission of the Convention, which was noticeable already in some of the minds that drafted the Convention, was that it should be some kind of European bill of rights, which would deal with isolated violations of human rights.[6] This ambiguity of the Convention's mission was felt by the members of the Commission, who were the first to interpret the rights it granted and decide on the shape these would be given. At the fifth anniversary of the Convention's entry into force the Commission's first president, C.H.M. Waldock, spoke of two ways to understand the Convention:

> If you regard the Convention as a constitutional instrument – as a European Bill of Rights for the individual – then it seems difficult to deny the importance of granting the individual a personal right to place his grievance before the Commission. If, on the other hand, the Convention is regarded rather as a pact for collective action to check the development of any totalitarian methods of government in member countries, then the individual's right of recourse to the Commission may seem less important than that of the Member States. The Convention compromised on this point.[7]

In the two decades following this speech, more and more states joined the Convention system and decided to recognise the individual right of

[4] E. Bates, *The Evolution of the European Convention on Human Rights: From Its Inception to the Creation of a Permanent Court of Human Rights* (Oxford University Press, 2010), preface.

[5] D. Harris, M. O'Boyle and C. Warbrick, *Law of the European Convention on Human Rights*, 1st edn (London: Butterworth, 1995), p. 2.

[6] Bates, *The Evolution of the ECHR*, note 4 above, pp. 65–74. Bates describes the ideas of Pierre-Henri Teitgen, arguably one of the Convention's founding fathers, with regard to creation of a European Union in which more than just a very limited number of rights would be protected.

[7] C.M.H. Waldock, 'Address by C.M.H. Waldock' in Council of Europe, *Fifth Anniversary of the Coming into Force of the ECHR: Brussels Exhibition, 3 September 1958* (Strasbourg: Council of Europe, 1959), reproduced in Bates, *The Evolution of the ECHR*, note 4 above, p. 367.

complaint.[8] It was subsequently observed that the anti-totalitarian function had remained 'largely dormant, coming to life in just a small number of inter-state applications' and that '[i]ncreasingly it [the Convention] ha[d] evolved into a European bill of rights, with the European Court of Human Rights having a role akin to that of a constitutional court in a federal legal system'.[9]

In Article 8 case law this process is reflected in *Marckx* v. *Belgium*, a case decided in 1979.[10] In this case, judge Sir Gerald Fitzmaurice, disagreeing with the interpretation of the scope of Article 8 given by the majority, gave his particular view on the nature of Article 8 and pointed out the anti-totalitarian purpose for its creation:

> It is abundantly clear (at least it is to me) – and the nature of the whole background against which the idea of the European Convention on Human Rights was conceived bears out this view – that the main, if not indeed the sole object and intended sphere of application of Article 8 . . . , was that of what I will call the 'domiciliary protection' of the individual. He and his family were no longer to be subjected to the four o'clock in the morning rat-a-tat on the door; to domestic intrusions, searches and questionings; to examinations, delaying and confiscation of correspondence; to the planting of listening devices (bugging); to restrictions on the use of radio and television; to telephone-tapping or disconnection; to measures of coercion such as cutting off the electricity or water supply; to such abominations as children being required to report upon the activities of their parents, and even sometimes the same for one spouse against another, – in short the whole gamut of fascist and communist inquisitorial practices . . . [I]t was for the avoidance of these horrors, tyrannies and vexations that 'private and family life . . . home and . . . correspondence' were to be respected.[11]

However, the majority in *Marckx* held a different view on Article 8 to that of Fitzmaurice, and included matters of intestate succession within its scope. This judgment, which faced strong opposition from Fitzmaurice, serves as a clear indicator that a majority within the Strasbourg organs had decided which road they were taking with regard to the overall mission of the Convention – for them the Convention was not merely a pact against totalitarianism.

Although, at the time, he was a clear minority, Fitzmaurice's opinion remains noteworthy for discussions of the scope of rights. It demonstrates

[8] Bates, *The Evolution of the ECHR*, note 4 above, pp. 133–6.
[9] Harris, O'Boyle and Warbrick, *Law of the ECHR*, note 5 above, p. 2.
[10] ECtHR, *Marckx* v. *Belgium*, 13 June 1979.
[11] See Dissenting Opinion of judge Sir Gerald Fitzmaurice in *ibid.*

that the understanding of the general aim of the Convention strongly impacts upon the scope of its rights. If the Strasbourg organs had followed his (and the drafters') understanding of the Convention rights, Article 8 ECHR would have a very narrow scope, and only the likes of the *Greek case* would have been declared admissible.[12]

2.2 'Living instrument'

A year prior to the *Marckx* judgment, described above, the Court delivered a judgment in the case of *Tyrer* v. *United Kingdom*, which coined the description of the Convention as a 'living instrument' – another element that went against the drafters' intentions and shaped the whole Convention and Article 8 with it.[13] This new term meant that the Convention 'must be interpreted in the light of present-day conditions'.[14] To determine present-day conditions the Court said it was influenced 'by the developments and commonly accepted standards . . . of the member States of the Council of Europe'.[15] Letsas notes that the interpretation of 'commonly accepted standards' has also experienced a transformation – it shifted from 'commonly accepted standards in domestic legislations to signs of evolution of attitudes amongst modern societies'.[16] The living instrument doctrine and its ability to transform played a part in widening the scope of Article 8. One of the cases in which the Court used the doctrine is that of *Christine Goodwin* v. *United Kingdom*.[17] The case concerned lack of legal recognition for the applicant's post-operative gender and the legal status of transsexuals in the United Kingdom. In previous similar cases the Court had held that the refusal of the United Kingdom government to alter the register of births or to issue birth certificates differing from the original recordings of gender could not be considered as an interference with the right to respect for private life,[18] and neither was there a positive obligation on the state to alter a register of births or issue new birth certificates.[19] But it had also stressed that, 'since the

[12] ECommHR, *The Greek case: Denmark* v. *Greece, Norway* v. *Greece, Sweden* v. *Greece, The Netherlands* v. *Greece*, decision, 31 May 1968, para. 251. The case concerned, *inter alia*, arrests that had been carried out at night.

[13] ECtHR, *Tyrer* v. *United Kingdom*, 25 April 1978. [14] *Ibid.* [15] *Ibid.*

[16] Letsas, *A Theory of Interpretation*, note 2 above, p. 77. See also the chapter by Mowbray in this volume.

[17] ECtHR (GC), 11 July 2002.

[18] See ECtHR, *Rees* v. *United Kingdom*, 17 October 1986, para. 35, and ECtHR, *Cossey* v. *United Kingdom*, 27 September 1990, para. 36.

[19] See *Rees*, *ibid.*, paras 35–46, and *Cossey*, *ibid.*, paras 36–41.

Convention always has to be interpreted and applied in the light of current circumstances, it is important that the need for appropriate legal measures in this area should be kept under review'.[20] Accordingly, when the Court examined the matter in the *Christine Goodwin* case it looked for a European consensus at the material time, and found that one still did not exist (as in previous cases). But the Court did not stop there this time. Sitting as a Grand Chamber it went on to transform the doctrine – it accepted as 'hardly surprising' that there was no consensus among the very diverse Member States, and decided to attach less importance to the lack of evidence of a common European approach than 'to the clear and uncontested evidence of a continuing international trend in favour not only of increased social acceptance of transsexuals but of legal recognition of the new sexual identity of post-operative transsexuals'.[21] Thus the doctrine, which had started as 'commonly accepted standards' in the Member States, was now a 'continuing international trend'. This development accompanied by other considerations led to the obligation to legally recognise the post-operative gender of transsexuals.

2.3 Going beyond the drafters' explicit intentions

Even though the 'living instrument' doctrine set the Convention rights free from what their meaning had been taken to be in the 1950s, there was still caution towards rights that had explicitly been excluded from its scope by the drafters.

In 1949, when the Convention was drafted, a proposal was laid before the Committee on Legal and Administrative Questions, to include in the Convention a provision that would guarantee to every person '[t]he inviolability of his private life, of his home, of his correspondence and of his family, in accordance with Article 12 of the United Nations Declaration'.[22] Article 12 of the Universal Declaration of Human Rights (UDHR) is noteworthy for the purposes of determining the scope of Article 8:

> No one shall be subjected to arbitrary interference with his privacy, family, home or correspondence, nor to attacks upon his honour and reputation. Everyone has the right to the protection of the law against such interference or attacks.

20 See *Cossey*, *ibid.*, para. 42; see also *Rees*, *ibid.*, para. 47.

21 *Goodwin*, note 17 above, para. 85.

22 *Travaux préparatoires* of the Convention, Art. 8, p. 2, available at: www.echr.coe.int/library/DIGDOC/Travaux/ECHRTravaux-ART8-DH(56)12-EN1674980.pdf (accessed on 10 February 2012).

Comparing Article 12 UDHR with the final, adopted version of Article 8 ECHR, one notices the difference regarding scope – the protection of honour and reputation was omitted from Article 8 ECHR. The *travaux préparatoires* for the Convention state that the 'omission was deliberate'.[23] Later in the drafting process the Committee of Experts explained that '[i]n accordance with the Assembly's intentions, only a certain part of the rights in Article 12 . . . of the Universal Declaration were included in the Convention'.[24] Thus it can be concluded without doubt that the omission was intended by the drafters, and a limit on the scope of Article 8 ECHR was set in this regard.

With regard to other Convention articles the Court has reasoned that in a legal situation like this it cannot derive a right that was not included in the Convention at the outset, 'particularly [not] . . . where the omission was deliberate'.[25] However, in another case the Court addressed the issue of omission and reasoned that the omitted matter struck at the essence of the right in question and could not be left outside its scope.[26] Similarly, with regard to the protection of reputation under the Convention, the limitation initially set by the drafters has been disregarded by the Court. To date, in several judgments this right has been included under the protection of Article 8 ECHR.[27] What is more, the issue of omission was not addressed in the judgments. Indeed, when introducing the right, the Court simply declared that 'protection of one's reputation is of course one of the rights guaranteed by Article 8'.[28] An explanation for the Court's decision not to make broader considerations could be that the idea that

[23] *Ibid.* [24] *Ibid.*, p. 5.

[25] ECtHR, *Johnston and others* v. *Ireland*, 18 December 1986, para. 53. The case concerned, *inter alia*, Mr Johnston's inability to remarry as it was not possible to dissolve his first marriage under Irish law. The Court held that the right to divorce cannot be derived from Art. 12 ECHR.

[26] ECtHR, *Young, James and Webster* v. *United Kingdom*, 13 August 1981. The Court was of a view that the substance of a right is important, downplaying any significance drafting history might have. The case concerned a negative aspect of the right to association – not joining an association. The applicants were dismissed after refusing to join a trade union, which was required from them under the 'closed shop' system in the United Kingdom. The 'closed shop' system was explicitly excluded from the scope of Art. 11 ECHR in the drafting of the Convention.

[27] See ECtHR, *Sidabras and Dziautas* v. *Lithuania*, 27 July 2004; ECtHR, *A* v. *Norway*, 9 April 2009; ECtHR, *Karako* v. *Hungary*, 28 April 2009; ECtHR, *Pfeifer* v. *Austria*, 15 November 2007; ECtHR, *Petrina* v. *Romania*, 14 October 2008; ECtHR, *Petrenco* v. *Moldova*, 30 March 2010.

[28] ECtHR, *Radio France* v. *France*, 30 March 2004, para. 31.

the 'explicit or imputed intention of the drafters is not relevant'[29] had been so firmly established by the early years of this century, when the reputation cases were heard, that it was thought irrelevant to invoke the *travaux préparatoires.*

2.4 Autonomous concepts

Another development that affected the scope of Article 8 was the introduction of the doctrine of 'autonomous concepts'. This doctrine was developed by the Court in *Engel and others* v. *The Netherlands*,[30] and means that the terms that the Convention uses do not necessarily have the same meaning as they have at the domestic level. In *Engel* the Court was faced with a classification of a particular offence as disciplinary rather than criminal. Given that Article 6 does not apply to purely disciplinary proceedings, the classification would escape review by the Strasbourg organs under that article. The Court found this situation worrisome, since it could be misused by states. Consequently, the Court declared that it would use the domestic understanding only as a starting-point for formulating the Convention meaning of concepts.[31]

All four Article 8 ECHR concepts – private life, family life, home and correspondence – have been given an autonomous meaning by the Strasbourg organs in the process of extending the article's scope by incorporating social, legal and technological developments.[32] 'Home' was explicitly declared an autonomous concept by the Commission in 1998.[33] More than a decade earlier, the Court was using a qualitative standard rather than relying on domestic formulations when deciding on applicability of the term 'home'.[34] According to the Court in the *Gillow* case, whether or not a particular premises constitute a 'home' that attracts the protection

[29] D. Spielmann and L. Cariolou, 'The rights to protection of reputation under the European Convention on Human Rights' in D. Spielmann, M. Tsirli and P. Voyatzis (eds), *The European Convention on Human Rights, a living instrument – Essays in Honour of Christos L. Rozakis* (Brussels: Bruylant, 2011), 579.

[30] ECtHR, 8 June 1976.

[31] ECtHR (GC), *Chassagnou and others* v. *France*, 19 April 1999, para. 100.

[32] U. Kilkelly, *The Right to Respect for Private and Family Life; A Guide to the Implementation of Article 8 of the European Convention on Human Rights*, Human Rights Handbooks, No. 1 (Strasbourg: Council of Europe, 2003), p. 10; available at www.echr.coe.int/library/DIGDOC/DG2/HRHAND/DG2-EN-HRHAND-01(2003).pdf (last visited on 15 January 2013).

[33] ECommHR, *Khatun amd 180 others* v. *United Kingdom*, decision, 1 July 1998.

[34] ECtHR, *Gillow* v. *United Kingdom*, 24 November 1986.

of Article 8 depends on the factual circumstances, namely, the existence of sufficient and continuous links between a person and a specific place.[35] 'Home' has been extended to include business premises,[36] and also unlawfully occupied premises.[37] 'Correspondence' has been developed to incorporate telephone conversations and new communication technologies.[38] As regards 'family life', the general principle applied by the Strasbourg organs is whether there are close personal ties between the parties. Thus, protection has been awarded not only to families based on marriage but also to relationships between unmarried couples with children,[39] and to relationships between parents and children born from an extra-marital or adulterous affair.[40] Based on the personal-ties standard, the relationship between an uncle or aunt and his/her nephew or niece, and even a relationship between persons with no blood tie,[41] can constitute 'family life'.[42]

'Private life' has been described by the Strasbourg organs as 'not susceptible to exhaustive definition'.[43] This understanding seems inherent in the notion itself and is not a Strasbourg construction. In 1970 (before most of the cases that led the development of the notion by the Commission and the Court) experts gathered for the Third International Colloquy on the European Convention on Human Rights to discuss privacy and human rights, and came to an agreement that 'private life' covers a broad field of law, the borders of which could barely be described.[44] It should be of no surprise, then, that new rights are born out of the right to respect for private life.

What the Strasbourg organs have done in defining 'private life' is not only to accept its broad nature but also to free it from how it is understood

35 *Ibid.* The standard was later used in ECtHR, *Buckley* v. *United Kingdom*, 25 September 1996.

36 ECtHR, *Niemietz* v. *Germany*, 16 December 1992.

37 ECtHR, *McCann* v. *United Kingdom*, 13 May 2008. For an elaborate list of premises protected as 'home' see Roagna, *Protecting Respect for Private and Family Life*, note 1 above.

38 For an extensive overview see the chapter by Mowbray in this volume.

39 *Johnston*, note 25 above.

40 ECommHR, *Jolie and Lebrun* v. *Belgium*, decision, 14 May 1986.

41 ECtHR (GC), *X, Y and Z* v. *United Kingdom*, 22 April 1997.

42 ECommHR, *Boyle* v. *United Kingdom*, report, 9 February 1993.

43 See ECtHR, *Costello-Roberts* v. *United Kingdom*, 25 March 1993, para. 36.

44 See J. Velu, 'The European Convention on Human Rights and the right to respect for private life, the home and communications' in A.H. Robertson (ed.), *Privacy and Human Rights; Papers by experts on an issue of growing importance given under the auspices of the European Convention on Human Rights* (Manchester University Press, 1973), 12–129.

by lexicographers and human rights scholars. In 1976 the Commission had to decide the case of *X* v. *Iceland*. The question before the Commission in that case was whether the freedom of an individual to keep a dog is protected under the Convention and, in particular, whether keeping a dog belongs to 'private life' within the meaning of Article 8 of the Convention. To answer the question about scope, the Commission turned to academic writings and even a law dictionary to inquire about what the notions might encompass.[45] The Commission found that '[f]or numerous anglo-saxon and French authors the right to respect for "private life" is the right to privacy, the right to live, as far as one wishes, protected from publicity'.[46] Indeed, the right to respect for private life was understood as a 'right to be left alone'.[47] Nonetheless, after consulting the work of lexicographers and scholars for the notion's meaning, the Commission formulated a more extensive understanding of it:

> In the opinion of the Commission . . . the right to respect for private life does not end there. It comprises also, to a certain degree, the right to establish and to develop relationships with other human beings, especially in the emotional field for the development and fulfillment of one's own personality.[48]

Again we see how the definitions given by others served only as a starting-point for the term's Convention meaning. As shown below, this particular development of 'private life' turned out to be an important one as it gave ground for multiple other interests to come within the term's scope.

The result of the freedom the concept has been awarded can be seen in the case of *Pretty* v. *United Kingdom* in which the Court gave an overview of the scope of 'private life':

> It covers the physical and psychological integrity of a person . . . It can sometimes embrace aspects of an individual's physical and social identity . . . Elements such as, for example, gender identification, name and sexual orientation and sexual life fall within the personal sphere protected by Article 8 . . . Article 8 also protects a right to personal development, and the right to establish and develop relationships with other human beings

45 The Commission indicates that it has noted numerous definitions of private life quoted by Velu, *ibid.*, and that it also consulted *Black's Law Dictionary*, 4th edn, 1951, under 'privacy'.

46 ECommHR, *X* v. *Iceland*, admissibility decision, 18 May 1976.

47 See Velu, 'ECHR and the right to respect for private life', note 44 above, pp. 27–8.

48 *X* v. *Iceland*, note 46 above. With regard to keeping a dog, the Commission held that, even though the 'dog has had close ties with man since time immemorial . . . this element alone is not sufficient to bring keeping of a dog into the sphere of private life of the owner'.

> and the outside world . . . Although no previous case has established as such any right to self-determination as being contained in Article 8 of the Convention, the Court considers that the notion of personal autonomy is an important principle underlying the interpretation of its guarantees.[49]

Here, the Court indicated the most important aspects of 'private life' and demonstrated the diverse spheres the concept has been extended to cover.[50] What is more, as will be shown below, these rights have developed further, flourishing like a growing tree.

3. Use of previous case law for further development

To understand the development of the scope of Article 8 we must also look closely at the inner workings of the article, and in particular, how one development of its scope impacts upon further case law.

Above I described how the right to develop relationships with other human beings was defined by the Commission. If we further examine the case law of Article 8 we can see this right being referred to again in other cases. One such case is *Bruggemann and Scheuten* v. *Germany*.[51] In this case the Commission reasoned that 'respect for private life comprises also, to a certain degree, the right to establish and to develop relationships with other human beings, especially in the emotional field, for the development and fulfillment of one's own personality, . . . and that therefore sexual life is also part of private life'.[52] We see here how one right was used to support further development of scope. Inclusion of sexual life within the scope of Article 8 was, in turn, used by the Strasbourg organs when considering whether to include within the scope of 'private life' a person's physical and moral integrity, as is further explored below.[53] What we can see from these cases is a 'tree-like mode' in which scope develops, where one 'branch' is the base and support for other 'branches' to grow.

In a tree, each branch can support *several* other branches. The same can be seen in Strasbourg case law. Not only was the right to develop relationships with other human beings the basis for including sexual activities within the scope of Article 8, but it also served as a basis for the Court's reasoning when it included professional activities within the

[49] ECtHR, *Pretty* v. *United Kingdom*, 29 April 2002, para. 61.

[50] No author to date seems to have produced a comprehensive list of rights and interests that are protected by Art. 8.

[51] ECommHR, decision, 19 May 1976. [52] *Ibid.*

[53] See ECommHR, *X and Y* v. *The Netherlands*, report, 5 July 1983, para. 76; ECtHR, *X and Y* v. *The Netherlands*, 26 March 1985, para. 22.

article's scope. In the case of *Niemietz* v. *Germany* the Court reiterated that respect for private life includes to a degree the right to establish and develop relationships with other human beings and that the 'outside world' should not be excluded from the protection of Article 8.[54] Including the 'outside world' was used further in the case. The Court reasoned that this understanding of private life also incorporates activities of a professional or business nature 'since it is, after all, in the course of their working lives that the majority of people have a significant, if not the greatest, opportunity of developing relationships with the outside world'.[55] And the tree continued to grow from there when the Court accepted that restrictions on employment interfere with 'private life'.[56] This latter development has considerable ramifications because it brings social and economic rights within Article 8,[57] and because it ensures a very strong horizontal effect.[58]

The tree-like mode of development is noticeable throughout the case law on Article 8, with smaller or bigger branches springing out from each new interest that has been accepted as forming part of the article's scope. To illustrate, the *Marckx* case, in which matters of intestate succession were included within 'family life', further developed to include matters of interpretation of testamentary dispositions.[59] The right to respect for the decision to become and the decision not to become a parent blossomed:[60] into rights to choose the circumstances of becoming a parent,[61] to choose to become a genetic parent,[62] to protect interests in conjugal visits,[63] and in access to IVF.[64] The right to physical and moral integrity has been further interpreted as covering strip-searches,[65] and it has been applied in cases about abortion and assisted suicide.[66]

54 *Niemietz*, note 36 above, para. 29. 55 *Ibid.*, para. 29.
56 *Sidabras and Džiautas*, note 27 above.
57 C. Ovey and R.C.A. White, *Jacobs and White: The European Convention on Human Rights*, 4th edn (Oxford University Press, 2006), p. 51. See also V. Mantouvalou, 'Work and private life: *Sidabras and Dziautas* v. *Lithuania*', (2005) 30 *European Law Review* 573–85.
58 See the horizontal effect in ECtHR, *Schüth* v. *Germany*, 23 September 2010 and ECtHR, *Obst* v. *Germany*, 23 September 2010.
59 ECtHR, *Pla and Puncernau* v. *Andorra*, 13 July 2004.
60 ECtHR (GC), *Evans* v. *United Kingdom*, 10 April 2007.
61 ECtHR, *Ternovszky* v. *Hungary*, 14 December 2010, para. 22.
62 ECtHR (GC), *Dickson* v. *United Kingdom*, 4 December 2007.
63 ECtHR, *Kalashnikov* v. *Russia*, decision, 18 September 2001.
64 ECtHR (GC), *SH and others* v. *Austria*, 3 November 2011.
65 ECtHR, *Wainwright* v. *United Kingdom*, 26 September 2006.
66 Abortion: ECtHR, *P and S* v. *Poland*, 30 October 2012, and see the case law cited therein. Assisted suicide: *Pretty*, note 49 above.

This mode of reasoning – relying on a previous case that shares an element with the new case – is preferred by the Strasbourg organs.[67] The preference is demonstrated by frequent use, as demonstrated above, and by the fact that in cases where the Strasbourg organs could have relied on other sources to interpret terms in Article 8, they chose to make links between their cases. If we take a look at one of the cases mentioned above – *X and Y* v. *The Netherlands*, which concerned the sexual abuse of a mentally disabled minor – the Commission and the Court could have limited themselves to interpreting 'private life' as encompassing the protection of physical and moral integrity. This would not have been an extraordinary move, as it had been suggested earlier by scholars and politicians.[68] Instead, the Commission referred to *Dudgeon* v. *United Kingdom* (which concerned homosexual relationships, at that time criminal offences in Northern Ireland),[69] and stated that *Dudgeon* 'implied' protection of physical and moral integrity.[70] When *X and Y* was referred to it, the Court did not mention *Dudgeon* but still accepted, as I read the case, that 'sexual life' is the common element that connects the 'branch' of 'physical and moral integrity' to the tree of 'private life'.[71] The Court reasoned this way despite the uncomfortable fact that it thus made a sexual assault on a mentally disabled girl her 'sexual life'.

The method for developing scope in which the Strasbourg organs refer to previous case law does not always resemble a tree and allow tracking the development back, branch by branch. It can also take a more cluster-like form where the links between the rights are not clearly visible. The new right then has some common element(s) with each of the rights in the cluster. Consider these two statements:

> The Court recalls that the concept of 'private life' is a broad term not susceptible to exhaustive definition. It covers the physical and psychological integrity of a person . . . It can therefore embrace multiple aspects of the person's physical and social identity . . . Elements such as, for example, gender identification, name and sexual orientation and sexual life fall

[67] For the use of analogy in the Court's case law see Gerards, 'The prism of fundamental rights', note 3 above.

[68] Robertson, *Privacy and Human Rights*, note 44 above. Parliamentary Assembly of the Council of Europe Resolution No. 428 (1970).

[69] ECtHR (GC), *Dudgeon* v. *United Kingdom*, 22 October 1981.

[70] See ECommHR, *X and Y*, note 53 above, para. 76. The Commission referred particularly to para. 39 of the *Dudgeon* judgment which describes the nature of legislation prohibiting homosexual activities.

[71] See ECtHR, *X and Y*, note 53 above, para. 22.

> within the personal sphere protected by Article 8 . . . Beyond a person's name, his or her private and family life may include other means of personal identification and of linking to a family . . . Information about the person's health is an important element of private life . . . *The Court furthermore considers that an individual's ethnic identity must be regarded as another such element.*[72]

And a smaller cluster:

> The Grand Chamber agrees with the Chamber that 'private life', which is a broad term encompassing, *inter alia*, aspects of an individual's physical and social identity including the right to personal autonomy, personal development and to establish and develop relationships with other human beings and the outside world . . . , incorporates the right to respect for both the decisions to become and not to become a parent.[73]

In both cases the broadness of the concept 'private life' is reiterated, then several elements are mentioned that seem to some extent to relate to the right that is about to be born, and finally the new right is introduced. The difference between the 'tree-like mode' and the 'cluster-like mode' is that in the former the Strasbourg organs indicate a single right out of which the new right is born. In the latter the new right is born out of a sphere that is formed by several rights.

4. Conclusion

Article 8 ECHR was strongly influenced by the developments and transitions that the Convention has experienced over time. The Convention was transformed from a pact against totalitarianism to a European bill of rights. The Strasbourg organs later freed the Convention from its drafters' intentions and formulated that into interpretation doctrines that see it as a 'living instrument' and the terms it uses as 'autonomous concepts'. Article 8 proved to be the battlefield on which contradictory views regarding the Convention have collided, so has helped shape the whole Convention.

Focus on the reasoning given by the Strasbourg organs when developing the scope of Article 8 reveals a strong reliance upon previous case law. The developments can take a tree-like form, in which a branch is a base from which another branch or branches grow. The reasoning can also be a more cloudy one where a cluster of rights from previous cases is presented and then the new right is introduced. Looking at both the processes in which

[72] ECtHR (GC), *S and Marper* v. *United Kingdom*, 4 December 2008 (emphasis added).

[73] *Evans*, note 60 above, para. 71.

the Convention has been transformed and the inner workings of Article 8 has brought us closer to understanding how Article 8 was shaped and has become such a content-rich part of the Convention.

The story of the development of Article 8 continues. Drawing from the development processes Article 8 has already experienced, further developments have been suggested. Relying on the consensus doctrine a right to marriage equality has been proposed;[74] the right to develop relationships with other human beings could be the basis for a right to community living;[75] opening 'family life' to non-conjugal relationships has been suggested;[76] and the right to personality in the context of (post-)genomic medicine has been identified as a potential part of 'private life'.[77]

[74] H. Lau, 'Rewriting *Schalk and Kopf*: shifting the *locus* of deference' in E. Brems (ed.), *Diversity and European Human Rights; Rewriting Judgments of the ECHR* (Cambridge University Press, 2012), 243–64.

[75] M. Burbergs, 'Rewriting *Kolanis* v. *the United Kingdom*: the right to community living' in *ibid.*, pp. 382–97.

[76] A. Gross, 'The *Burden* of conjugality' in *ibid.*, pp. 265–92.

[77] A. Krajewska, 'The right to personality in (post-)genomic medicine: a new way of thinking for the new frontier', (2011) 1 *European Human Rights Law Review* 54.

16

Discrimination as a magnifying lens

Scope and ambit under Article 14 and Protocol No. 12

ODDNÝ MJÖLL ARNARDÓTTIR

1. Introduction

The classic structure of analysis under Article 14 of the European Convention on Human Rights (ECHR; the Convention) asks first whether the non-discrimination guarantee is applicable to the case at hand and whether any *prima facie* discrimination has occurred, which refers to establishing the ground for the discrimination in question and the facts of the case against the Convention's operative concepts of discrimination. It is only when these questions have been answered that the second stage of analysis comes into play, namely assessing whether the *prima facie* discrimination so established constitutes actual discrimination or whether it only constitutes different,[1] or similar treatment.[2] Questions of material, personal and conceptual scope would therefore belong to the first stage of analysis, where the applicant bears the burden of persuasion. Only when those questions have been settled would the Court proceed to the second stage of analysis, where the respondent state bears that burden.[3]

This chapter will focus on the material scope of the protection under Article 14 and Article 1 of Protocol 12 ECHR. In open-model non-discrimination clauses the material scope of protection will be relatively wide, while it is limited to specific fields of activity in closed

[1] For example ECtHR (GC), *Stummer* v. *Austria*, 7 July 2011.

[2] ECtHR (GC), *Thlimmenos* v. *Greece*, 6 April 2000; ECtHR, *B* v. *United Kingdom*, 14 February 2012.

[3] On the burden of proof under Art. 14 ECHR see O.M. Arnardóttir, 'Non-discrimination under Article 14 ECHR: the burden of proof', (2007) 51 *Scandinavian Studies in Law* 13.

models.[4] Article 14 ECHR is in fact situated somewhere between the open and closed models in this respect. While not being quite as limited to specific spheres of activity as the EU non-discrimination directives,[5] it is not an independent equality clause that applies across the board to any activity. Instead, it is formulated as a guarantee 'accessory' to the enjoyment of the other rights protected by the Convention. There is, therefore, a fairly conspicuous 'gap' in the scope of protection that the article provides,[6] and it has sometimes been referred to as 'parasitic' on other Convention rights.[7] Protocol 12 was intended to amend this by introducing an independent non-discrimination guarantee into the Convention, but the ratification process has been extremely slow. Optimistic predictions on the future redundancy of the 'ambit' doctrine that governs the relationship between Article 14 and the other Convention right involved, put forward shortly after the adoption of Protocol 12, have therefore proven incorrect.[8] Article 14 continues to be the main source of protection against discrimination under the Convention and the issue of its relationship with other Convention rights continues to be of great relevance.

The ambit doctrine has hitherto been somewhat neglected in the literature on Article 14 and this chapter endeavours to fill that gap. It will begin by sketching the relationship between Article 14 and Protocol 12. The next section will analyse the case law with a view to elaborating the details of the doctrine. Here, the key contribution is the identification of three distinct kinds of magnifying effect that Article 14 can have in relation to other Convention rights. To foster a keener understanding of the doctrine, a closer look will also be taken at the interpretative exercise behind the development of the ambit of Convention rights and the way

[4] A.W. Heringa, 'Standards of review for discrimination. The scope of review by the courts' in T. Loenen and P.R. Rodrigues (eds), *Non-Discrimination Law: Comparative Perspectives* (The Hague: Kluwer Law International, 1999), 25–37, at p. 27 and S. Besson, 'Gender discrimination under EU and ECHR law: never shall the twain meet?', (2008) 8 *Human Rights Law Review* 647, at p. 660.

[5] For example Directive 2006/54/EC on the implementation of the principle of equal opportunities and equal treatment of men and women in matters of employment and occupation.

[6] R. Wintemute, '"Within the ambit": how big is the "gap" in Article 14 European Convention on Human Rights?', (2004) *European Human Rights Law Review* 366, at p. 367.

[7] D.J. Harris, M O'Boyle, E.P. Bates and C.M. Buckley, *Harris, O'Boyle and Warbrick, Law of the European Convention on Human Rights*, 2nd edn (Oxford University Press, 2009), p. 580.

[8] O.M. Arnardóttir, *Equality and Non-discrimination under the European Convention on Human Rights* (The Hague: Martinus Nijhoff, 2003), p. 38.

in which the ambit can function as an early-warning mechanism that identifies pressing interests that might in future be interpreted as falling within the more narrowly defined scope of a particular Convention right. The last section will conclude the discussion by addressing the fact that the perceived difference in material scope between Article 14 and Protocol 12 is slowly diminishing in many important fields of protection, most notably in relation to social security benefits. While these developments at the first level of analysis may seem to open the 'floodgates' for wide-reaching non-discrimination claims in the socio-economic sphere, it is concluded that at the second level of analysis the margin of appreciation doctrine functions as a gatekeeper and maintains an appropriate balance in the case law.

2. The relationship between Article 14 and Protocol No. 12

Although Article 14 is wide in scope, containing a non-exhaustive list of grounds on which discrimination might occur, it is quite limited in the fields of activity covered: it applies only to the enjoyment of the other rights and freedoms protected under the Convention. This has often been criticised as it means that Article 14 offers a lower level of protection than the general ban against discrimination in Article 26 of the International Covenant on Civil and Political Rights (ICCPR).[9] Also, with the exception of the rights to education and the protection of property, the ECHR focuses on protecting civil and political rights. One of the obvious consequences of the limited scope of the protection of Article 14, therefore, is the absence of a Convention ban on discrimination in the enjoyment of economic, social and cultural rights.

The purpose of adopting Protocol 12 to the ECHR in 2000 was 'the broadening . . . in a general fashion, [of] the field of application of Article 14'.[10] Its Article 1, therefore, provides a general prohibition of discrimination in the terms that 'the enjoyment of any right set forth by law shall be

[9] See e.g. Wintemute, '"Within the ambit"', note 6 above, p. 367; L. Wildhaber, 'Protection against discrimination under the European Convention on Human Rights – a second-class guarantee?', (2002) 2 *Baltic Yearbook of International Law* 71–82, at p. 82 and K.J. Partsch, 'Discrimination' in R.St J. Macdonald, F. Matscher and H. Petzold (eds), *The European System for the Protection of Human Rights* (Dordrecht: Martinus Nijhoff Publishers, 1993), 571–92, at p. 571.

[10] Protocol No. 12 to the European Convention on Human Rights, ETS no. 177, Explanatory Report, para. 10.

secured without discrimination' and that 'no one shall be discriminated against by any public authority'. According to the explanatory report to Protocol 12, and as clearly confirmed by the European Court of Human Rights (ECtHR; the Court),[11] the additional material scope of protection covers discrimination of the following types:

> (i) in the enjoyment of any right specifically granted to an individual under national law,
> (ii) in the enjoyment of a right that may be inferred from a clear obligation of a public authority under national law, that is, where a public authority is under an obligation under national law to behave in a particular manner,
> (iii) by a public authority in the exercise of discretionary power (for example, granting certain subsidies) or
> (iv) by any other act or omission by a public authority (for example, the behaviour of law enforcement officers when controlling a riot).[12]

At the date of writing, Article 1 of Protocol 12 has only been applied three times by the Court.[13] As regards all matters of interpretation, other than the difference of material scope, the Court has established that the two non-discrimination guarantees should be interpreted in the same way.[14] The difference in material scope and the relationship between the two Articles has also been clarified in these judgments. This obviously had negative consequences for persons belonging to ethnic minorities not included in one of them. Article 3 of Protocol 1 ECHR protects the right to free elections in the choice of the legislature, but not in the choice of the president. With regard to the former issue, the Court found that there had been a violation of Article 14 in conjunction with Article 3 of Protocol 1 and found it unnecessary to review the same issue under Protocol 12.[15] The choice of president, however, was not an issue where the discrimination claim arose in connection with the enjoyment of rights and freedoms otherwise protected by the Convention. This part of the complaint was therefore reviewed under Article 1 of Protocol 12, which was found to have been

11 ECtHR, *Savez crkava 'Riječ života' and others* v. *Croatia*, 9 December 2010, para. 104.
12 Protocol No. 12, note 10 above, para. 22.
13 Admissibility decisions rendered to date add no further detail to the picture of Protocol No. 12 presented by these judgments.
14 ECtHR (GC), *Sejdic and Finci* v. *Bosnia and Herzegovina*, 22 December 2009, para. 55.
15 *Ibid.*, para. 51.

violated.[16] In the second and third cases, *Savez crkava* and *Vuckovic*,[17] the Court found it unnecessary to review Article 1 of Protocol 12 since the facts at issue were the same as those that had already been found in violation of Article 14 in conjunction with Article 9 and Article 1 of Protocol 1 respectively. All three judgments, therefore, indicate that Article 14 will take precedence over Article 1 of Protocol 12 if both apply to the case at hand. This approach seems justified as, from the perspective of the Convention, discrimination in conjunction with other protected rights is a more serious violation than discrimination in other fields of life. Therefore, even though as a matter of principle Article 1 of Protocol 12 is applicable to all the instances that come under the scope of Article 14's protection, the latter continues to be of prime importance in the non-discrimination law of the Convention, as well as for states that have ratified Protocol 12.[18]

3. Article 14 as a magnifying lens

3.1 The autonomous nature of Article 14 and the ambit doctrine

It is clear from its wording that as Article 14 is an accessory guarantee it has no 'independent existence'.[19] However, as the applicability of Article 14 does not presuppose a violation of the other Convention right in question, it has been characterised as an 'autonomous' Convention guarantee nevertheless.[20] Doctrinally, this unique material scope of Article 14 has been described in the terms that for it to be engaged 'it is necessary but . . . also sufficient for the facts of the case to fall "within the ambit" of one or more of the Articles of the Convention'.[21] The Court has not been particularly elaborate, however, when it comes to explaining the ambit doctrine more specifically. Originally, when dealing with the relationship between Article 14 and other Convention articles, it did not use the term 'ambit'. In *National Union of Belgian Police* it referred to

16 *Ibid.*, para. 56.

17 *Savez crkava*, note 11 above, para. 115; ECtHR, *Vuckovic and others* v. *Serbia*, 28 August 2012, para. 89. *Vuckovic* has been referred to the Grand Chamber.

18 Contrary to the vision put forward by R. Wintemute, 'Filling the Article 14 "gap": government ratification and judicial control of Protocol 12 ECHR', (2004) *European Human Rights Law Review* 484, at p. 485.

19 ECtHR, *Case 'relating to certain aspects of the laws on the use of languages in education in Belgium'* v. *Belgium (Belgian Linguistics case)*, 23 July 1968, part I–B, para. 9.

20 ECtHR, *van der Mussele* v. *Belgium*, 23 November 1983, para. 43.

21 ECtHR (GC), *EB* v. *France*, 22 January 2008, para. 47.

the subject matter complained of as 'one of the modalities of the exercise of a right guaranteed'[22] and in *Schmidt and Dahlström* the Court stated that the subject matter was 'linked to the exercise of a right guaranteed'.[23] The concept of the ambit of other Convention rights was introduced in *Kjeldsen, Busk Madsen and Pedersen* and *Marckx*.[24] Following these judgments, and in concert with the general approach of the Court's jurisprudence, ambit doctrine has emerged without much elaboration in the abstract. It is, therefore, only through inductive analysis of the Court's case law that it is possible to theorise on the actual content of the doctrine.

3.2 *Three kinds of magnifying effect*

There are three distinct ways in which Article 14 leads to a certain magnifying of other Convention rights. The first is when another Convention article is in fact applicable, but the discriminatory element functions as an additional violation or an aggravating factor. The facts of the case, therefore, come within both the other article's scope of protection and that of Article 14 in the same case. The *Sommerfeld* judgment is a good example of this kind of magnifying effect.[25] The applicant fathered a child out of wedlock. His right to access to the child had been set aside by the German courts, which clearly comes under the scope of protection of Article 8. However, invoking the margin of appreciation given to the national courts in making such decisions, the Court considered the decision-making process of sufficient quality to protect his interests. There was, therefore, no violation of Article 8 under the relevant doctrines. However, since the statutory provisions applied by the German courts distinguished between fathers based on whether their children were born within or outside wedlock, the Court found a violation of Article 14 taken in conjunction with Article 8. The judgment in *Marckx* is another example, in which various limitations on the integration into her family of a child born out of wedlock clearly came under the scope of protection of Article 8.[26] The issues were reviewed under Article 8 in isolation and under Article 14 in

22 ECtHR, *National Union of Belgian Police* v. *Belgium*, 27 October 1975, para. 45.

23 ECtHR, *Schmidt and Dahlström* v. *Sweden*, 6 February 1976, para. 39.

24 ECtHR, *Kjeldsen, Busk Madsen and Pedersen* v. *Denmark*, 7 December 1976, para. 56; ECtHR, *Marckx* v. *Belgium*, 13 June 1979.

25 ECtHR (GC), *Sommerfeld* v. *Germany*, 8 July 2003. See also ECtHR (GC) *Sahin* v. *Germany*, 8 July 2003. Similarly ECtHR, *Hoffmann* v. *Germany*, 11 October 2001.

26 *Marckx*, note 24 above.

conjunction with Article 8, and violations of both articles were found. Finally, the judgment in *Salgueiro da Silva Mouta* v. *Portugal* is another good example.[27] Here the issue of a homosexual father's access to his child clearly fell under the scope of protection of Article 8, but the Court chose not to address the Article 8 issue in isolation, but to deal with the subject matter exclusively under Article 14 in conjunction with Article 8. It is clear from these judgments that Article 14 is applicable when the facts of the case come within the scope of the other article and that it does not, in principle, matter whether the other article has been violated or not.

The ambit doctrine, however, also gives Article 14 an autonomous field of application outside the scope of other Convention rights. The second kind of magnifying effect arises where the issue in question does not come within the legal scope of a Convention article, but the ambit doctrine leads to acknowledgement under the Convention, from the perspective of non-discrimination, of an additional interest related to that right. In this type of magnifying effect, there is no requirement that the state in question have voluntarily recognised the additional interest as of 'right' in its domestic legislation; the ambit doctrine can function completely independently of any such development. The judgment in *van der Mussele* is a good example.[28] Here, the Court found that obliging trainee advocates to do *pro Deo* work could not be regarded as compulsory labour since work or service that is within normal civil obligations is excluded from that concept under Article 4(3)(d). No compulsory labour had therefore occurred. When addressing the Article 14 issue, however, the Court noted that the criterion of activities within 'the normal course of affairs' took on a distinct, additional, substantive element when viewed through the lens of Article 14: 'work or labour that is in itself normal may in fact be rendered abnormal if the choice of the groups or individuals bound to perform it is governed by discriminatory factors'.[29] The complaint, therefore, came under the ambit of Article 4 and was reviewed for objective and reasonable justification under Article 14, although no violation was found. More recent examples of the same approach are to be found in the *Graziani-Weiss* and *Zarb Adami* judgments.[30] Other examples worth mentioning include *National Union of Belgian Police* and *Schmidt and Dahlström*, in which the Court

[27] ECtHR, 21 December 1999. [28] See note 20 above. [29] *Ibid.*, para. 43.

[30] ECtHR, *Graziani-Weiss* v. *Austria*, 18 October 2011; ECtHR, *Zarb Adami* v. *Malta*, 20 June 2006.

emphasised the general right of trade unions to protect the occupational interests of their members, and considered specific aspects of this right as coming within the ambit of the freedom of association under Article 11 when reviewed together with Article 14, although they were not considered to come within the more precise protective scope of Article 11 in isolation.[31]

Finally, a third kind of magnifying effect arises when a state has proceeded to protect a particular interest in national legislation as of 'right', over and above the minimum standards strictly required by the Convention. This additional protection, then, provides the ambit of the Convention right in question for the purposes of review under Article 14. This situation is clearly illustrated in the *EB* judgment.[32] The case involved a single person who was denied a licence to adopt a child because of her sexual orientation. It was not contested that Article 8 guarantees neither the right to found a family nor the right to adopt and that there was, therefore, no interference with Article 8 taken on its own.[33] However, when elaborating on the ambit test, the Court reasoned:

> The prohibition of discrimination enshrined in Article . . . 14 extends beyond the enjoyment of the rights and freedoms which the Convention and the Protocols thereto require each State to guarantee. It applies also to those additional rights, falling within the general scope of any Convention Article, for which the State has voluntarily decided to provide.[34]

Since the state had gone beyond its obligations under Article 8 in creating a right to adopt, the Court noted that it 'cannot, in the application of that right, take discriminatory measures within the meaning of Article 14'.[35] A violation of Article 14 taken in conjunction with Article 8 was consequently found to have occurred. Although the *EB* judgment gives unusually detailed explanation of the ambit test, it is by no means the only example of this kind of magnifying effect, which has, in fact, been a well known element of the case law ever since the *Belgian linguistics case*

[31] *Belgian Police*, 27 October 1975 [note 22 above]; *Schmidt and Dahlström*, note 23 above.

[32] *EB* v. *France*, note 21 above.

[33] See the earlier judgment in ECtHR, *Fretté* v. *France*, 26 February 2002, para. 32.

[34] *EB* v. *France*, note 21 above, para. 48. It should be noted that the Court somewhat confusingly gives the term 'general scope' the same meaning as the term 'ambit'. The former should not be confused with the actual and narrower scope of legal obligations flowing from each of the Convention rights. This terminology has been repeated in subsequent case law, see e.g. ECtHR (GC), *Konstantin Markin* v. *Russia*, 22 March 2012, para. 124.

[35] *EB* v. *France*, note 21 above, para. 49.

of 1968, the first judgment to deal with Article 14.[36] In that judgment the Court reasoned that, even though Article 2 of Protocol 1 does not entail any obligation on a government to create a particular kind of educational establishment (in this case teaching in a particular language), 'a State which had set up such an establishment could not, in laying down entrance requirements, take discriminatory measures within the meaning of Article 14'.[37] The case law on social security benefits is also illustrative of the third kind of magnifying effect. In *Stec*, the Grand Chamber settled the confusion as to whether the protective scope of Article 1 of Protocol 1 embraces non-contributory as well as contributory benefits.[38] It made clear that there is a right to the peaceful enjoyment of claims to all social security benefits as 'possessions' in the Convention sense insofar as they exist under national law. At the same time, however, the Convention itself does not provide any individual 'right to' them. Article 1 of Protocol 1 simply does not provide a right to become the owner of a property, a right to receive any pension or other social security benefit, or a right to social security benefits of a particular amount.[39] Accordingly, under Article 1 Protocol 1 states are free, in principle, to choose whether and how they provide social security benefits. However, if they proceed to provide such benefits, that provision falls within the wider ambit of Article 1 of Protocol 1 with the effect that benefits schemes must be organised in a manner that is compatible with Article 14.[40]

Upon close analysis, therefore, the case law shows that there is more to the ambit doctrine than meets the eye. It actually functions as a lens magnifying other Convention rights in three distinct ways. The suggestion put forward in the literature that the ambit of a Convention right should be understood in the context of Article 14 as 'the area in which a person is enjoying a right set out in the Convention, according to the ordinary understanding of the right in the relevant society',[41] therefore seems valid only for the third kind of magnifying effect.

[36] *Belgian Linguistics case*, note 19 above. [37] *Ibid.*, part I–B, para. 9.

[38] ECtHR (GC), Adm. dec., *Stec and others* v. *United Kingdom*, 6 July 2005.

[39] For example ECtHR (GC), *Kopecky* v. *Slovakia*, 28 September 2004, para. 35; *Kjartan Ásmundsson* v. *Iceland*, 12 October 2004, para. 39 and ECtHR (GC), *Andrejeva* v. *Latvia*, 18 February 2009, para. 77.

[40] *Stec*, note 38 above, para. 55.

[41] A. Baker, 'The enjoyment of rights and freedoms: a new conception of the ambit under Article 14 ECHR', (2006) 69 *Modern Law Review* 714, at p. 734.

3.3 *When do the facts of the case fall within the ambit of a Convention right?*

The question of what, more precisely, may fall within the ambit of a Convention article is a matter that must be resolved in the concrete context of each article. It is the result of the same kind of interpretative exercise as that involved in the determination of their (more narrowly defined) scope.

A few examples from the case law on Article 8 can be taken to illustrate this interpretative exercise. *EB* is, again, a good example. When subsuming matters related to adoption within the ambit of Article 8, the Court emphasised links with the interests protected by the wider notion of 'private life'. More specifically, it relied on the already established interpretation of Article 8 that the notion of 'private life' under that article is a broad concept that encompasses generally the right to establish and develop relationships with other human beings and the right to respect for both decisions to have and decisions not to have a child.[42] Similarly, in *Sidabras and Dziautas*, and even though neither the right to work nor the freedom of profession is protected by the Convention, the Court found that a far-reaching ban placed on former KGB officers against taking up employment in the private sector did affect their 'private life' within the ambit of Article 8 as it 'affected their ability to develop relationships with the outside world to a very significant degree and . . . created serious difficulties for them in terms of earning their living, with obvious repercussions on the enjoyment of their private lives'.[43] In *Petrovic* the Court conceptualised parental leave allowance as one of the key elements by which states 'demonstrate their respect for family life within the meaning of Article 8' with the effect that questions of entitlement to such allowance were reviewed under Article 14 in conjunction with Article 8.[44] In 2012 it was reiterated by the Grand Chamber that while Article 8 neither includes a right to parental leave nor entails a positive obligation to provide parental leave allowances, such leave comes within its 'scope'. More particularly, the Court argued that, since parental leave has the purpose of 'enabling one of the parents to stay at home to look after the children, parental leave and related allowances promote

[42] *EB* v. *France*, note 21 above, para. 43.

[43] ECtHR, *Sidabras and Dziautas* v. *Lithuania*, 27 July 2004, para. 48.

[44] ECtHR, *Petrovic* v. *Austria*, 27 March 1998, para. 29.

family life and necessarily affect the way in which it is organised'.[45] Finally, the judgment in *Bah* provides an interesting example. Here, it was clear that there is no right under Article 8 to be provided with housing. The Court nevertheless found that the legislation complained of fell within that article's ambit since it 'obviously affected the home and family life of the applicant and her son, as it impacted upon their eligibility for assistance in finding accommodation when they were threatened with homelessness'.[46]

Of course, the ambit of a Convention article still has its outer limits. Most cases in which the applicants' claims under Article 14 are farther removed from the essence of another Convention right are in fact filtered out as inadmissible. Some interesting examples of the outer limits of 'ambit' can nevertheless be found in judgments on property rights. With the exception of the developments regarding social security benefits that culminated in *Stec*,[47] it seems that the Court is not inclined to assign a generous ambit under Article 14 if the interest at stake does not fall squarely within the scope of Article 1 of Protocol 1 by fulfilling the conceptual requirement of being a 'possession' in the Convention sense.[48] In *Vilho Eskelinen*, for example, a claim that salary should continue at a particular level was not found to come within the ambit of Article 1 of Protocol 1 for the purposes of review under Article 14, as it did not have sufficient basis in national law to begin with.[49] Similarly, in *Roche*, under national legislation no claim in torts ever existed against another member of the armed forces or the state for personal injury occurring while on duty. This led to the finding that there was no possession that could come under either the scope of Article 1 Protocol 1, or its ambit when viewed through the lens of Article 14.[50] Moreover, in *Jasiuniene* hopes of recovering a plot of land that had been nationalised did not constitute a possession in the Convention sense with the effect that

[45] *Markin*, note 34 above, para. 130. In light of the clarity of the statement that there is no right to parental leave or allowance, the Court's reference to 'scope' as opposed to ambit seems misplaced.

[46] ECtHR, *Bah* v. *United Kingdom*, 27 September 2011, para. 40.

[47] In *Stec*, note 38 above, the Court brought together the conflicting case law as to whether non-contributory benefits come under the scope of Art. 1 of Protocol 1 or its ambit when reviewed in conjunction with Art. 14; *cf.* further discussion below.

[48] On the concept of 'posessions' see e.g. ECtHR (GC), *Draon* v. *France*, 6 October 2005, para. 65.

[49] ECtHR (GC), *Vilho Eskelinen and others* v. *Finland*, 19 April 2007, para. 94.

[50] ECtHR (GC), *Roche* v. *United Kingdom*, 19 October 2005, para. 133.

neither article applied.[51] And finally, *Prince Hans-Adam II of Liechtenstein* is a good example. The prince's claim to restitution (of a painting originally confiscated in 1945 from his father by former Czechoslovakia) was not considered to come within the scope of Article 1 of Protocol 1 since his claimed interest in the painting did not amount to a possession in the Convention sense. Following that finding, the Court simply concluded that 'he cannot therefore claim that in these respects he had been discriminated against in the enjoyment of his property rights'.[52]

In the context of Article 8, *Botta* is also an interesting example of the outer limits of the ambit test. In this case the applicant claimed a right under Article 8 to gain access to the beach and the sea during his holidays away from home, which hinged on the positive obligation of the state to remedy failures by private bathing establishments to provide disabled access. Article 8 was found inapplicable since the claim concerned such 'broad and indeterminate' interpersonal relations that there was no link between them and the state's obligation to protect private life under Article 8.[53] Even though the ambit test opens up possibilities additional to the actual scope of Article 8, the applicant's claim under Article 14 in conjunction with Article 8 was so far removed from the essence of Article 8 that it was considered to fall outside the ambit as well. Similarly, in *Haas*, an applicant who claimed discriminatory denial of inheritance rights had never been recognised as the 'illegitimate' son of the man he believed to be his father and had only had sporadic contact with that man. In contrast to cases involving emotional security, recognition of actual family ties or the applicant's personal identity, the applicant was found to be unable to 'derive from Article 8 a right to be recognised as the heir of a deceased person for inheritance purposes'.[54] The Court also found that his claims could not be 'accommodated within the ambit of Article 8'.[55] The conclusions in these judgments concerning Article 8 seem justified although the Court's comments, to the effect that since Article 8 did not apply Article 14 could not apply either, are rather misleading. Such comments seem to equate the scope of another Convention right with the scope of Article 14 through the ambit doctrine.[56] But as exhibited

[51] ECtHR, *Jasiuniene* v. *Lithuania*, 6 March 2003, paras 41–2.
[52] ECtHR (GC), *Prince Hans-Adam II of Liechtenstein* v. *Germany*, 12 July 2001, para. 92.
[53] ECtHR, *Botta* v. *Italy*, 24 February 1998, para. 35.
[54] ECtHR, *Haas* v. *The Netherlands*, 13 January 2004, para. 43.
[55] *Ibid.* [56] *Botta*, note 53 above, para. 39; *Haas*, *ibid.*, para. 45.

in numerous other judgments, the ambit doctrine does not strictly require the other Convention article at issue to be applicable *per se* to the facts of the case.[57]

3.4 The ambit test as a 'canary in the coal mine'

Clear acknowledgement of a particular interest as legitimately related to a Convention right in judgments involving the ambit doctrine under Article 14 may function as a prelude to that same interest being recognised as falling within the more strictly defined scope of that right in subsequent case law. It should be noted, however, that this is not a logical necessity. This early-warning effect may take a long time to develop and it might not happen at all.[58]

The *Thlimmenos* judgment is a good example. At the time of the judgment, while a certain consensus on the right to conscientious objection was rapidly evolving in domestic and international law, the Court had never pronounced on the issue. The best guidance was to be found in earlier decisions from the European Commission on Human Rights which had declared that there was no right to conscientious objection under Article 9 ECHR.[59] In *Thlimmenos*, the Court chose not to rule on the issue under Article 9, instead applying Article 14 in conjunction with Article 9.[60] Under the Article 14 approach it found that convicting Mr Thlimmenos of a serious offence for refusing to serve in the military, despite the fact that the refusal arose out of his religious beliefs and that his situation, therefore, was significantly different from that of other people convicted of felonies, came within the ambit of Article 9.[61] The complaint was reviewed on its merits and a violation was found. It was only in later case law, however, that the Court established that, taken on its own Article 9 does indeed protect the right to conscientious objection.[62]

The case law on social security benefits also provides a very interesting example of how developments under the ambit doctrine may predict future developments in the scope of another substantive article.

[57] For example *van der Mussele*, note 20 above.

[58] See the unchanged approach to Art. 4 in *ibid.* and *Graziani-Weiss*, note 30 above.

[59] For example ECommHR, *Grandrath* v. *Federal Republic of Germany*, 12 December 1966; ECommHR, *A* v. *Switzerland*, 9 May 1984.

[60] Thus following the most recent Commission cases; see e.g., *Peters* v. *The Netherlands*, 30 November 1994 and *Heudens* v. *Belgium*, 22 May 1995.

[61] *Thlimmenos*, note 2 above, para. 42.

[62] ECtHR (GC), *Bayatyan* v. *Armenia*, 7 July 2011, para. 110.

Originally, according to *Gaygusuz*, in order for the pecuniary interest to come under the ambit, let alone the scope, of Article 1 Protocol 1 entitlement to a social security benefit had to be linked to the payment of contributions to the relevant social insurance fund.[63] Following this judgment, however, the case law became misleading. In *Willis* the Court avoided dealing with the issue of whether this link is essential to establish the scope of Article 1 of Protocol 1, or its wider ambit under Article 14 review. The Court decided that it was not necessary to pronounce on 'whether a social-security benefit must be contributory in nature in order for it to constitute a "possession" for the purposes of Article 1 of Protocol No. 1',[64] before it proceeded to review Article 14 in conjunction with Article 1 of Protocol 1. This, of course, indicates that the interest at least fell under the wider ambit of Article 1 of Protocol 1 when reviewed with Article 14. A similar approach was taken in *Koua Poirrez*, where the Court found that a non-contributory benefit gives rise 'to a pecuniary right for the purposes of Article 1 of Protocol 1' and proceeded to the review of the discrimination claim.[65] In *Willis* and *Koua Poirrez*, the applicants actually claimed no violation of the protection of property in isolation, so the Court could rely on the more relaxed ambit approach under the non-discrimination angle. Subsequently, in *Kjartan Ásmundsson*, when faced with a complaint that raised both issues the Court reverted to the contributory benefits schemes criterion.[66] The issues were finally settled in *Stec* which cleared up the confusion as to whether non-contributory benefits 'fell within the "ambit" or "scope" of Article 1 of Protocol No. 1'.[67] In the interest of consistency within the Convention as a whole the Court found that the concept of 'possessions' under Article 1 of Protocol 1 should be interpreted consistently with the concept of 'pecuniary rights' under Article 6, where it makes no difference whether the benefits scheme in question is contributory or non-contributory.[68] Additionally, the Court found it 'important to adopt an interpretation of Article 1 of Protocol No. 1 which avoids inequalities of treatment based on distinctions which, at the present day, appear illogical or unsustainable'.[69]

[63] ECtHR, *Gagusuz* v. *Austria*, 16 September 1996, paras 39–41. It is not entirely clear whether the judgment was pronouncing on the scope or the ambit of Art. 1 Prot. 1 for the purposes of the Art. 14 review.

[64] ECtHR, *Willis* v. *United Kingdom*, 11 June 2002, para. 35.

[65] ECtHR, *Koua Poirrez* v. *France*, 30 September 2003, para. 37.

[66] *Ásmundsson*, note 39 above, para. 39.

[67] *Stec*, note 38 above, para. 41.

[68] See ECtHR, *Schuler-Zgraggen* v. *Switzerland*, 24 June 1993.

[69] *Stec*, note 38 above, para. 49.

It further noted the currently existing variety of funding methods for social security systems, which nevertheless confer entitlements on individuals as of right, and found that it appeared 'increasingly artificial to hold that only benefits financed by contributions to a specific fund fall within the scope of Article 1 of Protocol No. 1'.[70] The result was that non-contributory benefits were clearly brought under the scope of protection of Article 1 of Protocol 12.[71]

4. The 'floodgates' and the margin of appreciation

Although thirteen years have passed since the adoption of Protocol 12, only eighteen of the forty-seven Council of Europe Member States have ratified it.[72] This extremely slow process of ratification has been fuelled by twin fears of a flood of new cases to the already overburdened Court, and increased Convention interference in socio-economic policy and public spending.[73] Of course, it is true that ratification of Protocol 12 would mean that the non-discrimination obligation would not be restricted to the rights and freedoms otherwise protected in the Convention and filtered through the ambit doctrine. But at the same time it can be pointed

70 *Ibid.*, para. 50.

71 *Ibid.*, para. 56. Academic commentary still reflects certain confusion as to whether it was the issue of narrower scope or the wider ambit that was settled in *Stec* and the implications thereof. Compare e.g. E. Palmer, 'Protecting socio-economic rights through the European Convention on Human Rights: trends and development in the European Court of Human Rights', (2009) 2 *Erasmus Law Review* 397, who refers to the ambit of property rights at p. 422, with M. Cousins, 'The European Convention on Human Rights, non-discrimination and social security: great scope, little depth?', (2009) *Journal of Social Security Law* 120, at p. 123 and J. Gerards, 'The prism of fundamental rights', (2012) 8 *European Constitutional Law Review* 173, at p. 193, who refer to the scope of property rights. K. Kapuy, 'Social security and the European Convention on Human Rights: how an odd couple has become presentable', (2007) 9 *European Journal of Social Security* 221, refers at p. 229 to the scope of Art. 1 Prot. 1, but contrarily to the ambit doctrine seems to conclude that it is a precondition for Art. 14 review that the issue falls within the actual scope of property rights.

72 The states that have not ratified Prot. 12 include Germany, France, the United Kingdom, Ireland and most of the Nordic countries (Finland has ratified).

73 See, for example, U. Khaliq, 'Protocol 12 to the European Convention on Human Rights: a step forward or a step too far?', (2001) *Public Law* 457, at p. 459; J. Small, 'Structure and substance: developing a practical and effective prohibition on discrimination under the European Convention on Human Rights', (2003) 6 *International Journal of Discrimination and the Law* 45, at p. 46; Wintemute, 'Filling the Article 14 "gap"', note 18 above, p. 487; Wildhaber, 'Protection against discrimination', note 9 above, p. 81.

out that recent developments under that doctrine have, in fact, greatly reduced the actual difference between the protective scope of Article 14 and Protocol 12. This has occurred in areas such as housing and education,[74] and as regards social security benefits this difference seems *de facto* to have been erased completely.[75] In the final analysis, therefore, the ambit doctrine has at least gone some way to remedying the 'embarrassing' gap in the protection provided by the Convention when compared with Article 7 of the Universal Declaration on Human Rights of 1948 and Article 26 ICCPR.[76]

It is valid, however, to ask whether recent developments under Article 14, or the ratification of Protocol 12, do in fact open the floodgates to excessive intervention into legitimate policy choices in the socio-economic sphere. The first reason why that question should be answered in the negative lies in the simple fact that the scope of a Convention article is only a preliminary issue to be dealt with in the first stage of analysis. Even when the issue is found to fall within the scope of Article 14 (because it is within the ambit of another Convention right), or that of Article 1 of Protocol 12 (because it concerns any right or the activities of any public authority) the second stage of analysis remains, in which the state may advance objective and reasonable justification for the differentiations made. And this second stage of analysis is the 'appropriate mechanism for separating lawful and unlawful government distinctions',[77] not the formal aspects of scope dealt with in the first stage.

The second reason why there is not much cause for concern is the function of the margin of appreciation doctrine in the context of non-discrimination. It is well known that the Court distinguishes between discrimination grounds when reviewing objective and reasonable justification in the second stage of analysis. To this end, it has developed an approach under which certain discrimination grounds are 'suspect' and call for particularly strict scrutiny through the requirement that only 'very weighty reasons' can provide objective and reasonable justification for different treatment. The Court, in fact, has recently elaborated a 'vulnerable groups' approach to certain suspect grounds: sex/gender, sexual orientation, race/ethnicity and disability.[78] Under this approach,

74 Housing: *Bah*, note 46 above. Education: ECtHR, *Ponomaryovi* v. *Bulgaria*, 21 June 2011.

75 See e.g. ECtHR (GC), *Stec and others* v. *United Kingdom*, 12 April 2006, concurring opinion of Judge Borrego Borrego.

76 Wintemute, '"Within the ambit"', note 6 above, p. 367.

77 Baker, 'The enjoyment of rights and freedoms', note 41 above, p. 735.

78 ECtHR, *Kiyutin* v. *Russia*, 10 March 2011, paras 63–4.

the state's margin of appreciation is substantially narrower when it comes to groups that have been 'historically subject to prejudice with lasting consequences, resulting in their social exclusion'.[79] Additionally, the literature on Article 14 has identified as suspect three other grounds for discrimination:[80] nationality,[81] birth inside or outside marriage,[82] and religion.[83] At the same time, the Court has emphasised that states are given a wide margin of appreciation in cases involving 'general measures of economic or social strategy'.[84] It will therefore continue to be careful when reviewing cases that extend Convention obligations into the socio-economic sphere through the non-discrimination obligation in relation to Article 8 and Articles 1 and 2 of Protocol 1. Indeed, it stands out that, with the exception of the *Belgian Linguistics case*, findings of violations in judgments involving the third type of magnifying effect, where a state's provisions exceed the minimum requirements of the Convention, seem to be restricted to cases involving the suspect discrimination grounds nationality,[85] ethnic origin,[86] and sex/gender.[87] If the discrimination complaint is raised on a different ground, such as marital status,[88] status of residence permit,[89] place of residence,[90] or prisoner status,[91] or if differences based on sex/gender in relation to pension schemes are intended to correct factual inequalities,[92] the applicant is very unlikely to succeed.[93] Finally it should be emphasised that in such cases the states have decided of their own volition to make provision that exceeds the minimum standards

[79] *Ibid.*, para. 63. The vulnerable groups approach was first elaborated in a case about a disabled person's right to vote under Art. 3 Prot. 1; see ECtHR, *Alajos Kiss* v. *Hungary*, 20 May 2010, para. 42.

[80] For example Arnardóttir, *Equality and Non-Discrimination*, note 8 above, pp. 148–53 and J. Gerards, 'The application of Article 14 ECHR by the European Court of Human Rights' in J. Niessen and I. Chopin (eds), *The Development of Legal Instruments to Combat Racism in a Diverse Europe* (Leiden: Martinus Nijhoff Publishers, 2004), 3–60, at pp. 53–6.

[81] For example *Andrejeva*, note 39 above, para. 87.

[82] For example *Sahin*, note 25 above, para. 94.

[83] For example *Savez crkava*, note 11 above, para. 88.

[84] For example ECtHR (GC), *Carson and others* v. *United Kingdom*, 16 March 2010, para. 61 and *Andrejeva*, note 39 above, para. 83.

[85] *Ponomaryovi*, note 74 above; *Andrejeva*, note 39 above; ECtHR, *Luczak* v. *Poland*, 27 November 2007 and *Poirrez*, note 65 above.

[86] ECtHR, *Muñoz Diaz* v. *Spain*, 8 December 2009.

[87] *Markin*, note 34 above; ECtHR, *Runkee and White* v. *United Kingdom*, 10 May 2007; and *Willis*, note 64 above.

[88] ECtHR (GC), *Serife Yigit* v. *Turkey*, 2 November 2010.

[89] *Bah*, note 46 above.

[90] *Carson*, note 84 above.

[91] *Stummer*, note 1 above.

[92] ECtHR, *Andrle* v. *The Czech Republic*, 17 February 2011; *Stec*, note 75 above.

[93] See also J. Gerards, 'The prism of fundamental rights', note 71 above, p. 193.

of the Convention in the first place. It cannot, therefore, be said that state autonomy is severely interfered with.

5. Conclusions

The most recent doctrinal development in the elaboration of the ambit test occurred in the admissibility decision in *Stec* and was confirmed in the judgment in *EB*. It emphasises that the ambit encompasses 'those additional rights, falling within the general scope of any Convention Article, for which the State has voluntarily decided to provide'.[94] This does not tell the whole story, however, since the ambit doctrine can also encompass additional elements of the right in question, regardless of whether the state has voluntarily made any specific additional provision related to that right. Inductive analysis of the case law, in fact, shows that the ambit doctrine performs the following functions:

(1) detecting additional violations or aggravating elements within the minimum entitlements provided by the scope of Convention rights (i.e. where the protected interest comes under one of the operative concepts of a Convention article and there exists a 'right to' a certain state behaviour under that Article),
(2) detecting legitimate interests that are closely linked to Convention rights even though they fall outside the more precisely defined scope of those rights and have not been recognised in domestic developments (i.e. where the protected interest is sufficiently linked to one of the operative concepts of a Convention article but there exists no 'right to' a certain state behaviour under that article or in national law) and
(3) supporting domestic developments that exceed the minimum standards required for Convention rights (i.e. where the protected interest comes under or is sufficiently linked to one of the operative concepts of a Convention article, there exists no 'right to' a certain State behaviour under that article but such a right has been recognised in national law).

In the final analysis, therefore, Article 14 is not quite the 'parasite' sometimes alleged. It does not derive nourishment from the other article without benefiting it, but functions instead as a lens magnifying the interests protected by it.

[94] *Stec*, note 38 above, para. 40 and *EB* v. *France*, note 21 above, para. 48.

The question of when an interest actually falls within the ambit is a matter which must be resolved in the concrete context of each article through the Convention's ordinary means of interpretation. A clear link with the interests legitimately protected under the Convention must be established. The Court's approach to the right in question will determine whether the additional ambit is relatively wide or relatively narrow. For example, it accords with the general logic of the Article 8 case law for its additional ambit to be rather wide, whereas the general logic of the case law on Article 1 of Protocol 1 supports the more restrictive approach of the Court towards that article's ambit. Through identifying legitimate interests closely related to certain Convention rights, developments under the ambit doctrine can also pave the way for widening the scope of a Convention right in subsequent case law. Thus, it can function as the 'canary in the coal mine', providing early warning of emerging concerns and interests that need Convention protection in line with evolving conditions in the Member States.

When the ambit doctrine functions in support of domestic developments that exceed the minimum standards required by the Convention, this can lead to the extension of Convention guarantees into the socio-economic sphere. To begin with, judgments of this kind were few and far between: *cf.* the *Belgian Linguistics case* in 1968 and *Gaygusuz* in 1998. But the removal of the requirement that social security benefits must be contributory before they can come under the scope of Article 1 Protocol 1, and developments in common European standards as regards parental leave allowances under Article 8, have led to a dramatic increase in such judgments. Social housing and certain elements of the right to work have also been interpreted as falling under the ambit of Article 8, and it seems justified to ask when even more issues of a socio-economic nature will be interpreted as coming under the scope or ambit of Convention rights. The further into the realm of economic and social policy the Convention advances through the non-discrimination obligation under Article 14, the less will its protective scope differ from that of Protocol 12.

While at first sight these developments might raise concern over excessive intervention in the democratic prerogatives of Member States in the socio-economic sphere, there are certain elements inherent to the case law that minimise any cause for concern. The enlargement of the material scope of protection of Article 14, and the ratification of Protocol 12, are in any case only a question of formal scope in the first stage of analysis. Their real effect is not decided until the second stage of analysis, in which states can forward objective and reasonable justification for the distinctions made. As a general rule the state will in fact have a generous margin of appreciation for distinctions in the socio-economic sphere, the only exceptions being cases that involve certain 'suspect' grounds for discrimination. And even then, in many cases the advance of the non-discrimination obligation into economic and social policy hinges on states having decided of their own volition to provide more than required to by the minimum standards stipulated in the Convention. Guaranteeing that they do so without discriminating against certain vulnerable groups, therefore, does not involve a grave affront to the democratic prerogatives of the national authorities or great additional public spending.

INDEX

Cases listed in the index are ECtHR cases unless a parenthetical indicates otherwise.

Printed in Great Britain
by Amazon

61038461R00215